Sentient Ecologies

Studies in Environmental Anthropology and Ethnobiology

General Editor: **Roy Ellen**, FBA
Professor of Anthropology, University of Kent at Canterbury

Interest in environmental anthropology has grown steadily in recent years, reflecting national and international concern about the environment and developing research priorities. This major new international series, which continues a series first published by Harwood and Routledge, is a vehicle for publishing up-to-date monographs and edited works on particular issues, themes, places, or peoples that focus on the interrelationship between society, culture, and environment. Relevant areas include human ecology, the perception and representation of the environment, ethno-ecological knowledge, the human dimension of biodiversity conservation, and the ethnography of environmental problems. While the underlying ethos of the series will be anthropological, the approach is interdisciplinary.

Recent volumes:

Volume 31
Sentient Ecologies
Xenophobic Imaginaries of Landscape
Edited by Alexandra Coțofană and Hikmet Kuran

Volume 30
Living on a Time Bomb
Local Negotiations of Oil Extraction in a Mexican Community
Svenja Schöneich

Volume 29
Grazing Communities
Pastoralism on the Move and Biocultural Heritage Frictions
Edited by Letizia Bindi

Volume 28
Delta Life
Exploring Dynamic Environments Where Rivers Meet the Sea
Edited by Franz Krause and Mark Harris

Volume 27
Nature Wars
Essays around a Contested Concept
Roy Ellen

Volume 26
Ecological Nostalgias
Memory, Affect and Creativity in Times of Ecological Upheavals
Edited by Olivia Angé and David Berliner

Volume 25
Birds of Passage
Hunting and Conservation in Malta
Mark-Anthony Falzon

Volume 24
At Home on the Waves
Human Habitation of the Sea from the Mesolithic to Today
Edited by Tanya J. King and Gary Robinson

Volume 23
Edges, Fringes, Frontiers
Integral Ecology, Indigenous Knowledge and Sustainability in Guyana
Thomas Henfrey

Volume 22
Indigeneity and the Sacred
Indigenous Revival and the Conservation of Sacred Natural Sites in the Americas
Edited by Fausto Sarmiento and Sarah Hitchner

For a full volume listing, please see the series page on our website:
http://berghahnbooks.com/series/environmental-anthropology-and-ethnobiology

Sentient Ecologies

Xenophobic Imaginaries of Landscape

Edited by Alexandra Coţofană and Hikmet Kuran

berghahn
NEW YORK • OXFORD
www.berghahnbooks.com

First published in 2023 by
Berghahn Books
www.berghahnbooks.com

© 2023, 2025 Alexandra Coțofană and Hikmet Kuran
First paperback edition published in 2025

All rights reserved. Except for the quotation of short passages
for the purposes of criticism and review, no part of this book
may be reproduced in any form or by any means, electronic or
mechanical, including photocopying, recording, or any information
storage and retrieval system now known or to be invented,
without written permission of the publisher.

Library of Congress Cataloging-in-Publication Data

A C.I.P. cataloging record is available from the Library of Congress
Library of Congress Cataloging in Publication Control Number: 2022019094

British Library Cataloguing in Publication Data

A catalogue record for this book is available from the British Library

ISBN 978-1-80073-662-7 hardback
ISBN 978-1-80539-752-6 paperback
ISBN 978-1-80073-663-4 epub
ISBN 978-1-80073-766-2 web pdf

https://doi.org/10.3167/9781800736627

An electronic version of this book is freely available thanks to
the support of libraries working with Knowledge Unlatched. KU
is a collaborative initiative designed to make high-quality books
Open Access for the public good. More information about the
initiative and links to the Open Access version can be found at
knowledgeunlatched.org.

This work is published subject to a Creative Commons
Attribution Noncommercial No Derivatives 4.0 International License. The terms of the license can be found at
https://creativecommons.org/licenses/by-nc-nd/4.0/.
For uses beyond those covered in the license, contact
Berghahn Books.

Contents

List of Illustrations vii

Introduction 1
    Alexandra Coțofană

Part I. Reinventing the State

Chapter 1. Adamastor Unbound? Whiteness and Landscape in Post-1994 South Africa 23
    Scott Burnett

Chapter 2. Part of the Landscape: Quebecois Nationalism and Indigenous Sentience 43
    Philippe Blouin

Chapter 3. Ingrained Ontologies: How Romania's Institutionalized Processes Teach Us to Think with Xenophobic Sentient Landscapes 67
    Alexandra Coțofană

Chapter 4. Hostile Territory: Communal Politics and Sentient Landscape in Ladakh, Himalayan India 98
    Callum Pearce

Part II. Famous Fascisms

Chapter 5. Forests as the Sentient Bridge between German Landscape and Identity 121
    Hikmet Kuran

Chapter 6. Unruly Landscapes: Contested Desert Imaginaries in Post-Franco Spain 142
    Arvid van Dam

Chapter 7. Shinkoku: Reconsidering the Concept of
Sentient Landscapes from Japan 160
David Malitz

Chapter 8. Imagining Chile's South: The Making of a Phobic
Landscape of Prestige in the Forests 186
Georg T. A. Krizmanics

Part III. The Skeptics

Chapter 9. Can the Forests be Xenophobic? Migrant Pathways
through Croatia and the Forest as Cover 211
Sarah Czerny, Marijana Hameršak, Iva Pleše, and Sanja Bojanić

Chapter 10. Footsteps through the City: Encounters with
Social Justice in Czech Urban Landscapes 229
Susanna Trnka

Epilogue. Why Is It Vital to Scrutinize the Connection between
Landscape, Sentience, and Xenophobia in the Age of
Deepening Crises of Democracy and Ecology? 251
Hikmet Kuran

Index 263

Illustrations

Figures

1.1.	*T'kama/Adamastor* by Cyril Coetzee (1999). © Africana Collections, University of the Witwatersrand.	29
3.1.	Moldavian King Stephan fighting Hadım Suleiman Pasha's army in Almaş's book. © Valentin Tănase.	68
3.2.	Cover of *Gândirea* magazine, December 1921. © Central University Library Cluj.	72
3.3.	Cover of *Luceafărul* magazine, February 1904. © Wikicommons.	80
3.4.	Damirescu's book, tattered by time and misuse, in my childhood home. © Alexandra Coțofană.	84
3.5.	Almaş's volumes in my childhood home. © Alexandra Coțofană.	85
3.6.	Scan from Almaş. Romanian archers and the xenophobic sentient landscape attacking. © Valentin Tănase.	86
3.7.	Scan from Almaş. Beastly sentient others stealing riches from a Romanian boy. © Valentin Tănase.	87
3.8.	Scan from Almaş. Princess Dochia resisting colonization. © Valentin Tănase.	88
3.9.	Scan from Almaş. Battle of Posada. © Valentin Tănase.	89
3.10.	Scan from Almaş. Romanians attacking German tanks in World War II. © Valentin Tănase.	90
3.11.	Scan from Almaş. Horea and his capturers. © Valentin Tănase.	91
8.1.	Limache Cross. Source: Alonso de Ovalle's 1646 *Histórica Relación del Reyno de Chile* (Historical account of the kingdom of Chile) (between pp. 58 and 59). © memoriachilena.	197

Maps

3.1. The Romanian map with an arrow pointing to the
Prahova River. © Wikimedia Commons. 75

3.2. The Danube, Prut, and Olt Rivers. © Wikimedia Commons. 77

Introduction

Alexandra Coțofană

On January 14, 2021, the authors of this edited volume met over Zoom for a four-hour discussion. We had disseminated a reading list some months prior to the meeting and had received first drafts from thirteen authors for ten chapters in the weeks prior to the event. We had to work with an eighteen-hour time difference between our easternmost and our westernmost authors—some of them had just woken up for our Zoom meeting, while for others, it was already bedtime. The aim of the meeting was, as we, the editors, had envisioned it, to offer the authors food for thought, to allow them to present their chapters and listen to their peers' presentations, in order to assemble a cohesive manuscript from their revised, final submissions.

Equipped with enthusiasm and a foolproof plan, we welcomed everyone to the Zoom conversation that day. All the authors introduced themselves, and we proceeded with the presentations of our individual chapters. Halfway through the meeting, one author halfheartedly admitted to struggling with the concept of the edited volume, that of sentient landscapes capable of xenophobia. Later, three coauthors presenting one of the chapters focused their presentations on the various ways in which both the concept of sentience and that of xenophobia seemed to not fully fit their ethnographic experience. A long conversation followed on how other chapters could potentially inform and dialogue with the data from our skeptics' chapters. Perhaps naively, we, the editors of the manuscript, had not expected that any of our authors would feel conflicted about the core concept of the manuscript.

Months later, several drafts needed a third set of revisions, which were meant to create a more productive dialogue between the book's core concept and the authors' data. In our subsequent editorial conversations, after receiving the final versions of our authors' chapters, we noticed that some of this tension was still present in the narratives of our colleagues.

And so we tried to understand why. Why have our colleagues submitted substantial work to an edited volume focused on the notion of sentient landscapes capable of xenophobia while at the same time revealing apprehension toward the concept? This introduction is dedicated to our authors and is an attempt to untangle the ontologies of our disciplines, past and present.[1] Our goal is twofold, as our above question is itself twofold. On the one hand, the introduction will tease out the threads that make the concept of sentient landscapes capable of xenophobia a possible model to our authors.[2] On the other hand, the introduction will seek out the logics present in our disciplines that would make a scholar apprehensive toward fully embracing the term.

We chose to keep the name of the book centered around the concept of sentient landscapes capable of xenophobia not because it offers clear answers or, as we have seen, consensus, but because we believe the title's tensions and the uneasiness these create can be used productively. On the topic of the choices we make in naming a book, Anna Tsing made a fundamental point in her introduction to *The Feral Atlas* (2021). People in social sciences and the humanities use words poetically, as guidance, as a way to "simultaneously open up and drill down into meanings rather than cordoning them off as fixed and decided." To complicate things even further, the scholar is not a locus of objectivity. We come from different disciplines, each with our own disciplinary limits regarding what we can accept as real and what we cannot. We are all also actors and, equally, products of our unique upbringing, our experiences, our embodied interactions with the big concepts (nation, religion, gender, etc.). This, we believe, is a strength of the volume.

To better understand why the concept of sentient landscapes capable of xenophobia might create discomfort among moderns, the Latourian concept of hybridity comes in handy. The outofplaceness of sentient landscapes capable of xenophobia is in part due to the fact that the term does not fit with how we imagine modernity. Modernities, in whatever shape they may take, are all defined by the passage of time, in which we imagine a point of rupture, a break from an archaic past, producing an acceleration. In other words, hybridity produces a crisis: as scholars, we have heard of sentient landscapes, but they have always been associated with a romanticized image of indigeneity—just like the colonized, Indigenous people, sentient landscape could do no harm. To have to imagine, then, a sentient landscape capable of xenophobia, one which shares the ugly sentiments of moderns, means imagining a hybrid that is hard to grasp.

Before we move on, the Latourian hybridity of a sentient landscape capable of xenophobia needs some adjusting to fit our concept and context better. In most scholarship, the sentience is revealed only to the Indigenous tribes, as both humans and nonhumans share martyrdom at the hands of colonial actors. Scholarship has banalized the term of indigeneity to the point where it almost fully overlaps with a good spirit (Coletta and Raftopoulos 2016: xvii). We suspect this is in part due to the guilt stemming from the colonial history of anthropology. This metanoia results in anthropologists' needing to talk about the discipline's history as the handmaiden to European empires and to recognize the suffering this has produced for the colonized. While all these are historically accurate narratives, it is unhealthy for scholarship to romanticize a concept as big as indigeneity, and it also does not fit well with a moment in our disciplines when we are rethinking binaries. The Indigenous are not lesser beings with a more modest palette of emotions and wants—to suggest this would be to deny them coevalness (Fabian 1983). Thus, to be Indigenous or to be a sentient landscape does not mean to always be good. We must extend the argument to recognize the fullness and complexity of all sentient beings.

Furthermore, our own ontologies do not allow us to imagine the reality of sentient landscapes capable of xenophobia, and these ontologies have been long in the making. To be sure, the relationship between humans and nature has long been governed by the understanding of a Christian God. This understanding allows a constitution of moderns that enables us to imagine as much distance as possible between nature and society, a process started during the Reformation of the sixteenth century (Latour 1993: 34). Furthermore, the biblical moment of creation has imagined a violent separation between humans and everything else, a mode of thinking based on an apartheid between humans and nonhumans (Descola 2005). We are, as a result, incapable of seeing our human and nonhuman others as being able to cope with the same range of emotions as our own.

Theories and concepts are cultural objects just like any other cultural object—this means they change through time, through space, through the interdisciplinary translations they undergo (Guillaume 2015). How moldable they are reveals their plasticity, how transferable they are between disciplines and vocabularies reveals their elasticity, and what they can merge with reveals their hybridity. This volume should be read as a series of physics experiments on the concept of sentient landscapes capable of xenophobia, a first attempt at testing the plasticity, elasticity, and hybridity of the idea. We hope to witness an interesting diachronic curve for the concept, in the short, middle, or long term. At the same time, we acknowledge that we have very little control over how the term will be initially received, how it might be used, rejected, or reclaimed.

The title of the book is the result of the intellectual wandering of the editors. The authors generously responded to the general prompt, not always endorsing the analytical framework but instead engaging with diverse arguments and forms of evidence to experiment with the limits of the concept. In our January meeting and in their writing, the authors' diverse lenses revealed productive tensions that we hope will fuel future engagement with the term. Taken together, the chapters of the book endeavor to lay a few bricks toward the foundation of a more complex, and thus a more honoring, understanding of sentient landscape.

How, might one ask, can a narrative of xenophobia be respectful? In the book, we use the term xenophobia (from *xénos*, meaning "stranger, foreigner," and *phóbos*, meaning "fear") in its original meaning,[3] freeing it from today's very specific understanding of someone who has power and uses it to further disempower ethnoreligious others. The power dynamics between self and other differ greatly from one chapter to another, and this variety is intentional. The central question of the volume is how can we think with sentient landscapes without just romanticizing them as pure, kind, Gaia-like? Furthermore, how are the ways of thinking of sentient landscapes capable of xenophobia intertwined with human ontologies? We try to answer this question by lessening the human-nature divide.

If we are going to engage seriously with the concept of sentient landscapes, then we must accept that with their agency comes a full range of emotions. As the literature tells us, sentient landscapes see, smell, judge, and protect. This edited volume adds to that range of emotions by revealing ontologies in which sentient landscapes also fear, hate, dislike, and punish. Going even further, sentient landscapes capable of xenophobia should be treated as uneven—they do not behave the same everywhere, even when one important factor (fascist human ontologies) is present alongside several landscapes.

At this point, we must address a rather important question, one which we, together with some of our authors, have had to think about when explaining to peers, students, friends, and family what this book is about. How does one talk to a skeptic about sentient landscapes capable of xenophobia? The arguments are rather simple. First, no matter at what scale they gaze at a landscape (be it microbial, regional, or planetary), scholars and nonscholars alike can agree that landscape is imbued with life. Next, we must clarify what we mean by sentience. Tim Ingold understands sentience as "the inner essence, or soul, that holds the attributes of sentience, volition, memory and speech. Any being that possesses these attributes is a person, irrespective of the intrinsically unstable form in which it appears" (2000: 92). An experienced scholar, Ingold suspected that the skeptics would shriek that they have never seen the landscape speak. To this point, Ingold warns that we see sentience from a Western, Christian point of view. The fact that we have the ability to act on speech does not mean we have to do it. Or as Ingold puts it: "I may or may not choose to speak, or I may decide to say one thing rather than another, but as a being with intentions and purposes—that is, as a person—I am not the same as my speech" (2000: 102).

Communities that understand their survival is directly connected to the health of the landscape can choose to act on that instinct. Some scholars would argue that a partnership with the sentient landscape has ensured the success and longevity of great civilizations. For example, the Maya civilization flourished for millennia in a geographically diverse and climatically volatile region because of a fundamental belief in the vital essence of all sentient beings, including stones and streams, existing in dynamic cycles of interdependence (Coe and Houston 2015). It could be argued that communities that live closest to an environment and have a long-term practice of interacting with it will have its best interest in mind, and that we should learn from their wisdom.

We beg to differ, using a Hobbesian argument and statistical evidence. As human nature is corruptible, it happens more often than not that humans act against the health of the landscape. When hurt, misused and exploited, landscape reacts—rivers swell and destroy everything around them, boulders hurtle down in landslides onto communities, and post-deforestation landscape turns to desert. To some extent, even global warming could be understood through this logic: global warming just happens at a different pace than some of the other reactions of landscape, and we are yet to fully experience a violent moment of decompression, as we would understand it in our human time.

We will take this a step further and ask: Is landscape always good? Victimized? Just reactive? It could not possibly be that simple—but equally, the answers as to why it feels other things could be manifold. As any living sentient being would, landscape learns to adapt, but it also learns behaviors from other species. Just as humans have observed the landscape and learned from it virtues like patience, resilience, and nurturance, landscape could have observed predatory beasts (humans included) and learned how to hate, how to hurt. We could be confronted with a case of xenophobic cohabitations or symbiosis. We can understand the symbiosis of human-nature xenophobia as resembling how human capitalist extractivism cohabits and encourages species that decimate (rats, fungi, cockroaches). Is xenophobia then a product of colonial globalization that has been spread like a pest, has adapted, and can no longer be contained? Changing no longer just ecologies but the ontologies of ecologies?

There are certainly traceable cotemporalities between the colonial spread of European pests and diseases and European xenophobia. Have colonial humans, by reproducing the same ways of treating the environment back home, changed the way that colonized landscape understands itself and others? Has colonized landscape internalized the racism brought upon itself? Another option, borrowing the set of relationships described by Eduardo Viveiros de Castro and Peter Skafish in *Cannibal Metaphysics* (2014), could be that humans with their xenophobia are to the landscape what ticks with their Lyme disease are to humans. Or maybe landscape was the first teacher of xenophobia, making humans the student. We cannot be certain. The only certain thing is our lives are too short and we are too distracted by the monotone of whatever human culture we live within to ever be able to truly understand the logics of landscape. What we are learning to know—and this is a good thing—is that we do not know that much. And the more we look at what we know, the more we seem to understand how little it actually is, and how much of our time as a species we spend looking at ourselves.

Sketching a Conceptual Framework for Sentient Landscapes Capable of Xenophobia

The remainder of this introduction will follow sentience (when and where does it happen?), it will follow xenophobia (where and when does it happen, and which landscapes are stirred by it?), and it will follow landscape (what have people been trying or achieving when using certain narratives to talk about the environment?).

First, we cannot think of the agency of landscape without acknowledging the agency of humans. Human imaginaries about the landscape affect policies, which in turn change landscape itself. For example, in countries that take pride in their mountains, national parks will be created in an attempt to protect the forests, while the less compelling lowlands will be ignored, exploited, and not replenished, which in turn makes the mountains into the nation's favorite son. Yet this alone does not decide xenophobia—as with humans, both the privileged and the neglected could start harboring feelings of hatred towards a perceived other.

What ecologies do xenophobic landscapes and xenophobic people form together? Nonideal ones, as the nation rarely ends up carrying to term a landscape-protection project successfully; in the absence of an easy-to-blame, ethnoreligious other, the fragile eco-fantasy of a perfect nation-nature symbiosis crumbles. We see this more and more as conversations revolve around the Anthropocene, a term popularized in 2000 by Paul Crutzen, an atmospheric chemist, as a way to think about the planet's geological history and the effects that the Industrial Revolution has had. The term has since been adopted in discourse across social sciences and the humanities, art and activism, climate change scholarship and related fields, mainly as a starting point for a (legitimate) discursive self-flogging of our species. In these narratives, the modern human is seen as the root cause of dismal planetary changes, and the discussion then often extends to invasive species, toxic chemicals, and pathogens, whose behaviors and modes of existence mirror the same sort of colonial, totalizing, obliterating forms of greed towards fellow species.

It might then not be surprising that we are investigating and commenting on the xenophobia of landscapes at a time when the scholarly community has been focusing across the board on the detrimental consequences of human greed and the capitalist ethos. Despite holding on to our differences, we are following the connections between our fieldsites, and we have all, as authors present in the volume, harbored questions that we hoped the concept of "xenophobic landscapes" might answer. As the concept of the Anthropocene makes its way into the mainstream of scholarly debate, its meanings become schismatic, reproducing previously instituted imperial categories of class, race, and hegemony (Gilroy 2018).

The (Good) Sentient, the (Bad) Landscape, and the (Ugly) Xenophobic

A most useful theorization of sentient landscapes comes from Tim Ingold, who draws attention to the fact that landscape is not a stable object of knowledge, as "people's knowledge of the environment undergoes continuous formation in the very course of their moving about in it" (2000: 230). For Ingold, it is vital that people receive sensory education in order to be able to come to terms with the sentience of landscape. This education includes stories that explain the interconnectedness and reactions of sentient beings to each other. This interconnectedness, in turn, is what Ingold calls sentient ecology (2000: 10). To be part of a sentient ecology, one must live in it for a long time and have a commitment to the relationships that this interdependent ecology needs.

Donald Crosby coins the term *fellow thous* to refer to the other beings inhabiting this planet who are, in some ontologies, capable of conscious awareness: "I show that these creatures, and especially those capable of conscious awareness and feeling, are richly deserving of our moral recognition, respect, and responsibility" (Crosby 2013: x). While Crosby's intentions seem good, the problem is that this way of thinking remains anthropocentric—it is because other beings are like us, in that they are capable of conscious awareness (a superior, human capacity) that they deserve respect. What then happens to the entities that do not possess this capacity? Further, are those inferior entities not vitally intertwined with the thous? Can the thous be respected separately, while the non-thous are disrespected? Or is the balance of nature only formed of those deemed deserving—us and the thous? Furthermore, what do we do when the rights of thous come into conflict?

One theme that we see explored in current literature on sentient landscapes is that of scholars and their informants acknowledging the landscape's sentience and agency, and describing the landscape as kind, Gaia-like, and as siding with the marginalized and the colonized. The binary of modern/nonmodern has also superimposed a reality in which the modern is up to no good, driven by neoliberal, capitalist greed, while the ancestor imbued in the mountain or river is inherently good. This purifying, simplifying logic cannot be healthy to scholarship.

In some parts of the world, ontologies of sentience have been lost due to colonialism, and the concept of a sentient landscape was not the only one to be lost. The Amazonian Wari' used to consider the heart as the locus of knowledge, but after Protestant missionaries introduced them to their God and taught them mathematics in school, the Wari' started thinking of the brain as the site of knowledge (although the brain did not hold a place in their knowledge cosmology before) and started needing a numerological vocabulary to negotiate with white people. So they started using Wari' words as numbers: for example, the word for one is "alone" (Vilaça 2019). Christianity has also reinvented the relationship of the Wari' to their sentient others—before the colonial encounter the Wari' saw themselves and other animals as *wari'* (same, person) or *karawa* (prey). Christianity gave them a new cosmology in which no animal is off limits as prey because the Christian God made them all for humans to eat. This also normalized antisocial behavior (which, as refusal of socializing around food, used to be attributed to the fact that the person had turned jaguar, for example). In other places, the beliefs of locals had to be taken seriously by the scientific community and the elites out of a lack of alternatives. The Mount Paektu/Changbai stratovolcano, for instance, had not been within the reach of the elites, geographically and topographically, so the scientific expeditions to the mountain had to rely on a combination of rationalistic science and local beliefs in the mountain's sentience as data (Rogaski 2018).

Some of the current academic focus on sentience has followed the development of legal personhood around the world. Environmental personhood is the practice of granting parts of nature the status of legal person. Right now this means that they can be represented in a court of law and that their rights can be protected (Gordon 2017), but eventually the status might also be used in prosecuting landscape for crimes or for violating the rights of other sentient beings—how will a lawyer defend the intentionality of the land? Some authors have already started to reflect on this:

"Because the country is sentient, the ground, for Belyuen Aborigines, is always potentially liable to act for its own reasons" (Povinelli 1993: 150).

In March of 2017 the Whanganui River in New Zealand was granted the same legal rights as humans, after the Whanganui tribe's 140-year-long legal battle on behalf of their ancestor and living kin, the river. Days later the Yamuna and Ganges rivers in India were also legally recognized as living and legal entities (Chandran 2017). In Australia, the Belyuen Aboriginal community had tried to make the government understand that Old Man Rock listens, smells the sweat of the Aboriginals, and intentionally acts and reacts, as part of legal negotiations for granting the mountain legal personhood (Povinelli 1995). The Aboriginals and the Australian state think differently, not only in their ontologies regarding the mountains, but in how land should be used and in considering the economic value of acting one way or another—yet the balance of power between these groups is unequal at best.

Scholars have been discussing this phenomenon in the context of heterological societies, meaning cultures that extend membership to nonhuman others or *héteros* (Kwek and Seyfert 2018i). The questions that stem from this type of ontology have to rely on the framework of the material turn: How do nonhumans shape social life? How can we approach these nonhumans in their own terms? How can we understand these materialities and their agency?

Posthumanism and the focus on animals and nonhumans were earlier analytical steps toward answering these questions (Haraway 2003; Wolfe 2003). Yet all terms in the debate reveal Western, Cartesian ways of thinking, which separate humans from others. (See Latour's term "nature-culture," whereas Butler's "array of materialities" [1993: 97] and Ingold's idea of plurality in flux [2012] do not seem to agree on the conceptual framework.) Furthermore, we seem to disregard the very fact that we are made up of and in symbiosis with many types of nonhumans.

Outside of looking at environmental personhood, scholars fall under a few other categories in terms of how they construe sentience. It can be a country that is sentient, alive, and sensuous to those who can recognize it and know it (Biddle 2007: 12–13), a nod back to Ingold; or in the lens of new animism, sentience is simply personhood (Harvey 2005). For some authors, like Sylvie Poirier, the issue becomes something extremely important to communicate to the academic community: "When it is said that some rocks at Kutal are the ears of the ancestors that dwell there, this should be understood in a literal sense and not as a metaphor" (2005: 153).

Of all the accounts we encountered in the literature, two are ontologically closest to our volume. The first comes from the Yup'ik Eskimos, for whom the sentient cosmos (*ella* for the Yup'ik Eskimos), which perceives and engages, is understood as a large eye that can both hear and see. For their safety, people who were too loud (like mourners) or who had a specific scent (like menstruating women) had restrictions around their movement to make them pass unnoticed to the invisible eye (Fienup-Riordan 1994: 248). The other is from the Mapuche, for whom it is essential to be connected with ancestral land. The Mapuche believe that those who cannot trace their geographical ancestry have unpredictable, potentially dangerous behaviors (Di Giminiani 2018).

Some other authors have had engagements with the landscape in their fieldwork, and while there is a discussion about sentient landscapes in their work, it is unclear where they stand on the issue. Gaston Gordillo (2018) completes an analysis of terrain as an affective geography, inspired by Baruch Spinoza's term affective geometry, a term that analyzes the many ways in which bodies affect other bodies and are affected by them. These range from negative ways that could diminish the body's ability to act, to those that might positively expand the body's powers for action. The question guiding his work probes the ways in which bodies in motion affect and are affected by the terrain. The terms he uses—"bodies in motion" and "terrain"—manage to be more appropriate than the classic human/nonhuman binary. Still, the issue here remains the fact that Gordillo thinks of movement in human time and decides that terrain is not a body in motion, when in fact, as we well know, landscape also moves, constantly, it is just imperceptible to those of us perceiving in human time.

Gordillo's research maps US military interventions in the Korengal mountains and their valleys between 2005 and 2010 and uses the term "vectors of militarization" to refer to his main data source: a genre of film that normalized the presence and heroism of US troops in Iraq and Afghanistan while banalizing as terrorists the locals who were fighting back (2018: 54). For Gordillo, terrain is a process that includes not only land but also bodies of water, the atmosphere, and something that should also be conceptualized as political technology (laws, mapmaking, policing deployed for control of the terrain's volumetric physicality), since the dynamism of terrain can disrupt these technologies. Even though Gordillo cites Latour (2004) on the capacity of terrain to affect human action in either positive or negative ways as proof of the agency of matter, he goes on to say:

> But the very idea of terrain being an "actor" that has "agency" risks reifying and obscuring the multiple actions, pressure points, and affectations at play in these violent encounters. First, the capacity of steep rock formations to affect and slow down the march of Americans resulted not from their agency but from what Spinoza would call their power, that is, their capacity to affect other bodies. This is power that can be measured through its effects

(Viljanen 2014). But at the same time, the exhaustion felt by the soldiers was caused not only by the effect of those rocks on their exertion but also by these men's own efforts to move up carrying heavy loads. Likewise, it was the agency of the insurgency that turned the mountains into a weaponized field of action. (2018: 55)

Similarly, the title of Nicolas Peterson's work (2011) inquires: "Is the Aboriginal Landscape Sentient." The title localizes sentience as if it can be geographical—to draw a parallel, it would be the same as asking, Are Indigenous people alive? The problem here remains that there is a tendency to think it is the people who imbue the landscape with sentience, in the same way you would a stage puppet, which lies limp and lifeless once its human leaves. Last but not least, some engagements with the sentient landscape end up focusing completely on the human agent, making sentience a quality that humans can bestow on the land, instead of a feature intrinsic to the landscape itself. Take for example Simon Schama's reflection on his fieldwork: "Landscape is the work of the mind. Its scenery is built up as much from strata of memory as from layers of rock" (1995: 6–7).

The last thematic category that came out of our literature survey contains the work of scholars who try to understand where the problem lies by arguing that we do not grasp sentience to its full extent. Using their fieldwork data as a reference point, these scholars try to explain what exactly in the ontologies of the West might be lacking and thus preventing us from grasping the full meaning of a sentient landscape.

Take for example Julie Cruikshank's work (2006) in Athapaskan and Tlingit oral traditions from Yukon and Alaska, where glaciers can feel smells and listen, and where they punish the unjust and make moral judgements. One reason why this ontology may not have translated well to English-speaking settlers is the fact that, unlike some native languages that are rich in verbs and describe landscape through its actions, English does not have verb forms that differentiate between animate and inanimate subjects (Thornton 1995). That being said, this ontology has morphed through time: the sentience of landscape was not foreign to Europeans before the Industrial Revolution, yet their entire ontology ever since has been built on rejecting that possibility (Povinelli 1993: 12).

Following the Industrial Revolution and colonial encounters, shamanic ontologies have usually been dismissed as inferior by Western science, even though, for example, Amerindian shamanism has an understanding of syphilis and microbes in general that is close to modern-day biology (Giraldo Herrera 2018). Furthermore, shamans understood geological formations as having souls or spirits (Descola 1996). Even though we recognize that anthropology has gone through a process of self-reflection in the last few decades, trying to find some sense of cognitive justice and recognize the legitimacy of non-Western ontologies, we must also acknowledge that the binary of Western/non-Western still exists and is employed as if the world were as simple as literally non-white and white. At fault for the difficulty in grasping the ontological meaning of sentient landscapes could be the very anthropologists who create problems by trying to translate local vocabularies into Western terms. In any form of translation, a complete overlap can never happen; there are always shades of otherness that, despite their importance in the original context, can get lost through the work of academic translation.

As Giraldo Herrera puts it, translation is epistemic violence—and so is most research found in archives and museums, as forms of extractivist, colonial violence that split the world into modern and nonmodern, north and south, individual works of Western contemporary artists versus works exhibited as pertaining to an anonymous collective of nonmodern others (Marhöfer 2015). Anthropologists, historians, and their ken, have played important roles in the making and legitimation of these binaries and discourses. Not only is there violence in these discourses, as one of the binary terms always governs the other (Derrida 1990), but they also hinder our ability to imagine the multiple ontologies we inhabit. To speak of the nonhuman or other-than-human can further legitimate the zoning and segmentation of these ways of thinking.

The established procedures of knowledge production have a tendency to highlight human activity and make humans the reference point for everything (Marhöfer 2015). We may have been unable to escape this issue throughout the volume as the only language our ethnographers spoke was that of other humans, so their interlocutors were exclusively human. Not being able to talk to the landscape means we cannot assume things of its modes of thinking. Yet for so long we have been assuming it to be mother-like: generous, victimized, wanting to live in harmony—so perhaps one important move in unthinking colonial mindsets would be to also allow ourselves to imagine the opposite.

Even so, there is hope to recuperate colonial terminology and to use it to decolonize thought. Animism is an example of how this can be done: once a term used to talk about nonmodern ontologies, with the direct implication that they are epistemologically less than their Western counterparts, animism has been recuperated through the work of Descola (2013), Viveiros de Castro (2012), and Stengers (2010) as an academic tool that could help unthink and rethink Western beliefs.

In surveying the literature, we found a question posed by Ruth Rogaski (2018: 717) to be vitally productive for the purpose of the volume: "Do we need to know a mountain's nationality or can our knowledge about mountains transcend the political?" The question is an excellent starting point for investigating the links between the sentient landscapes capable of xenophobia and the sacralization of the nation. As the closest to the sky, mountain peaks have been the easiest to imagine as sacred. Additionally, there is an underlying assumption that uninhabited geographies are somehow pure and authentic and inspire a certain form of psychogeography. In fact, these landscapes remain uninhabited by way of government projects (the establishment of national parks or protected areas), or they are desolate, empty of infrastructure, and left wild with weeds, in a way that does not please the econationalist gaze.

From the sixteenth century on, mountains gained a sacred place in Europe in both religious and nonreligious fields (Mathieu 2006). We can notice that many of the Alpine peaks have names of saints (St. Moritz, St. Gallen, etc.) and so do valleys and passes (St. Bernhard, San Marco). Many of these had popular names for the longest time in history and were only given these Christian names as part of a rather nonreligious combination of topographical measurements and mountain tourism (Schorta 1988). Furthermore, the seventeenth century saw a boom in the creation of new pilgrimage places for Catholics, many of them overlapping with the topography of mountains. This happened less in Protestant countries, where God's omnipresence is central to the cosmology. In Southern Germany and Austria, the Santi Monti—artificially created mountains—have a whole pilgrimage devoted to them. All these pilgrimage sites were attempts of Europeans to recreate in Europe the mountain of Golgotha, thus topographically mimicking Jerusalem (Mathieu 2006).

Similarly, the root of far-right ecological thinking can be traced back to Romanticism, in the form of worries surrounding the shortage of wood and the risks surrounding the forests (Radkau 2014). This was coupled with a rejection of cold, uninvolved universalism in the favor of local uniqueness and diversity. With time, the nation and nature become a poetic, symbiotic ethnospace (Smith 2009). The discourses of protecting the environment and protecting the nation have a few elements in common— one is notably that both need to be protected against invasive species in the forms of plants, animals, or ethnoreligious others (Olwig 2003; Forchtner 2019). While these found an important place in fascist and National Socialist narratives of the mid-twentieth century, they have equally become an essential part of political imaginaries gathered under today's Nouvelle Droite or "new right," an ideology that supports nature as a partner of humans but also advocates for cultural and racial purity rather than mixing (de Benoist and Champetier 1999).

Perhaps most famously, the Nazis were very protective of the environment. In 1934, the Nazis mandated Dauerwald as the official silviculture doctrine of the German Reich through the law of 13 December 1934 Concerning the Protection of the Racial Purity of Forest Plants, whose aim was to "cast out the unwanted foreigners and bastards that have as little right to be in the German forest as they have to be in the German Volk" (Bruggemeier 2005: 44). Bruggemeier claims the policy was as the forest herself: green on the surface, and brown underneath (2005: 44), although he later oscillates between whether it was their intentions or their outcomes that were brown, meaning he is unclear on how much of the initial policy was racially motivated and how much of it had just the environment in mind.

Dauerwald is a form of *naturgemäße Waldwirtschaft*, or "natural forest management," a close-to-nature form of forestry that also produced many laws that were environmentally sound and progressive. The Dauerwald doctrine allowed for discourse that likened the German forest to the German volk—it was an easy tool to compare individual trees/individual Germans and the forest/nation. The Dauerwald had to only contain *bodenständige* (native) trees, which had always been rooted in German soil—and this was equally true of the volk. Ironically, the forest was seen as national even though its species were not, because the eighteenth-century German forests were planted with Norway pine and Scots pine. But they were planting monocultures, which had the same downfall as all monocultures, so scientific forestry fell out of fashion in Germany by the 1850s. Coniferous forests were held as particularly pure in German ideology, while broadleaf trees were considered "the stepchildren of forestry." However, the very idea of a national forest is rather artificial and noncongruent with the realities of the land: as landscape itself is not national, species will vary.

It can help us grasp the concept of sentient landscapes capable of xenophobia to recognize that German foresters in the 1930s famously spoke and wrote of the forest as an organism. Furthermore, one official is quoted saying, "Ask the trees, they will teach you how to become National Socialists!" (Modersohn 1939). The idea of a superior race was also maintained through parallels with a xenophobic sentient forest: "The balance among the components of the forest is maintained through the consumption of those who are superfluous, and that the survivors are those who are stronger and healthier, so that both the struggle and its victims serve the community. Thus, the forest teaches us the foundational laws of a völkisch and racially aware state such as the National Socialist one. And that is no coincidence" (Guenther 1936).

Tacitus's text *Germania* was a great influence on Protestant German scholars, who used it to create a lasting link between the noble savages of the past and the forest that could provide a legitimate source for the German national identity. This was not solely a political move—literary men like philosopher Johann Gottfried Herder used this connection to an idealized past as a tool against the globalizing effects of the French Enlightenment (Wilson 2012). In the late 1800s and early 1900s, the German forest became an important topic for works in botany, forestry, geography, history, literature, law, and politics, where the connection between the historical barbaric nation and its forests was praised in unison. The Germans were not alone in semiotically investing in the nature-nation connection: the British were deeply invested in connecting pastoral landscapes to the image of the nation, the Swedes were also praising the forest as a source of the nation, and French reforestation helped develop a sylvan nationalist discourse.

Chapter Summaries

We structured the book following concepts that matter in the ontological making of xenophobic landscapes: territory, nation, hostility, resources, who gets to speak with authority on who counts as Indigenous, and who counts as other. For example, the nation has resources and the know-how to protect nature, whereas the poor or marginalized lack both and are thus seen as dangerous to the landscape. In this sense, the nation is often discursively exempt from having negatively affected the landscape. In many of the chapters in this volume, geographical spaces have been the object of an ideological recovery in the service of right-wing ideologies.

One overarching theme that comes out of the narratives explored in the volume investigates who counts as other. In the first two sections of the book, the human populations inhabiting the sentient landscape see the land as coterminous with themselves, and they place human ethnoreligious others outside those boundaries. In this sense, the particular ontology of sentient landscapes explored in current literature (as kind, Gaia-like, siding with the marginalized and the colonized) does not match the findings of our authors. Such investigations illuminate ontologies in which the landscape is seen as more human than other groups perceived as less than human, whether historical or contemporary. The arguments against these less-than-human others go through the whole spectrum of disenfranchised others, including the Jew as both a contemporary colonial military other as well as a historically undesirable other in twentieth-century fascism (Coțofană's chapter), Japanese historical minorities in ethnoreligious nationalist Japan (Malitz's chapter), and competing Chilean discourses of human-landscape allegiances (Krizmanics's chapter).

The first part, "Reinventing the State," is made up of four chapters, each analyzing, with distinct ethnographic data and a distinctive lens, the tools and strategies that states concoct to imagine and narrate close bonds between a sentient landscape capable of xenophobia and their own political agendas. The book embarks on these conceptual and ethnographic explorations with the work of Scott Burnett. Burnett's study investigates the narratives and politics of South Africa's apartheid era. Here, he explores through anthems and poetry imaginaries of the connections between white South Africans and a sentient landscape. In Burnett's analysis, the sentient landscapes capable of xenophobia are revealed as both something to be feared and as a tool for a continued governing of the land. Next, Phillipe Blouin's work explores tensions between the settler institutions of Montreal and the Kanien'kehá:ka (Mohawk) Indigenous community. The Canadian settler population is appropriating logics of a partnership between the sentient land and humans to fit its ultranationalist, anti-immigration agenda. In the course of this ontological remolding, the sentient landscape itself becomes xenophobic, while the actual Indigenous people are imagined as part of the landscape. This attempt to self-indigenize is meant to legitimate the French settler's belonging to the land and give them the authority to speak against new waves of migration and refugees.

Coțofană's chapter traces the steady theme of sentient landscapes capable of xenophobia in Romania's long twentieth century, despite the many changes in political regimes and ideology. Her work looks at literary magazines and books assigned to primary school pupils, as well as at the discourse of Romanian politicians, journalists, and poets, to reveal how the concept of a xenophobic sentient landscape has come to the support of the Romanian people against both real colonizing political others (such as the Ottoman or Austro-Hungarian Empires) and imagined colonizing ethnoreligious others (such as the Jew in the early and mid-twentieth century). In the next chapter, Callum Pearce discusses his fieldwork in the Ladakh region of Himalayan India, focusing on tensions between Buddhists and Muslims that come accompanied by stories of how the sentient landscape attacks the Muslims, as they are not of that place.

The next part, called "Famous Fascisms," brings together ethnographic data from Nazi Germany, post-Franco Spain, Japan, and Chile. First, Hikmet Kuran's chapter sketches the historical context that we need to understand the connections between nation and the environment in Nazi Germany. Kuran's chapter alludes to the ways sentient landscapes capable of xenophobia become a trusted partner for the writing of Nazi history. In Arvid van Dam's chapter, we encounter a Spain like we have never seen before: eroded desert landscape and solitude inspire a cinematographic imaginary that includes hostile environments and the mirrored actions of the landscape's human counterparts. The section continues with the work of David Malitz on sentient landscapes capable of xenophobia in Japan.

Japan has at least four historical minorities, who differ from mainstream Japanese culture and have different legal status. These minorities are set against the concept of *shinkoku*, a term referring to the Japanese sentient landscape, imbued with deities, which throughout history has been reframed as connected to Japanese superiority, imperialism, and, later, to ultranationalism.

Last but not least, the ethnography of Georg T. A. Krizmanics illuminates ontologies of sentient landscapes capable of xenophobia in Chile. Settlers initially spoke of the relationship of the Indigenous Mapuche people with the sentient landscape, yet in the eyes of the Mapuche, the settlers, especially the Germans, had their own history of a bond with the sentient landscape, specifically the forest. Both forms had a rejection of foreigners at their core.

The last part, called "The Skeptics," concludes the book with two chapters that question the applicability of the concept. This section is vital as it opens new avenues for thinking with our concept. Sarah Czerny and her colleagues use their ethnographic fieldwork in Gorski Kotar, Croatia, to test the limits of the concept of sentient landscapes capable of xenophobia. Their work is extremely important as they are wary of European countries' xenophobic political history of associating the nation and nature. Susanna Trnka's work on Czech cities tests further directions in which the concept of sentient landscapes can be extended and applied, questioning whether the sentience of the built environment can exhibit xenophobia. Lastly, Hikmet Kuran delivers the concluding statements of the book.

Alexandra Coțofană holds a doctorate in anthropology from Indiana University Bloomington, with a doctoral minor in religious studies. Her research explores intersections of politics, modernities, and ontologies of governing. Alexandra's scholarly interests focus on political ecologies, the ontological turn, the study of political elites, and ways of governing, as well as on the occult as a tool for governing and discursive techniques employed in populist imaginaries to form racial, gender, and political Others. She is currently teaching and conducting research at Zayed University in Abu Dhabi as assistant professor of social sciences.

Notes

1. Ontology is the way we understand reality, the body of knowledge we have about being.
2. The word landscape comes from the Dutch word for flood fields, *landschap*, referring to the Dutch floodplains (Forchtner 2020), a topic of much artistic and literary interest during Romanticism.
3. We understand xenophobia as explained by Gregory Papanikos in his 2020 paper "Philoxenia and Xenophobia in Ancient Greece." Papanikos explains the complexities of the concept in ancient Greece—it was not used to mean solely fear or pure hatred but a complex set of emotions, rooted in the historical and political context in which the term emerged. The way our contemporaries use xenophobia today seems to carry the meaning of xenelasia (expulsion of foreigners). See https://www.atiner.gr/gtp/Papanikos(2020)-Philoxenia.pdf.

References

Biddle, Jennifer. 2007. *Breasts, Bodies, Canvas: Central Desert Art as Experience*. Sydney: UNSW Press.
Bruggemeier Franz-Josef. 2005. "Eternal Volk." In *How Green Were the Nazis? Nature, Environment, and Nation in the Third Reich*, ed. Franz-Josef Bruggemeier and Mark Cioc, 43–72. Athens: Ohio University Press.
Butler, Judith. 1993. *Bodies That Matter: On the Discursive Limits of Sex*. New York: Routledge.
Chandran, Rina. 2017. "India's Sacred Ganges and Yamuna Rivers Granted Same Legal Rights as Humans." *Reuters*, 21 March. Retrieved from www.reuters.com/article/us-india-water- lawmaking- idUSKBN16S109.
Coe, Michael D., and Stephan Houston. 2015. *The Maya*, 9th edn. London: Thames & Hudson.
Coletta, Michela, and Malayna Raftopoulos. 2016. *Provincialising Nature*. London: University of London Press.
Crosby, Donald A. 2013. *The Thou of Nature: Religious Naturalism and Reverence for Sentient Life*. Albany: State University of New York Press.
Cruikshank, Julie. 2006. *Do Glaciers Listen? Local Knowledge, Colonial Encounters, and Social Imagination*. Vancouver: UBC Press.
de Benoist, Alain, and Charles Champetier. 1999. "The French New Right in the year 2000." In *Alphalink*. Retrieved from http://home.alphalink.com.au/-radnat/debenoist/alain9.html.
Derrida, Jacques. 1990. *Positions*. London: The Athlone Press.
Descola, Phillipe. 1996. "Constructing natures: Symbolic ecology and social practice." In *Nature and society: Anthropological perspectives*, ed. Philippe Descola and Gisli Palsson, 82–101. London: Routledge.
———. 2005. *Par delà nature et culture*. Paris: Gallimard.
———. 2013. *The Ecology of Others*. Chicago: Prickly Paradigm Press.

Di Giminiani, Piergiorgio. 2018. *Sentient Lands: Indigeneity, Property, and Political Imagination in Neoliberal Chile*. Tucson: University of Arizona Press.
Fabian, Johannes. 1983. *Time and the Other: How Anthropology Makes Its Object*. New York: Columbia University Press.
Fienup-Riordan, Ann. 1994. *Boundaries and Passages: Rule and Ritual in Yup'ik Eskimo Oral Tradition*. Norman, OK.: University of Oklahoma Press.
Forchtner, Bernhard. 2019: "Nation, Nature, Purity: Extreme-right Biodiversity, Cultural Imaginaries of the Extreme Right." *Special Issue of Patterns of Prejudice* 53(3): 285–301.
———. 2020. *The Far Right and the Environment: Politics, Discourse and Communication*. London: Routledge.
Gilroy, Paul. 2018. "'Where Every Breeze Speaks of Courage and Liberty': Offshore Humanism and Marine Xenology, or, Racism and the Problem of Critique at Sea Level." *Antipode* 50: 3–22.
Giraldo Herrera, César E. 2018. *Microbes and Other Shamanic Beings*. London: Palgrave.
Gordillo, Gaston. 2018. "Terrain as Insurgent Weapon: An Affective Geometry of Warfare in the Mountains of Afghanistan." *Political Geography* 64: 53–62.
Gordon, Gwendolyn J. 2017. "Environmental Personhood." *Columbia Journal of Environmental Law* 43(1): 50–88.
Guenther, Konrad. 1936. "Preface." In *So lebt die Waldgemeinschaft: Eine Bildreihe in 3 Heften. 1. Heft: Biologische Gemeinschaftskunde*, ed. Hugo Keller, v–vi. Leipzig: Ernst Wunderlich.
Guillaume, Astrid. 2015. "The Intertheoricity: Plasticity, Elasticity and Hybridity of Theories." *HSS* IV(1): 13–29.
Haraway, Donna J. 2003. *The Companion Species Manifesto: Dogs, People, and Significant Otherness*. Chicago: Prickly Paradigm.
Harvey, Graham. 2005. *Animism: Respecting the Living World*. London: Hurst.
Ingold, Tim. 2000. *The Perception of the Environment: Essays on Livelihood, Dwelling and Skill*. London: Routledge.
———. 2012. "Toward an Ecology of Materials." *Annual Review of Anthropology* 41: 427-442.
Kwek, Dorothy H. B, and Robert Seyfert. 2018. "Affect Matters: Strolling through Heterological Ecologies." *Public Culture* 30(1): 35–59.
Latour, Bruno. 1993. *We Have Never Been Modern*. Translated by Catherine Porter. Cambridge, MA: Harvard University Press.
———. 2004. *Politics of Nature: How to Bring the Sciences into Democracy*. Translated by Catherine Porter. Cambridge, MA: Harvard University Press.
Marhöfer, Elke. 2015. "Ecologies of Practices and Thinking." PhD dissertation. Gothernburg, Sweden: Valand Academy, University of Gothenburg.
Mathieu, Jon. 2006. "The Sacralization of Mountains in Europe during the Modern Age." *Mountain Research and Development* 26(4): 343–49.
Modersohn, A. W. 1939. "Weltanschauung und beruflicher Einsatz." *Deutsche Forst-Zeitung* 8(15): 602–3.
Olwig, Kenneth. 2003. "Natives and Aliens in the National Landscape." *Landscape Research* 28(1): 61–74.

Peterson, Nicolas. 2011. "Is the Aboriginal Landscape Sentient? Animism, the New Animism and the Warlpiri." *Oceania* 81(2): 167–79.

Poirier, Sylvie. 2005. *A World of Relationships: Itineraries, Dreams and Events in the Australian Western Desert*. Toronto: Toronto University Press.

Povinelli, Elizabeth A. 1993. *Labor's Lot. The Power, History, and Culture of Aboriginal Action*. Chicago: University of Chicago Press.

———. 1995. "Do Rocks Listen? The Cultural Politics of Apprehending Australian Aboriginal Labor." *American Anthropologist New Series* 97(3): 505–18.

Radkau, Joachim. 2014. *The Age of Ecology*. Cambridge: Polity Press.

Rogaski, Ruth. 2018. "Knowing A Sentient Mountain. Space, Science, and the Sacred in Ascents of Mount Paektu/Changbai." *Modern Asian Studies* 52(2): 716–52.

Sampson, Fiona. 2018. "The Wilderness in Us." *Eurozine*, 28 February. Retrieved from https://www.eurozine.com/the-wilderness-in-us/.

Schama, Simon. 1995. *Landscape and Memory*. London: HarperCollins.

Schorta, Andrea. 1988. *Wie der Berg zu seinem Namen kam*. Chur, Switzerland: Terra Grischuna.

Smith, Anthony D. 2009. *Ethno-Symbolism and Nationalism*. Abingdon: Routledge.

Stengers, Isabelle. 2010. "Including Nonhumans into Political Theory: Opening the Pandora Box?" In *Political Matter: Technoscience, Democracy, and Public Life*. Minneapolis, MN: University of Minnesota Press.

Thornton, Thomas. 1995. "Tlingit and Euro-American Toponymies in Glacier Bay." In *Proceedings of the Third Glacier Bay Science Symposium*, 1993, ed. Daniel R. Engstrom, 294–301. Anchorage: National Park Service.

Tsing, Anna L., Jennifer Deger, Alder Saxena Keleman, and Feifei Zhou. 2020. *The Feral Atlas*. Stanford: Stanford University Press.

Vilaça, Aparecida. 2019. "Inventing Nature: Christianity and Science in Indigenous Amazonia." *HAU: Journal of Ethnographic Theory* 9(1): 44–57.

Viljanen, Valtteri. 2014. *Spinoza's geometry of power*. Cambridge: Cambridge University Press.

Viveiros de Castro, Eduardo. 2012. *Cosmologies: Perspectivism in Amazonia and Elsewhere*. Manchester: HAU Network of Ethnographic Theory.

Viveiros de Castro, Eduardo, and Peter Skafish. 2014. *Cannibal Metaphysics*. Minneapolis, MN: Univocal.

Wilson, Jeffrey K. 2012. *The German Forest: Nature, Identity, and the Contestation of a National Symbol, 1871–1914*. Toronto: University of Toronto Press.

Wolfe, Cary. 2003. *Animal Rites: American Culture, the Discourse of Species, and Posthumanist Theory*. Chicago: University of Chicago Press.

Part I
Reinventing the State

CHAPTER 1

Adamastor Unbound?

Whiteness and Landscape in Post-1994 South Africa

Scott Burnett

C. J. Langenhoven's 1918 poem "Die Stem" (literally "The Voice" but usually translated as "The Call"), the text for South Africa's apartheid-era national anthem, imagines a landscape that calls to the Afrikaner people to come together as a nation. In language that asserts possession of heaven and earth—"from the blue of *our* heaven, from the depths of *our* sea, over *our* eternal mountains"[1]—a voice is heard "from *our* beloved, from *our* land South Africa" that is answered by the people: "We shall answer your call, we shall sacrifice what you ask"[2] (Grové 1969: 72). The construction of intimate communion between an ethnic group and its homeland is not unusual in the Blut und Boden nationalisms of Europe. And yet, for Afrikaners, a culture had to be elaborated that squared their presence in and connection to Africa with their undeniable nonautochthonic status and their treasured European genealogy. In the parallel case of English-speaking white South Africans, who sang a broadly Anglo-inclusive translation of the hymn, the line "There's no land that shares our loving"[3] was less a statement of fact than an aspirational attempt to forge white racial unity from the lingering sense that these descendants of the imperial aggressors of the South African War (1899–1902) still owed their primary allegiance to Britain.

The figuration in "Die Stem" of a countryside calling out to white South Africans to come together to form a nation suggests a settler-colonial cosmopolitics in which landscape plays a central, even agentive, role. Generations of literary scholars, cultural geographers, and discourse analysts have indeed explored the myriad ways in which white South African identification has developed dialectically with both material and symbolic landscapes (e.g., J. M. Coetzee 1988; Foster 2008; Mpendukana and Stroud 2019). The landscape's agency—or *sentience*—has however not been explored as a dynamic of white identification, despite its ubiquity as a literary device. This chapter thus presents sociocultural analysis of three moments in white cultural production during the postapartheid period. These moments suggest that a lingering cosmopolitical uncertainty over whether whites are welcomed, or rejected, by the land haunts white identity projects. It will be argued that the provocative notion of a *xenophobic landscape* features both as a white anxiety and as a strategic resource for the continued domination of land.

Ethnographic explorations of sentient landscapes have tended to focus on Indigenous epistemologies, where land often plays a central role in pedagogy and knowledge production (e.g., Styres 2011, 2019), ecological justice (e.g., Strang 2020), or land justice (e.g., Di Giminiani 2018). Much of this work contrasts, explicitly or implicitly, Indigenous ways of knowing and thinking the land to those of an European colonial/imperial modernity that is alienated from a natural world treated as an inanimate resource to be exploited. To posit the existence of settler-colonial sentient landscapes might therefore seem something of a misclassification. Ethnographic accounts of Indigenous sentient landscapes have, however, repeatedly drawn attention to corresponding colonial constructions. Povinelli, for example, argues that the white Australian fixation on the productivity and ownership of land is as much an "unassailable totem" (1995: 506) as the idea that the land smells and feels human beings as they pass over it. Di Giminiani (2018) suggests that the principles that underlie neoliberal property discourses in Chile are not after all very different to those of the Indigenous Mapuche, only less well elaborated.

If the landscape is sentient, the question of whose side it will take—of whether it favors the *autochthon* and must therefore reject the *xenos*—is clearly an important concern for the establishment and development of settler-colonial societies. The symbolic production of the landscape is intimately interconnected with its material domination. As Roderick Neumann points out, the stakes of struggles for the meaning of landscapes are literally people's "livelihoods in place" (2011: 845). In this chapter, I read the symbolic production of the agency of the South African landscape by culturally dominant white settler-colonial groups as providing the conditions for their territorial domination. That the land might not welcome colonizing groups was an anxiety that needed to be overcome in the taming of the land, whose power then might be put to use as supportive of the rejection of new, unwelcome "others." Asking "Whose landscape?" is thus an important entry point into analysis of the symbolic and material (re)production of power relations that keep colonial and other social divisions in place, including race, ability, gender, and social class (see also Gilmore 2002).

In the next section, I discuss how landscape features in South Africa's territories of power. I describe how Adamastor, the monstrous mythological figure of the Cape of Storms in Luís de Camões's 1572 epic poem *Os Lusìadas,* has haunted the white literary imagination. I then present three moments from the past quarter century connected to ongoing processes of white identification. The first is from 1999 and relates to Cyril Coetzee's painting *T'kama-Adamastor,* which hangs in the University of the Witwatersrand's Cullen Library in Johannesburg. The second dates from May 2013, when the BBC aired a documentary feature framed by the question, Do white people have a future in South Africa? The third is the campaign against fracking the Karoo, seen through the lens of ethnographic material collected in 2016. In the concluding section, I connect Adamastor's haunting of the white imagination to the persistence of what Boaventura de Sousa Santos (2007) calls "abyssal thinking."

Space, Race, and the Social Life of Landscape

Racial hierarchies are frequently mapped onto spatial orders, and race and space co-occur in entangled and dialectical relationships. The production of socio-spatial epistemologies of race tends to associate particular places with specific racial identities and to restrict mobility in space (Lipsitz 2007; Natter and Jones 1997). Apartheid's development as the "enforced coincidence between spatial and 'racial' relations" (Cohen 1988: 8) was succeeded by "neo-apartheid" in South African suburban development enabled by neoliberal policymaking (Beavon 2000) and discourses naturalizing ongoing segregation (Durrheim and Dixon 2001; McEwen and Steyn 2013). White South Africans asserted a right to define "neighborhood character" (Ballard 2005) in discursive gestures aimed at keeping "African" cultural practices (and hence unruly Black bodies) out of their suburbs (see also Ballard 2010).

The "imaginative appropriation" of landscape was central to the historical forging of a white national identity in South Africa (Foster 2008). Specific landscapes become God-given "heartlands" threatened after apartheid by Black misrule (Burnett 2019). White constructions of landscape are, however, marked by nagging ambivalences about belonging, arising from histories of colonial dispossession. The landscape is as much a source of unease as of repose; generations of material and symbolic production were required for it to become "home." The alien trees of Johannesburg's artificial urban forest, for example, reflected back to its white habitués their European heritage, while row upon row of identical township houses for Black people reflected their supposed lack of an urban culture and the idea that their "real" home was in the homeland reserves set aside for them (Foster 2009: 192–97; Dlamini 2009: 151–52). The historical construction of urban (white) spaces as lush and green—so unlike the surrounding anarchic veld of Africa, "a place of unease, uncertainty and fear . . . [that] might erupt into violence" (Foster 2009: 201)—underwent significant revision towards the end of apartheid, when the idea of South Africa as a European bastion faded under the necessity of asserting a local, rooted, and Indigenous status, even as privatization and neoliberalization were segregating urban spaces into private and gated zones. While exotic green lawns remain important signifiers of "civilization" (Cane 2019), the assiduously marketed inclusion of local fauna and flora in exclusive "eco-villages" suggests an aspiration to Indigenous belonging (Ballard and Jones 2011; Raidoo 2020) even as African social realities are kept at bay.

South African literature has grappled extensively with its segregated locations of enunciation, the "tyranny of place" (Mphahlele 1987) characterized by "the diastole and systole of appropriation and renunciation, aggression and resistance" (van Wyk Smith 1990: 2–3). It is against this backdrop that two contrasting visions of the land appear in white writing: the pastoral, where a "dream topography" consists of "thousands of farms, each a separate kingdom ruled over by a benign patriarch" (J. M. Coetzee 1988: 6), and the antipastoral, where the landscape is mysterious, silent, and blank. The former requires of man that he prove his virtue in the rural idyll through honest toil; the fact that he is white, while it is Black people who labor, must thus be "[occluded] from the scene. . . . [For] how can the farm become the pastoral retreat of the black man when it was his pastoral home only a generation or two ago?" (1988: 5). Black people are similarly pushed into the background in the antipastoral tradition, which represents a "failure to imagine a peopled landscape" (1988: 9). Where communion with the land is allowed to happen, it brings forth monsters, "the return of what is repressed in the poetry of the silent landscape" (1988: 10). It is to just such a monster that we now turn.

Enter Adamastor

The story of Adamastor, claimed both as the origin of European-style literature and of literary criticism in South Africa, has been told and retold in a number of forms since Luís de Camões's 1572 epic poem *Os Lusìadas* (see Gray 1977). As the Portuguese explorer Vasco da Gama and his crew approach the Cape of Storms, they are filled with terror at a form emerging from darkness. A mysterious giant emerges in the rocky cape, cursing the imperialistic hubris of the Portuguese who dare to violate his realm (Graham 2012: 19). The ships will be wrecked, he warns, and catastrophe will befall those who reach land. Undeterred, da Gama commands the giant to identify himself. The giant explains that he is Adamastor, a Titan who loved and tried to ravish the sea nymph Tethys. As she escaped, she laughingly drew attention to his hugeness, which made their union impossible. Tethys and her mother lured Adamastor to a trysting point, where he embraced a decoy, falling under a spell that gradually turned him to rock. Adamastor became the massive form of Table Mountain, while Tethys herself was transformed into the waves, lapping tantalizingly and eternally around the giant's form.

Adamastor's frequent recurrence in South African poetry and prose often attends anxiety about race relations in South Africa (Gray 1977), where the giant's curse rings down the ages as a prediction of the inevitable failure of the European colonial project. This "punitively haunting Adamastor with his increasingly verified prophecies of racial revenge" (Crewe 1999: 81) was a European cultural invention, a repository for the symbolic elaboration of Africa, itself an "ancient text under revision [which] veered sharply between visions of paradise and purgatory, refreshment and desolation, fabled Christian empires and hazardous torrid zones" (Twidle 2012: 33). Adamastor's Latin etymological roots make him a rival to Adam, while in Greek he is "untamed" or "untamable":

> In the literature of colonial contact, then, the presence of the inanimate world, as it exceeds and threatens the biblical act of naming, all too easily becomes the maligned, mysterious Other. Such texts—in giving voice to coded, symbolically articulated threats to the colonial project while never dealing explicitly with the circumstances of indigenous resistance—then produce nature that does the work of culture. (Twidle 2012: 32)

Nature's resistance to colonization is thus necessary to the extent that the full agency of African people fails to find a place in the colonial moral and symbolic order. The figure of the savage Titan makes white explorers more human by contrast, reinforcing their own awareness of selfhood and agency, while legitimating subjugation of the threatening Other (Samin 2006). Africa's association with monstrous alterity furthermore generates sexualized "twin penetration anxieties": on the one hand the settler thrusting himself inland is "threatened with engulfment by the alien land," while on the other "his women are in danger of being penetrated and contaminated by the monstrous others who inhabit this territory" (Graham 2012: 18). This latter anxiety retraces the figure of the Black man as penis symbol, the "mainstay" of colonial white fear and desires (Fanon [1952]

2008: 150–51). It is against this threat, then, that white women constitute the "cherished frontier on which the status and superiority of the settler race depended" (Graham 2012: 18; see also Ahmed 2004). The figure of Adamastor as the savage would-be rapist of Tethys, cursing da Gama's colonial ships, has thus been a frequent preoccupation of the solipsistic settler imagination.

Taming Adamastor

The last five years of the twentieth century were a time of great hope and renewal in South Africa, a time when President Nelson Mandela was received by rapturous crowds around the world, when the country's admission to international sporting events resulted in a series of celebrated triumphs, when the end of the cultural and academic boycotts breathed new life into moribund social and cultural institutions, and when the ruling African National Congress's promise of a "better life for all" seemed just over the horizon. At the University of the Witwatersrand in Johannesburg, a bastion of liberalism throughout apartheid and the institution where Mandela had studied law, the question of how to reflect the dawn of this New South Africa was mooted. Professor Alan Crump convinced Vice-Chancellor Robert Charlton in 1994 to explore commissioning a new painting for a blank wall in the Cullen Library that faced two older paintings that celebrated the colonial project. The new commission would represent a break with that past and was intended to "reflect the radical transformation the country was undergoing" (Crump 2000: n.p.). Money was raised to pay for it, and the proposal of painter Cyril Coetzee to "reconstruct the colonial narrative of discovery metaphorically through the eyes of an indigenous African people" was approved (ibid.). The resulting painting was *T'kama-Adamastor* (figure 1.1), a version of the Adamastor myth inspired by an André Brink novella.

A handsomely produced art book with scholarly essays was published to accompany the painting. Celebrated author Ivan Vladislavić was recruited as editor, while prominent literary and art critics, as well as Coetzee and Brink themselves, contributed essays. The book engages elaborately with the archive of the Cullen Library, a repository of centuries of mostly European knowledge production about Africa. While Crump's claim about the perspective of the work being "through the eyes of" African indigenes engenders some unease from one of the critics—the iconography is after all exclusively European—the editor addresses the question of perspective by arguing that the painting "might fulfil Brink's proposition that the critical task for artists is not to look from the 'other'

Figure 1.1. *T'kama-Adamastor* by Cyril Coetzee (1999). © Africana Collections, University of the Witwatersrand.

side, but to find entirely new ways of looking" (Vladislavić 2000). Coetzee himself explains in his essay that he has tried to "make ironic and fantastic use of a variety of tropes and clichés of the colonial world-view" (C. Coetzee 2000: 3–4). This idea of "new ways of looking" that are "ironic and fantastic" is echoed in the volume's subtitle, "Inventions of Africa in a South African Painting."

Coetzee positions the painting as a metaphorical response, from the perspective of an (unnamed) Indigenous African people, to two other paintings that hang in the library—*Colonists 1826* by Colin Gill (1934) and *Vasco da Gama: Departure for the Cape* by J. H. Amshewitz (1935) (C. Coetzee 2000: 5–9). In Coetzee's painting, which follows the triptych layout also used by Gill and Amshewitz, the colonial contact narrative is fantastically reinvented with a visual vocabulary borrowed from Albrecht Dürer and Hieronymus Bosch, among others, and structured around Brink's story. In his novella, the Khoi chief T'kama is introduced as the first "avatar" of Adamastor. His desire to have sex with a white colonial woman (painted by Coetzee as Eve to T'kama's Adam) is thwarted by his long penis, which grows longer with every attempt. Eventually, he can wrap it around his waist. After a crocodile severs the offending member with a single bite, T'kama uses a more manageable clay phallus. The penis is however given a suggestive visual afterlife by Coetzee in the shape of the ostrich neck, which ascends from the Khoi chief's midriff.

Both works are ostensibly parodic of Eurocentric colonial contact narratives. In the account that Brink gives of his novella, "redefining that moment, redefining and reacknowledging Adamastor, is part of the demand that we redefine ourselves" (Brink and Nethersole 2000: 57). But Brink's deployment of Khoi mythology within a magical realist style arguably turns the precolonial world into a "site of wish fulfilment" (Twidle 2012:

42). The white writer arrogates to himself both the renovation of his own identity and the production of the "native" perspective on this process. One might expect the "invention" of Africa—through retelling the story of contact—to be "Adamastor's prerogative, not that of the invaders" (Klein 2018: 110). While Brink's (and by extension Coetzee's) ironic tone and postmodern destabilizations of his authorial reliability create room for the denial of intention or content, the white auteur is reinscribed as interpreter-in-chief of South Africa's colonial history.

This inscription is achieved through an act of ventriloquism. In both novel and painting, the powerful image of the ship as a bird dropping off boats like eggs from under its wings is supposedly produced from an Indigenous perspective. The image however "belongs to the same set of self-aggrandizing gestures that early modern European travel writers resorted to as a way of showcasing the seemingly effortless superiority of western technology over naïve indigenous world-views" (Klein 2018: 114). These gestures to centering an African perspective thus take place within an "almost exclusively European framework: the gaze mocked and ironized on the canvas through its many allusions to Renaissance artworks replicates the view from Europe, not Africa" (120). It is again whites who are doing the world making, passing off "more or less unreconstructed Eurocentric contact myths" (Hanzimanolis 2002: 256) as Khoi perspectives.

The bodily deformations visible in the painting reproduce gendered and sexualized anxieties associated with the colonial project (Hanzimanolis 2002). Adamastor's clay penis is paralleled by the abdomens of the Khoi maidens, hidden underwater. Margaret Hanzimanolis argues that these representations sterilize the Indigenous body, foreclosing the possibility of its populating the land, thereby opening up semiotic space for a new national identity to emerge. She reads the deformations of this painting in place as signifying "a reluctance, on the part of the formerly dominating culture, to relinquish command of certain enclaves of influence" (2002: 251). The Cullen Library, in which the painting hangs, contains one of the world's largest and most valuable collections of Africana, and is a popular research and working space for students at one of Africa's premier institutions of higher learning. It is a site intimately involved in ongoing knowledge production. With the decision to fill its only empty wall with this painting, "the door shuts rather loudly on an important opportunity" (2002: 263). Identities after colonialism and apartheid, and knowledge about Africa, are symbolically hemmed in.

So instead of marking a "transformative" moment and speaking back to the works by Gill and Amshewitz, the painting reaffirms elements of these colonial celebrations. In her essay in the edited collection that accompanied the painting, literary scholar Reingard Nethersole remarks on how the 1930s artists showed "the anxiety and uncertainty white pioneers had to undergo, and the defiant bravery they had to exhibit, in order to overcome adversity and make the country inhabitable" (2000: 37). This careless reproduction of terra nullius finds no real rejoinder from Brink or Coetzee, whose fantastical retreat from a reckoning with European colonial violence is in its own way an attempt to make the country "inhabitable"—for them and their families, in perpetuity, unburdened by decisive reparations or the centrality of perspectives on colonialism not structured by the white imagination. It is telling that every person described as involved in the commissioning, funding, and launch of the book and painting, bar one art critic, was white; and it is telling that every one of these white people, bar one literary scholar, was a man. We thus observe in the refiguration of Adamastor the next generation of "adamastorbation": white men having conversations with themselves about identity and belonging, rooted in their own anxieties and desires. A white cultural horizon as definitive of knowledge production in postapartheid South Africa is reproduced, and the figure of a landscape rejecting whiteness has been decisively tamed. T'kama-Adamastor has been emasculated, sterilized, his big penis replaced with a small clay pipe, while "his" perspective on colonial contact places European knowledge production at the very center, structured by the white, male gaze of scholars and artists.

"This Lovely Terrain Has Turned into a Battlefield"

The defiant bravery of white pioneers making a country "inhabitable" was powerfully evoked in May 2013, when the BBC broadcast a news insert by veteran journalist John Simpson asking the question, "Do White People have a Future in South Africa?"[4] The six-and-a-half-minute clip starts and ends at the Voortrekker Monument, the quasi-fascist neoclassical edifice in Tshwane-Pretoria that serves as a key site for the memorialization of Afrikaner nationalism. Over a sad, slow melody played on a mouth organ, Simpson calls the Voortrekkers "pioneers" who "carved out the Boer republics," and who went on to suffer terribly in British concentration camps. Lingering shots of statues of these brave souls from other vantage points in Pretoria create the sense that they continue to watch over the landscape. Simpson moves quickly through the rest of South African history: when these "pioneers" introduced apartheid, the "victims turned oppressors." Bringing his narration into the present day, he remarks that "now they voluntarily have given up political power altogether."

There is clearly little room for the liberation struggle, nor Black agency in any form, to intrude into history making in this summary account.

There is only the narrative arc of white victims turned oppressors, and then—as is shown in the rest of the clip—turned victims once again. While relations between white and Black are central to Simpson's framing of South African politics, the settings for the starting and opening sequences (the Voortrekker Monument), and the six intervening locations I will discuss below, suggest that racialized social relations are understood as *mediated* by the landscape, which emerges in tandem with specific subject positions. The first location is a primary school, where we see a visibly moved Simpson listening as a racially diverse hall of pupils sing songs together, before paging through the 1977 yearbook to point out his own daughters from the sea of all-white faces. He remarks that the school now "feels so much better and happier and freer." The location then shifts to the bars and restaurants of Vilakazi Street in Soweto, where a mostly Black clientele struggles to find parking space for their Porsches and BMWs, and where a festive atmosphere prevails, which, we are informed, is "in many ways . . . the dominant face of the new South Africa." When he interviews the "political activist" Mandla Nyaqela, who reminds him that white people still control most of the economy and the land, the camera does not focus on Nyaqela's face but on the beer bottle in front of him. The next location—another concession to lingering white power—is also presented as not entirely serious: it is a raucous scene of middle-class Afrikaners enjoying drinks and braaied (barbecued) meat served to them by Black staff, while *Boeremusiek* plays. Simpson concedes that many whites are still rich, but the anachronistic, folksy soundtrack that has been chosen undermines the seriousness of this characterization.

The tone then shifts abruptly, with a further change of location: "One ugly secret in the new South Africa is white poverty." In a white "squatter camp" called Sunshine Corner, we meet Frans de Jager, one of "at least two hundred thousand" whites living in poverty, who explains to Simpson that he cannot access social grants because "ninety-nine percent they don't help you because you're speaking to a Black person." Simpson ratifies the claim: "After all, white people never provided Blacks with a social security safety net when they ran the country." The location then shifts to the agricultural countryside. "But there's worse. Here, outside Pretoria, the killing ground begins." Simpson interviews a distraught Belinda van Noord, whose father and brother were killed during a robbery of their general store. As she moves past mounds of red earth dug for their graves, clutching their pictures, Simpson informs us that "two other white farmers" also recently murdered lie buried there. The police "don't seem to do much about it," and as for international media attention, "it's scarcely reported outside South Africa." Simpson concludes: "This lovely terrain has turned into a battlefield."

The tone shifts again with a new location. A cheerful acoustic guitar riff and a song in isiZulu accompany attractive shots of Church Square, once the "heart of Pretoria and of Afrikanerdom." But there is a problem: "Many whites feel like strangers in their own country, precisely as Blacks did under apartheid." This is explained visually and in Simpson's narration; the name of Pretoria is changing to Tshwane, while Black townspeople pose for pictures in front of the famous statue of Boer president Paul Kruger. "There's not a white face here," Simpson intones, "a living one at any rate." But Simpson is here to meet a white man, the deputy CEO of the Afrikaner rights organization AfriForum, Ernst Roets, who is presented as a brave crusader against growing government disrespect for the rule of law.

Simpson joins the Roets family on a bench at the edge of the square, where he asks Roets's wife whether she thinks there is a future for her child, on whose bright and happy face the camera lingers. She answers affirmatively, "If everyone just do their little bit to make this a better place then, ja, I am definitely sure there is a future for every one of us." This seemingly positive note occasions a transition back to the Voortrekker Monument, and a return to the tune of the lonely mouth organ. Of the five million white people "still" in South Africa, "many" will have a "good future," says Simpson. "But the wheel has turned. Just as it did when the Voortrekkers first arrived. And history can be pretty unforgiving."

This remarkable video, produced by a respected British journalist for an international audience, retraces tropes of central importance to maintaining South Africa as "inhabitable" by (and in the possession of) whites. Black people are represented as indulging in frenzied orgies of consumption on township streets, drunkenly pointing fingers at rich whites, while Black social workers supposedly deny social services to poor whites in acts of revenge for apartheid crimes. When the men of the Van Noord family are gunned down (by Black people), those meant to preserve law and order (also Black people) do nothing to bring the killers to justice and instead engage in an assault on a free judiciary (according to Roets). But this white suffering remains an "ugly secret" and farm attacks "scarcely reported"—except, that is, by brave journalists such as Simpson, who can pierce through the political correctness to ask tough questions about the New South Africa.[5]

Though this drama plays out in the acts of individuals and between social groups, the extent to which it is mediated through representations of the landscape is striking. In the opening and closing scenes, statues of the Voortrekker pioneers survey Pretoria sadly, memorialized as innocently "carving out" their republics from terra nullius, from land constructed as uninhabitable/uninhabited. Now we see the "habitability" that they created: the orderly white world of the monument and the school, with its prominently displayed honor rolls and racially mixed student body, strongly contrasted to the jumble of Black exuberance and wealth on the streets of Soweto, where expensive cars can barely find space to park. Subterranean monsters lurk in the rural areas, however, where red mounds mark the places on the "battlefield" where white farmers have fallen. On Church Square, the former "heart" of Afrikanerdom, the camera follows Black people clambering over Boer monuments, as if in triumph. The renaming of Pretoria to Tshwane and the predominance of Black faces on the square is articulated as having effects on white people similar to those apartheid had on Black people; white suffering is clearly inevitable if they no longer name and control the land. The idea of a white heartland, where white faces are not crowded out by Black, and where the semiotic landscape of colonialism and apartheid are left undisturbed, is normalized in Simpson's reportage as a reasonable response to a new dispensation in which they risk being finally "engulfed" by the land that they penetrated.

Spaces for white "self-determination," white "heartlands" with racially exclusive social institutions and extensive territorial control, are unstated but clearly adumbrated goals of a number of postapartheid white-run organizations, of which AfriForum is the most prominent. "Carving out" their own space on the postapartheid landscape requires exaggerating the scale of white poverty and vulnerability to violence, while also misrepresenting the government's response to it. To interrupt the perception of white South Africans as colonial victors living off the fat of the land, the land must be represented as still hostile, as persistently in need of taming. The threats of Adamastor must thus be allowed to resound once more, reminding the (white) world that "civilization" at the tip of Africa is dependent on whites being allowed to organize their own spaces, on their own terms.

"Locked Gates and Loaded Shotguns"

The arid plains of the Karoo hold a special place in the white imagination. For a colonial experience that started on the coast, the desert beyond the escarpment was hinterland, the unknown, the start of the "real" Africa. Inhospitable and vast, the blankness of the Karoo was particularly amenable to the fiction of terra nullius. Eventually parceled out into large white-owned agricultural plots supporting sheep and goats, a landscape of low farmhouses and ancient koppies on vast plains dotted with concrete dams and wind pumps came to be treasured as a place of calm, august beauty. The publication in 2011 of government-endorsed plans for Shell Oil and others to be granted prospecting licenses to explore the viability of hydraulic fracturing ("fracking") of natural gas thus drew fierce and immediate opposition from environmentalists and landowners (see Fig 2013). Horror stories from Australia and Pennsylvania of earthquakes, burning rivers, and poisoned water spread quickly through online and local social networks. Local "Karooists" and city-dwelling Karoo lovers alike cultivated the idea of a corrupt, despoiling government in cahoots with big oil and gas, representing an imminent threat to a treasured region outsiders neither knew nor loved (Burnett 2019). Landowners vowed to protect their lands with "locked gates and loaded shotguns."[6]

The most sustained environmental opposition came from the Treasure Karoo Action Group (TKAG), which under the leadership of CEO Jonathan Deal dominated much of the narrative of the fight against fracking. Environmental justice groups such as the Support Centre for Land Change (SCLC), which opposed fracking at the same time as advancing land restitution and reform, tried at times to work both with landowners and with TKAG, but with limited success. The leaders of SCLC are clear-eyed about the pitfalls of working with "mainstream" environmentalists in South Africa. "When the victory comes, they will say it was their victory," says Chriszanne Janse van Rensburg, who heads SCLC in Graaff Reinet. Phumi Booysen, one of SCLC's most prominent activists, agrees. On a previous campaign to prevent stretches of the Southern Cape coast from conversion into private golf estates, Booysen worked with white environmentalists. Once the campaign was won, white landowners resumed their opposition to land rights for people with whom they had recently stood "shoulder to shoulder against the golf estate."[7] For SCLC activists, fighting fracking is consistent with their opposition to colonial land appropriation and persistent injustice, even if they are forced to build alliances with landowners who only care about sustaining the "power that they unfortunately still have."[8]

When I meet TKAG CEO Jonathan Deal, he admits that when he started out he had a lot to learn about community organizing. He explains that his opposition to fracking was not underwritten by any constituency, least of all white landowners, and that it was love of the Karoo that motivated him.

> I have driven every single dirt road in the Karoo and I have been to every town. . . . So I think that out of people that would stand up to defend the Karoo I am well placed to understand how the culture works, the demographics, the way things are laid out, and the environment of the Karoo, sociopolitically, economically, from a tourism point of view.[9]

It is his cartographic, economic, and scientific knowledge of the land that underwrites Deal's authority to lead the campaign against fracking. In his attempts to forge broad alliances, he partnered with AfriForum, which resulted in prominent figures in the environmental justice movement distancing themselves from him.

> That was a ... bitter pill to swallow.... I've actually done much more for the poor and marginalized people and the farmworkers in the Karoo than I have for the landowners, because if fracking ever went ahead, and it created the type of disturbance that we anticipate that it would, farmworkers are going to be the first people to suffer.[10]

Deal thus considers his attempts to prevent fracking as long-term future wins for the farmworkers, which are more valuable than coalitions with land and environmental justice movements. This construction of the landless poor who labor on farms as benefiting from attempts to stop fossil fuel exploitation is also articulated by the president of the provincial agricultural union, who tells me that:

> The area they are targeting is particularly water scarce: the Karoo. Now how can we even think of going down that route, when we've had agriculture which has been sustained here for two hundred years plus? We've formed the economic backbone of rural communities for time immemorial.[11]

The "we" that forms the "economic backbone" is clearly not the Khoi herders or isiXhosa pastoralists who worked the land for hundreds of years before European colonization. The event two hundred years ago that made Western agriculture in the region profitable was the import of merino sheep by white farmers, and a boom in the price of wool. But it is water that connects the various narratives about how this backbone works. When the subject of land justice comes up in my conversation with Jonathan Deal, he says that he would sign over a few hectares to each of his three employees if it were not for the Land Tenure Act:

> The Land Tenure Act has got provisions along the lines that the entire family can immediately come.... And I could quite foreseeably after ten years be sitting with a few hundred people here. This land ... can't sustain that type of thing, and the Karoo water is not designed to sustain that kind of people.[12]

A landscape emerges here, constituted by the string of people who possess and control it, who together form its "backbone" and are engaged in intimate forms of knowing, mapping, and measuring it. Its lifeblood is the water table—the subterranean quantity of water only true insiders can understand—which serves as the basis for prognostications about whether the landscape will remain habitable. Both fracking (as envisioned by the national government) and land justice (as envisioned by decolonial activists) threaten to sap the water and thus to break the backbone. Only the status quo can keep the land habitable: and the status quo is a land of locked gates and loaded shotguns, a xenophobic landscape where outsiders are not welcome, where the land itself will reject and dehydrate interlopers. The effect of these discourses is to protect the Karoo as a white heartland, which is in turn produced as orderly, inhabitable, and sustainable in ways that make external influxes—whether from fossil fuel companies, or rapidly multiplying family members—threats against which gates must be locked, and shotguns loaded.

Conclusion: Into the Abyss

An outline emerges of something ever present, dark and monstrous, threatening to wipe the traces of white "civilization" from the map. Appearing as it does in the cultural production of (by their own account) progressive "Rainbow Nation" white South Africans, this figure is clearly entangled in complex postapartheid (re)negotiations of belonging. In order to construct the "unassailable totem" of rights to name, imagine, and occupy Africa, white settlers historically had to recognize themselves in the land—to belong there, so that the land might belong to them. As has been noted in a variety of settler-colonial contexts, the descendants of these settlers developed their own autochthonic myths (Burnett 2019; Dominy 2001; Garbutt 2006). This evolving articulation of an ethnic sense of place is not the denial of the sentience of the landscape but rather the remobilization of the sentient landscape as a tactic to shore up their property claim in the face of postcolonial calls for redistribution (see Dominy 2001).

Boaventura de Sousa Santos has suggested that the epistemological commitments of Western modernity that emerged in Europe during the Renaissance constitute "abyssal thinking" (2007). Beneath the metropolitan dichotomies and distinctions that uphold the rightness or wrongness of propositions, or make actions moral or immoral, legal or illegal, there is an invisible line beyond which "there is only nonexistence, invisibility, nondialectical absence" (2007: 2). This line is an epistemological cordon marking the border of the colony, a place in which such distinctions become unthinkable. Without an "abyss" between that side of the line and this, the universality of modern science and law would be fatally undermined. Whereas metropolitan sociopolitical contests play out between regulation and emancipation, in the colony there is only appropriation and violence—and it is the abyss between these worlds that enables the metropolitan distinction to function. Indigenous knowledges "vanish as relevant or commensurable knowledges" (Santos 2007: 4): their adherents are neither right nor wrong, as their knowledges are the raw materials for inquiry, not inquiry itself. The philosophical building blocks of the modern political order were by philosophers who situated the state of nature in the colonial peripheries, and who identified the emergence of civil society as abandoning this state to join European modernity. Before this modernity, there was nothing: their lands were *terra nullius*; their souls were *anima nullius* (Santos 2007: 8).

The polemical distinctions offered by Santos are complicated by the kind of (post)colonial settler-descendant cultural production analyzed in this chapter. European settler populations in Africa imagined themselves as bastions of modernity, while building their material foundations in the barbarous negation of Black humanity, constructed as perpetually in need of white guidance and "development" (Mpofu, 2018). Settler-colonial societies were built *on the abyss*—and the anxieties of (post)colonial whiteness relate mostly to finally sliding into it, finally and climactically being sublimated into the Other. The analysis presented in this chapter suggests that this anxiety attaches to the landscape's agency as ally or accomplice of Adamastor, bound or unchained. In *T'kama-Adamastor* the land persists as a site of Adamic wish fulfilment, where the ethical and imaginative borders of the New South Africa might be drawn by a cadre of white male intellectuals. In the moment the artists understand themselves as mocking the original settlers, they reveal their own desires to decisively tame/castrate Adamastor. The antifrackers and AfriForum have their own, perhaps earthier version of the solution: maintain the communion of man and land, lock those gates and load those shotguns. Simpson's BBC report hinges on what happens if this project fails: the "lovely terrain" controlled by "pioneering" whites will become a "killing ground." Surveying the site of their suffering, Boer statues sadly bear witness to the results of Adamastor's curse.

Anxieties about nonbelonging, and about violence repaid for bloody historical conquests, are thus in part projected onto a sentient landscape, whose agency in deciding who belongs is appealed to. The fear that Adamastor shakes himself free of all that is "modern" and "scientific" clearly animates the power/knowledge projects discussed here: repressing the violence of colonialism with postmodern irony in *T'kama-Adamastor*; revealing the "ugly secret" of Black postapartheid revenge against whites on the BBC; and producing the land as only truly knowable by white landowners and lovers of the land, who are its "backbone." Adamastor is the product of white abyssal thinking, a cultural phantasm reawakened by increasing calls for decolonization, and the redistribution of land and wealth.

Scott Burnett teaches and works at the University of Gothenburg's Department of Applied IT, Division of Cognition & Communication. Scott investigates, through a decolonial and post-Marxist lens, the construction and repair of racial hierarchies privileging whiteness in spatial and environmentalist discourse. His work has been published in leading journals such as *ACME: An International Journal for Critical Geographies, Discourse, Context & Media*, and the *African Journal of Employee Relations*.

Notes

1. Author's translation (emphasis added). The original reads: "Uit die blou van onse hemel, / Uit die diepte van ons see, / Oor ons ewige gebergtes" (Grové 1963: 72).
2. The original reads: "van ons geliefde, / Van ons land Suid-Afrika. / Ons sal antwoord op jou roepstem, / Ons sal offer wat jy vra" (Grové 1963: 72).
3. The original reads: "Deel geen ander land ons liefde" (Grové 1963: 72).
4. The insert and an explanatory article are available on the BBC website at https://www.bbc.com/news/magazine-22554709. The related quotes that follow are from this video.
5. When Simpson was challenged in the South African media for the numerous misrepresentations and inaccuracies in his piece, he published a response (https://www.bbc.com/news/magazine-22708507), which attributed the strong negative reaction to an offended self-image and vouched for his own nonracist intentions by referring to his joy when Nelson Mandela was elected president in 1994.
6. Quoted from coverage on http://karoospace.co.za/karoo-fracking-locked-gates-loaded-shotguns/.
7. Author's interview with Phumi Booysen, George, 1 December 2016.
8. Author's interview with Chriszanne Janse van Rensburg, George, 1 December 2016.
9. Author's interview with Jonathan Deal, Gecko Rock Private Nature Reserve, 2 December 2016
10. Author's interview with Jonathan Deal, Gecko Rock Private Nature Reserve, 2 December 2016
11. Author's interview with Dougie Stern, Graaff-Reinet, 29 November 2016
12. Author's interview with Jonathan Deal, Gecko Rock Private Nature Reserve, 2 December 2016

References

Ahmed, Sara. 2004. "Affective Economies." *Social Text* 22 2(79): 117–39.
Ballard, Richard. 2005. "When in Rome: Claiming the Right to Define Neighbourhood Character in South Africa's Suburbs." *Transformation: Critical Perspectives on Southern Africa* 57(1): 64–87.
———. 2010. "'Slaughter in the Suburbs': Livestock Slaughter and Race in Post-Apartheid Cities." *Ethnic & Racial Studies* 33(6): 1069–87.

Ballard, Richard, and Gareth A. Jones. 2011. "Natural Neighbors: Indigenous Landscapes and Eco-Estates in Durban, South Africa." *Annals of the Association of American Geographers* 101(1): 131–48.

Beavon, Keith S. O. 2000. "Northern Johannesburg: Part of the "rainbow" or Neo-Apartheid City in the Making?" *Mots Pluriels*, no. 13. Retreived from http://motspluriels.arts.uwa.edu.au/MP1300kb.html.

Brink, André, and Reingard Nethersole. 2000. "Reimagining the Past." In *T'kama-Adamastor: Inventions of Africa in a South African Painting*, ed. Ivan Vladislavić, 49–58. Johannesburg: University of the Witwatersrand.

Burnett, Scott. 2019. "Constructing White Autochthony in South Africa's 'Soul Country': Intersections of Race and Land." *Discourse, Context & Media*, no. 30 (January): 1–11.

Cane, Jonathan. 2019. *Civilising Grass: The Art of the Lawn on the South African Highveld*. Johannesburg: Wits University Press.

Coetzee, Cyril. 2000. "Introducing the Painting." In *T'kama-Adamastor: Inventions of Africa in a South African Painting*, ed. Ivan Vladislavić, 1–22. Johannesburg: University of the Witwatersrand.

Coetzee, J. M. 1988. *White Writing: On the Culture of Letters in South Africa*. New Haven: Yale University Press.

Cohen, Robin. 1988. *Endgame in South Africa? The Changing Structures & Ideology of Apartheid*. Trenton: Africa World Press.

Crewe, Jonathan V. 1999. "Recalling Adamastor: Literature as Cultural Memory in 'White' South Africa." In *Acts of Memory: Cultural Recall in the Present*, ed. Mieke Bal, Jonathan V. Crewe, and Leo Spitzer, 75–86. Hanover, NH: University Press of New England.

Crump, Alan. 2000. "Foreword." In *T'kama-Adamastor: Inventions of Africa in a South African Painting*, ed. Ivan Vladislavić. Johannesburg: University of the Witwatersrand.

Di Giminiani, Piergiorgio. 2018. *Sentient Lands: Indigeneity, Property, and Political Imagination in Neoliberal Chile*. Tucson: University of Arizona Press.

Dlamini, Jacob. 2009. *Native Nostalgia*. Auckland Park: Jacana.

Dominy, Michèle D. 2001. *Calling the Station Home: Place and Identity in New Zealand's High Country*. Lanham, MD: Rowman & Littlefield.

Durrheim, Kevin, and John Dixon. 2001. "The Role of Place and Metaphor in Racial Exclusion: South Africa's Beaches as Sites of Shifting Racialization." *Ethnic and Racial Studies* 24(3): 433–50.

Fanon, Frantz. (1952) 2008. *Black Skin, White Masks*. London: Pluto Books.

Fig, David. 2013. "Hydraulic Fracturing in South Africa: Correcting the Democratic Deficits." In *New South African Review* 3: The Second Phase—Tragedy or Farce? ed. John Daniel, Prishani Naidoo, Devan Pillay, and Roger Southall, 173–94. Johannesburg: Wits University Press.

Foster, Jeremy A. 2008. *Washed with Sun: Landscape and the Making of White South Africa*. Pittsburgh: University of Pittsburgh Press.

———. 2009. "From Socio-Nature to Spectral Presence: Re-Imagining the Once and Future Landscape of Johannesburg." *Safundi* 10(2): 175–213.

Garbutt, Robert George. 2006. "White "Autochthony."" *Australian Critical Race and Whiteness Studies Journal* 2(1). Retrieved 15 June 2021 from https://researchpor

tal.scu.edu.au/discovery/fulldisplay alma991012821117502368/61SCU_INST:Research Repository.
Gilmore, Ruth Wilson. 2002. "Fatal Couplings of Power and Difference: Notes on Racism and Geography." *Professional Geographer* 54(1): 15.
Graham, Lucy Valerie. 2012. *State of Peril: Race and Rape in South African Literature.* Oxford and New York: Oxford University Press.
Gray, Stephen. 1977. "The Myth of Adamastor in South African Literature." *Theoria: A Journal of Social and Political Theory*, no. 48 (May): 1–23.
Grové, A .P. 1963. *Afrikaans Poems with English Translations.* Translated by Charles John Derrick Harvey. Cape Town: Oxford University Press.
Hanzimanolis, Margaret. 2002. "Southern African Contact Narratives: The Case of T'Kama Adamastor and Its Reconstructive Project." *Kunapipi* 24(1–2): 251–71.
Klein, Bernhard. 2018. "Sea-Birds at the Cape of Storms, c. 1497." *Zeitsprünge. Forschungen Zur Frühen Neuzeit (Studies in Early Modern History, Culture and Science)* 22(3–4): 217–40.
Lipsitz, George. 2007. "The Racialization of Space and the Spatialization of Race" *Landscape Journal* 26(1): 10–23.
McEwen, Haley, and Melissa Steyn. 2013. "Hegemonic Epistemologies in the Context of Transformation: Race, Space, and Power in One Post-Apartheid South African Town." *Critical Race and Whiteness Studies, New Territories in Critical Whiteness Studies* 9(1): 1–18.
Mpendukana, Sibonile, and Chris Stroud. 2019. "Of Monkeys, Shacks and Loos: Changing Times, Changing Places." In *Making Sense of People and Place in Linguistic Landscapes*, ed. Amiena Peck, Christopher Stroud, and Quentin Williams, 183–200. London: Bloomsbury Academic.
Mphahlele, Es'kia. 1987. "The Tyranny of Place and Aesthetics. The Case of South Africa." In *Race and Literature: Ras En Literatuur*, ed. Charles Malan, 48–59. CENSAL (HSRC) 15. Pinetown: Owen Burgess Publishers.
Mpofu, William. 2018. "Decoloniality as a Combative Ontology in African Development." In *The Palgrave Handbook of African Politics, Governance and Development*, ed. Samuel Ojo Oloruntoba and Toyin Falola, 83–102. New York: Palgrave Macmillan.
Natter, Wolfgang, and I. I. I. Jones. 1997. "Identity, Space and Other Uncertainties." In *Space and Social Theory: Interpreting Modernity and Postmodernity*, ed. Georges Benko and Ulf Strohmayer, 141–61. Special Publication / Institute of British Geographers 33. Oxford: Blackwell.
Nethersole, Reingard. 2000. "Refiguring Colonial Identity: Cyril Coetzee's Answer to Amshewitz and Gill." In *T'kama-Adamastor: Inventions of Africa in a South African Painting*, ed. Ivan Vladislavić, 33–40. Johannesburg: University of the Witwatersrand.
Neumann, Roderick P. 2011. "Political Ecology III: Theorizing Landscape." *Progress in Human Geography* 35(6): 843–50.
Povinelli, Elizabeth A. 1995. "Do rocks listen? The Cultural Politics of Apprehending Australian Aboriginal Labor." *American Anthropologist* 97(3): 505.
Raidoo, Renugan. 2020. "The Unruly in the Anodyne: Nature in Gated Communities." In *Anxious Joburg: The Inner Lives of a Global South City*, ed. Nicky Falkof and Cobus van Staden, 132–51. New York: New York University Press.

Samin, Richard. 2006. "The Myth of Adamastor: The Ambivalent Metaphor of Otherness in South African Literature." *Commonwealth: Essays and Studies* 29(1): 59–69.

Santos, Boaventura de Sousa. 2007. "Para além do Pensamento Abissal: Das linhas globais a uma ecologia de saberes [Beyond Abyssal Thinking: From Global Lines to Ecologies of Knowledges]." Translated by Maria Irene Ramalho. *Revista Crítica de Ciências Sociais* no. 78 (October): 3–46.

Strang, Veronica. 2020. "The Rights of the River: Water, Culture and Ecological Justice." In *Conservation: Integrating Social and Ecological Justice*, ed. Helen Kopnina and Haydn Washington, 105–19. Cham, Switzerland: Springer International Publishing.

Styres, Sandra D. 2011. "Land as First Teacher: A Philosophical Journeying." *Reflective Practice* 12(6): 717–31.

———. 2019. "Literacies of Land: Decolonizing Narratives, Storying, and Literature." In *Indigenous and Decolonizing Studies in Education: Mapping the Long View*, ed. Linda Tuhiwai Smith, Eve Tuck, and K. Wayne Yang. New York and Abingdon: Routledge.

Twidle, Hedley. 2012. "First Lives, First Words: Camões, Magical Realism and the Limits of Invention." *Scrutiny* 217(1): 28–48.

van Wyk Smith, Malvern. 1990. *Grounds of Contest: A Survey of South African English Literature*. Johannesburg: Juta.

Vladislavić, Ivan. 2000. "Introduction." In *T'kama-Adamastor: Inventions of Africa in a South African Painting*, edited by Ivan Vladislavić. Johannesburg: University of the Witwatersrand.

CHAPTER 2

Part of the Landscape
Quebecois Nationalism and Indigenous Sentience

Philippe Blouin

With the abrupt spring thaw of 2017, the Saint Lawrence River, which circles around the island of Montreal, rose from its banks, flooding many villages on its shore, including the Kanien'kehá:ka (Mohawk) Indigenous community of Kanehsatà:ke. In neighboring settler towns, the Canadian Army was in charge of relief work, but for Kanehsatà:ke, whose memory was still scarred by the 1990 Oka Crisis—a two-month-long standoff between Mohawk warriors and the Canadian Army over the construction of a golf course on an ancestral cemetery—requesting assistance from the army was out of the question. Kanehsatà:ke community members thus called for volunteers to help clean up the rubbish that was left in the yards. Upon arriving there I found a large group of French Canadians who seemed fairly well organized, having brought their own shovels and pickup trucks. Many were wearing the same T-shirt depicting two hands shaking around planet Earth, under the printed word L'Alliance. I overheard the conversation they were painstakingly trying to hold with English-speaking Mohawks, attempting to overcome the age-old enmity between Mohawks and French settlers ever since explorer Samuel de Champlain slew three Mohawk chiefs with his harquebus upon their first encounter, in 1609. "Doesn't it feel good to be here together, having both lived on this land for so long?" said one of the members of L'Alliance, "especially when [Canadian Prime Minister Justin] Trudeau is opening the border for all those immigrants to sweep in."

Quick research revealed that the so-called L'Alliance was but an offshoot of the Storm Alliance, an ultranationalist anti-immigration group who made headlines when they staged protests at the US-Canada border against asylum seekers escaping Donald Trump's xenophobic policies. Later in the summer, another Quebec far-right paramilitary group called La Meute (The Pack) elicited criticism from Indigenous leaders after waving the Mohawk Unity Flag at the head of an anti-immigration protest in Quebec City. With limited success, La Meute sought to lure Indigenous members into its organization, using their traditional wolf paw print as its logo, and including environmental concerns on its militant agenda. At the same time, La Meute claimed that Francophone settlers also deserved to be considered Indigenous, by way of a Métis ancestry often dating back to the seventeenth century and shared by a majority of the population (Leroux 2019). One of La Meute's leaders, who renamed himself Sylvain "Maikan" after the Innu word for wolf, bluntly stated that "if you're a second-generation Quebecer, you are Aboriginal" (Curtis 2018). If such self-indigenizing efforts are not restricted to the far-right, they are increasingly present at the intersection of xenophobic and environmentalist narratives.[1] This chapter examines the role played by representations of Indigenous people by Quebec nationalists with regard to shaping such convergence between ecology and xenophobia. Or rather, it deals with colonial representations of Indigenous representations of the landscape and its nonhuman inhabitants as sentient, agentive beings, whom Quebecois settlers gradually imbued with xenophobic sentiments. Methodologically, this chapter takes the "imprint" of Indigenous worldviews within Quebec's territorial nationalism to be at once historically, spatially, politically, and semiotically layered. Drawing on Tsing, Mathews, and Bubandt's (2019: 187) invitation to retrace the historical emergence of landscapes' "patterns of human and nonhuman assemblages," it proposes to analyze the semiotic analogies that allowed Quebec nationalism to self-indigenize its spatial relationship with the nonhuman landscape, ultimately pitting its alleged sentience against later waves of immigration. In this process, I argue that the colonial animalization of Indigenous peoples and their "animistic" ecologies made them "part of the landscape" in such a way that their common sentience was simultaneously confiscated by, and excluded from, the constitution of Quebec's national territory.

To this end, I follow the historical development of Quebecois identity from its colonial inception to the moment it successfully marshaled a modern provincial state, paying attention to the key symbols on which it based its relationship with the Indigenous landscape. I start by articulating the core analogies that were drawn in the early colonial period between the nomadic and sedentary behaviors of French Canadian settlers and Indigenous peoples, and the two animal species whose behavior has the greatest impact on the eastern woodlands' landscape: wolves and beavers. By introducing a xenophobic interpretation of beaver ethology, the

French settlers' domestication of the landscape was set against the lupine nomadism of Indigenous populations, as the latter's adventurism was gradually put to the service of sedentary needs. I then analyze the impacts of British conquest on this semiotic scaffold, as French Canadians were debased into a paradoxical state of "colonized colonizers."

While its proponents faced British competition for settling new lands and tried to curb the mass emigration of French Canadians to the United States, the rural Catholic ideology hegemonic in French Canada throughout the nineteenth century gave rise to Romantic conceptions of the landscape, whose sentient qualities could help French culture survive against foreign intruders. The invisibilization and extermination of Indigenous peoples and animals, altogether relegated to details in the landscape, nonetheless raises the question of their spectral participation in the sentience of the landscapes that were cleared and settled at the time. To tackle this problem, I move on to the modern era, when Quebec nationalists, now with a secular and liberal demeanor, endeavored to build the then-biggest hydroelectric dams in the world on unceded Cree territory. Mobilizing the anthropology of infrastructures to understand how settlers simultaneously suppress and integrate prior landscape ecologies within their own "enchanted" sentience, I argue that their human exclusivism set the stage for a new resource-based xenophobia.

Wolves and Beavers: Keystones of Land Occupation

> I heard my host say one day, . . . "The beaver knows how to make all things to perfection: It makes kettles, hatchets, swords, knives, bread; in short, it makes everything."
> —French Jesuit missionary Paul Le Jeune, 1634

The French regime (1534–1763) that preceded British conquest provided Quebec with the raw materials of its identity, which acquired mythical import with time. Two contrasted figures are traditionally considered as the polar ends of early modes of land occupation. On one hand, the *coureurs des bois*, called "wood runners" or "bush lopers" by the British, symbolize the nomadic and free-ranging experience of the territory lived by these independent French traders, who were instrumental in the early exploration of the continent as they traveled to remote locations to exchange furs and other goods, thereby mingling with Indigenous peoples. The coureurs des bois reflect the French mercantile approach to the colonization of Canada, dispersed throughout an extensive network of inland trading posts in North America, by contrast with New England's intensive settler colonialism.[2]

On the other hand, the figure of the *habitant* designates French Canadian homesteaders who settled along the Saint Lawrence River on farms modeled after European agricultural and stockbreeding practices. Given that Indigenous peoples were then seen as "akin to the forests in which they lived and the animals they hunted" (Trigger 1985: 3), the opposite relations to the Indigenous landscapes nurtured by the coureurs des bois and the habitants are best evidenced by the analogies drawn within early colonial discourse between human and animal ways of dwelling. In particular, two animal species consistently emerge from these narratives as metaphors for nomadic and sedentary behaviors, coinciding with the two keystone species of the eastern woodlands of North America, whose behaviors deeply shape its landscape: wolves and beavers.

The presence of wolves is known to engender tremendous trophic cascades, determining the habitat of their herbivore prey, and consequently the distribution of vegetation. As the sovereign predators of both old and new worlds, they symbolized the threat of wild nature for early French settlers. Exhibiting colonizers' systematic fear of being beleaguered by the very people they invade (Hage 2017), French settlers consistently depicted their Indigenous foes as wolves prowling and howling about their precarious settlements. The French Governor Jacques-René de Brisay, Marquis de Denonville, who had attempted to curtail the freedom of movement of the coureurs des bois in 1685, also compared the Iroquois to "a band of wolves in a forest, who ravage those who live at the edge of the woods," suggesting that "to hunt them down, we would need good hounds, meaning other Savages"[3] (Prince-Falmagne 1965: 226). The coureurs des bois were at high risk of being contaminated by the lupine Indigenes they frequented, and seventeenth-century habitants of Quebec City, the colony's capital, called Montrealers "wolves," as their settlement bordered savage-ridden woodlands (Vincent and Arcand 1978: 33).

On the other hand, beavers fell on the side of habitants, as builders and dwellers. It is estimated that when the first Europeans arrived in North America, around 400 million beavers lived there, their dams creating vast wetlands harboring a wide variety of species.[4] With beaver felt hats trending in the European aristocracy, their pelts were a choice game for the coureurs des bois and accounted for 71 percent of exports from Canada (Delâge 2014: 16). For all these reasons, beavers truly "embodied the continent" (Feeley-Harnik 2001: 65), giving their name to the "Beaver Wars," which pitted the English and the Rotinonhsión:ni (Iroquois) against the French and their Huron-Wendat and Great Lakes Anishinaabek (Algonquin) allies for most of the seventeenth century. The Indigenous peoples living in Canada's boreal forest (Cree, Innu, Naskapi) acknowledged a special bond between beavers and humans, with a widespread myth suggesting that beavers had originally acquired their building capacities from a human who plunged in the waters to marry a beaver wife (Delâge 2014: 8). However, commercial overhunting soon broke this alliance between human and beaver nations, and natives accused colonial powers of having caused a war between them, becoming wolves to beavers (Parmenter 2010: 85).

Beavers piqued the nascent republican curiosity of the French. Based on Indigenous accounts, the proto-Enlightenment French writer Louis-Armand de Lom d'Arce, Baron de Lahontan, noted that beavers seemed to possess an "intelligent jargon," by means of which they consult among themselves "about everything that concerns the Preservation of their Commonwealth," in a way similar to what Lahontan witnessed in Native American councils (1905: 477). Acadian explorer Nicolas Denys described beaver dams as complex engineering projects, where a team of architects commandeered troops of specialized masons, carpenters, hood builders, and diggers (Delâge 2014: 30). Reappropriating Indigenous conceptions of beaver sentience, the French appended to them protophysiocratic theories of workflow management based on chains of command and division of labor. Indigenous myths, where the beaver played a cosmogonic role in shaping the "architecture of the world," were incorporated into a new "white myth" explaining the origins of society through communication, orderly work, and monogamous family units (ibid.: 39). A specimen was sent to Versailles, where renowned academician Georges-Louis Leclerc, Comte de Buffon, scrutinized its behavior. In Buffon's view, private property structured the beaver's republic to the extent that each family possessed its own lodge and did not "allow any strangers to settle within its enclosure" (1831: 437). This exclusive, not to say xenophobic, conception of beaver territoriality ignored the interspecies companionship that the Innu highlighted between beaver and muskrat nations, the latter being considered as the beaver's dogs, with whom they shared the same lodging and food (Clément 2012: 94).

Clearing the Way for the Nation

> These vast landscapes seem destined for the expansion of French Canadians, as the theater set aside by Providence for their action. Therein their children will be able to spread quietly without any stranger mixing with them for a long time.
> —Edme Rameau de Saint-Père, 1859

Following the British conquest of Canada, in 1763, the hope of reverting back to French rule sparked the first forms of French Canadian nationalism. While French Canadian traders stationed in the Great Lakes and the

Midwest played an important role in the 1763–66 anti-British rebellion by Pontiac, whose large Indigenous confederacy nevertheless failed to obtain effective support from the French, Canada's habitants attempted their own insurrection in 1837–38. Influenced by French republicanism, the Lower Canada rebellion, known as the Patriot's War in Quebec, also failed to ally with local Indigenous peoples. After Kanehsatà:ke Mohawks refused to lend their cannon to the Patriots who hastily required it, rumors spread in French Canadian and Mohawk towns to the effect that each was preparing to slaughter the other (Greer 1993: 348). In November 1838, the Patriots' secret society of the *Frères chasseurs* (Hunter Brothers), whose leaders were incidentally called "beavers," was ambushed on its way to disarm Kahnawà:ke Mohawks, an event that announced the insurrection's upcoming defeat (ibid.: 349). Thereafter, republicanism would vanish into thin air for more than a century, and as timber replaced fur as Canada's main export, the coureurs des bois were replaced by lumberjacks, whose nomadism was put at the service of the sedentary interests of the habitants (MacKay 2007: 17). To clear forests and build the nomadic British naval fleet, the coureurs des bois, once wolves to beavers, now became beavers themselves, or rather wolves to the forest.

Ultramontanism, a radical Catholic doctrine holding that the power of the pope must cross mountains (ultra-mons), filled the ideological vacuum left by the defeat of republicanism (Beauchemin 1997). Incidentally called "beavers" (Groulx 1952: 18), ultramontane priests sought to preserve French culture in America while advocating compliance with British authorities (Fahmy-Eid 1975: 55). Praising rural life as a site for religious edification "in the interests of a unified, religio-familial conception of society" (Beyer 1985: 46), this "conservationist ideology" (Juteau 1993) more or less put a halt to industrial development in French Canada, instead pushing families to breed in large numbers, a nationalist endeavor dubbed the "revenge of the cribs." In 1838, a prominent Whig intellectual, John Lambton Earl of Durham, was sent to Canada to investigate the underlying causes of the Patriots' rebellion. His report suggested that the socioeconomic inferiority of French Canadians was a consequence of their deeply embedded reluctance vis-à-vis progress and improvement. In addition to comparing them with Irish Catholics, Lord Durham explained the idleness of French Canadians by way of their historical proximity to Indigenous peoples.

As early as 1731, French Jesuit Pierre-François Xavier de Charlevoix had deplored "the scantiness, the aversion of assiduous work, and the independent spirit" of Canadians that resulted from their relationship both with Indigenous peoples and the landscape itself, as Charlevoix held "the air that we breathe in this vast continent" responsible for this idleness

(Vincent and Arcand 1978: 215). Such conflations were a constant feature of British slander against French Canadians. Jeremy Cockloft suggested in 1811 that the Canadians' "aversion to labor springs from pure, genuine, unadulterated indolence. Give a Habitant milk, a few roots, tobacco, wood for his stove, and a bonnet rouge, he works no longer;—like the native Savage, who seldom hunts but when driven thereto by hunger" (1960: 9). Yet this disparaging analogy did not drive French Canadians closer to Indigenous peoples; instead, nineteenth century French Canadian intellectuals increasingly worked to dissociate themselves from Indigenous defects (Smith 1974).

By contrast with French mercantilism, the British possessed a consistent ideology grounding private property in work. Provided that each man possessed his own body, John Locke's doctrine of improvement stated that "whatsoever then he removes out of the state that nature hath provided, and left it in, he hath mixed his labor with, and joined to it something that is his own, and thereby makes it his property" (quoted by Zimmer 2015: 144). Facing this powerful theory, as well as the massive arrival of Anglophone settlers, French Canadian conservatism was driven in a race to reconquer the soil it had purportedly already acquired. The roman du terroir (rural novel), the dominant French Canadian literary genre until the 1960s, contains stark examples of the "colonized colonizer" mentality that resulted from British competition. It advocated rural, agricultural, patriarchal, and religious lifestyles for French Canadians as a means both of taming the forest and resisting the rapidly expanding cities sparked by British industrialism, seen as dens of debauchery and race-mixing. In Félix-Antoine Savard's *Menaud, maître-draveur* (1937), lumberjacks and log drivers witness the British taking hold of the hinterland, while the protagonist of *Rivard le défricheur* (1874) has a dream suggesting that French Canadians should set out to clear land and create an "earthly paradise" before "the inhabitants of another hemisphere take over our forests before our eyes" (Gérin-Lajoie 1874: 20).

In these novels, the counterpart of the evil urban foreigner was the figure of the emigrant, as over one million French Canadians left for the United States between 1840 and 1930 (Courville and Séguin 1989). The relation between this wave of emigration and the nomadic tradition of the coureurs des bois is attested by the works of Quebecois emigrant Jack Kerouac, who pioneered the stream of consciousness writing style of the Beat Generation by writing the first draft of his road trip novel *On the Road* (1957) in a broken oral form of French. In the 1870s, Catholic authorities attempted to contain the nomadic dispersal of French Canadians by redirecting its flow northward in order to settle new regions—notably Abitibi and Lac Saint-Jean (Morissonneau 1978: 41).

The figure of the *défricheur* (land clearer) captured the mythical taste for adventure of the coureurs des bois yet regimented it into serving sedentary ends. Prominent priests such as curé Antoine Labelle framed their call for clearing new lands as a national endeavor to "conquer this land of America against the English philistines, . . . to conquer our conquerors" (Desbiens 2013: 88). Each new Anglophone settlement in the Laurentides north of Montreal (Rawdon, Morin Heights, etc.) had to be met with a French Saint-Côme or Saint-Michel-des-Saints (Morissonneau 1978: 47). Most importantly, the natural properties of the Laurentides's Matawinie mountains played an important part in the colonial advocacy of priests such as curé Théophile-Stanislas Provost, who associated them with the spiritual qualities required for the survival of French Canadian culture.

Drawing on the example on how mountainous landscapes offered a refuge for Balkan peoples, such as Montenegrins, to protect their culture against Turks, curé Provost suggested that "mountains protect and conserve particularisms," while "plains are an opening to the world, an obliged proximity with the other, the foreigner, or the enemy" (Morissonneau 1978: 43). Following this argument, mountainous landscapes were portrayed as inherently xenophobic, given their rugged, secluded, and enclosed wilderness. More than a mere geostrategic argument, curé Provost envisioned an analogic transfer of the landscape's properties to the people who would settle there, suggesting that rocky mountains would harden their souls and faith, thus buttressing their resistance to foreign influence (ibid.: 45). But in order to inherit the landscape's xenophobic seclusion, settlers would first have to break it open and tame its wilderness by clearing the ways for settler colonial infrastructure.

On the one hand, curé Provost's appeal to the xenophobic sentience of wild landscapes showcases the paradox William Cronon (1995) underlined regarding American Transcendentalists' cult of the "wilderness," which universalized the historical situation they witnessed, in which the landscape had been forcefully depleted of its Indigenous inhabitants by the mid-nineteenth century. The Matawinie mountains could therefore be presented as simultaneously wildly chaotic and passively empty, as fiercely xenophobic yet idly waiting for settlers to plant their roots therein. On the other hand, the Romantic appraisal of the sentient qualities of uncivilized landscapes paradoxically coincided with the call to civilize them. This equivocation seems to cut across the distinction Eric Kaufmann draws between two distinct forms of geographic nationalism: the nationalization of nature, which focuses on the imprint of civilization upon a fundamentally passive nature, and the naturalization of the nation, "praising the primeval quality of untamed nature and stressing its regenerative effect upon civilization" (1998: 669). This distinction collapses regarding Quebec nationalism, which comprises both the French inclination to civilize nature and the Romantic cult of wilderness found in "nations that possessed an abundance of unsettled landscape" (ibid.: 667).

The dialectic between these two orientations is particularly manifest in the writings of Lionel Groulx, a Catholic priest and historian whose clerico-nationalism exerted a tremendous influence on Quebec intellectuals in the first half of the twentieth century. On the one hand, Groulx suggested that "the people mark the land with their soul and personality" (1919: 87), while on the other he sensed that the "national milieu possesses a somewhat generative power. It creates a human variety, just as the soil, and the climate create biological varieties" (1937: 192). Groulx considered the "natural fatherland" (1922) as a result of this convergence between the ways in which the landscape "mirrors the features of those who have settled it" (1952: 175), and the ways in which settler behaviors reflect the ecological affordances of their land.

In *L'Appel de la race*, a major landmark of French Canadian nationalism, Groulx tells the story of a couple formed by a French husband and an English wife, whose kids consequently suffer from a "cerebral disorder," a "psychological duplication of mixed races" (1922: 130). A priest thus advises the family to take some rest in the forest, in the same Laurentides that curé Provost foresaw as French Canada's future cultural crucible. The family's confusion is rapidly cured by the wilderness, as they witness how the landscape itself seems to "naturally speak French" (ibid.: 120). In a crucial scene, the family witnesses oblate missionaries signing French Canadian folk songs on a lake, and the music resonates through the mountains as "the natural acclamation, the innate chant of the Canadian land" (ibid.: 119).

Incidentally, the oblates are paddling a canoe, relying on the utmost symbol of Indigenous culture. In this dramatic account of French Canadian nationalism, Indigenous culture is simultaneously included and excluded from the national sentiente of the Canadian landscape, relegated to a barely visible imprint in the landscape, albeit literally providing its vehicle. This approach is consistent with the stereotypical image of Native Americans that prevailed in Romantic artwork at the turn of the twentieth century, which ascribed to them psychological features that pertained to the landscape, depicting them from the back or at a distance, part of the scenery like mute and stoic mountains (Vincent and Arcand 1978: 226). This invisibilization superseded the prior association of Indigenous peoples with large predator animals, as both were largely decimated throughout the nineteenth century. No longer a threat, Indigenous peoples lost their wolf fangs, which could now be worn by French Canadians themselves, as evidenced by Lionel Groulx's invitation to engage in predatory behaviors to resist foreign powers: "In a world where wolves are kings, there is no future for sheep" (1937: 176).

The fact that French Canadian clerico-nationalism was the expression of an allegedly "oppressed" minoritarian culture does not necessarily argue against its proto-fascist character, as both Italian and German fascisms were formed in opposition to the colonial hegemony of France and Great Britain. Fascism might be conditioned by the will to overcome one's minoritarian status by subjugating other minorities. The most salient manifestation of fascism in French Canada, Adrien Arcand's swastika-adorned National Unity Party, also glorified the regenerating effects of pristine, untouched wilderness, by contrast with cities filled with foreigners and Jews, whom he deemed "more corrupting and degraded than any sort of Redskins" (Nadeau 2010: 74). Yet at the first assembly of his fascist "Goglus," Arcand's main proposal was the nationalization of forests, waterfalls, and dams, an idea that obsessed him (61). This project would reemerge some forty years later, when a new secular and liberal form of Quebec nationalism looked across the Laurentides to the land where Arcand planned to build concentration camps, and which curé Antoine Labelle already coveted in 1879: "the beautiful and fertile lands of James Bay" (Quoted by Auclair 1930: 182).

Sentient Infrastructures

> In this copper-snake, invented by Edison, he has wrested the lightning from nature.
>
> —Aby Warburg, 1923

Following the death of conservative Prime Minister of Quebec Maurice Duplessis after eighteen years of power in 1959, the newly elected Liberal Party put an end to the "Great Darkness" that had held French Canada under a Catholic shroud for more than a century (Rousseau 2005). In record time, the Liberals' "Quiet Revolution" transformed one of the most Catholic regions of the world into one of the most secular, as clerico-nationalism was superseded by a modern, industrious, and liberal form of nationalism. Out of this modernist strain stemmed a new Quebecois separatist movement, whose most radical faction formed the Quebec Liberation Front (FLQ), an armed revolutionary group whose 1970 kidnappings of a British diplomat and a minister were met with the Canadian army taking the streets. Following the repression of the FLQ's socialist and decolonizing stance, linked to Algerian, Cuban, and African-American revolutionary movements, the Parti Quebecois (PQ) took power in 1976, aiming for the separation of Quebec. Its leader, René Lévesque, had previously been instrumental in the Liberal Party's proposal to nationalize electricity, then in the hands of private interests, under the watchword *maîtres chez nous!* (masters at home). Yet the problem was that this home was not quite theirs (Nungak and Curley 2017).

In addition to nationalizing Hydro-Quebec's extant hydroelectric plants, the plan was to build new ones to meet the ever-growing needs of the population. In 1968, the largest multiple-arch buttress dam in the world was inaugurated: the Manic-5 dam on the Manicouagan River. Lévesque took great pride in insisting on using local expertise and on keeping all communications in French among construction workers and foremen. Clinging to the ambitious visions of Quebec engineers, notwithstanding the doubts of their international colleagues, the dam also featured the very first 735 kV power lines in the world. The republican beavers were back, with land clearers, pioneers, and lumberjacks being dramatically invoked in the project's propaganda material (Desbiens 2013: 169), as were the coureurs des bois, who were associated with the "cable-runners" (Fleury 1999) in charge of maintaining the thousands of miles of power lines in harsh conditions. It is as if the dam recapitulated and subsumed Quebec's entire history, closing the loop with the very mythical origins of the nation, while revealing its secular manifest destiny in the extraction of electricity from mighty pristine rivers idly flowing in the forest. Dams were, in a nutshell, as convenient politically as they were economically.

Regarding the new cultural awareness that replaced the self-denominator "French Canadians" with "Québécois" during the 1960s, the youth's nomadic tendency to desertion—instead of fleeing south as in the last century—was now increasingly turning inwards to threaten the state, as the FLQ's violent revolutionary methods gained widespread support. Seeking to deflect the youth's defection by creating thousands of jobs, and to distract attention from the separatist turmoil, the government sent the first engineers to James Bay in October 1970 to study the feasibility of a hydroelectric complex, at the exact same moment when the army was taking the streets against the FLQ.[5] Liberal Prime Minister Robert Bourassa announced the project by resorting to the old rhetoric of colonial rivalry:

> A territory cannot remain unoccupied. [James Bay] must be conquered, like the Europeans have conquered America, like the Eastern pioneers have conquered the West, like the Americans now want to conquer the moon. As for us, our heritage is that of the harsh territories of the North. Even still, we must conquer these territories if we want them to truly belong to us, otherwise they will belong to others. (Quoted by Desbiens 2013: 248)

As an alternative to the FLQ's anti-imperialist struggle, Bourassa thus suggested nothing short of a Quebecois invasion of Indigenous lands where, like the moon, no government official had set foot before the 1960s—and with no regard for the native inhabitants (Nungak and Curley 2017).

In 1965, the Pessamit Innu had been offered a meager $50,000 to allow the construction of the fourteen dams composing the Manic-5 complex (Binette 2018). The government was hoping to do the same with the Cree people living in their ancestral territory of Eeyou Istchee, around James Bay. But the world's then-largest hydroelectric project was met with fierce opposition both from Cree and Inuit communities, who won their case against all odds in the 1973 Malouf court ruling. Yet this ruling was quickly overturned on appeal, and no fewer than fifty-five thousand workers were sent up north, roughly as many as Canada's total Inuit population, where they proceeded to flood 11,000 square kilometers of boreal forest. Painstakingly reached in 1975, the James Bay and Northern Quebec Agreement was a unique example of modern treaty making, handing over more than 170,000 square kilometers of Eeyou Istchee territory to the Quebec government, while granting subsidies and exclusive hunting and fishing rights to the Cree. Throughout the court proceedings, Anglophone experts working with the Cree confronted the consistent attempts of Hydro-Quebec's Francophone experts to extinguish aboriginal claims, in the spirit of the federal 1969 white paper's proposal to municipalize Indian reservations. Thus, at the very same moment that Quebec was recognized as a "distinct society" within Canada, Indigenous peoples within its boundaries were proposed outright assimilation (Vincent 1995), as if the only way for the Quebecois to become a majority within their own society was to prove their "power to minoritize other cultures" (Handler 1988: 158). As journalist Boyce Richardson reported:

> After a decade of awakening, The Quebecois had shed much of the xenophobia they developed during their fierce struggle for survival. . . . But, oddly enough, it had become increasingly difficult to tell the difference between the Quebecois and the rest of the North Americans, apart from the fact that they spoke French. Like all other North Americans, they wished to embrace the technological dream. (1975: 22)

As Quebec nationalists now took pride in their own power to domesticate nature, the conflicts surrounding the James Bay project led to a frontal confrontation between Indigenous and colonial conceptions of the landscape, shedding light on their semiotic discrepancy.

One of the Cree's main contentions concerned the location of the first dam, LG1, projected to be built on one the most important sites for their subsistence and culture: the Grand River's Uupichun rapids. With its long and sharp slope engendering high water flows, Uupichun was a prime spawning spot for whitefish and was easily accessible to fishermen thanks to the wide rock platforms protruding over the waters. The Cree used to camp there in the summer, picking berries and drying fish, while elders allegedly predicted the future by reading its rapids. As geographer Caroline Desbiens points out, the very same "characteristics that made Uupichun such a strategic site for the Cree economy also made it highly desirable from the perspective of hydro engineering" (2013: 248). To this idea that the dam harnessed the same affordances of the landscape that sustained the Cree economy, I would add that it might be said to have captured Uupichun's fortune-telling properties as well, banking calculable amounts of electricity with what was previously a node of interspecies relationships.

Was the sentience of Uupichun also thereby captured by the hydroelectric complex? Would such infrastructure have the power to convert, or rather "transduct,"[6] the intricate ecological, economic, and spiritual interactions accounting for an Indigenous land's sentience into electricity, which, channeled through "copper-snakes," will come to animate the remotest human machines? What is this more-than-human animation to the less-than-human animism it supersedes on the same landscape? These questions point toward the nationalist sentience of hydroelectric power, which René Lévesque deemed "at once the engine and the mirror of the awakening and rise of francophone Quebec" (Desbiens 2013: 153)? It would seem that the mutually transformative relationship that Lionel Groulx indicated as shaping the "fatherland" now linked the Quebecois people to the energetic potential of its landscape, now the sole aspect accounting for its sentience, regardless of its other human and nonhuman inhabitants.

Repeating the nineteenth century's messianic call for land clearers to change nomadic desertions to serving sedentary ends, Quebec's infrastructures were now the object of its national pride, a nationalist "enchantment" that may have been drawn from the clearings that pertained to the interspecies sentience previously pervading its landscape. Martin Heidegger famously theorized the phenomenology both of hydroelectric dams and clearings, which in German (*Lichtung*) evokes at once an "opening" and a "lighting." The clearing designates the foundational aperture of Dasein, which "grants and guarantees to us humans a passage to those beings that we ourselves are not, and access to the being that we ourselves are" (1971: 53), that is, it grants access to the self as related to a plurality of other beings.

According to Heidegger, technology also operates a clearing, in the sense of a mode of revealing. Yet by analyzing the difference between hydroelectric dams and watermills, he identified a threshold whereby dams, instead of attending to the river's patterns, challenge them to deliver the sum of their energetic "standing reserve," extracted and stocked to the sole benefit of humans (1993: 320). Through this "en-framing," suggested Heidegger, technology "drives out every other possibility of revealing" (332), blocking access to other beings as possessing their own clearings, perceptions, and modes of revelation as it were, including those shared and communicated with humans. Heidegger further associated this totalizing logic of technology with the exclusionary imperialism of Western metaphysics, of which technology appears to be the accomplishment (244). He held technology's mode of revealing responsible for the disenchantment and vanishing of "any sense of awe and wonder in the presence of beings" (Wheeler 2018).

I would argue that, far from disappearing, the landscape's enchantment was confiscated by the James Bay hydroelectric dam, which subsumed and sublimated the beyond-the-human sentient landscapes that Indigenous sapience was previously attuned to. In other words, the infrastructure's abstraction and extraction of a sheer, countable, energetic potency out of Uupichun's complex set of interspecies interactions was tantamount to the dam "en-framing" the relational complexity that animated the Indigenous landscape into a monoculture of hydroelectricity. This is to say that the dam enchanted itself, and animated faraway machines, by transforming "the indigenous cultural and natural order to become part of this infrastructure" (Manning 2012: 60). The modern national landscape of Quebec thus simultaneously integrated and excluded the sentience of the Indigenous landscape it came to replace. On the one hand, the sentience previously shared by Indigenous and nonhuman forms of life was invizibilized, pushed into the background and absorbed into the backdrop of the national landscape throughout the nineteenth century. On the other hand, the infrastructures which heralded the colonial appropriation of the Indigenous landscape somehow incorporated the latter's sentience, endowing these infrastructures with an enchantment of sorts.

I would suggest that this analogic transduction of a sentient energy potential constitutes an important addition to the three features by which Penny Harvey and Hannah Knox (2012: 524–34) explain the "enchantment of infrastructure": the moral virtue of job creation and business opportunities (524); human labor, fueled by an epic battle with the elements (528); and the "encounters of stasis, rupture and blockade" (534)—in this case, the victory over Indigenous opposition. On the other hand, the infrastructure's exclusion of alterity—forbidding any alternative use of the territory for humans and nonhumans alike—seems to invalidate Jane Bennett's theorization of enchantment as a "surprising encounter" (2001: 5). This points to a recurring debate within the anthropology of infrastructures, whereby a certain "scale-blindness" (Bird-David 2018: 306) sometimes leads to universalize the concept of infrastructure to the point of encompassing what infrastructures replace and supersede—that is, what they "are after" in both temporal and intentional terms (Moten and Harney 2013: 92).

Strategic Indigenous reappropriations of this pervasive definition of infrastructure, like Uni'stot'en camp spokesperson Freda Huson's statement that the berry patches which the Wet'suwet'en people seek to defend against pipeline projects in northern British Columbia constitute their own "critical infrastructure" (Spice 2018: 40), are testament to the difficulty in defining the essence of infrastructures. Susan L. Star's (1999) oft-quoted suggestion that infrastructures are "by definition invisible," and only "become visible on breakdown," based on Heidegger's analysis of how tools reveal their essence when they are broken and lose their invisible readiness-to-hand, was contested by Brian Larkin (2013: 336) as failing to account for the fact that infrastructures are often staged in highly visible and spectacular forms. This was seen, for example, during the 1967 International and Universal Exposition in Montreal, where visitors were invited to watch a live transmission of the Manic-5 hydroelectric dam construction site on a widescreen display. Yet Larkin's definition of infrastructures as "matter that enable the movement of other matter" (229) would comprise phenomena as different as dams built with sand and gravel extracted on site, and canoes made from bark to travel the continental waterways using the affordances provided by the landscape for humans to encounter other beings through its natural river clearings. Larkin rightfully insists on how infrastructures, by contrast with non-transformative tools such as canoes, modify and recreate the basis of all relations within a landscape, as they are "things and also the relation between things"; that is, they are "objects that create the grounds on which other objects operate" (229). Yet what remains unaddressed is what lies beneath these news grounds and the imprint on which they are sealed: namely, the ontological difference in kind presumed by a technological difference in scale. Such a scale-blindness may stem from infrastructures' power to invisibly invisibilize what they are after.

Discussing the invasion of Afghanistan, Gaston Gordillo (2018: 61) argues that warfare technologies are essentially "efforts to fight the opacity of the countless forms, atmospheres, encounters, and lines of flight that make up the terrain of planet Earth." In this sense, the invisibility of the infrastructure's inner workings, as in the James Bay dam's underground power plant, is not opposed to visibility, but rather to an underlying opacity. This infrastructural leveling, where the landscape is thoroughly transformed to fit all-too-human grids of state legibility (J. Scott 1998), invisibilizes an "opaque" and "countless" entity by blocking access to its smaller relational scales, whose variegated multiplicity of "selves," with their own intersecting perspectives, or "clearings," are unintelligible to the all-too-human eyes of the state. Yet given the codependence of these perspectives for their mutual survival, their heterogeneous multiplicity nevertheless constitutes an undividable "whole," an emergent, self-contained, and self-consistent form. What infrastructures do is to technologically distinguish elements within this whole, to connect them afterwards as separated elements of a larger network and at a larger scale, both visible and invisible, but neither opaque, nor whole, nor multiple.

Drawing both on Charles Sanders Peirce's semiotics and Philippe Descola's typology of social ontologies, Eduardo Kohn (2019) suggests an "emergentist" understanding of this conversion, assessing the continuity and reliance of higher scale infrastructural networks on smaller scale relational patterns. Kohn suggests a parallelism between Peirce's view of all-too-human symbolic communication as relying on referential indexes, themselves ultimately composed of "icons,"[7] and Descola's ontological superposition of the "analogism" typical of imperial and colonial societies onto animist or totemic worldviews. "Analogism analogically emulates the logic of symbolic reference" (Kohn 2019: 5) by suspending indexical references to iconic qualities, allowing them to "leap-frog" symbolic abstractions over iconic animisms, "subsuming them in the process" (17).

In this sense, I would suggest that colonial infrastructures seem to naturalize human landscapes by subsuming Indigenous humanizations of natural landscapes. This is how the modern, disenchanted, and environmentally ravaged territory of Quebec can still feel sentient to its nationalists, whose infrastructures trapped, as trappers would do, animalized Indigenous humans underneath their new ground. By contrast with beavers, hydroelectric dams render impossible other use of the landscape, setting in concrete the Province of Quebec as the sole recipient of its potential energy. Under the pretext of thwarting Anglophone hegemony, the colonial nature of this appropriation qua transformation was obliterated in such a way that the state self-indigenized its exclusive grip on the landscape, resulting in a new form of resource-based nationalism, pitted against both Indigenous human and nonhuman forms of life alike. I would suggest that the indigenophobic and zoophobic nature of hydroelectric dams laid the groundwork for the subsequent return of xenophobic sentiments based on the exclusive use of Quebec's energetic powerhouse.

Immigrant Excursus

> He is one of the animals which roam the land. He is the predator on all others, but just as a wolf pack depends for its continued existence on the survival of the caribou herd, so this predatory man will not survive unless the animals continue to flourish.
>
> —Cree hunter Isaiah Awashish, quoted by Boyce Richardson, 1975

In a petition filed to the Minister of Indian Affairs to protest the James Bay hydroelectric project, Cree protesters stated that "only the beavers had the right to build dams on our territory" (Richardson 1975: 84). Humans should refrain from playing beaver, for if beavers once borrowed their construction skills from humans, it was in a mythical time when borders between animal bodies and nations had not yet been fixed. Should the white man awaken this liminality by acting as a beaver, he would bring about a tremendous ontological danger, which the Cree associated with the coming of a mythical blundering monster destroying the earth in a flood (C. Scott 1995: 38). The survival of a wolf-like keystone predator, such as the hunting man, "depends on knowing where he must stand" within an ecological equilibrium which took eight thousand years to achieve (Richardson 1975: 175). It also implies letting other beings shape their own landscapes and clearings. As the coureur des bois converged with the habitant through Quebec's mobile land clearing and dam building endeavors, the beaver was conflated with a wolf-like predator, and the wolf with a beaver-like constructor. And as gaps between perspectival beings were blurred to the benefit of an exclusively human keystone grip on the landscape, intercultural gaps incurred the same colonial filling, as the native "right to opacity" (Glissant 2010: 189) was denied through assimilationist policies.

Quebec separatists have had a hard time understanding the separatism of Quebec's own Indigenous peoples, as evidenced by nationalist geographer Louis-Edmond Hamelin's (1999) dismissal of the alliance protocol of the Rotinonhsión:ni (Iroquois), the Two Row Wampum, which suggests that different nations (human and beyond) can only follow the same direction if they remain in their own vessel on parallel rivers. Hamelin accused the protocol of eliciting a xenophobic fear of settlers, portrayed as "bad wolves." The 1980 and 1995 referendums on the separation of Quebec brought this issue to the forefront, as several Indigenous nations declared that they would separate from Quebec if Quebec separated from Canada. When asked if an independent Quebec would allow other sovereignties to access to their own independence, David Cliche, the spokesperson on

Indigenous affairs for the Parti Québécois, answered that Quebec would strive to protect its territorial integrity, as any state would do.[8] A minority at the scale of Canada, Quebec nationalists became a majority at their own provincial scale by minoritizing both Indigenous and immigrant people.

Quebec Prime Minister Jacques Parizeau's famous televised rant against the "money and ethnic vote" after the loss of the 1995 referendum marked a shift whereby the old conservationist xenophobia crept back into the modern, liberal, multicultural, and hydroelectricity-fueled nationalism. This brings us back to La Meute and its wolf paw print. Isaiah Awashish's quote, which opens this conclusion, suggests that when xenophobic movements take inspiration from wolves, they neglect how predators can only survive if their prey thrives. French philosopher Jean-Baptiste Morizot, who spent several years tracking wolf paths, suggests an altogether different way for humans to embody wolves. His "werewolf diplomacy" follows wolves' interspecies means of communication, acknowledging each form of life as an autopoetical "perfection with no model, a divergence with no canon." To relate with these others, which are only autonomous inasmuch as they are "tied to the biotic community," the werewolf diplomat "attends to the very force of things—and restricts itself to this attending" (2016: 53). Like a watermill rather than a dam, this way of relating to other beings acknowledges how one derives energy from smaller-scale forces, and that one's emergent higher pattern depends on the integrity of what it is grafted upon. As Eduardo Viveiros de Castro (2015: 11) suggests in reference to the "ontological wolf," such a diplomatic ethnography must "always leave a way out for the people you are describing"—that is, it must keep their own clearing intact.

If "Kanatiens"—the Kanien'kehá:ka (Mohawk) term for Canadians—designates those who have "embedded themselves on the land," their survival equally depends on their capacity to let other beings and their clearings crack through their new infrastructural grounds. This involves attending once again to the landscape onto which their "European elsewhere" (Taussig 1997) was superimposed; such an anamnesis would somewhat reverse their coloniality by way of assuming an immigrant conception of their presence in the landscape. To confront the current era, when people are increasingly divided between natives and foreigners, Achille Mbembe reminds us that "we are basically made of various loans to foreign subjects, and have therefore always been frontier beings" (2016: 46). When visiting the Western frontier around Michigan in the 1850s, Lewis Henry Morgan witnessed the remnants of hybrid forms of sociability and polyglot communication between Indigenous trappers, French immigrant traders, and beavers, each of them "using their knowledge of the others' distinctive ways of communication, what the trappers themselves called 'signs'" (Feeley-Harnik 2001: 75).

Involved in land speculation around projected railroad lines, Morgan became increasingly aware that colonial "improvement" was directly imprinted onto the geographies drawn by beavers, whose dams provided the frame for the colonists' roadbeds (Feeley-Harnik 2001: 67). Morgan grew weary of its "deadly appropriation of vital flows of earth, water, and blood" (80). Yet lacking a state, let alone infrastructure, as they were scarcely distributed throughout the West, the nomadic vestiges of French coureurs des bois on the frontier seemed to take part in the landscape's sentient interactions rather than superimpose new exclusive forms onto them. In this essay, I suggest that the difference in scale measured by the presence of infrastructures implicates the difference in kind between immigrant and colonial relationships with the landscape. The self-indigenization infrastructures brought about by transforming the landscape to fit the state's perception and needs seem to act as a threshold allowing former immigrant settlers to become xenophobic colonizers, jealously watching over the riches they incorporated from the landscape by becoming its apex predator on top of wolves, beavers, and people. This is to say that in settler-colonial contexts at least—and colonized-colonizer ones at best—the landscape appears xenophobic only once its sentience is funneled into fueling what destroys it.

Philippe Blouin writes, translates and studies political anthropology and philosophy in Tionni'tio'tià:kon (Montreal). His current research as a PhD candidate in anthropology at McGill University studies how the Kanien'kehá:ka (Mohawk) alliance protocol of the *Teiohá:te* (Two Row Wampum) challenges Western views of relating and belonging. Blouin has published articles in *Liaisons*, *Stasis* and *PoLAR: Political and Legal Anthropology Review*, and has edited the forthcoming oral history book *The Mohawk Warrior Society: A Handbook on Sovereignty and Survival*.

Notes

1. For instance, the title of the 2016 documentary *Footprints*, directed by Carole Poliquin and Yvan Dubuc, echoes La Meute's paw print, with the difference that it suggests that the Quebecois inherited left-wing values from their privileged contacts with First Nations: the search for peaceful, consensual solutions; gender equality; and an ecological respect for the land. It is also worth noting that in the 2019 Canadian elections, the Bloc Quebecois, historically formed by the convergence of left- and right-wing nationalists, won the ma-

jority of Quebec seats by campaigning on two issues purportedly prioritized by Quebec voters: restrictive immigration policies to protect Quebec culture and an ecological reluctance to build new pipelines.
2. In 1763, at the time of British conquest, there were fewer than seventy thousand settlers in Canada, whereas the British colonies already counted more than one million inhabitants (Barbieri and Ouellette 2012).
3. The French realized this by welcoming "domiciled Indians" within Catholic missions created near Montreal at the end of the seventeenth century and attempting to use them militarily against their Indigenous enemies—albeit with limited success.
4. If this number dropped to a historical low of one hundred thousand in 1900 because of overhunting, the beavers' wetlands still welcome up to 80% of the biodiversity on the West coast to this day (Worrall 2018)
5. According to the poet and filmmaker Pierre Perrault, the development of James Bay was expressly proposed to bring the population to forget the October Crisis (1973: 48).
6. Drawing on Simondon and Jakobson's idea of "transmutation" between nonverbal and verbal languages, Silverstein (2003) suggests the notion of "transduction" to highlight the materiality aspect of translating ideologies, using the metaphor of a motor's transducer which converts electrical energy into mechanical energy.
7. Icons constitute the most basic unit of signs, which are opaquely undifferentiated from their object, as they signify the "Quality of Feeling" in its "firstness", that is "regardless of aught else" (Peirce 1935: 32).
8. Cliche notably remarked that only a small triangle between Quebec, Drummundville, and Saint-Georges-de-Beauce is devoid of any Indigenous land claim (Vincent 1995: 222).

References

Auclair, Élie-J. 1930. *Le curé Labelle. Sa vie et son œuvre*. Montreal: Beauchemin.
Barbieri, Magali, and Nadine Ouellette. 2012. "La Démographie du Canada et des États-Unis des années 1980 aux années 2000: Synthèse des changements et bilan statistique." *Population* 67(2): 221–328.
Beauchemin, Jacques. 1997. "Conservatisme et traditionalisme dans le Québec duplessiste: aux origines d'une confusion conceptuelle." In *Duplessis. Entre la grande noirceur et la société libérale*, ed. Alain-G. Gagnon and Michel Sarra-Bournet, 33–54. Montreal: Québec/Amérique.
Bennett, Jane. 2001. *The Enchantment of Modern Life: Attachments, Crossings, and Ethics*. Princeton: Princeton University Press.
Beyer, Peter. 1985. "The Mission of Quebec Ultramontanism: A Luhmannian Perspective." *Sociological Analysis* 46(1): 37–48.
Binette, André. 2018. "Hydroélectricité: le vrai scandale sur la Côte-Nord." *Le Devoir*, August 23.

Bird-David, Nurit. 2018. "Size matters! The Scalability of Modern Hunter-Gatherer Animism." *Quaternary International* 464: 305–14.
Buffon, Georges-Louis Le Clerc. 1831. *Buffon's Natural History of the Globe*, Corrected and Enlarged by J. Wright. (To which are Added Elements of Botany). London: Thomas Tegg.
Clément, Daniel. 2012. *Le Bestiaire innu. Les quadrupèdes*. Quebec: Presses de l'Université Laval.
Cockloft, Jeremy. 1960. *Cursory Observations Made in Quebec Province of Lower Canada in the year 1811*. Toronto: Oxford University Press.
Courville, Serge, and Normand Séguin. 1989. *Rural Life in Nineteenth-Century Quebec*. Ottawa: Canadian Historical Association.
Cronon, William. 1995. *Uncommon Ground: Rethinking the Human Place in Nature*. New York: W. W. Norton & Co.
Curtis, Christopher. 2018. "La Meute Leader Claims He's 'Aboriginal' in Facebook Post." *Montreal Gazette*, 3 May.
Delâge, Denys. 2014. "Du castor cosmique au castor travailleur: histoire d'un transfert culturel." *Les Cahiers des dix* 68: 1–45.
Desbiens, Caroline. 2013. *Power from the North: Territory, Identity, and the Culture of Hydroelectricity in Quebec*. Vancouver: UBC Press.
Durham, John George Lambton. 1839. *Report on the Affairs of British North America*. Ottawa: The House of Assembly of Upper Canada.
Fahmy-Eid, Nadia. 1975. "Ultramontanisme, idéologie et classes sociales." *Revue d'histoire de l'Amérique française* 29(1): 49–68.
Feeley-Harnik, Gillian. 2001. "The Ethnography of Creation: Lewis Henry Morgan and the American Beaver." In *Relative Values: Reconfiguring Kinship Studies*, ed. Sarah Franklin and Susan McKinnon, 54–84. Durham, NC: Duke University Press.
Fleury, Jean Louis. 1999. *Les Coureurs des lignes: l'histoire du transport de l'électricité au Québec*. Montreal: Stanké.
Gérin-Lajoie, Antoine. 1874. *Rivard, le défricheur*. Montreal: J. B. Rolland & fils.
Glissant, Édouard. 2010. *Poetics of Relation*. Ann Arbor: University of Michigan Press.
Gordillo, Gaston. 2018. "Terrain as Insurgent Weapon: An Affective Geometry of Warfare in the Mountains of Afghanistan." *Political Geography* 64: 53–62.
Greer, Allan. 1993. *The Patriots and the People: The Rebellion of 1837 in Rural Lower Canada*. Toronto: University of Toronto Press.
Groulx, Lionel. 1919. *La Naissance d'une Race—Cours d'histoire à l'Université Laval*. Montreal: Bibliothèque de l'Action française.
———. 1922. *L'Appel de la race*. Montreal: Bibliothèque de l'Action française.
———. 1937. *Directives*. Montreal: Éditions du Zodiaque.
———. 1952. *Histoire du Canada français depuis la découverte*, vols. 3–4. Montreal: Bibliothèque de l'Action Nationale.
Hage, Ghassan. 2017. *Is Racism an Environmental Threat?* London: Polity.
Hamelin, Louis-Edmond. 1999. *Passer près d'une perdrix sans la voir ou attitudes à l'égard des autochtones*. Montreal: Grandes Conférences Desjardins.

Handler, Richard. 1988. *Nationalism and the Politics of Culture in Quebec.* Madison: University of Wisconsin Press.
Harvey, Penny, and Hannah Knox. 2012. "The Enchantments of Infrastructure." *Mobilities* 4(7): 521–36.
Heidegger, Martin. 1971. *Poetry, Language, Thought.* New York: Harper & Row.
———. 1993. *Basic Writings.* London: Routledge.
Juteau, Danielle. 1993. "The Production of the Québécois Nation." *Humboldt Journal of Social Relations* 19(2): 79–108.
Kaufmann, Eric. 1998. "Naturalizing the Nation: The Rise of Naturalistic Nationalism in the United States and Canada." *Comparative Studies in Society and History* 40(4): 666–95.
Kohn, Eduardo. 2013. *How Forests Think.* Berkeley: University of California Press.
———. 2019. "A Genuine Vocation: The Concept-Work of Philippe Descola in Times of Planetary Fragmentation." In *Au Seuil de la forêt. Hommage à Philippe Descola, l'anthropologue de la nature*, ed. Geremia Cometti, Pierre Le Roux, Tiziana Manicone, and Nastassja Martin, 537–54. Poullaouen: Tautem.
Lahontan, Louis-Armand de Lom d'Arce. 1905. *Lahontan's New Voyages to North America*, vol. 2, ed. Reuben Gold Thwaites. Chicago: A. C. McClurg & Co.
Larkin, Brian. 2008. *Signal and Noise. Media, Infrastructure, and Urban Culture in Nigeria.* Durham, NC: Duke University Press.
———. 2013. "The Politics and Poetics of Infrastructure." *Annual Review of Anthropology* 42: 327–43.
Leroux, Darryl. 2019. *Distorted Descent: White Claims to Indigenous Identity.* Winnipeg: University of Manitoba Press.
MacKay, Donald. 2007. *The Lumberjacks.* Toronto: Dundurn.
Manning, Paul. 2012. *Strangers in a Strange Land. Occidentalist Publics and Orientalist Geographies in Nineteenth-Century Georgian Imaginaries.* Boston: Academic Studies Press.
Mbembe, Achille. 2016. *Politiques de l'inimitié.* Paris: La Découverte.
Morissonneau, Christian. 1978. "La Colonisation équivoque." *Recherches Sociographiques* 19(1): 33–53.
Morizot, Jean-Baptiste. 2016. *Les Diplomates. Cohabiter avec les loups sur une autre carte du vivant.* Marseille: Wildproject.
Moten, Fred, and Stefano Harney. 2013. *The Undercommons: Fugitive Planning & Black Study.* New York: Minor Compositions.
Nadeau, Jean-François. 2010. *Adrien Arcand, Führer canadien.* Montreal: Lux.
Nungak, Zebedee, and Tagak Curley. 2017. *Wrestling with Colonialism on Steroids: Quebec Inuit Fight for Their Homeland.* Montreal: Véhicule Press.
Parmenter, Jon. 2010. *The Edge of the Woods: Iroquoia, 1534-1701.* East Lansing, MI: Michigan State University Press.
Peirce, Charles S. 1935. *Collected Papers of Charles Sanders Peirce*, vols. V–VI, ed. Charles Hartshorne and Paul Weiss. Cambridge: The Belknap Press of Harvard University Press.
Perrault, Pierre. 1973. "Préface." In *Le Mushuau Nipi à l'âge du caribou (Nouveau-Québec)*, by Louis-Edmond Hamelin. Quebec: Centre d'Études nordiques.
Prince-Falmagne, Thérèse. 1965. *Un Marquis du grand siècle.* Montreal: Leméac.

Rameau de Saint-Pierre, Edme. 1859. *La France aux Colonies: études sur le développement de la race française hors de l'Europe, les Français en Amérique, Acadiens et Canadiens*. Paris: Jouby.
Richardson, Boyce. 1975. *Strangers Devour the Land: The Cree Hunters of the James Bay Region*. Rexdale: Macmillan of Canada.
Ripple, William, and Robert L. Beschta. 2012. "Trophic Cascades in Yellowstone: The First 15 Years after Wolf Reintroduction." *Biological Conservation* 145(1): 205–13.
Rousseau, Louis. 2005. "Grandeur et déclin des Églises au Québec." *Cités* 3 (23): 129–41.
Scott, Colin. 1995. "Encountering the Whiteman in James Bay Cree." *Aboriginal History* 19(1): 21–40.
Scott, James C. 1998. *Seeing Like the State*. New Haven, CT: Yale University Press.
Silverstein, Michael. 2003. "Translation, Transduction, Transformation: Skating 'Glossando' on Thin Semiotic Ice." In T*ranslating Cultures: Perspectives on Translation and Anthropology*, ed. Paula G. Rubel and Abraham Rosman, 75–106. London: Routledge.
Smith, Donald B. 1974. *Le Sauvage: The Native People in Quebec Historical Writing on the Heroic Period (1534-1663) of New France*. Ottawa: National Museums of Canada.
Spice, Anne. 2018. "Fighting Invasive Infrastructures: Indigenous Relations against Pipelines." *Environment and Society* 9: 40–56.
Star, Susan L. 1999. "The Ethnography of Infrastructure." *American Behavioral Scientist* 43(3): 377–91.
Taussig, Michael. 1997. *The Magic of the State*. London: Routledge.
Trigger, Bruce G. 1985. *Natives and Newcomers: Canada's "Heroic Age" Reconsidered*. Montreal: McGill-Queen's University Press.
Tsing, Anna L., Andrew S. Mathews, and Nils Bubandt. 2019. "Patchy Anthropocene: Landscape Structure, Multispecies History, and the Retooling of Anthropology: An Introduction to Supplement 20." *Current Anthropology* 60(S20): S186–97.
Vincent, Sylvie. 1995. "Le Québec et les Autochtones: trois décennies de rapports politiques." In *Autochtones et Québécois. La rencontre des nationalisme*s, ed. Pierre Trudel, 116–25. Montreal: Recherches amérindiennes au Québec.
Vincent, Sylvie, and Bernard Arcand. 1978. *L'Image de l'Amérindien dans les manuels scolaires du Québec*. Montreal: Hurtubise.
Viveiros de Castro, Eduardo. 2015. "Who is Afraid of the Ontological Wolf?" *The Cambridge Journal of Anthropology* 33(1): 2–17.
———. 2019. "On Models and Examples: Engineers and Bricoleurs in the Anthropocene." *Current Anthropology* 60(S20): S296–S308.
Warburg, Aby. 1939. "A Lecture on Serpent Ritual." *Journal of the Warburg Institute* 2(4): 277–92.
Wheeler, Michael. 2018. "Martin Heidegger." In *The Stanford Encyclopedia of Philosophy*, ed. Edward N. Zalta. Retrieved from https://plato.stanford.edu/archives/win2018/entries/heidegger.
White, Richard. 2010. *The Middle Ground*. Cambridge: Cambridge University Press.

Worrall, Simon. 2018. "Beavers—Once Nearly Extinct—Could Help Fight Climate Change." *National Geographic*. Retrieved from https://www.nationalgeographic.com/animals/2018/08/beavers-climate-change-conservation-news/#close.

Zimmer, Zac. 2015. "The Enclosure of the Nomos. Appropriation & Conquest in the New World." In the *Anomie of the Earth,* ed. Frederico Luisetti, John Pickels, and Wilson Kaiser, 137–59. Durham, NC: Duke University Press.

CHAPTER 3

Ingrained Ontologies
How Romania's Institutionalized Processes Teach Us to Think with Xenophobic Sentient Landscapes

Alexandra Coțofană

In the 1475 battle of Vaslui between Moldavian Stephan the Great and the Ottoman governor of Rumelia, Hadım Suleiman Pasha, the landscape and weather conspired. Historian Dumitru Almaș[1] describes the battle in one of the three volumes of history for school children that he wrote and published in the 1980s:

> One of the greatest battles fought by Stephan the Great was the one in Vaslui. It was wintertime when the Turkish Sultan sent a great army to our country. The army was led by a great, skilled warrior, named Soliman Pasha. He believed he would defeat the Romanians and would subjugate their country easily. Stephan's army was three times smaller. . . . As I said, it was wintertime . . . [and] the army hid around a river's marshes, where the enemies would pass. . . . On the day that Soliman's troops came through, a thick fog settled on the valley of the river. Soliman advanced blindly. He could barely see a few steps ahead. Out of nowhere, from their hiding places, the Romanians stuck their enemies. They slayed many. Others were swallowed by the icy marshes. . . . The battle of Vaslui was a brilliant Romanian victory. Soliman Pasha returned to his country with whatever troops he had left. Such a shameful defeat had never before been suffered by a great Turkish general. (Almaș 1987: 41)[2]

The book illustrations below are from the same volume by Dumitru Almaș, representing the battle of Vaslui described above.[3] The reader can observe the fog descending onto the Ottoman army, while the marshes leave the occupiers immobilized. Stephan the Great (left, on a white steed) seems immune to the marshes and the fog, as he is about to strike an enemy with his gilded mace. Meanwhile, his opponent is restrained by the marsh, able only to shield himself. Behind the leader's white stallion, one Turk has been swallowed by the swamp whole, leaving only his human

Figure 3.1. Moldavian King Stephan fighting Hadım Suleiman Pasha's army in Almaş's book. © Valentin Tănase.

contour and turban as proof that he was there. On the bottom center right, another Ottoman soldier is stepped on, while the marsh consumes him. Taking full advantage of this pro-Romanian alliance of landscape and weather, Stephan's soldiers can be seen attacking, facing forward, dealing blows, as opposed to their numerous but defeated colonial opponents. What does a text like the fragment above respond to? Is it a way to manage real or imagined forms of colonialism? Why do they exist in books catering to young Romanian schoolchildren? What sort of historical and geopolitical factors must we turn our attention to in order to understand Romanian political continuities (both in terms of what is erased out of history, and in terms of what is repeated and centered)?

Romania's recent history has been marked by political disruption: from struggles for national union in the mid-1800s, to political regimes ranging from monarchy to an interwar far-right government to communism in a couple forms, and finally to a democracy, most recently as an EU member state. Even so, or perhaps because of these disruptions, various aspects of the national imaginary prefer continuity. The imaginary of a sentient landscape could be construed as one element that Romanians use to source their continuity. From school stories to national poets and, most recently, reactions in social media, the concept of a sentient landscape has bridged political disruptions and has provided a narrative of nature and nation as one. Throughout the last two centuries, in politics, literature, journalism, the public education system, and most recently in social media commentary, sentient landscape has appeared time and again, imbued with ethnic nationalism and imagined as punishing foreigners.

As the chapter unfolds, the sections chronologically follow the concept of a xenophobic sentient landscape, meaning a landscape that is imagined as having its own will, which it exercises through forms of xenophobia. Specifically, xenophobic sentient landscapes are often imagined in the literature as defending the nation from religious and ethnic Others—from the Muslim Other in the form of the Ottoman empire, to Catholic Others in the form of the Polish king and his armies, to, more recently, Jewish Others in their contemporary militarized forms.

First, it is important to understand the cultural and political factors that led to the association of nature and nation. The first section will introduce the politicians, journalists, and poets who have fostered xenophobic sentient landscapes in the national imaginary. Next, the chapter will focus on Mihai Eminescu, a Romanian poet, journalist, magazine editor, and political speaker who lived in the second half of the nineteenth century. Eminescu's persona was claimed by far-right groups, then by the communist regime, and he later kept his position as the country's national poet after 1989, only to recently be reclaimed by new far-right and conspiracy groups in the country. The poet is known for his verses that blend nation and nature, in many instances invoking the imaginary of a sentient landscape, tinged with the lyricist's own xenophobia.

In the subsequent section, the chapter focuses on a number of continuities: the national myths, especially the nature-nation connection and the erasure or highlighting of particular historical characters that were promoted before 1945 remained mostly intact and were even revived during the socialist regime, particularly by state-owned national presses that catered to school children. Some of these books were found frequently in homes after 1989 and their narratives were ingrained in the minds of several generations. This is particularly important as these people are now adults whose worldview includes the concept of xenophobic sentient landscapes, as we will see in the last section.

Elements of Xenophobic Sentient Landscapes in Nation Building

It is essential to understand how xenophobic sentient landscapes came to be an imaginable entity in the Romanian ontology. The principalities of Wallachia and Moldavia united in 1859 under Alexandru Ioan Cuza, and the country expanded even more in 1918, with the annexation of Bessarabia, Bukovina, and Dobrogea. While Romania's area more than doubled, its population grew by almost five million (Livezeanu 1995: 8). During this process, the country's bureaucrats and intellectuals relied on ethnic nationalism, ignoring the possibility of civic nationalism. In political writing, policies, poems, and literary texts, these figures smothered national minorities (Jews, Muslims, Roma, Greeks, Aromanians, etc.) by rewriting a pure, ethnocentric Romanian culture and history.

Several schools of thought emerged in Romania in the second half of the nineteenth century, some of which built the possibility of a xenophobic sentient landscape into the national imaginary. The creation and repetition in the collective imaginaries of a xenophobic sentient landscape that sided with the Romanians in their historical battles served to explain how improbable battles were won (when the Romanian troops were grossly outnumbered, for example), and to enforce the idea of Romanian indigeneity, through the trust that the landscape bestowed on Romanian military goals. Many of the intellectuals involved in these schools of thought were also political speakers and editors of prestigious magazines or newspapers. These publications sometimes took the names of sentient beings, as is the case for the newspaper *Luceafărul* (the morning star) (1902–1920), named after Mihai Eminescu's 1883 poem about an anthropomorphic morning star. The newspaper quickly became home to poems that eulogized sentient landscapes. Increasingly in the early twentieth century, these publications aligned with political narratives that centered the superiority of Romanian ethnicity and Orthodox Christianity, coupled with anti-Semitism, antiforeignism, and a focus on folk values and on the peasantry as being intrinsically pure and good.

With very few exceptions, such as playwright Ion Luca Caragiale and literary critic and politician Titu Maiorescu, the leading minds of Romanian intellectual life were captivated by anti-Semitism in the form of ethnic nationalism,[4] which was inflamed by the ethnic diversification that Romania experienced as a consequence of the territories won after World War I. They led public attitudes in a rapid rise in anti-Semitism grounded in the general acceptance of the authority of intellectuals. In some of the largest Romanian cities like Bucharest and Iași, it was seen as good form to be anti-Semitic (Stiehler 2015).

In the interwar period, the intellectual elite grew considerably, as a result of democratization and access to education. The percentage of urban young people grew, and with this came various consequences: they were more daring, more idealist, more inclined toward the extremes, more intolerant, but also prone to experiment. They did not wish to follow in the footsteps of previous generations and ideologically find a place within Europe, nor were they looking toward the East for solutions. Instead, they focused on—and in so doing invented—Romanianism (Boia 2012). Romanianism and a focus on Orthodox Christianity are the two discourses that fed ethnocentrism, although the deep interest of scholars like philosopher Emil Cioran and historian of religion Mircea Eliade in spirituality and the esoteric sometimes affected the direction of this discourse and allowed for the concept of a xenophobic sentient landscape to be imagined as legitimately part of the national imaginary.

Cioran and Eliade both called for a "spiritual" revolution in Romania, but this took different forms for each of them. Young Cioran was a National Socialist state scholarship holder, who believed the spiritual revolution had already been accomplished by Hitler in Germany (Cioran 2011: 140–45). He suggested that the driving force behind this revolution in Romania could be neither rural tradition nor its implicit Orthodox faith, but rather a Nietzschean ecstasy which, as xenophobia, has an inherent purifying power (Cioran 1936). For Cioran, Jews were dangerous because of their preeminence over traditional Romanian ways. For Mircea Eliade, anti-Semitism developed gradually, as he became inspired by the work of Mihai Eminescu and Nicolae Iorga. Eliade explained the interbellum Romanian right-wing group Garda de Fier (the Iron Guard) as an effort to reconcile Romania with God, in the sense that they completed what is laid out in tradition. Right before the 1937 elections, Eliade chose to express his faith in the Iron Guard by publishing his thoughts in the group's newspaper, *Buna Vestire* (The good news):

> I believe in the destiny of the Romanian people—that is why I believe in the victory of the Legionnaires' movement. A people who at all levels has demonstrated its creativity cannot fail at the edge of history, as a Balkanized democracy and civil catastrophe. . . . Is it possible that the Romanian people will end their days in the saddest decay that history has recorded, its days concluded, crushed by misery and syphilis, overwhelmed by Jews, torn to shreds by foreigners, betrayed and sold for a few hundred million lei? Whoever does not doubt the destiny of our people cannot doubt the victory of the legionnaires' movement. I believe in this victory because first of all I believe in the victory of Christianity. (Eliade 1936)[5]

Despite how things later progressed, Romanian nationalists were not very focused on religion before World War I. In fact, despite later associations between Romanianness and Orthodox Christianity as having always been one, the Romanian Orthodox Church was not recognized as an autocephalous church until the Ecumenical Patriarch of Constantinople's decision of 1885, and it did not become the national religion until its acknowledgement in the 1866 constitution. Yet, in the aftermath of World War I, there were major efforts in the young country of Romania to build a national identity that would contain the newly expanded state. These in-

Figure 3.2. Cover of *Gândirea* magazine, December 1921. © Central University Library Cluj.

cluded projects of religious nationalism introduced by Christian National Defense League (Liga Apărării Naționale Creștine, or LANC) founders Nicolae Paulescu and A. C. Cuza, as well as by the theologian Nichifor Crainic (1889–1972), who received funding from the Royal Foundations of Prince Carol and from the Ministry of Cults from the 1920s on and who became Minister of National Propaganda in the interwar right-wing regime (Ornea 1996).

For example, Crainic imagined and then aggressively promoted Orthodoxism, a form of nationalist Christianity that he believed should be the backbone of the new state. Crainic introduced Orthodoxy as an identity marker in the ultranationalist, anti-Semitic circles of the time, and used publications such as *Calendarul* (The calendar) to merge these ideas into new concepts of the nation. The *Sămănătorul* (Seed sower) newspaper heavily influenced and supported his work. This included strong propositions against civil rights or the right to live on Romanian territory for ethnic and religious minorities, and a complete rewriting of history that denied any connections between Christianity and Jesus on one side, and Judaism on the other (Crainic 1919). Below is the cover of the December

1921 *Gândirea* (Thinking) magazine, led by Nichifor Crainic. The artwork on the cover of the magazine was often influenced by Orthodox Christian imagery and depicted images of human-nature connections, as is the case for the below cover.

Interwar Europe abounded in nation-building projects that sought legitimacy through associating themselves with a religious identity, so this was not unique to Romania. From Germany to France, Hungary, Italy, and to fellow Orthodox-majority nations Serbia and Ukraine, this phenomenon was happening in many new (or newly refashioned) nation-states. The distinctive feature for the Romanian case was the fact that the strong move toward Orthodoxy came after a state expansion, more than doubling the nation's size, while in the rest of Europe, it came over dissatisfaction with lost territories, worries brought by secularization, or a reclaiming of purity (Clark 2012).

Secularism had, until that point, been fairly widely accepted. Even in the making of national imaginaries, groups such as The Transylvanian School (Şcoala Ardeleană), with their focus on the Latin heritage of Romania, or Paşoptiştii, who focused on secular nationalism and organized in Masonic Lodges, did not focus on Orthodoxy as a central element of Romanianness (Hitchins 1996). The Schopenhauer-inspired Junimea literary circle formed in the 1860s and identified the nation with the peasantry, imagining a collective identity that was pure, Indigenous, and increasingly biblical in its shepherding narratives. This literary circle inspired two currents—secular-leaning Poporanism, created by Moldavian socialists like political writer Constantin Stere, and antiforeign Sămănătorism, headed by Nicolae Iorga (1871–1940), which focused heavily on advancing the Romanian folk identity—although not focusing on Orthodoxy just yet.

Nicolae Iorga was a strong defender of values associated with an imagined way of living of the Romanian peasantry. Iorga lamented in the magazine *Sămănătorul* the way in which poet Mihai Eminescu was being undermined by the "invasion" of Jewish commerce in Iași and Suceava (see the issue from 10 November 1904), and in 1906 he advocated in the newspaper The Romanian People (*Neamul românesc*) (The newspaper coedited with scholar and right-wing LANC leader A. C. Cuza) for Romanization of the middle class by "eliminating"[6] the Jewish element (Stiehler 2015).

Iorga formed Nationalist Democratic Party (*Partidul Naţionalist Democrat*) in 1910. This meant that Sămănătorist ideas of antiforeignness—centering folklore, Orthodox Christianity, and anti-Semitic propaganda—became mainstream.[7] Nichifor Crainic's poems were heavily published by Nicolae Iorga's newspaper *Neamul românesc*, where Crainic also worked (and which ran until 1940), being influenced by the Sămănătorist movement to veer into organized anti-Semitism.

Some of Crainic's poems, like The Tree (*Copacul*)[8] invoked sentient landscape. In this poem, Crainic imagines himself as a tree, rooted to ancestral soil, having nationalistic pathos flow through him as sap.

Înalt și-ngândurat ca visătorul,	Tall and pensive like a dreamer,
Stând între cer și-ntre pământ stingher,	Waiting between skies and lonely earth,
Crescui și eu din veșnicul mister	I grew out of eternal mysteries
Din care toate își pornesc izvorul.	Out of which all things spring.
Când seva urcă-n trunchiul meu de fier,	When sap goes through my iron trunk,
Adâncul îmi trimite-n foi fiorul	Its depth sends shivers to my leaves
Și simt că-n mine năvălește dorul	And I feel growing inside of me
Pământului de-a fi mai lângă cer.	The earth's yearning to be closer to the skies.
Iar cerul peste vârful meu se-ndoaie	The skies bend over my tip
Și svonuri tainice din infinit	And from each leaf of mine they make
O gură fac din fiecare foaie.	Whispered secrets into infinity.
Și-n freamătul de foi nelămurit,	In the incomprehensible move of the leaves,
Cu șoaptele veciei se-ntretaie	The tired earth's cries mingle
Suspinele pământului trudit.	With the soft voice of eternity.

In Crainic's political work, the nation-nature imaginary was as strong as it is in his poems. In his essay entitled "Parsifal," Crainic likens the nation to "a bloc of unconscious force, ripped out of the wildness of nature." He believes peasant life is essential to the nation, saying "it has no history, it sinks into nature," while Orthodoxy is proof of the soul being naturally Christian (*anima naturaliter christiana*). Crainic claims Orthodoxy alone has the ability to rescue his "virgin nation," this "naïve child of nature," from the depravities of Western civilization, including secularism (Crainic 1924). In his courses held first at the University of Chișinău and later at the University of Bucharest, Nichifor Crainic opposed Western rationalism, preferring Eastern mysticism and claiming that true value, and Romanian identity, spring from the latter. Crainic claimed that Romanian peasants will never accept anything other than Orthodoxy, despite religious Romanianism being a movement created in the cities, by intellectuals, and not something inherently in the flesh and blood of the Romanian peasants.[9]

Another regular author in *Semănătorul* is George Coșbuc (1866–1918), who also edited the magazine from 1901 to 1902 (Cioculescu 1973).

Coșbuc's own contribution to the imaginary of sentient landscapes comes in the form of several poems, some of which anthropomorphize and give sentience to rivers. Three such poems are "Prahova" (1893), "Prutul" (1896), and the Danube and the Olt ("Dunărea și Oltul") (1904). These three river poems are important for the fact that all three rivers represent historical borders of the nation. (Prahova arises at the limit between Muntenia and Transylvania, the Prut represents the natural eastern border of the country, between Romania and the Republic of Moldova, and the

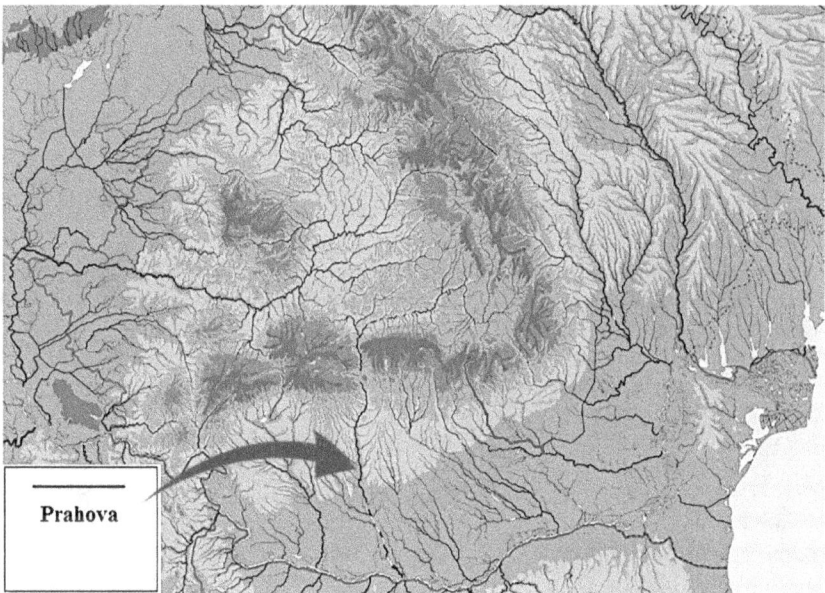

Map 3.1. The Romanian map with an arrow pointing to the Prahova River. © Wikimedia Commons.

Danube is currently the natural border between Romania and Bulgaria and has traditionally been depicted in the national imaginary as the body of water that has kept Ottomans out of the Romanian territories). The three rivers have kept enemies out, but they have been reimagined, as is the case of Prahova, as being at the core of the nation ever since Transylvania was annexed. The mountains where the Prahova River arises have been battlefields in both World War I and World War II and have traditionally been a tall, hard-to-cross, natural border. Yet since 1918, when Transylvania was annexed, the Carpathians, despite naturally separating Transylvania from the two other Romanian regions of Muntenia and Moldavia, have been reimagined as being an inclusive, not a divisive topographic element.

In the poem "Prahova," Coşbuc refers to the river by the same name as a female lover, whose route he traces but whose body he eroticizes, even though at the end of the poem he reveals he walked her to her groom (also a river):

Potriveşte-ţi părul bine;	Style your hair well;
Strânge mijlocelul tău,	Cinch your tiny waist,
Pieptul plin ca să-ţi răsară!	So that your full bosom can be seen!
S-or uita flăcăi la tine,	Young men will look at you,
Şi copile tinerele:	And so will young women.

The poem "Prutul," published two years later, continues the theme of a sentient river, but this time adds the element of xenophobia, specifically against Romania's long-term Muslim Others, the Ottomans and Tatars. The poem is a dialogue between the author and the male river, as Coșbuc notices the violent river carrying down limbless bodies:

- Prutule, tu vii turbat	Prut river, you arrive violently,
Și cu sânge-amestecat,	And mixed with blood,
Și n-ai pace și-alinare	You have no peace or comfort,
Și n-ai loc cum vii de mare:	And there is no room for your size:
Ce ți-e iar de spumegare?	Why are you foaming again?
Și-aduci arme ghintuite,	You bring with you spiked weapons,
Trupuri de voinici ciuntite,	And the severed bodies of young men
Steaguri de oștiri păgâne	Flags of pagan armies,
Și cai roibi fără de frâne!	And red-haired horses without reins!
Iar de maluri tu izbești	You hit against the banks
Capete moldovenești	Moldavian heads
Și prin rădăcini încurci	And through roots you weave
Bărbi cărunte, bărbi de turci!	Grey beards, Turkish beards!

The river answers, expressing his aversion toward the colonizing Muslim Other:

Ce văzui n-am mai văzut!	What my eyes saw then, they had never seen before!
Cât cuprinzi cu ochii-n zare	
Numai tunuri, numai care,	As far as the eyes could see
Numai turci bătrâni călare,	Only cannons, only war chariots,
Numai turci, numai cazaci ...	Only old Turks on horseback,
Barba lor bătea-le brâul	Only Turks, only Cossacks ...
Și țineau cu dinții frâul,	Their beards touched their waist sash,
Pe-unde trec ei duc pustiul!	And their teeth were holding the horses' reigns,
Și când i-am văzut, creștine,	Wherever they go, they bring destruction!
Că iau calea către mine,	And when I saw them, Christian man,
Și când le-am văzut mai bine	Galloping toward me,
Ochii cu fulgerătura,	And when I got a better glimpse
Pletele cu zbârlitura,	At their lightning eyes,
Bărbile cu-ncâlcitura,	Their tousled hair,
Eu de maluri m-am izbit	Their unkempt beards,
Prins de friguri și-ngrozit,	I hit the banks,
Că mi se negrea vederea	Captured by chills and terrified,
Și mi se topea puterea	My sight went dark
Și-amărât stăteam ca fierea!	My powers melted
	And I stood there bitter as bile!

In Coșbuc's dialogue, the river is capable of Orientalism. This is revealed through the word choices meant to portray the many savage, barbaric features of the Ottomans and Cossacks. The river also identifies

Map 3.2. The Danube, Prut, and Olt Rivers. © Wikimedia Commons.

Coșbuc as a "Christian man," a confidant who could understand the fright that the river felt upon meeting these barbarous Others, with their unkempt facial hair and their bloodcurdling eyes. The river itself tries to escape, hitting its banks, yet much like the Romanians, the river has nowhere to escape to—it is trapped in its banks, like the humans are trapped within the boundaries of their territories, captive to barbarian attacks.

The Prut River (above, in bold, in the northeast) is the natural border between Romania and the Republic of Moldova, and it eventually flows into the sprawling Danube, right before the latter flows into the Black Sea. The third poem is a dialogue between the Danube, Europe's second-longest river after the Volga, and her son, the Olt River, the longest river flowing exclusively through Romania, which arises in Transylvania, crosses Muntenia north to south, then flows into the Danube. The poem starts with the Danube asking her son why he always flows down troubled and unsettled. The Danube wonders if the cause for his distress comes from the heavy rains in the Carpathian Mountains, or perhaps it is simply in his character. The Olt River answers:

Dar nu-i asta, maică sfântă,	This is not the reason, holy mother,
Nu de asta-s tulburat,	This is not why I am troubled,
Ci de câte văd mi-e milă,	It is because of all the things I see,
Maică, și-i păcat!	I feel pity, mother, and it is such a shame!

Tu, pe unde-alergi prin lume,	For you, wherever you cross the world,
Vezi și țări și munți frumoși,	You see countries and beautiful mountains,
Neamuri ce-și vorbesc ferice	Peoples who happily speak
Graiul din strămoși . . .	Their ancestral tongues . . .
Eu de unde vin, mâhnitul,	Where I come from, troubled,
Furios spre șes scobor,	Furiously I descend into the plains,
Căci de unde vin, e spaimă.	For where I spring there is only dread,
Groază și fior.	Terror and fright.
Tot români sunt și pe-acolo,	Romanians live there too,
Neam din veac pe-aici adus,	Peoples who have been here forever,
Dar pe gâtul lor și astăzi	Yet their neck is weighed even today
Jugul este pus.	By the yoke.
Ei n-au voie să-și vorbească	They are not allowed to speak
Graiul strămoșesc ce-l au,	Their ancestral language
Iar în coasta lor de-a pururi	And in their ribs endlessly
Sulițele stau	Spears poke.
Sfânta libertate este	Holy freedom is
Nume gol pe-al lor pământ:	An empty word on their own land;
Cei nedrepți sunt cei puternici,	The unjust are in power,
Singuri au cuvânt!	The only ones who can decide!
Ah, de mila lor eu, maică,	Oh, holy mother, it is out of pity for them,
Vin așa de tulburat,	That I flow so unsettled,
Și de ciudă pe dușmanii	And out of wrath toward their enemies,
Cei ce l-au călcat.	Who have stepped on them.
Iar de-nec și mal și oameni,	If I drown banks and people,
Nu mai știu ce fac nici eu	It is because I get lost in my own feelings
Că mă simt de-atâta jale	Because of so much grief,
Tulbure mereu!	I feel eternally gloomy!

In a very interesting understanding of xenophobic sentient landscapes, the Olt River, known for producing terrible floods and destroying communities, explains its destruction of Romanian communities as an unwanted consequence of its anger toward Romania's oppressive colonial Others, the Catholic Austro-Hungarians. The Olt explains to the Danube—a river with origins in Germany that actually flows through Austrian and Hungarian cities before reaching Romania—that the cultural and linguistic oppression of Romanians is simply too much to witness and leads it to be blinded by rage and sorrow, causing it to hurt the very people whose fate it mourns.

The National Poet and Xenophobic Sentient Landscapes

Nichifor Crainic, George Coșbuc, and many others disseminated their ideas in the *Luceafărul*, the newspaper named after Mihai Eminescu's poem about an anthropomorphic morning star (see the magazine cover below). The collaboration of these authors with the magazine is important not only because of the political ideas of Mihai Eminescu but also because of the editorial makeup of the magazine. Started in 1902 by diaspora students in Budapest, the editorial committee included Octavian Goga, who later became Romania's right-wing prime minister (1937–1938) and was buried, as per his wish, with a swastika on his casket.[10] Goga's xenophobia did not just affect the direction of *Luceafărul*, it also helped shape the ideological line of the *Semănătorul* magazine, led by George Coșbuc, where Goga published frequently (Constantin 1997).

The fact that *Luceafărul* was named after Eminescu's poem alludes to the political direction inspired by the poet. Mihai Eminescu (1850–1889), considered Romania's national poet, is the subject of this section, as his political beliefs and work have been celebrated through the many Romanian political regimes of the twentieth century. Even though elements of his work became subject to censorship throughout the period, his work and personality were still celebrated in the communist rewriting of the nation's history. The poet is known for his general xenophobia (and specifically his anti-Semitism), his criticism of Western atheistic values, as well as his attachment to Romanian Orthodoxy, rurality, and the nature-nation connection, revealed in his prose, poetry, and political discourse (Stan and Turcescu 2012).

Eminescu's xenophobia reflected the mentality of many intellectuals and scholars at the time. In the interbellum literary, journalistic, and political sphere of influence of right-wing LANC, A. C. Cuza often cited Eminescu's xenophobic ideas. The 1848 Union of the Romanian Principalities ensured peoples felt united, and ethnicity became a reason for pride. In this context, terms like homeland and nation became heavily used in literary and journalistic texts, while more and more inhabitants of Moldavia, Muntenia, and Transylvania felt increasingly Romanian (Părpăuță 2012).

During the previous century, called the Phanariot century, the Romanian principalities were administered by foreign princes, Greek nobility from the Phanar neighborhood of Istanbul. They became wealthy from their short and indifferent terms, which led Romanian intellectuals to feel a sense of betrayal despite a Greek-Romanian Orthodox Christian connection and presumably shared anticolonial sentiments against the Ottomans. Among political leaders and writers of the time, there was a general

Figure 3.3. Cover of *Luceafărul* magazine, February 1904. © Wikicommons.

consensus that the Phanariot century kept the Romanian principalities from developing a well-formed bourgeoisie. Furthermore, Romania's social stratum of merchants and craftsmen was equally underdeveloped, making the young country unable to partake as a peer in the celebrations and successes of the age of nations (Călinescu 1972). The 1829 Treaty of Adrianople redressed this deficiency through the arrival of a high number of craftsmen and merchants of Russian Jewish origin who settled in Moldavian cities. This triggered the discontent of Romanian journalists, intellectuals, and other members of the bourgeoisie, whose anti-Semitism spread like wildfire.

Eminescu's interest in nature and landscape strengthened when he became the founder of The Orient, a literary circle in 1869; the group focused on collecting traditional stories, fairytales, popular verse, and documents regarding the nation's history and literary traditions (Călinescu 1972). Like many Romanian utopians, Eminescu developed a fixation on immortality, which often took the form of an ecstatic communion with Nature (Aramă 1993). Between 1872 and 1883, Eminescu composed several works of prose in which sentient nature is seen as paradisiacal and utopian and signifies immortality. Even though utopia as a literary form was rejected as a Marxist import by Romania's interbellum right-wing regimes, as well as by the communist regime led by Nicolae Ceaușescu (Polek 1989), Eminescu's work and persona were centered and celebrated by both regimes, and on into the postsocialist period.

Between 1870 and 1883, Mihai Eminescu mixed ecopoetry and radical nationalism as he wrote several versions of "Doina," a poem named after a generic style of traditional poem, characterized by its focus on grief.[11] In "Doina," Eminescu expressed his anger toward invading foreigners, particularly Russians, Greeks, Ukrainians, Jews, Germans, and Hungarians. The poem has been a part of the Romanian school curriculum since the 1890s, invoking an endangered dream of a Greater Romania.

De la Turnu 'n Dorohoiu	From Turnu to Dorohoi
Curg dușmanii în puhoiu	Enemies pour in overwhelmingly
Și s-așează pe la noi;	And they settle on our lands;
Și cum vin cu drum de fier,	As they come with their iron roads
Toate cântecele pier,	All song dies out,
Sboară paserile toate	All birds fly away
De neagra străinătate.	From the gloom of the foreigners.
Numai umbra spinului	The shadow of the thorn alone
La ușa creștinului.	Adorns the door of the Christian.
Își desbracă țara sânul,	The country unveils her chest,
Codrul—frate cu Românul	The forest—the Romanian's brother
De secure se tot pleacă	Collapses under the strike of the axe
Și isvoarele îi seacă	And its springs dry
sărac în țară săracă!	Poor in an impoverished country!

The above section of Eminescu's "Doina" evokes antitechnicist, anti-Western discourse by criticizing the effects of the foreign "iron road," the railway built by the Austrians. In Eminescu's ecopoetic view, this railway destroys nature ("all songs die out, all birds fly away"), evoking a nature-nation union where Romanians and their landscape are equally destroyed by Westerners and their modernizing disruptions. In the second stanza, Eminescu's eco-worries are further explored. Forest exploitation is seen as a defilement of the nation, as her silvan shirt is ripped by immoral foreigners, exposing her geological breast. Later in the poem, Eminescu's anger is formulated as a curse peppered with racial slurs:

Cine ne-au adus Jidanii	Whoever brought us the kikes,
Nu mai vază zi cu anii	May they not see the light of day
Ci să-i scoată ochii corbii	May their eyes be removed by ravens

Să rămâe 'n drum cu orbii	May they roam the paths with the blind.
Cine ne-au adus pe Greci	Whoever brought us the Greeks,
N'ar mai putrezi în veci	May they rot for eternity
Cine ne-au adus Muscalii	Whoever brought us the Russians,
Prăpădi-l-ar focul jalei	May the fire of mourn consume them
Să-l arza să-l dogorească	May it burn them, may it scorch them,
Neamul să i-l prăpădească!	May their bloodline be forever lost!
Cine ține cu străinii	Whoever sides with the foreigners
Mânca-i-ar inima cânii	May the dogs eat their hearts,
Mânca-i-ar casa pustia	May their home be swallowed by hell,
Și neamul nemernicia!	May their bloodline be swallowed by wretchedness!

Around the same time, Romania's national poet also published "Scrisoare a treia" (The third letter) (1881), another poem which has been a part of the Romanian school curriculum since the 1890s, despite (or perhaps thanks to) its xenophobic hatred. The poem has two parts: the first contrasts the patriotism of Romanian soldiers to the false nationalism of their foreign counterparts; the second describes the battle of Rovine, where Mircea the Elder's army fought the Ottoman army commanded by Sultan Bayezid I. In his veiled threats to Bayezid, Mircea equates the Romanian people to a xenophobic, sentient Danube:

Eu nu ti-as dori vreodata să ajungi să ne cunosti,	I would never wish upon you that you get to know us,
Nici ca Dunarea să'nece spumegand a tale osti.	Nor that the Danube frothingly swallow your armies.

Mircea continues by claiming that the pure, simple patriotism of Romanians is supported by a sentient landscape that sees the Ottomans as enemies:

Imi apar saracia si nevoile si neamul. . . .	I defend my poverty, my needs, and my people . . .
Si de-aceea tot ce misca'n tara asta, raul, ramul,	This is why all that moves in this nation, from rivers to woodlands,
Mi-e prieten numai mie, iara tie dusman este,	Are friends to me alone, and enemies to you,
Dusmanit vei fi de toate, far' a prinde chiar de veste;	You will be loathed by them all, before you will even know.

Even though Mircea the Elder wins the battle against the Ottomans, Eminescu's anger toward foreigners moves into his own era, more violent, eugenicist, and radical than before.

Bulgaroi cu ceafa groasa, grecotei cu nas subtire;
Toate mutrele acestea sunt pretinse de roman,
Toata greco-bulgarimea e nepoata lui Traian!
Spuma asta-nveninata, asta plebe, ast gunoi
Să ajunga-a fi stapana si pe tara si pe noi!
Tot ce-i insemnat cu pata putrjunii de natura,
Toti se scursera aicea si formeaza patriotii,
Incat fonfii si flecarii, gagautii si gusatii,
Balbaiti cu gura stramba sunt stapanii astei natii!

Thick-necked Bulgarians, thin-nosed Greeks,
All these mugs that claim to be Roman,
All the Greco-Bulgarians claim to be the grandchildren of Trajan!
This venomous froth, this scum, this refuse,
Are now ruling over us and our land!
Everything that nature has marked with decay,
Has dribbled here, feigning patriotism
With their lisps, their gabbles, these twits with lardy scruffs,
Stuttering cripples are reigning over this nation!

Xenophobic Sentient Landscapes at Home

The fact that Eminescu's poems have been part of school curricula in Romania for so long is but one of many continuities that have allowed for an imaginary of a xenophobic sentient landscape to emerge in the national ontology. These continuities relate to the building of national imaginaries, accepted historical narratives, and popular/hidden memory transmissions. In this section, the chapter focuses on some of these continuities. Specifically, it is crucial that the national myths promoted before 1945 remained mostly intact and were even revived during the socialist regime, particularly by state-owned presses that catered to school children. Some of the published books were found frequently in homes after 1989 and their narratives were ingrained in the minds of several generations.

It might seem contradictory that the green ecology of the peasant-loving interwar Romanian right would be easily adapted by the industry-heavy socialist regime that followed. The reality is that the Socialist Republic of Romania (SRR) embraced green ideology, as it could provide some much-needed credibility to Ceaușescu's totalitarian regime, especially after the 1970s, when ideological means for mass mobilization were becoming scarce (Tascu-Stavre and Stanca 2011). Furthermore, the Romanian Communist Party and green ideology shared anticapitalist, anticonsumerist ideas.

Growing up, my parents' library held two books that many Romanian children born in the 1980s had in their homes. As you can see below, these books were read many times, perhaps too many times. These books were

Figure 3.4. Damirescu's book, tattered by time and misuse, in my childhood home. © Alexandra Coțofană.

some of the first stories my generation, among others, ever read, and they formed readers' ideas about the Romanian nation and its Others. The first book below, Delia Damirescu's *Din Legendele Românilor* (From the legends of the Romanian people), was published by the Ion Creangă publishing house in 1990. The Ion Creangă publishing house pioneered local book illustration, signing contracts with recognized artists who forged the way for rich, colorful, and innovative visual art, which contrasted with other aspects of the lives of children under the communist regime (Radu 2009).

The visual art in Damirescu's book is eerie, and there is something almost esoteric about it. The text is remarkable, too, as it evokes imaginaries of sentient landscapes that side with Romanians against foreign attackers. Most stories in the book tell the legend of a particular place in the geography of the country: a cave, a mountaintop, a lake, etc. In many of the stories, Romanians turn into stone, imbuing the landscape with a national sense of sentience. For example, in the story of "Pietrele Muierilor" (Women's Rocks), the legend says that Tatars were invading the village of Solca. While the men of the village went to war, the women and children went

Figure 3.5. Almaș's volumes in my childhood home. © Alexandra Coțofană.

into the mountains to hide. Almost defeated, the Tatars ran from the Solca men into the mountains, where the Solca women attacked them and won. The sharp rocks where the women stood are called the Women's Rocks and are imbued with their spirits, which sometimes still haunt the cliffs, shrieking with their hair undone (1990: 121–22).

Written in the form of a series of stories that a grandfather tells his three grandchildren as they walk through a history museum, the three volumes of Dumitru Almaș's *Povestiri istorice pentru copii și școlari* (Historical stories for children and pupils) were published in the mid- to late 1980s by Editura Didactică și Pedagogică. These stories follow the Romanian nation chronologically, from its Dacian protoform to the current era. The intention of the author is made clear in the preface of the first volume: "I wrote this book specifically for primary school pupils, as support material when they start learning the country's history in class . . . [M]y yearning [is] to help our young pupils to start discerning from an early age the truth of history and the light of our nation's legends. . . . Heard since childhood, I have faith that the deeds of our ancestors will be ingrained deep in the consciousness of our children and never be forgotten" (8: 1984).[12]

Figure 3.6. Scan from Almaș. Romanian archers and the xenophobic sentient landscape attacking. © Valentin Tănase.

The narrative of the stories is consistent. Dacians and later Romanians find themselves outnumbered, battling occupying foreigners and trying to reason with greedy Others who refuse their offers of peace and friendship. The technologies of the Romanians/Dacians is always behind, their leaders always autochthonous. The Romanians/Dacians prevail by devising clever plans involving the xenophobic sentient landscape, winning against all odds. The ethnic and religious military Other is often left at the mercy of the Romanian landscape, which guarantees victory for the Romanian army. The forest thickens and fog blinds the enemies at just the right time, leaving them surrounded by local archers; the valleys narrow before the enemies grasp the danger, allowing Romanian peasants to crush them under a deluge of boulders; swamps slow them, giving the Romanians the perfect opportunity to attack.

Dehumanizing Others is often used as a narrative technique. In these stories, time and again, the Tatars and Turks are compared to predatory animals—either to wolves preying on herds of Romanian sheep (a biblical image), or to black, croaking ravens waiting for honest, hard-working Romanians to go to sleep so they can steal their shiny belongings (see below), or to wild forest beasts hunting as a pack, at night, targeting peasant women and children (reminiscent of the Ottomans attacking

Figure 3.7. Scan from Almaș. Beastly sentient others stealing riches from a Romanian boy. © Valentin Tănase.

and abducting women and children). In one story, King Petru Rareș believes that to go to the sultan's palace is like willingly shoving yourself in the lion's mouth: "ca și cum te-ai băga, de bună voie, în gura leului" (54). In another story, the Turks fighting Mihai Viteazul are portrayed as packs of wolves and groups of wild boars charging at the Romanians: "Năpustindu-se, înghesuindu-se, lovind năprasnic în români, au trecut podul peste apa Neajlovului și au umplut locul, ca niște haite de lupi și turme de mistreții" (66). The revolutionary Tudor Vladimirescu addresses Phanariot rulers by calling them wolves and venomous snakes: "Până aici, hapsânilor și lupilor și șerpilor veninoși! Cu arma vă vom alunga din țarăl" (99).

Even from early Dacian times, the locals are imagined as preferring death to foreign submission. When losing the battle against the Roman emperor Trajan around AD 103–105, the Dacian king Decebal prefers to die by his own sword rather than surrender. Facing the reality of colonialism, Dacians pray to their gods and turn to rock. Reclaiming the theme of humans turned into landscape, Dacian princess Dochia, at the end of the

Figure 3.8. Scan from Almaș. Princess Dochia resisting colonization. © Valentin Tănase.

same battle, refuses to leave for Rome to become Trajan's bride and turns to stone, becoming one with the mountain.

> "I will not leave here, I wish to be buried here, in Dacia's holy land. . . . Trajan was angered at the news that Dochia took a flock of sheep, became a shepherdess and escaped to the mountains. . . . "I will take you with me against your will. I will abduct you!" And he signaled to the soldiers to seize her. Scared, Dochia raised her hands to the skies and whispered, "I will become a cliff and remain here in my country." Truly, within the blink of an eye, beautiful Dochia together with her flock turned to stone, rooted in the mountain". (14)[13]

Shocked, Roman emperor Trajan exclaimed: "There is nothing I can do, the men and women of Dacia are tied to their land like mountains and cliffs" (14).[14]

The landscape often exhibits sentience in the narrative of Dumitru Almaș, in stories that explain the perplexing victories of the small, unarmed Romanian peasant armies against colonial Others. In AD 1330, King Basarab I hid his army in the woods, waiting to attack Hungarian King Charles Robert, whose colonizing ambitions had to be stopped:

Figure 3.9. Scan from Almaș. Battle of Posada. © Valentin Tănase.

He hid in the mountains and forests. Because the mountain forest is brother of the Romanian and will protect him. There, he waited, in a gorge with very tall walls and so narrow that it wouldn't fit more than ten to twelve horsemen. That place is called Posada. The king ordered his soldiers to go up in the mountains and track the approaching enemy. Eager to capture Basarab, like you would a bear in its den, King Charles Robert advanced conceited, believing no one can defeat him. And he drove his troops into the Posada strait. Before he could realize it, they were caught in a deluge of boulders, logs, rocks, spears, and arrows. It seemed the mountains themselves were collapsing, ravaging them. (20)[15]

The exact same framing is used in the third volume, the one that tells stories from nineteenth- and twentieth-century Romania. In this volume, we see an almost identical story about a mountain village fighting "in the plight against the fascists" (1984: 42). This time, the colonizing enemy is equipped with tanks and trucks full of ammunition, and in describing the battle, the author references the Posada battle of AD 1330: "It was as if the old times had come back to life, when the Romanians were fighting in Posada, led by King Basarab" (42).[16]

Figure 3.10. Scan from Almaș. Romanians attacking German tanks in World War II. © Valentin Tănase.

Sharing in the suffering of the martyred Romanian revolutionaries fighting against Austro-Hungarian colonization, the sentient landscape acts and reacts, mourning the arrest and upcoming execution of the freedom fighter Horea.

> Horea was extremely tired, you could say he crawled more than he walked. The metal cuffs were causing his ankles to bleed; his hands were going numb under the weight of the iron, and his neck was stiff in its cuff.... On top of all this, a great thirst was also tormenting him; he simply could not wait to come across a spring and quench his thirst. After a long period of agony, finally, there it was, a spring on the side of the road. A spring overflowing with clear, cold water. Horea stopped and bowed to take a sip. But the mounted soldier who had him tied jerked his chains and did not let him cool his lips. Horea looked at him in anger and uttered: Drought! They say that from that day on, the spring stopped giving water, it went dry. So the people who imprisoned Horea could not quench their thirst either. (95)[17]

It is important to note that the word for drought (*secătură*) can also translate as an offense brought upon a human, the equivalent of "wretch." This speaks to the fact that Horea was not an entirely powerless prisoner, as he defiantly insulted a member of the imperial military forces while at the same time asking the spring to go dry.

Figure 3.11. Scan from Almaş. Horea and his capturers. © Valentin Tănase.

Postcommunist Xenophobic Sentient Landscapes

After 1989, Eminescu's appeal grew once more. One of the best-known Romanian far-right groups, called the New Right (Noua Dreaptă), claims Eminescu as the absolute national poet. The Romanian far right has a deep element of martyrdom in its self-narrative: not only were a large number of their interwar elites assassinated by the regime of King Carol II but the oppression grew even harsher under communism. Of particular interest are the waves of arrests that took place from the late 1950s to the mid-1960s and resulted in almost four thousand nuns and monks being arrested. The police raided monasteries and monastic seminaries for former supporters of the Iron Guard (Beeson 1975).

The New Right are not alone. Leaders of the governing center-left Social Democratic Party have, for some years now, relied on unfounded arguments targeting philanthropist George Soros, while Romanian social media froths with terminology like "Judeo-communism" and "the occult elites," and is prone to xenophobic panics. This quasi-mysticism relies not on historical data or proof but on an imported discourse meant to produce panic around the Jewish minority that has not only suffered two pogroms at the hands of Romanians but has mostly disappeared from the country.

Xenophobia is grown online and in political discourse. At the same time, esotericism as a scholarly interest finds its way back to Romania through new authors and new publications, but somehow rehashing old arguments. Scholarly esotericism gained momentum in the 1950s in the French academic milieu, emulating (but also trying to differentiate itself from) the scholars of the Eranos meetings, among whom was Mircea Eliade (Raveca Buleu 2019). Following communism, scholarly esotericism has found its way back to Romania in the form of books such as Radu Cernătescu's *Literatura Luciferică* (2013). In the book, Cernătescu insists that Romanian prose and poetry should not be read simplistically but with an effort to understand the hidden meaning behind the author's words and intentions, claiming all authors share a mystogenetic matrix (2013). Many famous Romanian novelists and poets, including Mircea Eliade, Mihai Eminescu, and Mihai Sadoveanu, are interpreted by Cernătescu as being driven by motives stemming from their secret Freemasonry. Cernătescu also devotes an entire chapter to Romanians' spiritual relationship with mountains and claims that all literary references to mountains are indeed driven by Freemason and Rosicrucian affinities.

Alexandra Coțofană holds a doctorate in anthropology from Indiana University Bloomington, with a doctoral minor in religious studies. Her research explores intersections of politics, modernities, and ontologies of governing. Alexandra's scholarly interests focus on political ecologies, the ontological turn, the study of political elites, and ways of governing, as well as on the occult as a tool for governing and discursive techniques employed in populist imaginaries to form racial, gender, and political Others. She is currently teaching and conducting research at Zayed University in Abu Dhabi as assistant professor of social sciences.

Notes

1. Dumitru Almaș was the literary pseudonym of Dumitru Ailincăi, a twentieth-century prose writer, publicist, historian, and author of historical novels, who was born in 1908 in Neamț county in the Romanian northern Carpathians. He was awarded a bachelor's degree in history and geography from the university of Bucharest (1928–1933) and received his doctorate for a thesis titled "Historical Voltaire." In the 1930s he worked as an editor for various newspapers, taught history in high schools (1938–1949), and taught as a university lecturer (1949–1972) and then as a tenured professor (1972–1975) at the University of Bucharest. Almaș reimagined the regional identities of the times

around the battle of Vaslui through the lens of the new Romanian nation-state of the mid-1800s by repeatedly calling the different regions "our country" and the regions' inhabitants "Romanians," leading the young reader to imagine that the various intricate political geographies of past times have always been today's Romania, forcefully partitioned by colonial others. More on the academic and editorial career of Almaș can be found here: https://zch.ro/dumitru-almas-cel-mai-prolific-scriitor-din-neamt/.
2. The original reads: "Una din cele mai mari bătălii a dat-o Ștefan vodă la Vaslui. Era vreme de iarnă, când sultanul turcilor a trimis o mare armată asupra țării noastre. O conducea un general iscusit, mare războinic, numit Soliman Pașa. El credea că-i va înfrânge pe români și țara lor o va supune repede. Ștefan vodă avea o oștire de trei ori mai mică. . . . Cum am spus, era iarnă . . . așezat oastea pe malul unui râu mocirlos, în lungul căruia se afla drumul, pe care aveau să treacă dușmanii. . . . În ziua când armata lui Soliman pașa a ajuns în dreptul românilor, pe valea râului s-a lăsat o ceață deasă. Soliman a intrat cu toată oastea în valea râului. Dar, din pricina ceții, abia vedea la câțiva pași. Înainta orbește. Și, deodată, . . . din adăposturile lor, românii au tăbărât asupra dușmanilor. Pe mulți i-au ucis. Pe alții i-au împotmolit în mlaștina cu sloiuri de gheață. . . . Bătălia de la Vaslui a fost o strălucită biruință românească. Soliman pașa cu armata, câtă i-a mai rămas, s-a întors în țara lui. Asemenea rușinoasă înfrângere nu mai suferise, până atunci, nici un alt mare general turc.""
3. Unless otherwise stated, all images are scans from my personal archive. The book illustrations are from pages 54–55.
4. Some notable names include poet Vasile Alecsandri, philosopher Vasile Conta, political figure Cezar Bolliac, national poet and political speaker Mihai Eminescu, diplomat Ion Ghica, essayist Ion Heliade-Rădulescu, statesman and historian Mihail Kogălniceanu, novelist Constantin Negruzzi, philologist Bogdan-Petriceicu Hașdeu, writer and journalist Ioan Slavici.
5. The original reads: "Cred în destinul neamului românesc—de aceea cred în biruința mișcării legionare. Un neam care a dovedit uriașe puteri de creație, în toate nivelurile realității, nu poate naufragia la periferia istoriei, într-o democrație balcanizată și într-o catastrofă civilă. . . . Poate neamul românesc să-și sfîrșească viața în cea mai tristă descompunere pe care ar cunoaște-o istoria, surpat de mizerie și sifilis, cotropit de evrei și sfîrtecat de străini, demoralizat, trădat, vîndut pentru cîteva sute de miloane (sic!) de lei? Cine nu se îndoiește de destinul neamului nostru, nu se poate îndoi de biruința mișcării legionare. Cred în această biruință, pentru că, înainte de toate, cred în biruința duhului creștin."
6. The call for ""elimination,"" which A. C. Cuza grounded in the irreconcilable struggle between Christian and Jewish culture, does not initially relate to their physical destruction but rather to the expulsion of Jews from key economic positions within the state.
7. See more in N. Iorga, Problema evreiască la Cameră (Vălenii de Munte, Tipografia Neamul Românesc, 1910).
8. The only mention of a publication date for the poem comes in his memoir *Zile albe, zile negre* (Good days, bad days), published posthumously in 1991:

"After my Native Lands volume was published, Dragomirescu dedicated an entire evening to the volume, in the presence of his circle of writers, where he himself read the entire volume, remarking on what he believed was special. I remember that in one sonnet called 'Copacul,' he said I had imbued it with a true 'Bergsonian spirit.'" (The original reads: "După apariția 'Șesurilor natale,' Dragomirescu le-a închinat o ședință a cenaclului său de scriitori, unde a citit el singur tot volumul remarcînd ce i se părea mai realizat. Mi-aduc aminte că într-un' sonet, 'Copacul,' găsea că am pus un adevărat 'elan Bergsonian.'") The volume mentioned here was published in 1916; it seems from Crainic's comment that the poem was part of that collection.

9. Perhaps unsurprisingly, Nichifor Crainic was a mentor to Arsenie Boca, a mystic and an Orthodox priest who was martyred by the Communist regime and reclaimed by the Romanian new far right as well as by the Romanian Orthodox Church, which has recently decided to canonize Boca.

10. Goga represented the National Christian Party (PNC), formed in 1935 through the fusion of A. C. Cuza's LANC and Goga's National Agrarian Party. PNC's logo featured a swastika. See Claudiu Padurean, Expoziție inedită de fotografii – Octavian Goga, înmormântat cu un simbol oribil pe sicriu, ClujToday, February 27, 2020. Retrieved from https://clujtoday.ro/expozitie-inedita-de-fotografii-octavian-goga-inmormantat-cu-un-simbol-oribil-pe-sicriu/.

11. Several versions of the poem are circulated, with unclear dates. Websites published by the legionnaire movement in Romania host uncensored versions of the poem (See miscarea.net and legiunea.com), where the word *jidani* (kikes) appears several times. According to Arthur Gorovei, Eminescu wrote "Doina" in 1883 in Ion Creangă's country home (Gorovei 1930). Creangă and Eminescu's friendship was infamous, and in Gorovei's writings, Creangă recalls Eminescu's declining mental health and that Eminescu once arrived with a revolver, which he claimed would defend him from unnamed enemies (Călinescu 1972).

12. The original reads: "Am scris această carte anume pentru cei mici, care n-au ajuns încă în clasa a IV-a, când încep a învăța istoria patriei după manual . . . râvna de a ajuta micuții noștri preșcolari și școlari, copiii noștri dragi, să înceapă a desluși, încă din fragedă pruncie, câte ceva din adevărul istoriei și din lumina legendelor patriei. . . . Auzite încă din copilărie, am credința că faptele strămoșilor se vor imprima în conștiința copiilor adânc și de neuitat."

13. The original reads: "Eu însă de aici nu plec, voiesc să mă îngrop aici, în pământul sfânt al Daciei. . . . Traian când a aflat că Dochia a luat o turmă de mioare, s-a făcut păstoriță și a urcat în munți, departe, s-a supărat foc. . . . 'Te iau cu de-a sila. Te răpesc!'" Și a făcut semnal ostașilor s-o prindă. Speriată, Dochia a ridicat mâinile spre cer și a șoptit: "'Stană de piatră mă fac și rămân aici, în tara mea!'" În adevăr, cât ai clipi din ochi, Dochia cea preafrumoasă, cu toate mioarele ei răspândite pe pajiște, s-au prefăcut în stânci, înfipte în piatra muntelui."

14. The original reads: "N-am ce face; dacii, bărbați și femei, sunt legați de țara lor ca munții și stâncile lor.""

15. The original reads: "Apoi s-a retras, cu grijă, din calea vitezei și numeroasei oștiri a lui Carol Robert. S-a retras în munți și în codri. Că doar codrul e frate cu românul și-l apără. Acolo l-a așteptat, la o strâmtoare cu pereții foarte înalți și așa de îngustă, că abia încăpeau zece-doisprezece călăreți alături. Acelui loc i-a zis Posada. Voievodul a poruncit ostașilor lui să se urce pe munți, deasupra acelei strâmtori, și să pândească apropierea dușmanului. Foarte dornic să-l prindă pe Basarab, ca pe un urs în culcușul lui, precum zisese, Carol Robert a înaintat semeț și încrezător că nimeni nu-l poate birui. Așa a vârât oastea în strâmtoarea de la Posada. Dar iată că, tocmai când nici gândea, de sus, din munte, din piscuri, din vârfuri de brazi, au început să cadă, ca un potop: stânci, butuci, bolovani, suliți și săgeți. Părea că toți munții se prăbușesc asupra lor, potopindu-i."
16. The original reads: "Parcă reînviaseră vremurile bătrîne, cînd românii luptau la Posada ocîrmuiți de Basarab Întemeietorul."
17. The original reads: "Foarte, foarte ostenit, Horea mai mult se târa decât mergea. Gleznele îi sângerau din pricina cătușelor; mâinile îi amorțeau sub povara fierului, iar gâtul îi înțepenise în cătușă. . . . Peste toate acestea îl mai chinuia și o sete grozavă; de-abia aștepta să întâlnească în cale un izvor să și-o potolească. După o îndelungă suferință, iată, în sfârșit, un izvor, la marginea drumului. Un șipot cu apă multă, limpede și rece. Horea s-a oprit și s-a aplecat să bea apă. Dar soldatul călare, care-l ținea legat, a smucit lanțul și nu l-a lăsat să atingă apa ca să-și răcorească buzele. Horea l-a privit, cu mânie, și a rostit: '"Secătură!"' Se zice că din clipa aceea, izvorul a încetat să mai curgă: a secat. Așa că nici cei care-l păzeau pe Horea n-au maj avut cu ce-și potoli setea."

References

Almaș, Dumitru. 1984. *Povestiri istorice pentru copii și școlari, șoimi ai patriei și pionieri (III)*. București: Editura Didactică și Pedagogică.
———. 1987. *Povestiri istorice pentru copii și școlari—șoimi ai patriei și pionieri (I)*. București: Editura Didactică și Pedagogică.
Aramă, Horia. 1993. "Utopias Are Written in Romania as Well." *Utopian Studies* 4(2): 144–49.
Beeson, Trevor. 1982. *Discretion and Valor. Religious Conditions in Russia and Eastern Europe*. 2nd ed. Philadelphia: Fortress Press.
Boia, Lucian. 2012. *Capcanele istoriei. Elita intelectuală românească între 1930 și 1950*. Bucharest: Humanitas.
Călinescu, George. 1972. "Mihai Eminescu." In *Istoria literaturii române. III: Epoca marilor clasici*, ed. Șerban Cioculescu, Ovidiu Papadima, and Alexandru Piru, 159–242. București: Editura Academiei.
Cernătescu, Radu. 2013. *Literatura Luciferică*. Bucharest: Cartea Românească.
Cioculescu, Șerban. 1973. *Istoria literaturii române III. Epoca marilor clasici*. București: Editura Academiei Republicii Socialiste România.
Cioran, Emil. 1936. *Schimbarea la față a României*. București: Vremea.

———. 2011. "Eindrücke aus München. Hitler im Bewusstsein der Deutschen." In Ders.: *Über Deutschland. Aufsätze aus den Jahren 1931–1937*, 140–45. Berlin: Suhrkamp Verlag .Original in *Vremea* 346, 15 July 1934.

Clark, Roland. 2012. "Orthodoxy and nation-building. Nichifor Crainic and religious nationalism in 1920s Romania." *Nationalities Papers. The Journal of Nationalism and Ethnicity* 40(4):525-543.

Constantiniu, Florin. 1997. *O istorie sinceră a poporului român*. București: Editura Univers Enciclopedic.

Crainic, Nichifor. 1919. "Problema biblică." In *Icoanele vremii*. București: Editura H. Steinberg.pp. 203-207.

———. 1924. "Parsifal." *Gândirea* 3.8–9–10: 181–86.

Damirescu, Delia. 1990. *Din Legendele Românilor*. București: Editura Ion Creangă (ilustrații de Adrian Mihăilescu).

Dietrich, Donald J. 1988. "National Renewal, Anti-Semitism, and Political Continuity: A Psychological Assessment." *Political Psychology* 9(3): 385-411.

Dragomirescu, Mihail. 1934. *Istoria literaturii române în secolul XX, după o nouă metodă. Sămănătorism, poporanism, criticism*. București: Editura Institutului de Literatură.

Eliade, Mircea. 1937. "De ce cred în biruința Mișcării Legionare?" *Buna Vestire* An I, 17 Decembrie, nr. 244: 1–2.

Gorovei, Arthur. 1930. *Alte vremuri. Amintiri literare*. Fălticeni: J. Bendit.

Hitchins, Keith. 1996. *The Romanians, 1774–1866*. Oxford: Clarendon.

Iordachi, Constantin. 2004. *Charisma, Politics and Violence: The Legion of the "Archangel Michael" in Inter-war Romania*. Trondheim, Norway: Trondheim Studies on East European Cultures & Societies.

Iorga, Nicolae. 1910. *Problema evreiască la Cameră*. Vălenii de Munte: Tipografia Neamul Românesc.

Livezeanu, Irina. 1995. *Cultural Politics in Greater Romania: Regionalism, Nation Building, and Ethnic Struggle, 1918–1930*. Ithaca NY: Cornell University Press

Ornea, Zigu. 1996. *Anii Treizeci, Extrema Dreaptă Românească*. București: Editura Fundașiei Culturale Române.

Părpăuță, Radu. 2012. "Xenofobia lui Eminescu." In *Confluențe literare*.

Polek, Fran. 1989. "Red Stars and Eternity: Hidden Realities in Contemporary Romanian Poetry." *Pacific Coast Philology* 24(1/2): 72-82.

Radu, Cristina. 2009. "Ilustrația de carte. Un domeniu minor?" *Ziarul Financiar*, Feb 27.

Raveca Buleu, Constantina. 2019. "Esotericism and Secrecy in Alternative Literary Histories." *Dacoromania Literară* VI: 47–57.

Stan, Lavinia, and Lucian Turcescu. 2012. "The Romanian Orthodox Church. From Nation-Building Actor to State Partner" *KZG/CCH* 25: 401-17.

Stiehler, Heinrich. 2015. "Zur Geschichte des rumänischen Antisemitismus", *Zeitschrift für Balkanologie*, Vol. 51, No. 2, pp. 254-262

Tascu-Stavre, Miroslav, and Cristina Stanca. 2011. "When Green Cleans Red. Or Why Romanian Communists Turned to Green Ideology," *State of Nature 2nd International Workshop of the NATURE AND NATION Network*, București, 2–4 December 2011.

Zelea Codreanu, Corneliu. 1998. *Scrisori studenţeşti din închisoare*. Bucureşti: Editura Ramida.

———. 2003. *Doctrina mişcării legionare*. Bucureşti: Editura Lucman.

CHAPTER 4

Hostile Territory
Communal Politics and Sentient Landscape in Ladakh, Himalayan India

Callum Pearce

Introduction

In December 2014 I was conducting fieldwork in Ladakh, an arid and mountainous region of Himalayan India at the western edge of the Tibetan Plateau and (at that point) part of the state of Jammu and Kashmir. While staying outside the regional capital of Leh, I heard a story from a student originally from the village of Kumdok in the eastern part of the region.

There, he said, near his home, are two small lakes inhabited by *lu* (Tibetan: *klu*), subterranean spirits of water and fertility known across the Himalaya and routinely identified with the Indic *nāga*. While *nāga* are typically represented in Buddhist art as serpentine creatures, and while Ladakhi *lu* are often described as taking the form of worms, lizards, or fish (Dollfus 2003a: 9), the pair living within the two lakes are locally said to take the forms of a yak and an Indian ox (*glang to*). In the brief story the student related, a Muslim[1] man had approached one of the lakes as he made his way on foot from one village to another. Stooping down, he cupped his hands and made to drink when the surface of the water suddenly broke, and the resident *lu* rose up out of the lake in the form of an immense and angry ox. It charged at the man, chasing him away from the water as far as the next village; there, it suddenly crashed down into the earth, turning back to water and leaving behind a new lake in its place.

This account employs several elements that are common to stories from Ladakh and across the Himalaya: it describes landscape features inhabited and embodied by sentient beings who may enrich or punish those they encounter, and a landscape that moves and changes in response to shifting relations with humans. The description of the moving lake sits alongside accounts of mountains that fly from place to place, lakes drained after battles between Buddhist missionaries and *lu*, and whole valleys sealed up to be hidden from the outside world (Allen 1997; Buffetrille 1996; Samuel 2021). In Ladakh, stories of the capricious entities of land and water often describe them bestowing wealth on households to repay individual acts of kindness—or, alternatively, striking down those that seek to exploit them. There is an underlying violence to many of these accounts, something that reflects the difficulties of life in Ladakh's cold and dry climate. Yet in stories like the one from Kumdok, the violence spills over into the divisions between people.

The student presented his story as an instance of just retribution: the Muslim receiving the punishment he deserved, the ox-*lu* rising out of the water like a bovine avenger. Springs and pools linked to *lu* are routinely associated with prohibitions on the use of water for washing or drinking, and the man's actions demonstrate either ignorance or deliberate disregard for such customs. The story marks him as an outsider and identifies this status with his religious background. The subtext is a commentary on the place of Muslims in Ladakh, with an embodiment of the land itself emerging to drive off an outsider. This is characteristic of stories told by Buddhist Ladakhis to demonstrate the power of local spirits and deities: such stories routinely describe outsiders falling prey to spirits, often simply because they failed to take the necessary precautions and were in the wrong place at the wrong time. Common accounts of migrant workers from Nepal falling ill after encountering unidentified figures on the road at night provide an object lesson in the resident dangers of the Ladakhi landscape, illustrated by figures who cannot recognise the beings that have harmed them. Yet the role of the outsider-victim is regularly given to Ladakhi Muslims instead, reflecting tensions that have emerged between Buddhists and Muslims in the region over the past sixty years. These stories may describe Muslims being chased off by *lu* or struck down by a goddess dwelling in a tree (see below); or a Muslim neighbour struck down with paralysis after meeting a red-skinned *tsan* (*btsan*) spirit near his house, who is only able to overcome his affliction by accepting the help of a Buddhist ritual specialist. These accounts all emphasise the idea—encouraged by political activists—that Muslims are not truly Ladakhi.

Taking the population of the region as a whole, Muslims in Ladakh outnumber Buddhists—though the groups are largely divided between the two administrative districts of Shia Muslim-majority Kargil and Buddhist-majority Leh.[2] Yet in recent years Buddhist activists have mobilised religious affiliation for political ends in a way that Muslims have not, and have increasingly sought to characterise Ladakhi identity as defined by Buddhism. While this programme depends on the exclusion and marginalisation of the significant and long-established Islamic presence in the region, this is rarely acknowledged openly and tends to be carefully obscured in public discourse (van Beek 2003: 294). The politicisation of Buddhist identity rests on an undercurrent of hostility toward Muslims, a subterranean politics that rises to the surface in occasional moments of violence.

This deliberate silence mirrors the attitude of Buddhist activists to the role of the sentient landscape in religious life. While the practice of Buddhism in Ladakh is inseparable from relations with the spirits and deities that embody and inhabit the land, public representations of the religion typically depict it in a sanitised and rationalised form influenced by modernising trends developed over the course of the twentieth century. This has usually involved characterising Buddhism as a fundamentally peaceful, egalitarian, and scientific tradition focused on mindfulness and meditation (McMahan 2008: 5–8). Yet on a practical level, Buddhist ritual in areas such as Ladakh operates primarily as a framework for organising relations with worldly gods and the land (Mills 2003: 346). This was always most evident in historic forms of state ritual carried out by monasteries on behalf of the kings of Ladakh; but local spirits and divine protectors continue to play a central role in daily and seasonal ritual for laity, and social organisation remains dependent on the maintenance of household and village deities. Thus, while Buddhist activists have sought to carve out a political programme based on religious identity, the coherence of this depends on unspoken elements. In stories like the one from Kumdok, these emerge intertwined with the anti-Muslim sentiments that form a key part of Buddhist identity politics in Ladakh.

Anthropologists drawing on discussions of ontology have often sought to characterise concerns with sentient landscape as standing radically apart from dominant Western and colonial modes of being, offering alternative configurations of personhood, politics and relations with non-humans and the land (cf. Ingold 2000: 107–10; Hage 2015: 83, 201–3). Blaser, writing about a conflict between an Innu First Nation group and the government of the Canadian province of Newfoundland and Labrador, has described a clash between separate worlds established on incommensurable grounds: authorities imposed a hunting ban on caribou that disregarded indigenous relationships with the "spirit master" of the caribou (or *atîku*), and the need to maintain those relationships through hunting (Blaser 2016: 545–48).

The existence of the spirit master and the responsibilities that Innu people owed to him were rendered "unrealistic" and "irrelevant" by the "reasonable politics" of the provincial government, which dismissed Innu needs out of hand. This led Blaser (drawing on Latour 2004) to argue for an expanded understanding of politics that leaves space for both "ontological multiplicity" and dialogue between "multiple worldings" (Blaser 2016: 563). This depends on a "cosmopolitics" that leaves open "the question of who and what might compose the common world": a space of political dialogue that allows these separate worldings to coexist without presupposing the conditions of reality (ibid.: 548). In practice this involves an emphasis on "homonymic" actions that seek to address incommensurable concerns simultaneously ("not a matter of either/or but of both/ and"), sidestepping the need for agreement of a single common ground (ibid.: 565). Yet framing arguments to appeal to another party's interests— while leaving open questions of contested claims and responsibilities—is simply how ordinary political negotiation works.

Applying this emphasis on ontological multiplicity to Ladakh presents complications. The organisations that claim to speak on behalf of Buddhists in Ladakh do not publicly recognise the worldly spirits and deities of the region, regardless of the continued relevance of these beings to everyday life and their importance for institutional Buddhism, and these groups have adopted their own form of "reasonable politics" shaped by Buddhist modernism and the demands of life in modern India. Yet accounts of sentient lakes, trees, and mountains routinely follow the dominant mode of Ladakhi politics, often displaying the same underlying hostility toward Muslims that characterises activist constructions of Buddhist identity. In contrast to Blaser's depiction of discrete "worldings," the political values of modern India and local concerns with gods and spirits flow into and shape one another. Ladakhi Buddhist activists may employ constructions of religious identity that obscure the role of spirits and deities, but Buddhist practice remains grounded in relations with sentient landscape; and the beings that embody this landscape have not been unaffected by the growth of "communal" politics in Ladakh. Alternative modes of being are not sealed off from dominant forms of politics, or immune to the power of divisive political movements; nor do sentient landscapes necessarily align with the interests of the marginalised and oppressed.

In what follows, I will argue that these issues operate on the level of rhetoric and not ontology: that to treat apparently incommensurable representations of religion, landscape, and belonging as radically distinct is to mistake political processes for essentialised cosmologies. I work from the understanding that people inhabit worlds characterised not by the unity of ontology but by what Lambek terms "a plurality of unities," navigating between incommensurable and contradictory systems of knowledge and modes of being on a daily basis and seeking to resolve this fragmented state through narrative. The images of life contained in stories about spirits, communicated informally and circulating in rumour, are less ontological artefacts than "the fragile, contingent, evanescent products of conversation and practice" (Lambek 1993: 379).

Communal Politics in Ladakh

Stories like the one from Kumdok can only be understood in the context of Ladakhi politics, which in recent decades has become increasingly dominated by the role of "communalism": a broad term used in South Asia to refer to various attempts to define political interests according to ethnic or religious identity, and often associated with violence between communities. Both the growth of communalism in Ladakh and the divisions between Buddhists and Muslims that it has encouraged result from the region's complicated history with India and with Kashmir.

Ladakh joined the newly independent state of India in 1947 as part of the former princely state of Jammu and Kashmir, to which it had been forcefully annexed in the 1830s. For a little over seventy years, the state of Jammu and Kashmir (J&K) maintained a special federal status within India: retaining its own flag, its own constitution, and a degree of autonomy, governed by an elected assembly based in the Kashmiri capital of Srinagar and arguably dominated by the interests of the Sunni Muslim Kashmiri majority. For many Ladakhi activists, however, this situation represented little more than a continuation of Kashmiri colonialism, a view that parallels the attitudes of Kashmiri separatists towards the state of India (van Beek 2004: 195–6). Throughout the 1960s and 1970s, Buddhist activists led by the Ladakh Buddhist Association (LBA),[3] the most prominent such organisation in the region, agitated for increased regional autonomy. This led to the creation of the Ladakh Autonomous Hill Development Council (LAHDC) as a form of local administration in 1995 (van Beek 1999: 439–40). Yet from the 1980s on, political campaigns began to focus on a bigger goal: the granting of "Union Territory" status to Ladakh, involving separation from J&K. This demand was strongly identified with the ideal of true regional autonomy, to be achieved through freedom from perceived Kashmiri oppression (Aggarwal 2004: 42).

This resentment of Kashmir coincides with Hindu nationalist attitudes towards what was India's only Muslim-majority state, and over the last few years Buddhist activists have formed an uneasy alliance with the Hindu nationalist Bhāratīya Janatā Party (BJP), leading to local electoral success for the BJP in 2014 and 2019. The BJP's wins in Ladakh resulted largely from their support for the Union Territory demand, with their political platform centred on the promise to formally separate Ladakh from J&K; but when the government elected in 2014 failed to achieve this, the BJP member of parliament representing Ladakh resigned in protest citing "false promises" made by the party leadership ("False Promises And Unwise Decisions" 2018). Yet in August 2019, the BJP-dominated Indian parliament revoked Article 370 of the Constitution of India and formally set in motion the dissolution of J&K's special status. Ladakh was to be separated from the state from 31 October 2019 as a Union Territory administered directly from Delhi with no regional legislature of its own, while the regions of Jammu and Kashmir were to remain together as a separate Union Territory. The Indian parliament simultaneously revoked Article 35A of the constitution, enabling non-residents to purchase land in these regions for the first time since 1947 and effectively opening up the lands of the former princely state to settlement by outsiders.

The BJP's success in Ladakh and the eventual realisation of the Union Territory demand were both founded on the growth of communal politics in the region. Buddhist support for a Hindu nationalist party may be little more than political expediency, but the BJP and activist groups like the LBA share a common antipathy towards Muslims and a willingness to exploit communal divisions for political ends. The LBA have encouraged divisions between Buddhists and Muslims to further their political goals, mirroring wider trends in Indian politics since the 1970s, and have increasingly identified Ladakhi identity and the goal of regional autonomy with communal values. This rose to a climax in 1989, when the LBA extended its agitation in support of the Union Territory demand to a "social boycott" of the largely Sunni Muslim "Argon" community in Ladakh, characterising this minority group as agents of Kashmir; yet this boycott was soon extended to cover Shia Muslim Ladakhis as well after they failed to support the LBA's campaign. During the boycott, which lasted until 1992, Ladakhi Buddhists were pressured to avoid social contact and intermarriage with Muslims and to shun Muslim-owned shops (Aggarwal 2004: 43). This period was marked by sporadic outbreaks of violence between Buddhists and Muslims, leaving deep scars in Ladakhi society that remain to this day—further exacerbated by a later social boycott enacted in the outlying region of Zangskar between 2012 and 2018 ("Buddhists End 6-year-old Social Boycott of Zanskar Muslims" 2018)—and cemented the association of the Union Territory demand with communal politics. The results of this became particularly visible in late 2019.

The inauguration of Union Territory status was greeted in Kashmir by government-instituted curfews, the house arrest of leading politicians, and violent clashes between police and protesters ("Jammu and Kashmir" 2019; Ghoshal and Bukhari 2019). By contrast, as I witnessed on 1

November 2019, the predominantly Buddhist Ladakhi capital of Leh was dominated by celebrations: the main bazaar was decorated with the flags of India and the BJP, while local groups organised displays of dances and the unveiling of a highly romanticised statue of Senge Namgyal, a seventeenth-century king of Ladakh famous for his patronage of Buddhist institutions. Meanwhile the mood in the largely Shia Muslim Ladakhi town of Kargil was far more muted: local councillors described the 31st of October as a "black day" and spoke of their fears that Kargil would be marginalised within the new Union Territory of Ladakh (Donthi 2019; "Ladakh UT formation" 2019). In the months that followed, the initial jubilation of many Buddhist Ladakhis faded to be replaced by fears for the future: by concerns that Ladakhi language and culture would be under threat in the new Union Territory, that outsiders would buy up land in the region to establish tourist resorts, and that the BJP would fail to protect Ladakhi interests. On social media, Ladakhis shared images from a Hindi television programme describing Ladakh as the home of the Hindu god Shiva to illustrate fears of the "saffronisation" of the region: the colonisation of Ladakh by Hindu nationalists, with the imposition of Hindu values at the expense of local religions and cultures.

Whatever happens next, the LBA's apparent success in achieving their political goal has at least demonstrated the efficacy of communal tactics in modern India. This is starkly demonstrated by the fact that Buddhist activists and Hindu nationalists have been able to set the agenda in a region where the population is around 46% Muslim, while Ladakhi Muslims themselves have effectively been marginalised by their failure to organise along communal lines. This may, in turn, partly reflect Sunni/Shia divisions in Ladakh (van Beek 2003: 304). As the BJP have demonstrated on a national scale since the 1980s, the Indian political system rewards those who successfully appeal to communal interests by enabling them to mobilise religious communities as voting blocs. The rise of communal politics in Ladakh follows these nationwide trends, with Ladakhi Buddhist activists responding to the perception that democracy in modern India requires communal representations of group identity (ibid.: 292–93). This is not a direct reflection of the form of the system itself—which primarily organises Ladakhis into eight "scheduled tribes"[4] that are little more than creations of state bureaucracy—but rather shows political activists attempting to respond to what van Beek terms "the perceived rules of the game" (2000: 549).

Buddhist leaders from Leh have thus been able to claim to speak on behalf of all Ladakh, while the region has become publicly identified with Buddhism and is routinely advertised in India and elsewhere as the "land of lamas" or as a "little Tibet." Muslim representatives from Kargil have become increasingly marginalised as a result, despite attempts to reclaim their identity as Ladakhis (Gupta 2013: 44). Yet the association of Ladakhi identity with Buddhism and its construction in opposition to Islam is a modern development, and a representation that works by obscuring historical Buddhist-Muslim relations as well as the very real divisions between Ladakhi Buddhists themselves. Marriage between Buddhists and Muslims has become socially unacceptable, a casualty of the boundary-policing begun during the 1989 social boycott. Both Buddhist and Muslim activists in Ladakh have become increasingly sensitive to perceived threats to communal identity, with rumours of forced conversions periodically circulating on either side. At the same time, the construction of a bounded and homogeneous Buddhist religious identity has involved papering over differences rooted in wealth, class, and caste, in regional divisions and sectarian affiliations.

This representation of a unified Buddhist identity depends on a distinctly modern formulation of Buddhism, one that has been labelled variously as "Protestant Buddhism" or "Buddhist modernism": terms popularised by the anthropologist Gananath Obeyesekere (1970) and the historian Heinz Bechert (1984) respectively. These labels cover a range of movements originating in Sri Lanka and Southeast Asia that tend to represent Buddhism as a rationalised philosophy (or "way of life") rather than a religion; that stress the compatibility of Buddhist doctrine with science, emphasising mindfulness meditation while downplaying ritual, the veneration of images, and apotropaic practices; and that stress a universalist and secularised emphasis on social values of peace and equality over either pragmatic ritual or other-worldly soteriology.

Buddhist modernists tend to represent Buddhism in a laicised form, where the religion is no longer purely the preserve of dedicated renouncers (i.e. monks and nuns) but is something practised by ordinary people on a day-to-day basis (McMahan 2008: 7). This places requirements on laity beyond their normal role of supporting monastic establishments, with this interpretation of a secular vocation transforming non-renouncers into the preservers of Buddhist culture. In Ladakh, this is visible in the LBA's campaign to persuade Buddhist laity to become vegetarian on the principle that nonviolence is supposedly a core Buddhist doctrine (though most Ladakhi Buddhists, both renouncers and laity, continue to eat meat). It is also apparent in the organisation's campaigns against abortion and some forms of contraception, on similar grounds, with the LBA circulating the statement that "Abortion is a cause to sever oneself from human rebirth in the next lives" (Aengst 2013: 29–30).

Yet each of these campaigns is "homonymic," to use Blaser's term, in that they speak to both modernist ideals and a communal opposition to

Muslims: butchers in Ladakh are overwhelmingly Muslim, so a prohibition on meat-eating would achieve similar effects to a social boycott; similarly, attitudes to abortion are motivated as much by fears of Muslim expansion and a declining Buddhist population as by interpretations of doctrine (Smith 2009: 209–10). The universalist and rationalised representations of Buddhist modernism emerge intertwined with hostility toward the presence of Muslims in Ladakh. As one young man told me in Zangskar in 2014, during the early stages of the social boycott there, "Buddhism is peaceful, like all religions. Except Islam. Muslims believe they must kill *kāfirs* [i.e. unbelievers]."

Buddhist Modernism and Sentient Landscape

It is relatively unusual to hear anti-Muslim sentiments expressed as openly as this. Modernist representations of Tibetan Buddhism more usually follow the official line set by the fourteenth Dalai Lama,[5] encapsulated in blandly inoffensive statements that characterise Buddhism as concerned primarily with "happiness" and social harmony or as "not a religion but a science of the mind" (Dalai Lama XIV 1990: 115; Lopez 1998: 184–86). This tendency is especially pronounced in representations aimed at non-Tibetan audiences, but it is also apparent in the public reformist campaigns directed by groups like the LBA. In emphasising a rationalised and modernist form of Buddhism, these tend to obscure the major role played by worldly spirits and deities to represent local religion as defined by meditation, the study of Buddhist texts, and the observance of stringent ethical precepts. Yet for Buddhist laity in Ladakh, these are not the defining features of religious practice. While dedicated laity may take on temporary one-day semi-monastic vows (*bsnyen gnas*) on special occasions, and while people often turn towards the reading and repetition of religious texts in their old age as a way of acquiring merit in preparation for rebirth, on a day-to-day basis Buddhist ritual essentially operates as a framework for organising relations with the entities that embody the sentient landscape.

Life in Ladakh is conditioned by the presence of various spirits and deities who inhabit and embody the land, controlling the fragile water supply and watching over houses and villages by a kind of contractual obligation to their human tenants. Each village is linked to its own named deity, the *yul lha*, while every household belongs to a *phaspun* group centred on a shared deity, the *phas lha*, who functions somewhat like an apical ancestor for the group. On a more basic level, the land used for houses and fields belongs to the normally anonymous *sadak* (*sa bdag*), spirit "landlords" who must be ritually appeased before the start of building projects, while water and fertility are influenced by subterranean *lu* like the yak- and ox-shaped beings from Kumdok. These figures are all propitiated through ritual, their favour sought to ensure the smooth progress of life, and are usually housed in small shrines constructed by laity: the gods in cubic *lha tho* built from mudbricks or stone topped by sheafs of juniper branches, decorated and renewed annually during New Year celebrations, and the *lu* in small white "storehouses" (*klu bang*) situated beside springs, pools and streams. Just as *lu* inhabit water sources in the immediate landscape, so *yul lha* are sometimes linked to specific mountains that provide glacial meltwater to the villages below. There is an essential ambiguity to descriptions of these figures, who are treated almost interchangeably as the invisible *inhabitants* of the landscape and as the living *embodiments* of mountains, lakes, streams, and even trees (cf. Pommaret 1996: 42). The group identity of Ladakhi laity—organised into households, *phaspun*, and villages—is bound up with these beings, who embody places and the people who live within them.

For the most part, the ritual propitiation of these beings remains the preserve of Buddhist laity. Thus, laity perform the very basic ritual of *sangs* on a daily basis: an offering of juniper smoke made to cleanse the house and appease the *lha* and *lu*, often accompanied by the repetition of Buddhist mantras. Buddhist renouncers do not take part in these domestic rites, or in the annual renewal of the *lha tho* dedicated to the gods of villages and households. Yet monastic establishments have their own worldly protectors who play an equivalent role to the *yul lha* and *phas lha*, watching over Buddhist *gompa* (loosely, monasteries) and residing in their own rooftop shrines decorated with juniper branches. These are deities of the same kind as those venerated by laity, though with a superior status in local hierarchies, and in many cases possess biographies that describe their association with important local families before they became protectors of Buddhism. Such figures remain rooted in the landscape, ideally separated from ordinary agricultural practice but with a role in watching over particular villages and the gods associated with them.

Lay households annually sponsor Buddhist renouncers to perform *skangsol*, a ritual that repairs contractual relations between these divine beings and local people by offering atonement for wrongs committed by laity over the course of the year. Rituals like this place Buddhist laity in a three-pointed network of reciprocity: reliant on the protection and goodwill of worldly deities, lay households support local Buddhist *gompa*; and these *gompa*, in turn, provide ritual practitioners who can maintain and reinforce lay relationships with divine protectors. In practice, to be Buddhist in Ladakh is to be embedded in these networks of reciprocity that bind together laity, monastic institutions, and the landscape itself.

Political action in Ladakh was historically bound up with these forms of ritual practice, with the propitiation or invocation of local deities and the construction of religious architecture used to lay claim to territory, to prevent disaster, or to pacify the land and the people within it. This depends on the understanding that people are embedded in the landscape, tied to relations with non-human beings, and subject to influences emanating from the land itself. Ritual means could thus be used against human threats, and Mills describes local claims that the eighteenth-century *gompa* at Rangdum, situated on a hill before the high pass that separates the largely Shia Muslim Suru Valley from Buddhist-dominated Zangskar, was constructed as a geomantic counterweight (*kha gnon*) against Muslim influences emanating from Kashmir (Mills 2003: 21).[6] Where the story of the ox-*lu* from Kumdok shows the landscape itself rejecting Muslim presence, modern accounts of the foundation of Rangdum *gompa* work on the understanding that the landscape can be used to affect those living within it by ritual means.

Buddhism thus offers a hierarchical framework that harnesses and orders the sentient landscape; and for laity, involvement in Buddhist ritual is more normally connected to these pragmatic concerns than to soteriology or mindfulness. It goes almost without saying that none of this receives any official recognition from either the Indian state or local Buddhist activist organisations like the LBA, with the presence of local gods almost entirely obscured in representations of Ladakh and Ladakhi Buddhism. This silence does not necessarily indicate erasure, however, just as the modernist rhetoric employed by the LBA does not necessarily translate to changes in practice. Ladakhi Buddhist laity continue to annually renew *lha tho* and make offerings to local deities, though the sacrifice of animals to *yul lha*, still known around fifty years ago (Kaplanian 1979: 133) has now almost entirely been replaced by vegetarian offerings. Similarly, while anthropologists have predicted the disappearance of apotropaic behaviour used to divert harmful spirits (Dollfus 2003b: 303), in my experience protective diagrams were still visibly displayed on newly built houses in Leh as of 2019. Despite the irrelevance of local gods to Indian conceptions of Ladakh as a border territory, Indian troops operating on the "line of control" between Ladakh and Pakistan commonly make offerings to the prominent local deity Zangnam before heading to postings on the contested Siachen Glacier.

In other words: although the role of sentient landscape is silenced in public discourse, this does not mean that it is actively marginalised. As Mills has argued in discussing Tibetan refugee governmentality, concerns with ritual practice and relations with landscape are "hidden in plain sight" in Tibetan (and Ladakhi) politics: they remain implicit because while they provide the basis for legitimate authority and structure the ceremonial processes of governance, they are not the *object* of political activity (2006: 202–3). In practice, modernist representations of Buddhism do not conflict with ritual practice oriented towards local spirits and deities; rather, they regularly appear entwined with one another, with ritual actions aimed at repairing or establishing relations with sentient landscape recast in the modernist language of peace and happiness. This can be seen in various "World Peace" projects undertaken by Buddhist leaders, whereby tantric empowerments and the construction of religious architecture used to pacify the landscape are represented as working for global "peace and harmony" (Mills 2009: 95, 98–100). These claims are not disingenuous; it is simply that they leave the *means* of bringing about their aims unspoken.

Modernist representations thus stand for the reasonable *face* of political action. Just as Ladakhi Buddhist activists employ communal tactics while publicly denying or downplaying any hostility toward local Muslims, so the group identity of Buddhist laity remains fundamentally grounded in and defined by unspoken relations of reciprocity with local spirits and deities. The rationalised and sanitised representations of Buddhist identity that form the public face of communal politics in Ladakh are influenced by these factors, which operate beneath the surface and shape one another. These issues remain absent from public political discourse, as irrelevant to the rhetorical mode of political representation in modern India, yet they remain present and emerge intertwined in popular stories like the account of the *lu* from Kumdok. These stories connect issues of belonging to frameworks of reciprocal relations with the landscape that are usually obscured, yet they recast these concerns in the light of communal interests to portray Muslims as outsiders ignorant of proper behaviour towards Ladakhi deities.

Thus, a story well-known among Buddhists in Ladakh's capital of Leh describes the Tsugtor Lhachang, a "god tree" (*lha lcang*) inhabited by the local goddess Tsugtor Gyalmo and situated in one of the narrow streets of Leh's predominantly Muslim old town. One of the branches of the tree grew through the window of a nearby house, leading its Muslim owner to take an axe to it. According to the story, he was immediately struck down by paralysis: the deity punishing him for an act of violent disrespect. As with the account of the *lu* from Kumdok, this dramatizes communal conflict from a Buddhist perspective: the Ladakhi landscape itself lashing out against perceived Muslim intrusion. Yet this portrayal is a consequence of the growth of communal politics since the 1980s and of the deliberate exclusion of Muslims from ritual involvement with *phas lha* and *yul lha*: Muslim intermarriage with Buddhists was not uncommon before the social boycott of 1989, and many Ladakhi *phaspun* still encompass both Buddhist and Muslim households. In some areas of Ladakh, Muslims actively participated in annual offerings to local deities until relatively recently (Nawang Tsering Shakspo 1995: 186–87). What stories like this demonstrate is not that Muslims are inherently outsiders, but that Buddhist understandings of the sentient landscape of Ladakh—embodied in the gods and spirits of its lakes and trees—have fallen in line with the dominant, communal mode of modern politics in the region.

Politics, Ontology, and Rhetoric

To return to the issues with which I began this chapter: while it is tempting to characterise concerns with sentient landscape as radically distinct from the politics of modern neoliberal nation-states, or to speak of "ontological multiplicity" and a separation between fundamentally incommensurable modes of being, in Ladakh accounts of local spirits and deities reflect an active involvement with the communal politics of modern India. Ritual relations with the landscape are entangled with issues of Ladakhi identity and with recent Buddhist-Muslim conflict, despite the widespread use of modernist rhetoric that leaves these topics deliberately unspoken; and religious identity in Ladakh remains grounded in networks of reciprocity with sentient landscape that have not remained unaffected by the growth of communalism in the region. The "homonymy" that Blaser describes as a solution to conflicts between incompatible worlds is a normal feature of Ladakhi political action and representation: the LBA routinely promote campaigns informed simultaneously by the apparently contradictory interests of Buddhist modernism and communal rivalry, while Buddhist leaders like the Dalai Lama engage in ritual practices that address modernist ideals through the pacification of the landscape. These actions draw on several conflicting sets of rationales at once, with multiple frameworks of interpretation apparently encompassed within a single rhetorical frame.

Yet it would be a mistake to assume that modernist representations of Buddhist identity are little more than an insincere front. Ladakhi Buddhist activists are not operating solely within the frame of Indian communalism, of Buddhist modernism, or of an underlying Ladakhi ontology established on ritual relations with tutelary deities; rather, they are operating within all of these at once. People routinely move between apparently incommensurable modes of being without confronting the apparent contradictions—between communal hostility and the modernist emphasis on peace and harmony, between a rationalised model of religious identity and the continued reliance on networks of local gods—because these different modes do not operate as separate ontologies or ideologies, and because people do not normally try to work out the full implications of any one mode in isolation. As Lambek has argued in reference to religious and medical knowledge in Mayotte, things "do not fully tie together": people normally "live happily (as happily as any of us) in a partially fragmented world without being terribly conscious of the fissures." And it is through narrative, not theorising or world-building, that people seek resolution (Lambek 1993: 379–80).

Thus, in stories about a *lu* rising out of a lake or a tree lashing out against a threat we see communal politics flowing together with a concern for the responsibilities due to the gods and spirits of the land. Like someone trying to reconcile a modernist emphasis on peace and universalism with a fear of Islam, the storyteller begins from the assumption that the different values and entities encompassed by the narrative exist in a single shared world. These representations may not exhibit much internal consistency if examined closely—identifying Muslims as ignorant outsiders while neglecting the continued involvement of Ladakhi Muslims in ritual practices aimed at local deities—but that is only a problem for the anthropologist seeking a unifying, underlying order. Like life, stories are messy and incorporate contradictions. It is a mistake to treat these as referring to self-contained, ordered, and stable realities, the ontologies and cosmologies described by anthropologists, which are little more than post-hoc systematisations of various actions and representations. While Blaser adopts the term "worldings" to escape the static implications of some of these arguments and to emphasise the processual quality of any mode of being, this nevertheless reproduces the two main problems inherent in these approaches: a basic essentialism (cf. Blaser 2014: 51–52) and the issue of ontological closure, whereby different ways of understanding and being in the world are characterised as radically separate realities.

The discussion of cosmopolitics is grounded in these assumptions, beginning with the idea that people normally inhabit worlds governed by abstract conceptions of cosmology, categories of being, and relations between humans and non-humans: Blaser builds on Latour, while Latour, in turn, establishes his arguments on Descola's attempt to globally categorize and delineate four different ontological modes (Latour 2004: 457–58; Descola 1996: 87–89). This leads directly to the perception that ontological multiplicity presents a problem for political dialogue, and that the politics of modern nation-states necessarily require disputants to acknowledge the limits of a single shared reality. This misrepresents the tangled reality of how people live—regularly moving between incommensurable conceptions of life, identity, and the world—and misunderstands the function of political rhetoric. When Ladakhi activists invoke modernist representations of religion as the foundation for Buddhist identity in modern Indian politics, this involves a silencing but not an erasure of the role played by the sentient landscape in Ladakhi life. Activists adopt the language and forms of reasonable politics in modern India without necessarily taking on the assumptions and values these seem to imply. As such, political actions are *routinely* "homonymic": addressing different interests and understandings simultaneously without requiring a common ground. Political rhetoric works by providing a contextual illusion of a defined and agreed common world, enabling dialogue between conflicting interests in the absence of any genuine consensus.

This is not to say that dominant forms of politics have no impact on other modes of being. The hostility toward Muslims that forms the *substance* of modern Ladakhi Buddhist communalism—but which is not typically represented in public discourse—has brought about distinct changes in Ladakhi society and in understandings of identity, social organisation and relations with the land; but this is a consequence of actions like the social boycott and not simply a product of adopting the rhetorical forms of modern Indian politics. Where this has spilled over into accounts of local spirits and deities, the sentient landscape of Ladakh is depicted as reflecting not only communal interests but also many of the values promoted by the Hindu nationalists that form the current Indian government. This is essentially an alignment with dominant forms of state politics, one that contrasts starkly with the situation of indigenous groups described by anthropologists employing the language of ontology. These concern contexts where relations between indigenous groups and settler-colonial states offer clear political dichotomies; yet these approaches simply do not apply to Ladakh, where Buddhist activists invoke colonialism to justify a hostility toward Kashmir that fits neatly with the agenda of the state.

Conclusion

Buddhist identity in Ladakh remains bound up with networks of reciprocity with the gods and spirits of the land, enacted through ritual action addressed to the deities that embody corporate groups and the various nameless spirits that inhabit the land and water. Yet the role of sentient landscape is typically obscured in the modernist representations of Buddhism and Buddhist identity that play a key part in the growth of communal politics in Ladakh, with Ladakhi identity represented as synonymous with this rationalised image of religion. Ladakhi Buddhist activists have employed communal and modernist representations of identity as means of achieving their political goals in the context of modern Indian democracy, seeking regional autonomy and separation from Kashmir. Yet in practice this has resulted in growing tensions between Buddhists and Muslims in Ladakh—with initial hostility towards Sunni Muslims later expanded to cover Ladakh's substantial Shia Muslim population—and in the political marginalisation of non-Buddhist voices. The inauguration of Ladakh's Union Territory status in 2019 seemingly demonstrated the success of these communal tactics, but the reality of the new situation may turn out to be quite unlike the ideal.

Throughout this chapter, I have tried to show that the adoption of dominant forms of political discourse by Ladakhi Buddhist activists has involved the strategic use of political rhetoric: that the apparent silencing of particular interests does not equate to an erasure or denial of those interests. As with modernist representations of Buddhist ritual, activist campaigns routinely address different goals simultaneously without resolving the contradictions through the establishment of a single common ground. This is possible because people normally move between multiple different understandings of identity, selfhood and the world on a daily basis. People do not normally mark ontological distinctions, but rather inhabit what they assume to be a single, continuous world that encompasses every aspect of life. This is reflected in narrative, as in the accounts of the ox-*lu* of Kumdok or the Tsugtor Lhachang in Leh, where the fragmented experience of ordinary life reaches towards a rough sort of resolution. Here the implications of communal politics emerge combined with the entities that embody Ladakh's sentient landscape, in narratives where modernist rhetoric is completely absent.

As these stories should make clear, a concern with sentient landscape does not necessarily offer an alternative to dominant forms of politics: in Ladakh, accounts of spirits of deities increasingly align with the hostility toward Muslims that characterises the domination of modern Indian politics by Hindu nationalism. An analysis that points to radically distinct worlds or essentialist ontologies is an awkward fit for this context, where dichotomous characterisations of different modes of being are basically unhelpful. In contrast to accounts from indigenous groups in North America, Ladakhi Buddhist stories depict the landscape siding with power: turning against the marginalised and enforcing a politics of exclusion and division.

Callum Pearce is an anthropologist of Tibetan and Himalayan religion. He is interested in religion in Asia (especially South Asia, Tibet, and the Himalaya), landscape, spirit possession, the anthropology of religion, and the history of Western involvement with Asian religions. His research focuses on landscape, the role of perception, and the relationship between Tibetan Buddhist ritual authority and local spirits and deities in the Ladakh region of Himalayan India.

Notes

1. "Muslim" here translates *kha che* in Ladakhi, i.e. "Kashmiri." This regional term is used to refer broadly (though often inaccurately) to Sunni Muslims, as a counterpart to the equally inaccurate Balti (*sbal ti*, i.e. someone from Baltistan) for Shia Muslims. However, many Buddhist Ladakhis now use *kha che* to refer to Muslims in general without distinguishing between Sunni and Shia.
2. The 2011 census gives a total population of 108,761 Buddhists (with 88,635, or 81%, resident in Leh district) and 127,296 Muslims (with 108,239, or 85%, resident in Kargil district). The total population of Ladakh (both districts) at the time was 274,289: 46% Muslim and 40% Buddhist, with the remaining 14% consisting of Hindus, Sikhs, and Christians ("Kargil District Population Census" 2011; "Leh District Population Census" 2011). The census data does not distinguish between Sunni and Shia Muslims.
3. Or Ladaks Nangpe Tsogdus in Ladakhi (*la dwags nang pa'i tshogs 'du*), roughly "the association of Ladakh insiders." *Nangpa*, literally "insider," is a formal term used by Buddhists in Ladakh to refer to themselves as an alternative to the more common *boto*. It is contrasted with *chipa* (*phyi pa*), "outsider," formerly used to refer mainly to Hindus but increasingly used as a synonym for Muslim. The modernist explanation for these terms claims *nangpa* refers to the Buddhist concern with the mind and other "inner" states, in contrast to a supposedly Hindu or Muslim concern with external ritual and purity. Due to the communal associations of these terms, their use has been discouraged by the fourteenth Dalai Lama.
4. Specifically: Balti, Beda, Bot, Brokpa, Changpa, Gara, Mon and Purigpa. None of these groups really exist as "tribes" in any meaningful sense. As van Beek shows, these categories do not map neatly onto religious affiliation: while the Bot group largely covers sedentary Buddhist Ladakhis resident in the Leh Valley, it also includes Muslims and Leh's small Christian population (1997: 35). The designation of eight official "tribes" omits several other groups recognized locally, such as the predominantly Sunni Muslim Argons.
5. The fourteenth Dalai Lama has also played an active role in opposing communal agitation in the Ladakh region, urging an end to the Zangskar social boycott in 2016 and 2018 ("Buddhists End 6-year-old Social Boycott of Zanskar Muslims" 2018; Maqbool 2018).
6. Similarly, the fifteenth century Namgyal Tsemo temple, situated on a hill overlooking the regional capital of Leh, is described in local histories as having been constructed to invoke divine protection to repel an invading "Hor" (i.e. Central Asian or Mongol) army (Francke 1926: 103).

References

Aggarwal, Ravina. 2004. *Beyond Lines of Control: Performance and Politics on the Disputed Borders of Ladakh, India*. Durham, NC: Duke University Press.

Allen, N. J. 1997. "'And the Lake Drained Away': An Essay in Himalayan Comparative Mythology." In *Mandala and Landscape*, ed. Alexander W. Macdonald, 435–51. New Delhi: D. K. Printworld.

Aengst, Jennifer. 2013. "The Politics of Fertility: Population and Pronatalism in Ladakh." *Himalaya* 32(1): 23-34.

Bechert, Heinz. 1984. "Buddhist Revival in East and West." In *The World of Buddhism: Buddhist Monks and Nuns in Society and Culture*, ed. Richard Gombrich and Heinz Bechert, 272–85. London: Thames and Hudson.

Blaser, Mario. 2014. "Ontology and Indigeneity: on the Political Ontology of Heterogeneous Assemblages." *Cultural Geographies* 21(1): 49–58.

———. 2016. "Is Another Cosmopolitics Possible?" *Cultural Anthropology* 31(4): 545–70.

"Buddhists End 6-year-old Social Boycott of Zanskar Muslims." 2018. *Kashmir Observer* 24 July. Retrieved from https://kashmirobserver.net/2018/07/24/buddhists-end-6-year-old-social-boycott-of-zanskar-muslims/.

Buffetrille, Katia. 1996. "The Blue Lake of A-mdo and Its Island: Legends and Pilgrimage Guide." In *Reflections of the Mountain: Essays on the History and Social Meaning of the Mountain Cult in Tibet and the Himalaya*, ed. Anne-Marie Blondeau and Ernst Steinkellner, 77–89. Wien: Verlag der Österreichischen Akademie der Wissenschaften.

Dalai Lama XIV [bstan 'dzin rgya mtsho]. 1990. "The Nobel Evening Address." In *The Dalai Lama A Policy of Kindness: An Anthology of Writings by and about the Dalai Lama*, ed. Sidney Piburn, 108–16. Delhi: Motilal Banarsidass.

Descola, Philippe. 1996. "Constructing Natures: Symbolic Ecology and Social Practice." In *Nature and Society: Anthropological Perspectives*, ed. Philippe Descola and Gisli Pálsson, 82–102. London: Routledge.

Dollfus, Pascale. 2003a. "De quelques histoires de klu et de btsan." *Revue d'Etudes Tibétaines* (2): 4–39.

———. 2003b. "Comments on van Beek, Martijn. The Art of Representation: Domesticating Ladakh 'Identity.'" In *Ethnic Revival and Religious Turmoil: Identities and Representations in the Himalayas*, ed. Marie Lecomte-Tilouine and Pascale Dollfus, 302–6. Oxford: Oxford University Press.

Donthi, Praveen. 2019. "'In J&K's reorganisation, Kargil is the Biggest Loser': Asgar Ali Karbalai." *The Caravan*, 30 October. Retrieved from https://caravanmagazine.in/politics/kargil-asgar-karbalai-leh-ladakh-union-territory-370.

"'False Promises And Unwise Decisions': Ladakh BJP Lawmaker On Resigning." 2018. *NDTV*, 21 November. Retrieved from https://www.ndtv.com/india-news/false-promises-and-unwise-decisions-ladakh-bjp-lawmaker-thupstan-chhewang-on-resigning-1950792.

Francke, August Hermann. 1926. *Antiquities of Indian Tibet. Part (Volume) II: The Chronicles of Ladakh and Minor Chronicles*. Calcutta: Superintendent Government Printing, India.

Ghoshal, Devjyot, and Fayaz Bukhari. 2019. "Kashmir Protesters Defy Restrictions, Clash with Security Forces." *Reuters*, 23 August. Retrieved from https://fr.reuters.com/article/uk-india-kashmir-idAFKCN1VD0HC.

Gupta, Radhika. 2013. "The Importance of Being Ladakhi: Affect and Artifice in Kargil." *Himalaya* 32(1): 43–50.

Hage, Ghassan. 2015. *Alter-Politics: Critical Anthropology and the Radical Imagination*. Carlton: Melbourne University Press.

Ingold, Tim. 2000. *The Perception of the Environment*. London: Routledge.

"Jammu and Kashmir: India Formally Divides Flashpoint State." 2019. *BBC News*, 31 October. Retrieved from https://www.bbc.co.uk/news/world-asia-india-50233281.

Kaplanian, Patrick. 1979. "The Constituent Elements of Architecture and Urbanism in Ladakh." In *Cambridge Undergraduate Ladakh Expedition, Matho: Continuity and Change in a Ladakhi Village*, 123–55. Unpublished report.

"Kargil District Population Census." 2011. *Census of India*. Retrieved from http://www.census2011.co.in/census/district/622-kargil.html.

"Ladakh UT formation: Leh celebrates; Kargil observes black day." 2019. *Business Standard*, 31 October. Retrieved from https://www.business-standard.com/article/pti-stories/ladakh-ut-formation-leh-celebrates-kargil-observes-black-day-119103101354_1.html.

Lambek, Michael. 1993. *Knowledge and Practice in Mayotte: Local Discourses of Islam, Sorcery, and Spirit Possession*. Toronto: University of Toronto Press.

Latour, Bruno. 2004. "Whose Cosmos, Which Cosmopolitics? Comments on the Peace Terms of Ulrich Beck." *Common Knowledge* 10(3): 450–62.

"Leh District Population Census." 2011. *Census of India*. Retrieved from http://www.census2011.co.in/census/district/621-leh.html.

Lopez, Donald S. 1998. *Prisoners of Shangri-La: Tibetan Buddhism and the West*. Chicago: University of Chicago Press.

Maqbool, Majid. 2018. "Six Years On, 'Social Boycott' of Minority Community in Zanskar Continues." *The Wire*, 31 March. Retrieved from https://thewire.in/communalism/six-years-on-social-boycott-of-minority-community-in-zanskar-division-of-kargil-continues.

McMahan, David L. 2008. *The Making of Buddhist Modernism*. Oxford: Oxford University Press.

Mills, Martin A. 2003. *Identity, Ritual and State in Tibetan Buddhism: The Foundations of Authority in Gelukpa Monasticism*. London: Routledge.

———. 2006. "The Silence in Between: Governmentality and the Academic Voice in Tibetan Diaspora Studies." In *Critical Journeys: The Making of Anthropologists*, ed. Geert de Neve and Maya Unnithan-Kumar, 191–205. Aldershot: Ashgate.

———. 2009. "This Circle of Kings: Modern Tibetan Visions of World Peace." In *Boundless Worlds: An Anthropological Approach to Movement*, ed. Peter Wynn Kirby, 95–114. London: Berghahn.

Nawang Tsering Shakspo. 1995. "The Significance of Khuksho in the Cultural History of Ladakh." In *Recent Research on Ladakh 4 & 5: Proceedings of the Fourth and Fifth International Colloquia on Ladakh*, ed. Henry Osmaston and Philip Denwood, 181–87. Delhi: Motilal Banarsidass.

Obeyesekere, Gananath. 1970. "Religious Symbolism and Cultural Change in Ceylon." *Modern Ceylon Studies* 1(1): 43–63.
Pommaret, F. 1996. "On local and mountain deities in Bhutan." In *Reflections of the Mountain: Essays on the History and Social Meaning of the Mountain Cult in Tibet and the Himalaya*, ed. Anne-Marie Blondeau and Ernst Steinkellner, 39–56. Wien: Verlag der Österreichischen Akademie der Wissenschaften.
Samuel, Geoffrey. 2021. "Hidden Lands of Tibet in Himalayan Myth and History." In *Hidden Lands in Himalayan Myth and History*, ed. Frances Garrett, Elizabeth McDougal and Geoffrey Samuel, 51–91. Leiden: Brill.
Smith, Sara H. 2009. "The Domestication of Geopolitics: Buddhist-Muslim Conflict and the Policing of Marriage and the Body in Ladakh, India." *Geopolitics* 14(2): 197–218.
van Beek, Martijn. 1997. "The Importance of Being Tribal, or: The Impossibility of Being Ladakhis." In *Recent Research on Ladakh 7. Proceedings of the Seventh Colloquium of the International Association for Ladakh Studies*, ed. Thierry Dodin and Heinz Räther, 21–41. Ulm: Universität Ulm.
———. 1999. "Hill Councils, Development, and Democracy: Assumptions and Experiences from Ladakh." *Alternatives* 24: 435–60.
———. 2000. "Beyond Identity Fetishism: 'Communal' Conflict in Ladakh and the Limits of Autonomy." *Cultural Anthropology* 15(4): 525–69.
———. 2003. "The Art of Representation: Domesticating Ladakh 'Identity.'" In *Ethnic Revival and Religious Turmoil: Identities and Representations in the Himalayas*, ed. Marie Lecomte-Tilouine and Pascale Dollfus, 283–301. Oxford: Oxford University Press.
———. 2004. "Dangerous Liaisons: Hindu Nationalism and Buddhist Radicalism in Ladakh." In *Religious Radicalism and Security in South Asia*, ed. Satu P. Limaye, Mohan Malik, and Robert G. Wirsing, 193–218. Honolulu, HI: Asia Pacific Center for Security Studies.

Part II.
Famous Fascisms

CHAPTER 5

Forests as the Sentient Bridge between German Landscape and Identity

Hikmet Kuran

In 1910, Rudolf Düesberg, one of the major figures in the formation of racial superiority doctrines, anti-Semitism, and the "nature-based" claims and policies of the Nazi regime, published a book titled *Der Wald als Erzieher* (Forest as educator). The main premise of the book was that both the German people and the German forest were the products of the same entity and thus should be evaluated in the same manner. He asserted that forests are the source of knowledge and must be perceived as "educators" for social order. According to him, the order in and of the German forests suggests a valid and comprehensive example for German society to follow. The forests, he wrote, are "deeply rooted, sedentary, [and have] risen to greatness in the struggle with rough climate and through hard work on poor soil," while German society "forms a model for those institutions necessary for the strengthening of Germandom. In this manner, the forest can become the educator of the German Volk [people]" (Düesberg 1910: 139; Imort 2005a: 67). From a similar viewpoint, Düesberg also criticized the capitalist mode of production and again came up with the same recipe to protect German identity, social order, and landscape. For him, "the dominant laws for the cultivation of a forest apply equally to the rationally organized human community," and "in this way the forest becomes an educator" (Düesberg 1910: 138–39; Wilson 2012: 194–95).

Not content with the forest's role in "educating" or identity building, Düesberg also finds in it justifications for anti-Semitism. As Imort (2005a: 69) shows, his views of German forests had deep-seated links with xenophobia.

> Düesberg thus used the forest to exemplify the idea that the community, not the individual, was the basic unit of German society. At the individual level, trees served as placeholders in which Germans were to recognize

themselves. At the collective level, the forest community became a simile of the national community. At the political-economical level, the dichotomy of "Germanic" forestry versus "Semitic" husbandry was the base line for drawing racial boundaries between "us" and "them": idealistic Germans who were rooted in the soil and live cooperatively so as to further the common good as opposed to materialist Semitic nomads who roamed the land in their capitalist pursuit of personal profit.

In a way similar to arguments that glorify the original German character (blood) as being sylvan and deeply rooted (soil), Düesberg pointed out the threats from the fundamental elements of capitalism such as competition, productivity, and monopoly (especially on land ownership). He proposed a connection between these capitalist elements and a nomadic worldview in order to ground his racial claims about Jewish people and culture. According to him, "the basis of the modern state and institutions of public life are neither Christian nor Germanic," and because "they represent a nomadic, Jewish worldview," Germany risked its forests and national character being dominated by Jewish culture (Düesberg 1910: 139–52; Wilson 2012: 196; Imort 2005: 68).

Consistent with previous beliefs, enhanced by contemporary and later thinkers, and echoed in national and anti-Semitic imaginaries of forests, Düesberg's arguments are crucial to understanding how the bridge between nature and nation is built upon sentient agencies.

This chapter seeks to scrutinize both the historical path and the theoretical construction of nationalist and xenophobic imaginaries of German landscape based on sentience. By revealing that connection, it aims to pave the way for interrogating how xenophobia, anti-Semitism, and nation-building discourses interact in a historical context—one which can help us understand similar constellations today, including movements on the global far right.

There are several profound multidimensional theorizations that assert that landscapes mean much more than just their natural components to thinkers, artists, politicians, and nations as a whole. Landscapes are both perceived and instrumentalized beyond their physical existence and form. As Simon Schama (1995: 61) pointed out, "landscapes are culture before they are nature; constructs of the imagination projected onto wood and water and rock."

It is vital to illuminate the relationship between these understandings so that the interaction between nature (landscape) and nation (national identity) can be resolved and a bridge to sentient landscapes can be seen. As Ernest Gellner asserts, a nation is something "invented" by nationalism, and it requires differentiating aspects of the nation's character to bring it into being (Gellner 1964: 169). For Schama, the role of landscape as a differentiating and defining feature of the nation brings it into direct contact with nationalist discourse theoretically and historically. It is also clear that these imagined landscapes "can function as projection screens for manifold cultural constructions, political agendas, and public perceptions" (Zechner, 2011: 19). Therefore, the theoretical framework referenced in this chapter links the historical or cultural dimensions to the social and political fields.

Germans have had quite a special relationship with forests throughout the country's history. This strong bond provides a unique opportunity to question and resolve the "sentience bridge" between landscape and race (i.e., between nature and nation) in the German case. Called "forest-mindedness" (Imort 2005a: 55), this German affinity for ascribing physical, spiritual, religious, and sentient qualities to natural features warrants attention, as it provides not only cultural and environmental discourses for analysis but also societal, racial, and political discourses. For this reason, investigating the correlation between landscape and elements of nationalism in the German case offers a fruitful perspective on xenophobic landscapes.

It is well known that Germans have a peculiar perception of their forests. Historically, forests have been the subject of many thinkers, artists, politicians, poets, and civil activists, who intended to create, define, or strengthen a sentience bridge between German landscape (forests) and nation-based agendas, ranging from defining the ancestral roots of the German nation to legitimizing claims regarding anti-Semitism, xenophobia, and racial purity and superiority. With these issues as a basis, this chapter aims to elaborate on a framework that can offer a clearer understanding of xenophobia and racial claims that derive from natural elements.

To this end, the historical background of German perceptions of landscape must be examined with an eye to the intellectual, conceptual, and sociopolitical breaking points that enabled German forests to be instrumentalized in favor of racial incentives and motives. The historical origins of those breaking points will be discussed first, followed by the theoretical conceptualizations and practical dimensions of the German xenophobic landscape, approached through National Socialist ideology and policies.

Historical Dimension: Ancestral Roots of German Perceptions of the Forest

Although the sentience bridge became heavily emphasized after the nineteenth century, the arguments for it go back to 100 CE. Tacitus, the notorious Roman historian, mentions the forests as the origin of Germanic tribes in his book *Germania* (Zechner 2011: 20). He also defines two crucial national characteristics of Germans that directly relate to the forest in Germany—wildness and freedom—and which were later used by German nationalists and theoreticians as grounds for tying landscape and race together through common characteristics (Feshami, 2020).

Additionally, Tacitus played a vital role in underlining the "legitimate" ancestral roots for othering, so much so that he "emphasized the Germans' wildness and freedom, comparing them favorably against their more servile and decadent counterparts in the Roman Empire" (Feshami, 2020). According to him, Germans, thanks to their forest-based characteristics, were different from their Roman counterparts. This was not only a conceptualization of national characteristics but also a distinction based on forests. As Imort points out (2005a: 57–58), Tacitus's claims connecting forests and Germans led Romantics to cast the former as the home of the latter and also as the primary source of Germans' strength.

The Battle of Teutoburg Forest serves as another historical source for mystification and glorification of the German past through entities in nature. One of the most prominent German heroes, Hermann (Arminius), on account of his victory against three Roman legions in the Teutoburg Forest, was frequently referred to by Romantic nationalist thinkers (Wilson 2012; Imort 2005a). Major Romantic figures pointed out that Hermann's victory taking place in the woods was not only a symbol of German heroism and opposition to all "foreign" occupation but also of the strong bond between German "destiny" and German forests. It is not surprising that the mythical narrative of this battle was a reference point for critics of Napoleon's occupation of several German states. As will be discussed later, Romantic thinkers and artists in particular cited the story of Hermann while directly referencing the French occupation. Foreign invasions were critical to the process of understanding the xenophobic landscape perceived by the German Volk.

Urge for Unification

The relatively belated unification process to form the German state was also crucial in linking nation and nature. Before analyzing the role of German landscape, namely forests, it seems beneficial to analyze how the arguments for national unification were expressed through natural entities.

As Wilson (2012) argued, a sylvan discourse sprouted from several German historical roots and myths. First, Germans had a unique reverence for the woods, based solely on their supposedly barbaric historiography. Second, this special relationship was kept alive over a long period of time, providing a convenient source for Nazis to enrich their political discourse. With the rise of capitalist production, the commodification and loss of forests became another issue animating nationalist figures and organizations and later National Socialists as well. Not surprisingly, this discourse carried a "differentiating" aspect used to build and justify xenophobia and othering. This use is apparent in the example of labeling Jews as the "offspring of the desert" (Zechner 2011: 22), in contrast to arguments about the vitality of forests as a component of German national identity.

According to these arguments, there is a direct relationship between national rootedness and forests. As Wilson notes, "Southern European cultures had already decimated their forest in ancient times and declined as a result" (2012: 5). From this point of view, the discourse not only offers a direct correlation between natural elements and national "destiny" but also lays the foundations for the "sentience bridge." As will be discussed later, claims regarding Romanticism or opposition to industrialization, urbanization, and scientific forestry were also tied to this sylvan discourse. Moreover, traumatic defeats by France played a decisive role in nationalistic discourse.

Forests were the focal point of the political project aimed at "unifying German-speaking people against the occupation of their Heimat by Napoleon" (Imort 2005a: 57). Realizing the need to unify and to find historical, mythical, and differentiating roots for that purpose, Germans put massive importance on forests on a broad scale. The collective effort to define Germans as a "woodland nation" was carried out by foresters, geographers, historians, archaeologists, ethnographers, and botanists (Wilson 2012: 18), as well as by artists and thinkers. As Wilson pointed out, "Their ideas were echoed widely throughout society, finding resonance in the popular press, in schools, and among hiking enthusiasts.... Private citizens and all manner of voluntary organizations—botanical societies, hiking clubs, and the Heimat movement for instance—developed and propagated this new image of the nation" (2012: 18).

Therefore, the French occupation was an alarm indicating the need for national unification in order for Germans to survive on cultural, philological, historical, national, and political levels, which were all tied to their sentimental claims concerning landscape and the German forest. It is critical to analyze those claims and those who asserted them and to point out the links they used to create a relationship between nation and nature.

Theoretical Dimension: Figures, Arguments, Conceptualizations

German philosopher Johann Gottlieb Fichte was one of the primary theoreticians who founded his arguments mostly on the "peculiarities" of German identity. In his book *Addresses to the German Nation*, published in

1808, Fichte clearly attempted to acquaint the German people with their different historical, linguistic, and spiritual characteristics. One of the fundamental questions he attempted to answer was, What is the German in opposition to other peoples of Teutonic descent? (Fichte 2008: 100). For him, language is the most important component of the formula to define and differentiate a nation. In other words, the German language is the basis of German uniqueness (Moore 2008: xxiv). Fichte's efforts to create philosophical links between language and identity were founded upon this notion. As he wrote in *Addresses to the German Nation;*

> To begin with, and above all else, the first, original and truly natural frontiers of states are undoubtedly their inner frontiers. Those who speak the same language are already, before all human art, joined together by mere nature with a multitude of invisible ties; they understand one another and are able to communicate ever more clearly; they belong together and are naturally one, an indivisible whole. No other nation of a different descent and language can desire to absorb and assimilate such a people without, at least temporarily, becoming confused and profoundly disturbing the steady progress of its own culture. The external limits of territories only follow as a consequence of this inner frontier, drawn by man's spiritual nature itself. And from the natural view of things it is not simply because men dwell within the confines of certain mountains and rivers that they are a people; on the contrary, men live together—and, if fortune has so arranged it for them, protected by mountains and rivers—because they were already a people beforehand by a far higher law of nature.
>
> Thus lay the German nation, sufficiently united by a common language and way of thinking, and clearly enough separated from the other peoples, in the middle of Europe, as a wall dividing unrelated tribes. It was numerous and brave enough to protect its frontiers against any foreign incursion, left to its own devices and little inclined by its whole way of thinking to take notice of the neighboring peoples, to meddle in their affairs or provoke their hostility by harassing them. In the process of time its auspicious fate preserved the German nation from an immediate share in the rape of other continents—the event which more than any other has determined the course of recent world history, the destinies of peoples and the greater portion of their ideas and sentiments. (2008: 166–67)

Formulating his intellectual efforts around the urge to build a "German" identity, Fichte constantly emphasized the importance of unity, which can be realized by Germans "qualifying" themselves as a nation. For this purpose, language is the trademark and specific criterion to define their "German" identity, which "differentiated them from 'foreign' elements like the French" (Feshami 2020).

Not surprisingly, Fichte interpreted the French occupation took place between 1794-1814, in an alarming manner, claiming foreign control had devastating repercussions on the morals, values, ideals, cultures, and languages of a nation. "Germandom" offered both the intellectual conceptualization that would guide the building of the nation and the defining criterion of national identity deriving from the peculiarity of the German language.

Ernst Moritz Arndt, considered to be one of the founders of German nationalism (Mosel 2010: 7), was a decisive figure in the building of a nationalist framework in a sentient manner that encompassed German nature, nation, and identity. Focusing on the moral principles of freedom through claims based on cultural norms, Arndt asserted that those principles should be directly related to one's dedication to and engagement with the public's consuetudo (Mosse 1974: 103). In this way, Arndt played a decisive role in shaping both a nation-based natural sentience perspective and a theoretical and historical ground for racial superiority claims that were followed by his intellectual, political, and artistic successors. In a political atmosphere defined by French occupation, he developed a chauvinistic and anti-French vision apparent across all his works—one focused on a unified Germany (Hughes 1988: 27).

This perspective was reflected in Arndt's song "The German Fatherland," published in 1813, which described Germany as a place "where fury exterminates foreign trash" and "every Frenchmen is called enemy" (Arndt 1845: 322–333). Therefore, his intellectual vision was embodied by patriotic devotion to the homeland and was justified by racial and linguistic purity (Kuran 2018: 52). This dual support of his xenophobic perspective inevitably informed his racial superiority claims as well. The passage below reveals Arndt's pursuit of historical rootedness, the "causality" of purity and superiority, and the "othering" of other races.

> The Germans are not bastardized by alien peoples, they have not become mongrels, they have remained more than many other peoples in their original purity and have been able to develop slowly and quietly from this purity of their kind and nature according to the lasting laws of time; the fortunate Germans are an original people. For our ancestors we have a great piece of evidence from one of the greatest men who ever lived, from the Roman Tacitus. This extraordinary man who with his prophetic eyes penetrated the depth of the human heart and the depths of nature, the present time and the future, clearly saw the worth of our fathers, and prophesied their splendid future; and so far, history has not contradicted him. But of all things he saw most clearly how important it was for the future greatness and majesty of the German people that they were pure and resembled only themselves, that they were no mongrels; for he saw his Italy, which had once been the mistress of the world, a bastardized canaille, cursed and outcast, defile the memories of the Fabricians and Cornelians and the proud Roman soul bled and writhed because there were no longer any true Romans. (Arndt 1815: 115; Kohn 1949: 791–92)

The urge to define historical roots for building a national identity can also be observed in Arndt's works. In an attempt to create a German cultural revival, he argued that the cultural characteristics of the Hohenstaufen, a dynasty that reigned between the twelfth and thirteenth centuries near Stuttgart, included freedom, bravery, purity, and discipline (Kuran 2018: 52). His mythical glorification of the German homeland tied with patriotism was one of the most prominent themes in his writing:

> Where God's sun first appeared to you, where stars of heaven first twinkled at you, where lightening first revealed to you God's almighty power and where his storm-winds roared through your soul producing holy terror, there is your love, there is your fatherland. Where the first human eye bent longingly over your cradle, where your mother first held you joyfully on her lap and your father burned into your heart the lessons of wisdom and Christianity, there is your fatherland. (Hughes 1988: 27)

German forests were likewise colored by such a patriotic perspective and became one of the most important embodiments of Arndt's arguments. With his intellectual positioning against the French occupation and in favor of a united, "purified" nation, the meaning of forests was crucial for him. His warning that "without its forest, Germany will be no more" (Arndt 1820: 71; Imort 2005a: 60) was a cry for the need to create a shield composed of forests near the French border (Imort 2005: 60).

Another crucial figure in constructing the bridge between the forest and Germandom was Wilhelm Heinrich Riehl. Parallel to the environmental determinist discourse, Riehl suggested a link of sentience between the national character and the German landscape, particularly forests (Imort 2005a: 60). According to Riehl, the fundamental characteristics of the Germans had been shaped by their environment, where the forests were predominant (Imort 2005a: 59). Riehl stated that forests are the primary entity shaping the German cultural and national atmosphere by forging "the strength and character that made and sustained it [Germany] as a nation" (Imort 2005a: 60). As a student of Arndt, Riehl also emphasized the vital importance of forests for German national unity and identity from a sentient perspective that later served as a touchstone for social movements, environmentalists, National Socialist theoreticians, and last but not least, Nazi political figures. Although focused more on an "environmental" point of view, Riehl justified his claims unsurprisingly with a racial motivation. Cherishing nature was central to nationalist ideas:

> If you wish to see society reduced to a bland parlor culture, where everything is identical in color and finish, then uproot the forests, level away the mountains, cordon off the sea. We must retain the forest not only to keep our stoves from going cold in wintertime but also to keep the pulse of our national life beating warmly and happily. We need it to keep Germany German. (Riehl 1857: 52; Staudenmeier 1995: 6)

Again, similar to Arndt, Riehl emphasized the role of forests in the freedom of nations. He clearly defined a contrast between the modern Western concept of freedom and the concept of German freedom rooted in, and made possible by, its forests. For him, Germany is "deeply rooted in its wooded wilderness," and the political freedom of the West is radically different from Germany's self-sufficiency thanks to its forest (Zechner 2011: 21). Riehl also implied that the urge to protect forests is a differentiating point between Germans and others, which is again derived from a nationalistic perspective. Claiming that preserving the forest was more a patriotic necessity than an economic or silvicultural one (Zechner 2011: 21), Riehl plainly presented the value of natural entities as derived not from environmental or historical concerns but from attempts to justify national unification and racial superiority via othering.

Changing Times and the Need for Stabilization

Apart from the figures mentioned above, the connection between the forest and Germandom was also common in the cultural landscape of early Romantic thinkers and artists like Caspar David Friedrich, Friedrich Hölderlin, and Ludwig Tieck (Imort 2005a: 57). Their works served not only to aestheticize but also to politicize the forests for the purpose of national unification and the creation of a German identity. In other words, "this reevaluation of the forest was more than just another reorientation of aesthetics; it was also a deliberate political project to unify the German-speaking people against the occupation of their Heimat by Napoleon" (Imort 2005a: 57).

As we have seen, Tacitus's *Germania* and the Battle of Teuteburg Forest were regarded as starting points for the myth of the German people's unique affinity with their forests. These narratives provided Romantics with solid ground for praising forests both "as the ancestral home of the German people and the source of strength for their future resurgence" (Imort 2005a: 57–58), especially in times of French occupation. Caspar David Friedrich's painting *The Chasseur in the Forest* provides a substantial example. Feshami's (2020) interpretation of the painting discusses the early Romantics' efforts regarding the mobilization of landscape for the sake of nationalist causes.

> Friedrich's painting *The Chasseur in the Forest* (1814) depicts a lonely French soldier standing on a forest path, surrounded by imposing trees which tower over him. His arms hang at his sides and his shoulders appear slumped, lending him an air of helplessness and despair. A raven sits on a stump in the foreground, portending the soldier's death in the wilderness.

By taking these early Romantics into consideration along with intellectuals such as Arndt, Riehl, and Fichte, it can be seen how they all helped to popularize a nationalist political project based on forests by representing them "as the spiritual conduit between a heroic Germanic past and a future united Germany" (Imort 2005a: 58). In the eighteenth and early nineteenth centuries, with the influence of Romanticism, forests were redefined in a nationalist framework within the sociocultural and political conditions of the period, quite apart from their material reality and meaning. This bridge between landscape and the identity, history, and future of the nation influenced the theoretical approaches and practices that were later embraced by the Nazis (Kuran 2018: 51).

Völkisch Nationalism and Oppositions

Founded upon premises and mythical arguments from a sylvan perspective, völkisch nationalism represented a unique perception of the bridge between the natural landscape and Germandom. With the contributions of thinkers such as Fichte, Riehl, and Arndt, this nationalist understanding came to play a crucial role in the twentieth century. Still, völkisch nationalism encapsulated more than has been mentioned thus far. Taking into consideration the turbulent times of political uncertainties (foreign occupations, lack of national unity), economic failures (high unemployment and inflation, the effects of the Great Depression, etc.) and accelerating social and technological change (industrialism, urbanization, Enlightenment, modernity, etc.), völkisch nationalism also developed diverse perspectives.

The theoretical ground of the völkisch movement was shaped by Arndt and Riehl via ethnic populism and nature mysticism driven by a severe reaction to modernity in all its senses (Staudenmeier 1995: 7). Völkisch thinkers attacked the values of modernity, linking the "heroic" and "different" past of Germans with present-day attempts to realize national unification and racial purity and "prove" their racial superiority, all based on landscape. "They sought to reconstruct society into one that was sanctioned by history, rooted in nature, and in communion with the cosmic life spirit" (Mosse 1964: 29). Despite this aspiration, their accusations of a lack of national unity and calls to protect the natural landscape changed to attacks on "rationalism, cosmopolitanism, and urban civilization" by blaming Jews for the changes they opposed. (Staudenmeier 1995: 7).

This conservative declaration of war against modernity targeted any kind of progress or change and was justified by nationalist figures' xenophobic and anti-Semitic discourses. According to Hughes (1988: 142–43), the main characteristics of völkisch nationalism were "adoration of heroes and soldiers, the idealization of a rural way of life, romanticization of the past, an irrational rejection of modernity, deep pessimism about the future, and a total rejection of foreigners and foreign ideas." Völkisch nationalism gave arguments concerning racial purity, racial superiority, and anti-Semitism another platform, allowing them to reach a greater audience, both civil and political. With shifts such as the rise of industrial capitalism, urbanization, modernity, and the Enlightenment, German society was precarious and unwieldy, both intellectually and practically. This allowed the theoretical and organizational work of the völkisch movement to gain momentum and later strengthen the radical policies and initiatives of the Nazi period (Kuran 2018: 66).

Serving as a bridge between the nineteenth and twentieth centuries by transmitting Romantic, anti-Semitic, anti-modern, and anti-Enlightenment perspectives, völkisch nationalism meant much more than a temporary sociocultural trend (Kuran 2018: 66). As Staudenmeier (1995: 7) points out:

> Reformulating traditional German anti-Semitism into nature-friendly terms, the völkisch movement carried a volatile amalgam of nineteenth century cultural prejudices, Romantic obsessions with purity, and anti-Enlightenment sentiment into twentieth century political discourse. The emergence of modern ecology forged the final link in the fateful chain which bound together aggressive nationalism, mystically charged racism, and environmentalist predilections.

Furthermore, völkisch nationalism was highly organized, both theoretically and practically, before the Nazis came to power, and this process aligned with another mystical and nature-based discourse—that of Blood and Soil.

Enlarging the Bridge: Blood and Soil

At this stage, it should also be underlined that Blut und Boden (Blood and Soil) mysticism was directly related to the perception of the forest and was fed by many of the figures mentioned so far. Assuming a unity between German national characteristics and German national landscape, Blood and Soil played a major role, especially during the reign of the Nazis, who declared it the official party doctrine. Although more than forests were associated with German national characteristics, Blood and Soil paved the way for the bridge between nation and nature. Figures such as Friedrich

Ratzel, Emil Adolf Rossmäsler, Rudolf Düesberg, and Friedrich von Hellwald offer a useful framework to observe this ambiguous and indistinct transition.

The "ethnicised forest" (Köstlin 2000; Zechner 2011: 21) perspective profoundly influenced contemporaries of Arndt and Riehl and served as a sentient and historical ground to build xenophobic claims. Friedrich Ratzel, for instance, founded his claims about the intersection between nature and nation solely on Riehl's writings. According to Ratzel, recognizing the mutual influence between people and environment was crucial. Working from this, with an environmental determinism approach, Ratzel argued for protecting the purity of nature (Dominick 1992: 23–24), not from an environmentalist standpoint but from a nationalist, othering perspective. He glorified and distinguished Germany, in contrast to Austria-Hungary and France, as a "land of forests and pastures, of green landscapes from one end to the other" (Ratzel 1909: 5; Wilson 2012: 20).

Defining German forests as more than their material being was also the main concern of other crucial thinkers such as Rossmäsler and Düesberg, who took the sentient landscape perspective a step further. For instance, Rossmäsler studied the "social life" of trees and tried to create a correlation between forests, class divisions, and national unity. According to him, the forest is "a beautiful and powerful union of forms and phenomena, in which no part is completely the same as any other, but in which nonetheless everything completely harmonizes in a sublime unison, plucking at the chords of every unspoiled breast" (Rossmäsler 1863, quoted in Wilson 2012: 181–82). Claiming the forest is "an integrated, organic unity" (Heske 1938: 42), Rossmäsler too made a landscape-based justification for the call for national unity.

Friedrich von Hellwald was another important figure. His main contribution to the process of "nation building via landscape" was introducing the social Darwinist discourse of forests, employing a racial perspective that he used to justify othering. Considering the forests as a model for society, Hellwald appreciated the Darwinist concepts of "struggle between species" and "drive for dominance and territory" as natural phenomena. Linking nature to the nation, he "encouraged a racialized understanding of the sylvan metaphor with implications for human society" (Wilson 2012: 187).

The social Darwinist perspective was promoted in German society with the comprehensive studies of Raoul France, who focused on decoding nature to extract lessons from it and apply them to social issues (Wilson 2012: 190). His perspective on human-nature relations derived from a monistic worldview inspired by Ernst Haeckel. Emphasizing unity between human and nature, France focused on the two main concepts of Darwinism—cooperation and competition—to identify and solidify a sentience bridge between human life and the forest. According to France, "the union of competition and cooperation is the law of the forest and thus a likeness of human life" (1908: 7; Wilson 2012: 190).

France's approach, which served to build an ethnicized forest, made racial deductions via social Darwinist claims regarding forests. His metaphorical statements about non-native plants clearly assume they are at a disadvantage trying to fit into German forests, using a German forest analogy to justify the exclusion of "outsiders" and "foreigners."

Practical Dimension: Nazi Era

Widening the Ground for Xenophobic Claims: Political Practices

The Nazi period stands out as a decisive turning point in the perception of landscapes as xenophobic. The Nazis embraced the historical views that connected German forests and the German national character, and which gave the forests sentience, bringing them to the forefront of German society using National Socialist ideology. The Nazi era represents a critical turning point regarding nature-nation relationships because it added to the landscape's sentience a layer of xenophobia with legal, administrative, political, and institutional dimensions.

With Blood and Soil mysticism becoming the official doctrine of the Nazi regime, and *Dauerwald* its mainstream silvicultural strategy and propaganda theme (one backed up by institutional and legal changes), claims of racial superiority and purity grew on the expanding foundation of sentient landscapes. The fundamental reason for those developments and race-based claims lay in the fact that the claims in question were processed not only through German forests but also through the German natural landscape with a holistic perspective. In this context, Walter Darré stood out by advocating for organic agriculture and for farmers to take into consideration German identity and culture. He emphasized the abovementioned opposition to urbanism, Enlightenment, modernism, and industrialism, and their corrosive influence on German national identity. Darre's arguments and actions as a political figure are quite important in an examination of the Nazi regime's perspective on nature-nation interaction.

Darré, who joined the Nazi Party in 1930, was the very person who convinced Hitler that the party should solicit peasant and farmer support to get more votes in elections. With the success of this strategy, he made rapid promotions within the party and became Minister of Agriculture in 1933 (Bramwell 1985). At only age thirty-eight, he succeeded in taking control of all agricultural organizations in the nation and received the title of "Reich Peasant Leader" (Frei, 1993). As one of the leading actors in Nazi ecology, Darré's efforts both in the Blood and Soil propaganda process and in the agricultural policies of the Nazi Party were considerable.

His most fundamental theoretical argument was that peasants are necessary for the unity of the German race and to fulfill the Blood and Soil ideology. According to him, peasants are the "conveyors" of German historical genetic heritage, the source of youth for the German nation, and the backbone of national defense (Dominick 1992: 94). They are vital to maintaining the existence of the German nation and its cultural heritage.

Throughout his career, Darré was concerned with the problems of peasants and made arguments connecting nationalism with rural values. He saw the unity of Blood and Soil as a solution for protecting peasants from racial extinction and national disintegration (Lekan 2004). The basis of legitimacy for the implementation of Blood and Soil ideology as an official state policy was formed by Darré.

One of Darré's main concerns was for the health of the soil, which enabled the implementation of organic farming methods. Describing the soil as a living organism, Darré argued that degradation of the soil disrupts the vital cycle of nature (Bramwell 1985). In parallel with his concern for soil health, Darré also undertook a great responsibility for integrating organic farming methods into national agricultural policy. With this political move, which he called "farming according to the laws of life," Darré was able to lead the institutionalization of organic farming and its nationwide spread, and he became the main actor in the Nazi government's support for agricultural planning via organic farming (Staudenmeier 1995).

One of the most prominent political figures of the Nazi Government's environmental wing, Darré also provided some striking insights and arguments about the impacts of cities and urbanization on rural values, villagers, and national consciousness. Describing big cities as machines vacuuming up the villagers from rural lands, Darré accused urbanization of tearing apart the ties between people and the soil. With the restoration of the unity between Blood and Soil, villagers could be reconnected to the land, and thanks to this, national solidarity could be rebuilt (Lekan 2004). What underlies Darré's arguments about agriculture, environment, antiurbanism, and peasant problems and values is strikingly related to his belief in the supremacy of the German race. When the subtext of the exaltation of peasantry and rural values, the emphasis on organic farming methods and soil health, and antiurbanism are examined carefully, the results show that they derive from a racist framework. Darré's advocacy for healthier soil and strengthening the ties between villagers and the land is an attempt to achieve racial purity and integrity. Darré's political moves to protect peasantry and peasant values from racial extinction and national deterioration do not arise from an environmental consciousness. The antiurbanist Darré also claimed that Nordic blood is polluted by foreigners mixing with native-born people in Nordic cities. He thought the only hope of preserving racial purity was to preserve peasant farmers and their land as the "reservoir of the best German blood" (Dominick 1992: 95).

Darré's key political position and close relationship with Hitler made him crucial not only to the process that enabled Blood and Soil mysticism to be put into practice but also to the growing perception of xenophobic landscapes, regarding soil (organic farming), farmers, and rural values. Although labeling his ideas and arguments as xenophobic might seem inexact, Darré played a major role in the process of constructing a bridge between the German nation and nature. This made racial purity and superiority, which were rooted in and derived from natural entities and processes, Darré's main themes. His warning that "to remove the German soul from the natural landscape is to kill it" (Darré 1938: 86–87; Dominick 1992: 95) reveals both the bridge he worked on and his theme.

Dauerwald

In this context, there is another crucial figure whose approach played a vital role in the perception of nature based on racial claims such as purity and superiority. Alongside the Blood and Soil mysticism that became official Nazi doctrine was *Dauerwald* (meaning "sustainable forestry" or "eternal forestry"), a program put into practice by another prominent Nazi figure, Alfred Möller. Dauerwald represents the peculiar relationship Germans had with their forests during the Nazi era, but it also offers a data set that limits the extent to which the politics of landscapes can be perceived as xenophobic and even fascist.

Möller, a member of the Prussian Forest Academy, put Dauerwald forward as a new alternative to scientific forestry management. This German nationalist and nature conservationist view was directly related to the sentience perspective, which was derived from antimodern, anti-Enlightenment, and anticapitalist views. The basis of Dauerwald was to create and implement an alternative system of forest management based on a more nature-oriented approach rather than on economic interests or scientific factors. In this way, a more diverse forest structure would be formed, and the focus would shift from economic gains to quality and sustainability (Imort 2005a: 71), which fits perfectly with the perception of the German forest as sentient. It should be noted that this "anti" perspective that is in favor of diverse forest management directly contradicts unidimensional, profit-centered, and "efficient" forestry.

Dauerwald quickly emerged as the primary forest management system for the Nazis. Hermann Göring, who had strong ties with völkisch nationalism and was one of the most important actors in the Nazi regime, made legal, political, and institutional efforts to realize Dauerwald nationwide, and his thoughts about nature-nation interaction also reveal the sentient bridge in the political realm. Underlying the implementation of Dauerwald were race-based arguments and political linings, and the program was perceived by the Nazi government as extremely fertile ground for Nazi political ambitions and propaganda, while also pointing to the intellectual legacy concerning theories of race that were part of National Socialist ideology. With this propaganda process, the sentient bridge between the German forest and German identity, which was beginning to be built long before, was advanced to the next stage by the Nazi regime in general, and by Göring in particular. His desire for the forest to be a main factor in the creation of national identity (Göring 1939: 245-255, quoted in Zechner 2011: 22) reveals the fundamental motivation behind Nazi forest policies and propaganda claims.

Dauerwald, declared the official forestry policy of Nazi Germany by legal decree in 1934, basically defined forests as a holistic organism rather than a collection of trees. Accordingly, its principles were shaped by applications focused on diverse silviculture. For instance, Dauerwald favored natural regeneration over planting, multilayered structure over uniformly tall and even-aged stands, and the selection of different plant species over monoculture (Imort 2005b: 47). Despite its innovative forestry methods, its appearance and use in the political arena was the direct product of propaganda and the racial claims of Nazi ideology. Under Göring's leadership, the intersection between völkisch nationalism and the idea of a sentient German forest and corresponding forestry practices was the driving force behind Dauerwald's popularity during Nazi rule. Connecting organic forestry techniques and Germany's "organic" heritage for National Socialist political purposes, Göring took legal, administrative, and institutional steps to make Dauerwald mandatory for the entire Reich (Imort 2005b: 48). Göring established and led a new Reichforstamt, giving it authority on a national level with the Law of July 1934 Concerning the Transfer of Forestry and Hunting Affairs to the Reich.

Imort (2005b: 52–53) lists the intersections between the theoretical and practical elements of the Dauerwald approach and Nazi ideology as follows:

- Only native, site-adapted tree species were allowed to be a part of the Dauerwald forest; similarly, only those Germans that were of the "proper" racial heritage could be *Volksgenossen*, or members of the national community.

- Individual trees played an important role as components of the Dauerwald forest, but they did so at their "proper station," with some dominating and others serving within the greater organic whole; similarly, every *Volkgenosse* was assigned to a task and a position that most benefited the corporatist *Volksgemeinschaft* [people's community], rather than himself or herself.

- The best trees in the Dauerwald forest were to be privileged in terms of light and space so a greater share of the growth might accrue to them; similarly, those Volksgenossen of the "best race" were to receive incentives and rewards for child rearing and other ways of "serving the nation."

- Selective cutting, thinning, and pruning ensured that the stand was continually improved in terms of phenotype and "race"; similarly, those individuals who did not fit the National Socialist vision of "race" were to be "removed" from the collective of the Volk.

- Selective cutting meant that while individual trees were removed constantly, the stand was never cleared entirely and the forest as a whole was perpetual; similarly, while the individual Volksgenossen were dispensable and lived only for a relatively short time, the Volksgemeinschaft as a whole was perpetual, or, in Nazi parlance, "eternal."

One place where these intersections can be determined most clearly are the statements of Göring and several proponents of the Dauerwald approach. According to Göring, "forest and people are much akin in the doctrines of National Socialism." In this ideology, "eternal forest and eternal nation are ideas that are indissolubly linked" because "the people is [sic] also a living community, a great, organic, eternal body whose members are the individual citizens" (Imort 2005b: 54). As A. W. Modersohn, another Dauerwald proponent, claimed, "the Dauerwald idea has much in common with our National Socialist idea of life, of the state, of race, blood, and soil. . . . Ask the trees, they will teach you how to become National Socialists!" (Modersohn 1939: 602–3; Imort 2005b: 54).

Not surprisingly, the implementation phase of Dauerwald silviculture, brought to the fore through propaganda, was pushed into the background by other priorities of the fascist regime. Despite the fact that the Nazi regime cultivated forests in the process of constructing a bridge between National Socialist conceptualizations of race and the German Volk (Imort 2005b: 68), economic development, autarky, and warfare clearly overrode the practical implementations, legal arrangements, and administrative organizations of silviculture. Therefore, Dauerwald was merely used as a propaganda tool for the Nazis, who were clearly in search of political gains and justification for their racial arguments, just as they were in their ecological conceptualization and practice of Nazi ecology. They regarded environmental protection as a rich source of propaganda resources, as it had historically helped them remain in power (Kuran 2018: 89), which is also the case for Blood and Soil and Dauerwald.

Conclusion

The implications of the historical, theoretical, and practical dimensions of the sentient bridge built to tie German forest to national identity can be listed as follows:

- There is a historical link between German forests and national identity. Views on this link were expressed more strongly and comprehensively as time progressed, especially when the notion of the nation-state was invoked. The justifications for those views were directly linked to racial superiority, racial purity, and xenophobia.

- Natural landscape, forests in this case, was considered to be the main factor, facilitator, and ground for the conceptualization of and justification for the sentient bridge.

- This sentient bridge, whose foundations were laid between natural landscape and the nation through forests, was historically built on nationalist, particularist, and othering claims, and it reached its peak under Nazi rule.

- The sentient bridge in question was also used as the main impulse and source of motivation for political propaganda, embodied in the examples of Blood and Soil and Dauerwald. Therefore, this perception of the German forest stands out as a case of the xenophobic landscape concept.

As a result, the construction of the sentient bridge reveals and summarizes the historical, intellectual, and political factors that played significant roles in the interaction between landscape and xenophobic views, not only on conceptual and perceptual bases but also in practice through German forestry.

Hikmet Kuran is assistant professor at Cappadocia University in the Department of Urban, Environmental, and Local Government Policies. He has research and teaching interests in environmental ethics, environmental politics, and Nazi ecology. Hikmet received his PhD in political science from Ankara University, and his most recent monograph, *Sehir Hakki; Neoliberal Kentlesme Ve Sinif Mücadelesi* (Right to the city: neoliberal urbanization and class struggle), came out in 2021 with the Turkish publishing house Nika Yayinevi.

References

Arndt, Ernst Moritz. 1815. "Fantasien zur Berichtigung der Urteille über Künftige Deutsche Verfassungen." In *Ausgewahtle Werke*, eds. Heinrich Meisner and Robert Geerds,77-83, Leipzig: M. Hesse.
———. 1820. *Ein Wort über die Pflegung und Erhaltung der Forsten und der Bauern im Sinne einer höheren d.h. mensschlichen Gesetzgebung*. Schleswig: Kgl. Tabustummen Inst.
———. 1845. "The German Fatherland." In *The Poets and Poetry of Europe*, ed. Henry Wadsworth.322-333, Philadelphia: Carey & Hart Press.
Bramwell, Anna. 1985. *Blood and Soil: Richard Walter Darre and Hitler's 'Green Party.'* Buckingamshire, UK: Kensal Press.
Darré, R. Walther. 1938. *Neuadel aus Blut und Boden*. Munich: Lehmanns Verlag.
Dominick III, Raymond. 1992. *The Environmental Movement in Germany: Prophets and Pioneers 1871–1971*. Bloomington: Indiana University Press.
Düesberg, Rudolf. 1910. *Der Wald als Erzieher: Nach den Verhaltnissen des Preussischen Ostens Geschildert*. Michigan: University of Michigan Library.
Feshami, Kevan. 2020. "A Mighty Forest is Our Race: Race, Nature, and Environmentalism in White Nationalist Thought." *DrainMag*. Retrieved from http://drainmag.com/a-mighty-forest-is-our-race-race-nature-and-environmentalism-in-white-nationalist-thought/.
Fichte, Johann Gottlieb. 2008. *Addresses to the German Nation*, ed. Gregory Moore, Cambridge Texts in the History of Political Thought. Cambridge: Cambridge University Press.

France, Raoul H. 1908. "Gesetz des Waldes." *Kosmos* 5(1): 100-105.
Frei, Norbert. 1993. *National Socialist Rule in Germany: The Fuhrer State: 1933-1945*. New York: Wiley-Blackwell.
Gellner, Ernest. 1964. *Thought and Change*. London: Weidenfeld and Nicolson.
Göring, Hermann. 1939. "Ewiger Wald—Ewiges Volk. Rede auf der Tagung des Deutschen Forstvereins am 17 August 1936." In *Hermann Göring: Reden und Aufsätze*, ed. Erich Gritzbach, 245–55. München: Zentralverlag der NSDAP.
Heske, Franz. 1938. *German Forestry*. New York: Oxford University Press.
Hughes, Michael. 1988. *Nationalism and Society: Germany 1800–1945*. Baltimore, MD: Edward Arnold.
Imort, Michael. 2005a. "A Sylvan People: Wilhelmine Forestry and the Forest as a Symbol of Germandom." In *Germany's Nature*, ed. Thomas Lekan and Thomas Zeller, 55–80. New Brunswick, NJ: Rutgers University Press.
———. 2005b. "Eternal Forest—Eternal Volk: The Rhetoric and Reality of National Socialist Forest Policy." In *How Green Were the Nazis? Nature, Environment, and Nation in the Third Reich*, ed. Franz-Joesf Bruggemeier, Marc Cioc and Thomas Zeller, 43–72. Athens: Ohio University Press.
Kohn, Hans. 1949. "Arndt and the Character of German Nationalism." *The American Historical Review* 54(4): 787–803.
Köstlin, Konrad. 2000. "Der Ethnisierte Wald." In *Der Wald—Ein Deutscher Mythos? Perspektiven Eines Kulturthemas*, ed. Albrecht Lehmann and Klaus Schriewer, 54–65. Berlin and Hamburg: Dietlich Reimer Verlag.
Kuran, Hikmet. 2018. *Nazi Ekolojisi* (Nazi ecology). Ankara: Ekoloji Kolektifi.
Lekan, Thomas M. 2004. *Imagining the Nation in Nature: Landscape Preservation and German Identity 1885-1945*. Cambridge: Harvard University Press.
Modersohn, A. W. 1939. "Weltanschauung und Beruflicher Einsatz." *Deutsche Forst-Zeitung* 8(15): 602-603.
Moore, Gregory. 2008. "Introduction in Addresses to the German Nation." In *Fichte*, Cambridge Texts in the History of Political Thought. xi-xxxvi, Oxford: Cambridge University Press.
Mosel, Jamie. 2010. "Conservation, Naturschutz, and Environmental Policy in Nazi Germany." History Research Paper, Holocaust and History, Fall 2010. Retrieved from https://www.jemosel.com/uploads/5/6/4/4/5644599/natur shutz_germany.pdf.
Mosse, George. 1964. *The Crisis of German Ideology: Intellectual Origins of the Third Reich*. New York: Grosset & Dunlap.
———. 1974. *The Culture of Western Europe: The Nineteenth and Twentieth Centuries*. New York: Rand McNally.
Pundt, Alfred G. 1935. *Arndt and the Nationalist Awakening in Germany*. New York: Columbia University Press.
Ratzel, Friedrich. 1909. "Die Deutsche Landschaft, Dürer Bund." In *Flugschrift zur Ausdruckskultur* 55 (October): 1-24.
Riehl, Wilhelm Heinrich. 1857. *Feld und Wald*. Stuttgart: Deutscher Wald e.V..
Rossmäsler, Emil Adolf. 1863. *Der Wald*. Leipzig: C. F. Winter'sche Verlagshandlung.
Schama, Simon. 1995. *Landscape and Memory*. New York: Vintage Books.

Staudenmeier, Peter. 1995. "Fascist Ideology: The 'Green Wing' of the Nazi Party and Its Historical Antecedents." In *Ecofascism: Lessons from the German Experience*, ed. Janet Biehl and Peter Staudenmeier.5-31, Edinburgh: AK Press.

Wilson, Jeffrey K. 2012. *The German Forest: Nature, Identity, and the Contestation of a National Symbol, 1871–1914*. Toronto: University of Toronto Press.

Zechner, Johannes. 2011. "Politicized Timber: The 'German Forest' and the Nature of the Nation 1800-1945." *The Brock Review* 11(2) : 19-32.

CHAPTER 6

Unruly Landscapes
Contested Desert Imaginaries in Post-Franco Spain

Arvid van Dam

Departing from Granada in a southeasterly direction, the A-92 that winds through the foothills of the Sierra Nevada begins to descend. Gradually, the pine and oak forests become thinly spread and make way for shrubs and grasses. The grey, solid granite turns to pale and crumbly limestone. The view extends in every direction as the hills flatten and vegetation becomes increasingly sparse. The landscape takes on craggy, eroded shapes. These are the arid landscapes of Almería, an Andalusian province in the southeast of Spain, also dubbed "the desert of Europe." Located in the eastern shadows of the Sierra Nevada mountains, the region is characterized by extremely low and irregular rainfall, averaging between 200 and 300 mm per year, concentrated in torrential rains that can spike up to 90 mm on a single day (AEMET 2019). Moving further into this desert landscape, every now and then whitewashed villages pass by. Some buildings are worn down and collapsed, abandoned by their inhabitants recently or decades ago. Then, turning a corner, the eye adjusts to the simmering reflection of the Mediterranean sun upon plastic sheets that extend to the coastline tens of kilometers away. In thousands of greenhouses, fruits and vegetables grow for Spanish and European markets.

This arid landscape shows paradoxical signs of desolation and development. On one hand, ruins of farms, villages, and industries draw scars in the landscape. On the other hand, the desert has been converted, subdued it seems, into landscapes centered on capitalist extraction through greenhouses, olive plantations, and quarries. Trucks of all types and sizes, carrying tomatoes, gravel, and plastics can be seen passing by shanty houses and workers on bicycles, and the regulars of a village bar may be heard discussing the latest controversies over intensive irrigation in a place where water is scarce. How do these modes of existence come to coincide in one place? How, if at all, do they relate? And what ideological underpinnings do these landscapes conceal?

In this chapter, I explore the contested landscape imaginaries at play in this arid corner of Spain. My focus in exploring the landscape's sentience, then, lies in the stories it inspires through its materiality and its various transformations—stories that seek to explain this landscape and that (re)produce it in doing so—and in the persistence of these stories over time and through developmental interventions. I take an interdisciplinary approach, bridging the environmental humanities and anthropology, and juxtaposing analyses of representations of the landscape in popular films and TV series with ethnographic material collected in the region between 2016 and 2019. By discussing the landscape's harsh imagery, its fascist legacies, and its various contemporary forms of capitalist exploitation, I show that the landscape has collected a range of violent images that are a significant burden to farmers living and working in the region. These farmers are implicated in this imaginary and are protagonists of the material practices that give substance to its proliferation. At the same time, they are the ones who have historically struggled to improve life for themselves and their workers, who continue to do so, and who are eager to present a different image. It appears, however, that they are struggling against the landscape itself—a landscape that is persistently antagonistic to the various attempts to bring it in line.

In this discussion, I view the (un)making of landscape as a project of both representation and physical engagement. I draw on new materialist approaches, understanding materiality as the conjuncture of the social, the discursive, and the material without presuming dominance of one over the other, so that the landscape "is made up of matter *and* meaning" (Dolphijn and van der Tuin 2012: 91; see also Knappett 2007). Imagination, then, is not just cognitive: it is culturally shared and embedded in symbols, objects, and environments, while material engagement is always discursive and infused with cultural images. This implies that "practice and representation are intrinsically intertwined in the construction of the landscape" (Benson 2010: 64). New meanings can emerge from new material forms, and new forms can emerge from altered meanings. In this way, making and unmaking landscape is something humans do all the time—it is about making sense of the environment, telling and retelling its stories, and redefining its forms. Throughout this chapter, I show how different imaginaries have been developed and challenged, as part and parcel of the "lines of becoming" (Ingold 2011) of people and landscape. The landscape is always changing, co-constituting, growing; it is "continually coming into being and never complete" (Ingold 2020: 585), though not as an idyll, but as a site of friction. In its perpetual process, landscape justifies particular modes of action and intervention, or the absence of these. It creates, but also confines, possibilities for design activities, shaping the ways in which people experience and physically alter it. The landscape, then, is not just subject to politics, but intrinsically political.

The desert provides a particular but also exemplary case to explore the unruly becoming of landscape. Deserts have taken a complex and problematic position in western cultural and environmental history. On one level, the desert has biblical connotations and is associated with divine presence and spiritual connection, coupled with a view of its extreme climate conditions as divine ordeal or punishment (Davis 2016; Gersdorf 2009; Lane 1998). On another, the desert has an uneasy place in the narrative of European expansion into the Americas, Asia, Africa, and Australia. Due to environmental determinist views, desert landscapes long served to confirm the otherness and backwardness of these regions while posing Europe as the center of civilization and modernity (Davis 2016; Gersdorf 2009). The desert gained connotations of unproductive, degraded land, unfit for human habitation and mismanaged by native populations (Davis 2016). Such tropes spurred efforts to convert desert landscapes into productive, cultivated terrains. Here, too, biblical notions of Eden and of garden versus barren wilderness have played a role, often at the cost of native pastoral livelihoods. Nowadays, this rings true for example in the various "reforestation" projects that are implemented even in regions that never were forests. As such, "desert landscapes have been and are increasingly subject to global efforts to increase food production through agricultural expansion into arid lands" (Davis 2016: 8). The UN- and African Union–backed "Great Green Wall" project, which is supposed to surround the Sahara with a belt of vegetation with the aim of producing agricultural landscapes, is a case in point, as is the expansion of center pivot irrigation in Saudi Arabia since the early 1990s. The Almerian desert, which is the focal point of this chapter, with its thousands of greenhouses and superintensive olive plantations, testifies to this view of desert landscapes as being in "need" of transformation—as well as to its tendency to resist being tamed. Rather than simply reiterating these imaginaries, my aim is to analyze them as they appear in public debates and films produced in the region, to show how they seem to have become engrained in the landscape, and how they have been contested. My starting point for this is the prominence of cinematic representations of the Almerian landscape.

Desert Imaginaries in Spaghetti Westerns

With its steep, eroded hillsides and deep, dry riverbeds, it is no wonder that the spectacular Almerian landscapes have attracted not only geologists interested in rock formation but also filmmakers looking for settings for their work. The movie industry in Almería began in the 1950s but expanded exponentially in the early 1960s with the emergence of the "spaghetti western" genre, an umbrella term for European westerns (Hughes 2004). Though film experts tend to agree that most of the more than five hundred spaghetti westerns made by the late 1970s can be considered pulp (Hughes 2010), some *did* become successful and have gone on to gain legendary status, notably Sergio Leone's Dollars trilogy, to which I will limit my discussion in this section. The trilogy comprises the films *A Fistful of Dollars* (1964), *For a Few Dollars More* (1965), and *The Good, the Bad, and the Ugly* (1966). These films have played a catalyzing role in the Almerian film industry and are famous for their emblematic photographic portrayal of the desert landscapes of Almería. What binds the three films is not the narrative but the setting, and the imagined world this setting represents. The films share a set of archetypal characters often played by the same actors. In particular, the reappearance of Clint Eastwood in his signature outfit (poncho, hat, and cigar) became a leitmotif in the three films.

In *For a Few Dollars More*, Eastwood's nameless character rides into town on a mule, passing a group of tobacco-spitting men in cowboy attire. They jeer at the traveler, ridicule his looks, and fire their pistols at the mule's feet, scaring it and causing it to run away. The traveler jumps off, recomposes himself, and returns to confront the gang. He insists that the men apologize to his mule, which of course they refuse to do. As they draw their guns, he quickly shoots each of them in the heart and, one by one, they drop down in the sand. The undertaker, who has been watching the scene from a distance, smiles gleefully at the sight of his new clients. Cinematic spectacle aside, the traveler's response to the mocking behavior of the men appears excessive, to say the least. What does this reveal about the traveler, who seems not only indifferent to danger, but to life itself? And what does this tell about the landscape he travels through, which not only allows but seemingly encourages, such random acts of violence?

To me, this iconic scene demonstrates a central message of the Dollars trilogy, namely that in the desert, both the environment and the people that dwell there are wild and hostile. This is a place for outlaws, bounty hunters, grave diggers: merchants of death who reflect, and are in turn framed by, the normative desert landscape through which they ride. This link between man and landscape is continually highlighted, as close-ups of the main characters alternate with wide shots that emphasize that they are embedded in their environment. Their figures are framed by bare hills and distant mountains so that character and landscape merge seamlessly: man emerges from the desert, imitates it, becomes like it, and returns to it in death (French 1997; Tompkins 1992). Nothing is revealed of his past or future, other than that he came from the desert and that he will ride off into it again when the film ends. Indeed, his identity lies not in a name, but in the landscape itself—both man and place are nameless, placeless, timeless.

The Dollars trilogy, and spaghetti westerns in general, are a celebration of heteronormative masculinity. Almost all of the characters are men, the plot takes place in public spaces, physical action and body language are dominant over speech, emotions are hardly expressed at all, pain and discomfort are stoically endured, and death is faced fearlessly (French 1997; Tompkins 1992). Meanwhile, women, when they appear at all, are generally either widows, prostitutes, or damsels in distress; others are mute figures in black dresses who flee the streets as gunmen ride into town. This reveals more than just impoverished stereotypes of traditional gender roles, for which the films have been criticized extensively. Rather, these westerns actively oppose femininity and associated forms of institutional life (Tompkins 1992). In this sense, the desert is a landscape not only characterized by a lack of water but by a lack of institutions. There is no justice, at least not of the kind provided by conventional law and order. Justice exists only in the form of compassion or, more often, the cruelty of personal revenge. Absolute freedom goes hand in hand with the possibility of crimes that will never be punished because there are no laws to criminalize them. And it is the landscape that facilitates this. It offers hiding spots for criminals in the cracks of its mighty rocks, ruined buildings, and desolate graveyards. Quite often, the bandit does not even have to hide, for he is already in a place where the tentacles of civilization do not yet reach. The desert is portrayed as a place where the only ruling entity is the landscape itself, but while this landscape dictates where one can or cannot live and how one can or cannot move, it does not distinguish between what is good or bad. The absence of law and law enforcement are thus but a superficial reflection of a much deeper absence, of what might be called moral law. In the absence of this, the landscape is not so much *im*moral as it is *a*moral: it is profoundly indifferent to the moral constraints that circumscribe civilized human life (French 1997).

The films thus convey the idea that the desert offers people only unsophisticated cultures and savage habits. However, despite their displays of graphic violence, spaghetti westerns are intensely nostalgic, romanticizing a natural landscape that has yet to be corrupted by civilization. This romanticism can easily slide into a form of environmental determinism.

The desert landscape, in this sense, is not just a passive background to the regular occurrences of deceit, theft, violence, and revenge; instead, it makes these human acts possible. It actively *produces* them. But while humans live, fight, and die, the landscape remains changeless. The desert exists on a timescale beyond that of the various human figures who enter it, dwell in it, and must eventually either abandon it altogether or convert it into something else. And precisely this conversion is a recurring theme in the western genre, which shows how the advance of civilization—the coming of the railroad, so to speak—brings an end to the frontier.

Without exception, each of the Dollars films ends in a final standoff. Three men walk onto a paved threshing circle, where they know that at least one of them will die. Staring intensely at each other, they make to draw their guns. Assisted by Ennio Morricone's evocative soundtrack, the scene builds up slowly to its climactic violence. The act of violence itself, when it finally happens, passes in a split second. Today, the cameras are now long gone, the films' actors ageing, but the threshing circle is still in place: a touristic landmark. An accompanying information sign displays a still of this final scene, accompanied by a brief description in four languages. In the background, pulling me back into the present, is a series of long plastic greenhouses, draped over the hills. This is where the Plastic Sea starts.

Landscape Transformation

It is thought-provoking that many of the establishing shots from the Dollars trilogy would be impossible today due to the development of greenhouses. With this and other developments, the arid regions of Almería have undergone an immense transformation over the past half century, resulting in what is now popularly known as the Plastic Sea. This "sea" is an expanse of roughly two hundred square kilometers that is blanketed by plastic greenhouses. At first sight, this human-made landscape offers a stark confrontation with the materialization of a domesticated desert: it is an image of what comes after the western's credits have faded to black, when civilization has been allowed to advance. These greenhouses are used to increase temperatures in winter, producing fruits and vegetables for export to other parts of Spain and Europe. The all-year-round high temperatures inside the greenhouses are a significant competitive advantage in the European food market, and Almería has consequently become an important region in terms of European food security.

Indeed, transforming the desert into a hyperproductive landscape has changed the very patterns of human habitability, not just in relation to subsistence or livelihood, but also in broader cultural terms. There is understandable pride in the transformation of a place previously considered to be "nothing but a desert" into "the orchard of Europe," with the intensive agriculture answering to a long history of drought and the economic and social deprivation that is supposed to come with it. As such, the Plastic Sea relays the conviction that "the fundamental consequences of drought are due to underdevelopment, and only development can remedy drought" (Anderson 2011: 71). In Spain, such economistic thought, known as *regeneracionismo* (regenerationism), built momentum in the nineteenth century. It portrayed the Spanish nation as having declined in the wake of decolonization in the Americas and instead demanded from society a focus on internal development. Under regeneracionismo, such thinking suggested, the desert could be tamed.

In my own conversations with farmers in Almería, a common explanation I heard for the development of plasticulture was that farmers in the 1950s accidentally found their crops grew better when protected from the dusty winds with plastic sheets instead of traditional fences. Indeed, several early experiments with plasticulture have been recorded. Marín Martínez (2016), for example, writes of a particular grape farm that was the first in Almería to construct a greenhouse in 1959. Although beset by numerous failures in the beginning, it grew through the 1950s and 1960s from a family farm into a business with a workforce of 1,500 men, women, and children. Nevertheless, it would be a romantic fallacy to ascribe this "Almerian miracle," as the Plastic Sea is also called, to the sheer inventiveness of the farmers. Without dismissing their role, it should be stressed that this development owes much to the National Colonization Institute (Instituto Nacional de Colonización, or INC), which was established by General Francisco Franco's regime in the immediate aftermath of the Spanish Civil War in 1939 and was a brainchild of regenerationist ideology (Martínez Rodríguez 2018; Rivera Menéndez 2000).

The INC was a response to severe problems in rural Spain in the twentieth century, where a dichotomy between landowners with extensive but scarcely productive plots and peasants living in dire poverty was causing social tensions. Under Franco, Spain became oriented toward self-sufficiency, which meant that the primary sector had to be developed to the extent that Spain was capable of feeding itself. Modernizing agriculture thus became a key element in the ideology of *Franquismo*, or "Francoism" (Centellas Soler, Ruiz García, and García-Pellicer López 2009). This ideology served multiple needs at once: it would increase the productivity of the primary sector, offer better living conditions in rural areas, and prevent urbanization, which was seen as a source of civic unrest and thus a threat to the regime (Pérez Escolano 2009).

Functioning under the Ministry of Agriculture, the INC's main objective was to instigate such developments. It sought to counter the problematics of rural Spain through the organized settlement of families in prefabricated towns, with plots allocated to each family. The basic idea was to increase productivity by populating previously unproductive territories and improving irrigation systems. So, although colonization was primarily a technological reform, it also encompassed a redistribution of land, which in Almería has resulted in a large number of small landowners (Centellas Soler, Ruiz García, and García-Pellicer López 2009; Rivera Menéndez 2000). Selected for colonization were poor, landless nuclear families with five or six members. Rather than placing families in traditional *cortijos* (farmhouses) separated from existing villages, the INC constructed neatly ordered villages for the inhabitants of the new countryside. These new villages were built in modernist architectural style and highly planned: they were to be populated by 80 to 200 families, housing between 500 and 1,000 people, with the distance between the plots and the family residence not to exceed 2.5 km, meaning that the towns were designed to be constructed at 5 km apart (Centellas Soler, Ruiz García, and García-Pellicer López 2009).

Between 1939 and 1971, the INC established around 130 villages in Andalusia, fourteen of them in the province of Almería, of which twelve are in the plains of Dalías and Níjar (Centellas Soler, Ruiz García, and García-Pellicer López 2009). It is no coincidence that these are also the places in which the Plastic Sea is now located. Blessed with large and accessible bodies of groundwater, these regions formed an excellent base for the development programs of the INC, which led "an anxious search for water" by introducing new technologies to extract and distribute groundwater (ibid.: 13; see also Rivera Menéndez 2000). Moreover, this development program was a form of propaganda for the authoritarian state. The new clean, white towns, furnished with modern services, favored functionalism and rationalism over romantic nationalism and became emblematic of modern life—the long-envisaged regeneration of the rural environment (Centellas Soler, Ruiz García, and García-Pellicer López 2009), as well as an exertion of state control, and with it, human dominance, over the arid landscape.

In short, the colonization campaign was aimed at preventing, and even reversing, the depopulation of rural Spain and at increasing the efficiency and productivity of its agriculture. Rather than a romanticization of the countryside, or simply an attempt to improve the lives of poor farmers, it was also a regulatory (and repressive) mechanism to prevent excessive urbanization and political resistance. Either way, in Almería, its effects have been overwhelming, and the success of the Plastic Sea is something that no one could have foreseen (Pérez Escolano 2009). While the introduction of new technologies through the INC, and with them access to groundwater, stimulated a steady growth of plasticulture, this only spiked when Spain entered the European Economic Community in 1986 and access to the European market opened up (Molina Herrera 2005). Both the inward gaze of *Franquismo* and the resistance of other EEC members to admitting the authoritarian regime had prevented Spain from entering the EEC before Franco's death in 1975. The transition to democracy opened up new possibilities for the export of Almería's products. Accordingly, the symbolism of agriculture in the most arid region of Europe appears to have changed drastically. Having long been at the margin of the Spanish national imaginary, the development of plasticulture suddenly propelled Almería into national and European space in new and unexpected ways.

Perhaps not surprisingly, the narrative of Francoist development has remained strongly present in Almería. While I certainly would not suggest that this reflects the perspective of all farmers in the region, several of my interlocutors openly and without being asked expressed appreciation for Franco's development programs. For example, during the lunch break of a seminar on regional water scarcity, in which the irrigation schemes of the INC had been discussed, a farmer at my table spoke up, saying that Franco had been preoccupied primarily with making sure people had food to eat. "We have forgotten," he said, "what it is like not to have food, to be hungry. But that was the case in the past. And that is why Franco developed a large and stable agricultural sector." Knowing that he touched upon a sensitive topic in defending Franco's policy, he added, "And you may or may not like that." For many people in the region and beyond, the Plastic Sea is nothing less than a symbol of modernity and globalization, and it is looked upon in awe: finally, humans have conquered the hostile desert.

Contested Imaginaries

Yet the exceptionality of the local landscape remains (Rivera Menéndez 2000: 15). Nowhere else has agriculture developed into such forms which, while not necessarily "miraculous," still border on the bizarre. Comparing economic growth and migration patterns with other provinces in Spain confirms Almería as a case apart (Molina Herrera 2005). In discursive as well as material terms, the changes are not straightforward. Particularly, the landscape of greenhouses suffers from a bad image. What becomes apparent in media representations of the region, and what I also noticed during my fieldwork, is that the Plastic Sea is popularly associated with groundwater abuse, pesticides, ugliness, unnatural plastics, the destruction of a natural landscape, and, even more so, illegal migration and labor exploitation—all calling into question to what extent the unruly desert landscape has indeed been subdued to modern civilization.

A very interesting example of this imaginary can be seen in the Spanish detective television series *Mar de Plástico* ('Sea of Plastic' directed by Norberto López Amado, Javier Quintas, and Alejandro Bazzano and first aired by Antena 3 in 2015). Set in a fictive town amidst the greenhouses, the story it tells is not a pretty one. A girl disappears in the night in an alley between two greenhouses. The next morning, her blood is sprayed through the sprinklers in one of the greenhouses and her head is found in a water basin. This gruesome discovery is the prelude for a series of hostile events in a small town in the middle of the Plastic Sea where everyone knows and hates each other, and where everyone has secrets. Racial tensions between white Spanish managers and Black African migrant workers escalate after it becomes known that the girl, who was white, secretly had a Black boyfriend. And while the plot takes the form of a classic detective story, with some love affairs between the characters and plenty of suspects with fraught alibis, the title, *Mar de Plástico*, indicates what this series really is about: the landscape of plastic greenhouses itself.

Although the series was popular throughout Spain, with nearly five million viewers tuning in to the first episode (Migelez 2015), it was not well received in the Almerian province. The mayor of El Ejido, Francisco Góngora, weighed in and is reported to have said that he did "not believe there is a single *Almeriense* who liked that series" (Estrella Digital 2015). Already before the TV series was aired, farmers' associations expressed their concerns with the "negative stereotypes and exaggerations" it portrayed (León and Martínez 2014). One farmers' association even called upon its members not to watch the first episode and to avoid feeding into the controversy on social media, hoping that the series might be discontinued when viewers' numbers turned out to be low (Vargas 2015). One reason behind this suspicion was that the accents of the actors did not represent Almerian ways of speaking and were considered more similar to Sevillan accents (Rodríguez and Martínez 2015). More importantly, farmers' communities and officials in Almería felt misrepresented with regard to the theme of racism and xenophobia in the series. Jesús Muñoz, president of the provincial separatist group Action for Almería (Acción Por Almería), was reported to have rejected *Mar de Plástico* as "a series that shows our land as a sinister place where indiscriminate crimes and beatings occur" (Rodríguez and Martínez 2015).

Indeed, there is quite graphic, and often racialized, violence shown throughout the series. On some occasions, the greenhouses themselves are used as tools for torture or as accomplices to crime, their material characteristics making possible the forms of violence that occur. Just as the desert was represented as a landscape where the rule of law could not reach, so the Plastic Sea is portrayed as offering space to a range of illegal activities, with drug deals, prostitution, beatings, and killings happening in and between the greenhouses. Many of the Spanish villagers are introduced as white supremacists, who aggressively deny people of color access to their spaces, and who carry swastika tattoos beneath their shirts. The "immigrants," on the other hand, are portrayed as living in uncomfortable shacks, in poor conditions, and without access to rights or services. Only gradually do the two clashing groups begin to accept each other as they come to realize they are both suffering from the same crime. Here, *Mar de Plástico* reveals that progress has not brought morality to the desert. On the contrary, it has brought greed and lies, social inequality and violence. Compared to the lynching by racist mobs that is graphically shown in *Mar de Plástico*, the violence of the outlaw figures in spaghetti westerns appears almost innocent. And instead of a standoff between anachronistic emblems of masculine superiority, *Mar de Plástico* exposes the disturbing violence of modernity itself in a transformed yet far from tamed landscape.

Two weeks before the first episode was due to air, Andrés Góngora Belmonte, Secretary of COAG Almería, a major farmers' union, sent a letter to Atresmedia, stating that "there is much concern in the region for the image that the series 'Mar de Plástico' could project of our province and our agriculture" (Góngora Belmonte 2015). The letter urged the producers to base their representation of the agrarian sector on "reality" instead. Góngora emphasized that people with migrant backgrounds had found in Almería a place "to live and thrive," sketching a situation of mutual respect and harmonious labor relations in which different cultures productively coexist. How fragile this harmony might turn out to be was revealed when he then wrote, "We fear that series like 'Mar de Plástico' can distort this reality and generate situations of irritation and tension." The main message was that a misrepresentation of the region would have the potential to damage labor relations, to tarnish the image of the sector in national and international markets, and ultimately to "cause serious economic damage to the province." "Should you not respect the reality of our sector," the letter ominously ended, "COAG Almería reserves the right to undertake as many legal and media actions as are necessary to restore the good image of the Almerian agriculture and farmers, which have cost us so many years to build."

Unions and politicians are certainly not the least influential parties in Almería, and their concern over the image of plasticulture was immediately responded to by Atresmedia with a statement that *"Mar de Plástico* is fiction," and with a promise to include a corresponding statement at the beginning of the series (León 2015). As a result, each episode of the series starts with a white text on black background that reads: "The facts and personages that appear in this series, as well as the locality of Campoamargo, are totally invented." Still, one cannot escape the feeling that this statement signifies precisely the opposite. After all, it was only fifteen years before, on 5 February 2000, that riots had broken out in the municipality of El Ejido. The riots lasted for three days and followed the deaths of three people who had been killed by immigrants. Although both suspects were detained, the events triggered an outbreak of violence that was directed primarily at its Moroccan population, but also at immigrants more generally. Several main access routes were blocked, and establishments and homes of immigrants were attacked, with fire set to buildings and vehicles. The national police were called in from the neighboring provinces to suppress the uprising. The events were discussed in national newspapers in terms of xenophobia, racism, and, as one article in the post-Francoist national newspaper *El País* commented, "racist barbarism" (Constenla and Torregrosa 2000).

Mar de Plástico may be fictional, but its resemblance to the events of February 2000 is hardly a coincidence. No wonder the Almerian agricultural sector feared for its image: framing the local population as xenophobic could potentially rake up old sores. The sector has had to cope with a bad image in terms of its social dynamics. Both national and international media feature pieces on the labor conditions for migrant workers in the greenhouses on a regular basis. *Mar de Plástico* gleefully built upon this negative image of the greenhouse landscape and its inhabitants; the landscape itself may be flooded with light, but the imaginary it reproduces is unremittingly dark.

Making a Moral Landscape

The imaginaries I have described so far stand in stark contrast to the experiences and views of the farmers I encountered during my fieldwork. If anything, these farmers share a sense of pride in their work and in the achievements of their sector and their province. Many of them had committed themselves to sustainability principles, both ecological and socioeconomic. There are many unions and cooperatives in Almería that represent the interests of farmers in the region and in the international market, but which also push for responsible cultivation among their constituents. Environmental concerns, including biodiversity and landscape design, are taken seriously, as is responsible water use. When it comes to labor, there are numerous social workspaces, and all farmers I spoke with were eager to point out that they paid their laborers fair wages throughout the year. However, nearly all of them also admitted that, every now and then, when the workload exceeded the capacity of the farm's regular labor force, they would temporarily employ undocumented day laborers. For example, Andrés, a small-scale, ecological farmer with three greenhouses of about two hectares total, explained to me:

> In agriculture, you may need one person today and tomorrow you need five. The work needs to be done, but of course it's difficult to just find five people and hand it to them. Honestly, throughout the year, you will occasionally have a person who does not have papers. Definitely. Just once, but you will have them. Because you have to do the work, and if there are no people, what will you do?

Like Andrés, my interlocutors did not deny that there was inequality and tension in their industry when it came to labor. Rather, they openly discussed this, often empathizing with migrant laborers while also pointing to structural discrepancies in the national and European immigration policies. For farmers themselves this also posed serious challenges. As Andrés continued:

> It is very poorly regulated. There are many people without documents in Spain and in Almería. But if the government lets them stay here, then these people need to work. If you go to Campohermoso or San Isidro in the morning, there will be a lot of Africans there who are asking for work. And there the authorities do not intervene. But later they come to your greenhouse and fine you for employing these people. So, I don't see it. This needs to be regulated, and then we would all be more at peace.

As they were very much aware of the negative imaginary of the Plastic Sea, several local farmers, farmers' unions, and politicians have actively been trying to change this image. A case in point is Lola, a farmer who has opened her greenhouses to the public with guided tours for schools, tourists, and professionals. During these tours, she points to the sustainable modes of production and the technological innovations that have been implemented in the farm, including advanced water circulation, automated systems, and the abolishment of pesticides, as well as to her commitment to providing good labor conditions, fair wages, and social security.

Similarly, Hortiespaña, a sector-wide collaborative, has launched a campaign to improve the image of greenhouse agriculture in the Spanish southeast, adopting the slogan "We are doing it well" (*Lo estamos haciendo bien*). Opposing the image of the Plastic Sea as ugly and unnatural, the campaign makes a bold statement: for a large number of reasons, the Almerian system of production is "one of the most sustainable in the world" (Almería en Verde 2017: 6). As part of this campaign, Hortiespaña has produced two short videos that are, interestingly, directed at the farmers themselves. The idea behind it, Fransico Góngora Cañizares, president of Hortiespaña, explained during a public roundtable discussion in Almería, is that farmers need to start believing in themselves to then convince the consumer in Spain and Europe. "Farmers feel proud, but they have to manifest the same externally," Góngora said.

Both videos show images of the Plastic Sea from above—a view that allows its immense scale to be apprehended—as well as from within the greenhouse, in this way seeking to disclose what happens underneath the plastic. This is captured in images of smiling farmers and workers, ripe vegetables, and green leaves. The first video is titled "The reality of cultivation in greenhouses" (*Realidad del cultivo en invernadero*, Hortiespaña 2017a). In two and a half minutes, it seeks to debunk the idea that food produced in greenhouses tastes bad. People in a marketplace are asked what they think of food from a greenhouse, which elicits answers referring to tastelessness, artificiality, and pesticides. Even though we are in the twenty-first century, the narrator says, the image we have of greenhouses seems to be stuck in the 1970s. Being in the twenty-first century means caring for the environment. The video then compares the plastic greenhouse with a plastic rain cover for a baby stroller. "It is our natural instinct to protect what is most important to us." The video reassures its audience—the Almerian farmers themselves—that there are plenty of arguments for a better public image for Almería. The landscape transformation from "desert" to "orchard" forms a central argument: "If we have been able to convert this arid region into an example of work, evolution, and respect, we are going to be able to change the perception of society." The video finishes with the statement that this is "a change that starts today."

The title of the second video, "A sea of reasons to believe in what we do" (*un mar de razones para creer en lo que hacemos*, Hortiespaña 2017b), refers directly to the Plastic Sea. The video starts by recognizing explicitly that plastic is considered unnatural, and that it leads consumers to believe that products from greenhouses are artificial and contaminated. Then it asks: "But what if society, including ourselves, was aware of what really happens underneath this sea of plastic?" The music changes to a happy tune, and once more, landscape transformation is called to the fore. The only thing this region used to export half a century ago, the narrator says, was its own inhabitants who emigrated to find work. Now, Almería is the largest exporter of vegetables in Europe. With this, Almería has also become an example of successful immigration and social integration. The greenhouses are further praised for being independent from subsidies, and for being a model for production that has been adopted across the globe. Also, in terms of biological (as opposed to chemical) pest control, the narrator asserts, Almería is a world leader. Within Spain, the narrator continues, the southeast is the most efficient in its water use, while within Europe, the Spanish greenhouses use "twenty-two times less energy." Finally, it is argued that the white plastic reflects sunlight and in so doing combats global warming. "We are doing it well," the video concludes.

The campaign, and the agricultural practices behind it, demonstrate that in the making of landscape, material transformation and imagination go hand in hand, continuously informing one another. The Almerian farming industry has, as any thriving industry perhaps, been in a process of ever-proceeding innovation. The implementation of automated irrigation systems and biological pest control, as well as discussions of what type of greenhouse is most sustainable and profitable, are examples of how, on an everyday basis, the Plastic Sea is materially transformed. At the same time, the campaign and the narratives of the farmers I spoke with also highlight that these changes need discursive validation, as they seek to frame the landscape in terms of sustainability and quality. Changes in the image of landscape and changes in its materiality require constant reassessment in the face of one another. In a way, the campaigns discussed here continue the transformation from "desert" to "orchard" instigated by the INC decades ago. Only now, the transformation occurs not so much through the material instalment of new technologies as a means of human dominance over harsh terrain, but by trying to influence how the landscape is perceived.

Conclusion

While its materiality and aesthetics have changed profoundly in the transformation from the "desert of Europe" to the "orchard of Europe," it seems as if the arid landscapes of Almería have somehow retained their unruly character. Effectively going against the dominant desert imaginary, this transformation involved eradicating poverty and enhancing human habitability as well as allowing selected nonhuman species to thrive in a controlled environment. This connected in turn to the perceived Europeanness of the landscape by establishing direct links with the European market. But the transformation from "desert" to "orchard" also suffers from a bad image, not least due to rumors of lawlessness. Now, the desert is productive and fertile, though it is still represented as a wild place, fundamentally "other" to civilized society, which suggests that the landscape imaginary has not been transformed to the same extent as its materiality.

However, there has been a significant symbolic transformation in the nature of hostility in the desert: once associated with wild and uncivilized masculinity, then with fascist-enforced modernizing development, now it is associated with twenty-first century capitalist exploitation of people and the environment. In the process of taming the desert through agricultural development, it has received an entirely new narrative, namely that of social inequality; and while this is in itself highly undesirable, it might ironically be the ultimate proof that the desert has indeed become a human, habitable place.

This is not to say that imagination and experience influence one another in a direct or necessarily reciprocal manner. I would certainly not suggest that spaghetti westerns, or any other films produced in Almería, have had a direct impact on the way the landscape has been materially transformed. Rather, the images that circulate of the landscape give direction to how it may be experienced and transformed, while the material transformation of landscape inevitably engenders new ways of imagining and representing it. This directional impulse to the "lines of becoming" (Ingold 2011) of people and landscape can be tied to particular characteristics of the landscape itself, primarily its exceptional aridity, but it also relates to more broad-based beliefs in technological innovation and modern progress.

Those farmers who have been struggling against the grain of the desert environment to produce a landscape that is no longer infertile and uninhabitable, but productive and profitable, continue to struggle against the imaginaries associated with it. They face pressure from a European market that demands miserably low prices for their products, migration policies through which member states defer responsibility and leave humanitarian crises to unfold, and media outlets that criticize their entire industry for permitting poor labor conditions. Their efforts to present counternarratives, to demonstrate that they "are doing it well," are then not a matter of whitewashing an undesirable situation but may be better understood as a step in the modern project of "civilizing" the persistently unruly desert landscape.

Arvid van Dam received his PhD in environmental anthropology and the environmental humanities from the University of Leeds, where he explored the making and unmaking of landscape in the arid southeast of Spain. Critically examining processes of modernization, he argued for a perspective that is attentive to the entanglement of progress and decay. As part of this work, van Dam was a visiting doctoral fellow at the Rachel Carson Center in Munich. After obtaining his doctorate, van Dam has been a postdoctoral fellow at the University of Bonn and currently works as a researcher at KWR Water Research Institute. He holds bachelor's and master's degrees in cultural anthropology from Utrecht University.

Dr. van Dam would like to thank his interlocutors in Spain for making this research possible; Prof. Graham Huggan for his tireless support; and the editors, Dr. Alexandra Coțofană and Dr. Hikmet Kuran, for their support and their efforts in bringing this volume together. This research has received funding from the European Union's Horizon 2020 research and innovation program under the Marie Skłodowska-Curie grant agreement No. 642935.

References

AEMET. 2019. OpenData. Retrieved from http://www.aemet.es/es/servicioscli maticos and https://datosclima.es.

Almería en Verde. 2017. "Un Mar de Razones para Apoyar a los Cultivos de Invernadero." *Almería en Verde* 157.

Anderson, Mark D. 2011. *Disaster Writing: The Cultural Politics of Catastrophe in Latin America*. Charlottesville: University of Virginia Press.

Benson, Michaela. 2010. "Landscape, Imagination and Experience: Processes of Emplacement among the British in Rural France." *The Sociological Review* 58(2): 63–77.

Centellas Soler, Miguel, Alfonso Ruiz García, and Pablo García-Pellicer López. 2009. *Los Pueblos de Colonización en Almería: Arquitectura y Desarrollo para una Nueva Agricultura*. Almería: Colegio Oficial de Arquitectura de Almería; Instituto de Estudios Almerienses.

Constenla, Tereixa, and Ana Torregrosa. 2000. "Vecinos de El Ejido Armados con Barras de Hierro Atacan a los Inmigrantes y Destrozan sus Locales." *El País*, 6 February. Retrieved from https://elpais.com/diario/2000/02/07/es pana/949878022_850215.html.

Davis, Diana K. 2016. *The Arid Lands: History, Power, Knowledge*. Cambridge: MIT Press.

Dolphijn, Rick, and Iris van der Tuin. 2012. *New Materialism: Interviews & Cartographies*. Ann Arbor: Open Humanities Press.

Estrella Digital. 2015. "El Ejido y los Agricultores Claman Contra 'Mar de Plástico.'" *Estrella Digital*, 23 September. Retrieved from https://www.estrella digital.es/articulo/television/ejido-y-agricultores-claman-mar-plastico/ 20150923163823254553.html.

French, Peter A. 1997. *Cowboy Metaphysics: Ethics and Death in Westerns*. Oxford: Rowman & Littlefield.

Gersdorf, Catrin. 2009. *The Poetics and Politics of the Desert: Landscape and the Construction of America*. Amsterdam: Rodopi.

Góngora Belmonte, Andrés. 2015. Carta de COAG a Atresmedia por la Emisión de la Serie "Mar de Plástico." Almería: COAG.

Hortiespaña. 2017a. *Realidad del Cultivo en Invernadero*. Retrieved from https:// actualfruveg.com/2017/07/02/video-mar-razones-favor-la-huerta-almeria/.

———. 2017b. *Un Mar de Razones para Creer en lo que Hacemos*. Retrieved from http://www.hortiespana.eu/index.php/2017/08/09/un-mar-de-razones-para-apoyar-nuestros-cultivos-de-invernadero/.

Hughes, Howard. 2004. *Once Upon a Time in the Italian West: The Filmgoers' Guide to Spaghetti Westerns*. London: I. B. Tauris & Co.
———. 2010. *Spaghetti Westerns*. Harpenden: Kamera Books.
Ingold, Tim. 2011. *Being Alive: Essays on Movement and Description*. London: Routledge.
———. 2020. "Preface." *Social Anthropology* 28(3): 585–87.
Knappett, Carl. 2007. "Materials with Materiality?" *Archaeological Dialogues* 14(1): 20-23.
Lane, Belden C. 1998. *The Solace of Fierce Landscapes: Exploring Desert and Mountain Spirituality*. Oxford: Oxford University Press.
León, Manuel. 2015. "Atresmedia: 'Mar de Plástico es Ficción.'" *La Voz de Almería*, 17 September. Retrieved from https://www.lavozdealmeria.com/noticia/20/economia/90602/atresmedia-mar-de-plastico-es-ficcion.
León, Manuel, and Evaristo Martínez. 2014. "Los Agricultores Observan con Recelo la Serie de Antena-3 'Mar de plástico.'" *La Opinion de Almería*. Retrieved from https://www.laopiniondealmeria.com/2014/09/los-agricultores-ven-con-recelo-la.html.
Marín Martínez, Porfirio. 2016. "La Finca de Huechar: Una Historia Milenaria." *El Eco de Alhama de Almería* 21(36): 84–93.
Martínez Rodríguez, F. Javier. 2018. "El Aprovechamiento de las Aguas Subterráneas en la Modernización de la Agricultura Española del Siglo XX: Cambio Tecnológico e Iniciativa Estatal." PhD dissertation. Almería: Universidad de Almería.
Migelez, Xabier. 2015. "'Mar de Plástico' (29,2 percent) Seduce a Casi 5 Millones de Espectadores en su Estreno en Simulcast." *Formulatv*, 23 September. Retrieved from https://www.formulatv.com/noticias/49503/mar-de-plastico-seduce-casi-5-millones-espectadores-estreno-simulcast/.
Molina Herrera, Jerónimo, ed. 2005. *La Economía de la Provincia de Almería*. Almería: Instituto de Estudios de Cajamar.
Pérez Escolano, Víctor. 2009. "Prólogo." In *Los Pueblos de Colonización en Almería: Arquitectura y Desarrollo para una Nueva Agricultura*, ed. Miguel Centellas Soler, Alfonso Ruiz García, and Pablo García-Pellicer López, 8–11. Almería: Colegio Oficial de Arquitectura de Almería; Instituto de Estudios Almerienses.
Rivera Menéndez, José. 2000. "La Política de Colonización Agraria en el Campo de Dalías (1940–1990)." PhD dissertation. Almería: Historia Instituto de Estudios Almerienses y Cajamar.
Rodríguez, Marta, and Evaristo Martínez. 2015. "División de Opiniones en el Estreno de 'Mar de Plástico.'" *La Voz de Almería*, 23 September. Retrieved from https://www.lavozdealmeria.com/noticia/5/vivir/91066/division-de-opiniones-en-el-estreno-de-mar-de-plastico.
Tompkins, Jane. 1992. *West of Everything: The Inner Life of Westerns*. Oxford: Oxford University Press.
Vargas, Fransisco. 2015. "Y Tú, ¿Qué Vas a Hacer?" *Almería 360*. Retrieved from https://almeria360.com/principal-opinion/opinion/y-tu-que-vas-a-hacer/.

CHAPTER 7

Shinkoku

Reconsidering the Concept of Sentient Landscapes from Japan

David Malitz

Introduction

Japan is often considered an ethnically and culturally homogenous society—by cultural nationalists, tourist guidebooks, and the business literature alike. In reality, Japanese society always was ethnically diverse and multicultural, and many of the Japanese traditions demonstrating the assumed cultural homogeneity must be considered invented traditions (Vlastos 1998: 1). Until the end of World War II, this diversity was embraced to justify the Japanese imperial project (Oguma 2002).

Today, the four main cultural and ethnic minorities in Japanese society are the Indigenous Ainu people of the northern island of Hokkaidō; the Burakumin, who are commonly described as descendants of outcast groups in feudal Japan; the Ryūkyū Islanders from the prefecture of Okinawa; and Korean long-term residents known as *zainichi Kankokujin* 在日韓国人 (CERD 2018; Ohnuki-Tierney 1998: 31–32; Lie 2004: 3). From a contemporary standpoint, these minorities differ considerably in how they diverge from mainstream Japanese society, culturally and legally. What they have in common, however, is that their status as outsiders can be linked to the conception of the Japanese archipelago as the "country of the gods (*shinkoku* 神国)," a sentient landscape in which gods, bodhisattvas, tutelary deities, and ancestral spirits are manifest in specific sites forming the Japanese ethnoscape as the territorial embodiment of Japan.

This term shinkoku is nearly as old as Japanese (written) history itself. Unsurprisingly for such an old term, its meaning was neither static nor did it always imply Japanese superiority. In fact, it implied Japanese inferiority in the Middle Ages. In the nineteenth century, however, it became intimately tied to Japanese imperialism, as the Japanese socialist Kōtoku Shūsui (1871–1911) critically observed already in 1901 (Kōtoku 1901: 17; Tierney 2015: 149). The term also features in the 1937 official summary of the ideology of Japanese "ultranationalism," the *Kokutai no hongi* 国体の本義, translated as *Cardinal Principles of the National Entity* (Monbushō 1937: 64; Gauntlett and Hall 1949: 105). When Prime Minister Mori Yoshirō 森喜朗 (b. 1937, in office 2000–2001) therefore publicly stated in 2000 that Japan was the "country of the gods," a backlash both domestically and internationally was ensured (Watts 2000).

The term sentient landscape was introduced in anthropological scholarship in the context of the study of Indigenous societies in former settler colonies. While there is no shared and widely agreed upon definition of the term, common traits can be identified in the literature (Peterson 2011: 167–68). Sentient landscapes are territories inhabited by Indigenous peoples, whose collective identities are shaped by and dependent on their interaction with those landscapes. They are not thought to be sentient per se, but are considered as such, because the landscapes are understood to be populated by ancestral and other spirits or deities. These divine beings have shaped the community in the past and continue to communicate with community members (Sharp 2002: 58). Therefore, sentient landscapes are necessarily also social spaces shaping the community's identity in the present (Cruikshank 2005: 152). In the literature employing the term, it is usually implied that out of a community's dependency on a territory, not only economically but also culturally, there arises an exclusive right to it. Sentient landscapes are thus to be differentiated from what Henri Lefebvre has called the "abstract spaces" of capitalist modernity, the measurable and exchangeable plots of lands that are treated as commodities (Cruikshank 2005: 259; Lefebvre 1991: 307; Povinelli 1993: 217–18). The necessarily exclusionary nature of a sentient landscape due to a community's dependence on it is not problematized. Rather, the concept is applied only for Indigenous minorities struggling to preserve such landscapes (as well as the sustainable economic activities and cultural identities dependent on them) against the onslaught of an exploitive neoliberalism often linked to an Anglo-Saxon and Protestant majority culture—an assessment in line with the United Nations Declaration on the Rights of Indigenous Peoples (United Nations 2007).

Yet sentient landscapes are at the same time strikingly similar to what the scholar of nationalism Anthony D. Smith has labeled "ethnoscapes." These are sacred national homelands, and constitutive elements of nations, created through the territorialization of collective memories of historical events and persons, through which the nation's "geobody" and people merge. As is the case with the sentient landscapes, the nation's identity and the ethnoscape are mutually dependent on and definitional of each other. Ethnoscapes differ from sentient landscapes in the former's clearly defined boundaries, and because the mosaics of ethnoscapes' *lieux de mémoire* are the product of conscious historical projects. Yet most importantly for his volume, they differ because sentient landscapes remain "enchanted gardens," in which ancestral and other spirits or gods are really existing, while the national homeland is sacred but not considered sentient (Smith 2009: 49–51, 72, 77–78, 94–95; Nora 1989: 8; see also Wehler 2007: 40).

Japanese nationalism and its conception of the archipelago as the country of the gods—*shinkoku* 神国—offers a case study to interrogate these concepts and especially their exclusionary nature. Contemporary Japan is not just an ethnoscape of sites of national significance but simultaneously a sentient landscape, where national, local tutelary, and other deities remain accessible in a myriad of shrines.

This chapter will first provide an overview of the genealogy of shinkoku as a concept limiting claims to political legitimacy. Defining the Japanese islands as a sentient landscape also always meant creating a social hierarchy between those closest to divine authority and thus to political legitimacy, and those farther removed and excluded from the exercise of legitimate power. With the introduction of the novel ideas of nationalism and scientific racism to Japan from the late nineteenth century onward, the Japanese islands additionally became an ethnoscape to which the Japanese nation as a whole had a unique relationship. Whether specific sites are considered to be really inhabited by gods or spirits or are simply sites of national memory depends, of course, on individual belief.

The second part of the chapter delineates how various forms of exclusion in postwar Japan experienced by the Burakumin, the Ainu of Hokkaidō, and the Ryūkyū Islanders have their roots in shinkoku thought. Due to a lack of space, the Korean residents of Japan (*zainichi Kankokujin*) are not covered here. As immigrants or descendants thereof, the denial of their ties to the country of the gods as literal outsiders is also the most straightforward one.

A Short History of the Country of the Gods

The term shinkoku, the "country of the gods," is nearly as old as Japanese history itself. It describes Japan not only as created by the gods, but also as a territory in which gods as well as ancestral and tutelary deities are manifest, interacting with its inhabitants. Shinkoku appears first in the *Chronicles of Japan* (*Nihon Shoki* 日本書紀), composed in 720. The text describes an invasion of the Korean peninsula by the mythical Empress Jingū. The King of Shilla is overawed by the disembarking force of her "divine soldiers (*shinpei* 神兵)" crossing over from the country of the gods, ruled by just and wise kings (*seiō* 聖王), who carry the titles of "heavenly sovereigns" or *tennō* 天皇 (Kuroita 1962a: 118; Aston 1896a: 230). Shinkoku was thus already in this very first known instance a political concept linking the notion of Japan as the country of the gods—a country with an identity distinct from Korea, and by extension China—to the legitimacy of the royal court of the Yamato clan (Itō 2003: 80). The Yamato had established their hegemony over other clan groups by the end of the sixth century and ruled over Western Honshu and Northern Kyushu from their base in present-day Nara prefecture. To create legitimacy for their suzerainty, they systemized the ancestral myths of the various clans around their own ancestral deity, the sun goddess Amaterasu-Ōmikami, and crafted a common ritual system (Mori 2003: 14–26). In the *Nihon Shoki*, these myths were written down, creating a history linking creation to the establishment and expansion of Yamato rule. In this sentient realm, ancestral and local tutelary deities were ever present, shaping the lives of the people and providing legitimacy to the continuing authority of local clans.

When Buddhism was introduced from the Korean peninsula, the bodhisattvas appear to have been first understood as foreign deities intruding into this sentient landscape. To avoid angering the local deities, the veneration of the newcomers was initially limited to members of a powerful immigrant clan of the nobility (Kuroita 1962b: 48; Aston 1896b: 65–68). Being associated with the civilizations of the powerful states of China and the Korean peninsula, however, the court began to embrace Buddhism and to use it to legitimize the centralization of its power. The expansion of seventh-century Yamato power was thus contemporaneous with the establishment and spread of Buddhist practices and beliefs throughout the country (Como 2008: 15).

In the second half of the seventh century, a centralized bureaucratic polity based on Chinese models was built. An important difference from the Chinese blueprint was the inclusion of a so-called "Ministry of Kami (gods, divine beings) Affairs" or *Jingikan*, which ritually ordered the sentient landscape of the realm's deities through a network of officially recognized and centrally administered shrines, complemented by a similar network of temples. (Mori 2003: 29, 38, 44, 50). Territorial expansion occurred through the conquest of lands in northern Japan from the people referred to as *Ezo* or *Emishi* 蝦夷. There territories were also understood as sentient landscapes. And so, integrating the new territories into the realm meant not only defeating the Ezo but also pacifying through the establishment of shrines the tutelary deities that might otherwise take revenge for the clearing of forests (Breen and Teeuwen 2010: 25). In this process of territorial and ritual expansion, the sentient landscape of the country of the gods was thus understood to be congruent with the realm of the imperial court in Kyoto.

Shinkoku: From Marker of Inferiority to Proof of Superiority

The coexistence of the two religious frameworks and the simultaneous use of them by the court appears to have caused the search for an overarching framework accommodating both Indigenous gods and foreign bodhisattvas. This was found in the original Japanese paradigm of "original forms of deities and their local traces (*honji suijaku* 本地垂迹)," which first took shape in the eighth century. It interpreted Japanese deities as local incarnations of the bodhisattvas and thus subordinated the former to the latter (Teeuwen and Rambelli 2003). By the turn of the second millennium, the court's ability to maintain a centralized administration throughout the realm had broken down and a feudal polity began to take shape. This extended to the ritual sphere, where shrines and temples were increasingly independent from imperial control. In 1185 the first government by a military noble (samurai) was established in Kamakura. Territorial expansion had led to the amassing of estates effectively outside the court's control by local nobles and temples shifting power from the capital. With the disintegration of the bureaucratic institutions, order broke down. For contemporaries, the age of *mappō* (末法), the period of the degeneration of the Buddhist teachings, had arrived (Mori 2003: 64–65, 79). At this time, long after the Buddha had acquired nirvana, and in this country far from India, the bodhisattvas could only reach and save the people by showing themselves in the form of local gods (Bialock 2007: 208). Japan at the time was thus the "country of the gods" precisely because of its inferiority.

This interpretation was reversed following the failed invasions of the Mongols. While they had overrun China and Korea, their invasion fleets were destroyed by typhoons that became to be known as "divine winds (*kamikaze* 神風)" of the gods of the Japanese islands (Mori 2003: 81). The deities manifest in the archipelago, making it a sentient landscape, had defended the country of the gods from foreign invaders.

Yet the defense preparations caused an economic and political crisis that led to the fall of the government in Kamakura in 1333. Competing imperial courts, a northern one in Kyoto and a southern one in the town of Yoshino, emerged and would compete for dominance until 1392. To support the claim of the Southern court, the aristocrat Kitabatake Chikafusa 北畠 親房 (1293–1354) around 1340 wrote the *Jinnō Shōtōki* 神皇正統記 (*Chronicles of Gods and Sovereigns*). Drawing on the *Nihon Shoki*, its famous opening lines explicitly call Japan the "country of the gods" because its dynasty had descended from the sun goddess, making Japan not just unique but superior to all other countries (Kitabatake 1914: 1; Varley 1980: 49). In the end, however, the Northern court, supported and controlled by the shoguns of the Ashikaga clan, won and cemented the political dominance of the warrior (samurai) class.

This was reflected in the 1480 political memorandum *Shōdanchiyō* 樵談治要 (Principles of ruling the realm according to a humble woodcutter), written by the courtier Ichijō Kaneyoshi 一条 兼良 (1402–1481) for the shogun Ashikaga Yoshihisa 足利 義尚 (1465–1489). The text stated that all people in the "country of the gods," high and low born, were descendants of the gods, thereby extending the divine legitimacy to the warrior ruling class (Ichijō 1480). By this time, however, a succession struggle following the death of a shogun in 1467 had already turned into a full-blown civil war. It caused the imperial court to lose control over the remaining hierarchy of shrines, and the court also lost access to its estates in the provinces, severely diminishing its income. This created opportunities for religious innovators. The most successful and brazen of them was Yoshida Kanetomo 吉田 兼倶 (1435–1511), a shrine priest from a family of court officials.

By cultivating ties with the imperial court and the shogun in the capital as well as with local shrines' priests in the provinces, Yoshida was able to secure his access to both funds and religious authority. In 1473 the emperor declared Yoshida's shrine the most important one in the country of the gods and, in 1489, even accepted the claim that the gods of the Ise Shrine, intimately linked to the imperial dynasty, had migrated there. More importantly, Yoshida invented a new doctrinal system partly based on texts made up by himself. Its main text explicitly addressed the idea of the country of the gods as defined by the divine descent of the emperor from the sun goddess. Yoshida reversed the former hierarchy and argued that the Japanese gods had come first and Buddhism as well as Chinese philosophy were secondary to them (Hardacre 2017: 208–22). This worldview made Japan superior over all other countries due to its direct relationship with the gods and thus the sentient nature of its landscape.

His descendants continued to cultivate relationships with feudal lords. This might have included the warlord Toyotomi Hideyoshi 豊臣秀吉 (1537–1598), who came close to uniting the Japanese archipelago through conquest in the late sixteenth century (Hardacre 2017: 230; Kang 1997: 90, 96, 101). Yoshida's thought might have been particularly attractive for Toyotomi, as he had been born a peasant and lacked both the descent from an emperor that shoguns had shared so far and a high education focused on the Chinese classics and Buddhism. But Hideyoshi also used Yoshida's interpretation of Japan as a divine and therefore superior country to legitimize a new and aggressive foreign policy. In 1591, after he had conquered the southern island of Kyushu, whose warlords had entertained close relations with Portugal and Spain, Hideyoshi outlawed Christianity, explicitly referring to Japan as the "country of the gods" in a letter to the governor-general of Portuguese India announcing his ban (Saitō 2006: 205).

A year later, Toyotomi launched an invasion of Korea with the aim to conquer China and have the Japanese emperor rule over all three countries. A visit to the shrine of Empress Jingū prior to the troops' embarkment likened this endeavor to the history in the *Nihon Shoki*. The Japanese forces were able to subdue Korea but soon found themselves bogged down on the peninsula once Ming China intervened on behalf of its vassal. After Toyotomi's death, a council of elder vassals was supposed to administer Japan until the maturity of his heir. The most powerful member, Tokugawa Ieyasu 徳川家康 (1543–1616), was however quickly able to make himself the ruler, unify the country, and make peace with Korea.

Claiming the Sentient Landscape of the Gods for All "Japanese" through Early Modern Scholarship

The political system that Tokugawa Ieyasu and his heirs established proved to be remarkably successful. It lasted until the mid-nineteenth century, when Japan was opened to trade by the colonial powers. Its legitimacy rested on an amalgamation of ideas from various traditions, among them a deification of the founder after his death, which associated Ieyasu with a bodhisattva but also with the sun goddess. Like his predecessor, he employed the discourse of the divinity of Japan to justify outlawing Christianity (Saitō 2006: 206).

To maintain the new political order, feudal lords were required to attend court every other year in the shogun's capital. When they were in their own domains, they had to leave their wives and children as hostages in the capital. This necessitated the construction and maintenance of a road network traversing the whole country, which would impress nineteenth-century European visitors. More importantly, however, peace, mandatory traveling, and infrastructure boosted economic growth, especially in the towns along roads. And so, during the period of the "great peace," as the Tokugawa period would come to be known, a protocapitalist economy emerged. While theoretically they occupied lower rungs in the social hierarchy than the samurai and peasants, town-dwelling merchants and craftsmen benefited most from this. And this state of affairs would then be reflected in the religious landscape. New doctrines and practices found adherents promising them their own agency and thus challenging the established institutions and lineages. With prosperity and safe roads, commoners began to travel to important shrines and temples. The print industry in the large towns churned out manuals for the travelers explaining "foreign" manners to them but also providing information about the landscapes and sacred sites in them.

In texts such as the *Jingikun* written by Kaibara Ekiken 貝原 益軒 (1630–1714), sites of local significance were linked to the myths of the imperial court and the archipelago. This simultaneously made such sites accessible to ordinary people and confirmed that Japan was indeed a sentient landscape in which various deities were present, thereby truly making the islands the "country of the gods" (Ethington and Toyosawa 2015: 76–87). One particularly important sentient site was Mount Fuji, which had long been recognized as sacred. Jikigyō Miroku 食行身禄 (1671–1733). The sixth leader of the confraternities of the Fuji cult introduced the notion that the mountain replaced Mount Sumeru, the axis mundi in the Buddhist cosmography, precisely because it was located in the "country of the gods" (Earhart 2011: 118–19).

In the seventeenth century a scholarly tradition also emerged that applied philological methods to analyze the most ancient Japanese texts to derive an understanding of the pure Japanese "heart," or authentic nature, as it was assumed to have existed before any Chinese influence. *Kokugaku* 国学, as it later became known to differentiate this line of inquiry from the study of Chinese sources, naturally came to the conclusion that Japan was the country of the gods and superior over China and India. The unbroken line of emperors descending from the sun goddess was an essential element in this conception of Japan (Antoni 1998: 133). At the same time, Confucian scholars in Japan grappled with the problem that the concept of China as the Middle Kingdom rendered Japan inferior. But with the fall of the Ming dynasty to the Manchus and the establishment of the new Qing dynasty by this "barbarian" people, Japanese Confucianists increasingly embraced the notion that Japan had become the true middle kingdom, replacing China (Wakabayashi 1999: 29).

While *kokugaku* scholars tended to be hostile toward everything Chinese, the two lines of thought could be reconciled easily enough in what has since been named *Mito-gaku* 水戸学 after the name of the feudal domain where it emerged. Japan could be imagined as both: it was the "middle kingdom" precisely because it had a virtuous court with an unbroken line of emperors descending directly from the sun goddess, which simultaneously made it the "country of the gods" (Wakabayashi 1999: 29, 56–57). This was made explicit in *Mito-gaku's* most famous text. The "New Theses

(*Shinron* 新論)" were written by the samurai scholar Aizawa Seishisai 会沢 正志斎 (1782–1863) in 1825 (Wakabayashi 1999). Due to its influence on the movement that would later succeed in overthrowing the Tokugawa in the Meiji Restoration, it has been labeled the restoration movement's "bible" (e.g., Shimazono 2010: 113).

Likewise, in the early nineteenth century the scholar Hirata Atsutane 平田 篤胤 (1776–1843) broke with the philological approach of his *kokugaku* peers, who concentrated on literary sources. For him the true Japanese identity remained accessible in the lives of the peasantry; unsurprisingly, rural elites were the most important segment of paying students in his academy. Indeed, for Hirata, all Japanese, including commoners, were descended from the gods and therefore superior to other people (McNally 2005: 4, 9, 13, 186–87, 197, 199, 206, 210, 212). Hirata developed his own theology, in which all ancestors were lifted to the status of emperors as "manifest deities" (*arahitogami* 現人神). The daily prayers introduced by Hirata to his disciples imagined the Japanese islands as overlapping and hierarchically ordered sentient landscapes. Practitioners would start their day by praying to the deities of the whole realm before "working their way down" through the deities of their provinces and local communities to those of their household and their ancestors (Hardacre 2017: 337–38). To be Japanese for Hirata meant to consciously live in a sentient landscape. Explicitly excluded from this imagined community were the outcastes due to their perceived ritual impurity (Maeda 2014: 44).

The Sentient Landscape of the Gods as the Basis of Japanese Modernity

By the mid-nineteenth century, the theoretical engagements with the identity of Japan as a country of the gods in which the deities were manifest had sparked a movement demanding a return to imperial rule. At this time, Japan suffered from a protracted economic crisis as the feudal and agrarian economy had reached its limit of growth while the population kept growing. At the same time, Western ships came close to Japanese shores with increasing frequency, challenging the strict controls of foreign trade and travel introduced by the early Tokugawa rulers. In 1854 the shogun was finally forced to open the country. This, however, only served to worsen the economic crisis while also demonstrating the weakness of the shogun's government. Under siege domestically and pressured by the colonial powers, the shogun visited the emperor in Kyoto to gain his support. This endeavor was not only unsuccessful but also demonstrated the shogun's acceptance of the higher status of the emperor, further emboldening his opponents. In early January 1868, forces from the two powerful

Western domains of Satsuma 薩摩 and Chōshū 長州 occupied the imperial palace and had the sixteen-year-old Emperor Meiji (1852–1912) declare the restoration of imperial rule (the Meiji Restoration).

The following decades saw a protracted and often violent struggle over the future of the Japanese archipelago between factions ranging from traditionalists, who aspired to return to a utopian age of the gods, to modernizers striving to adopt Western "civilization" wholesale. In the end, the Meiji system codified in the Constitution of the Empire of Japan (1898) and the Imperial Rescript on Education (1890) combined the institutional framework and constitutional mechanisms of nineteenth-century Europe with an ideology essentially derived from *Mito-gaku*. The conception of the Japanese archipelago as a sentient landscape of the gods served as the ideological foundation for the modern Empire of Japan.

The constitution of imperial Japan was comparable to those of contemporary European nations, if not more liberal. It granted the freedom of religion as long as the exercise of one's faith did not violate one's duties as an imperial subject (Josephson 2012: 138, 226–32). At the same time, the participation in the cult of the imperial dynasty as well as the paying of respect to historical loyalists and fallen soldiers at national shrines was defined as nonreligious and a patriotic duty for all Japanese. At school, the myths were taught as history and the constitutional mechanisms that removed the emperor from close to all decision making remained largely unexplored. Apart from a small minority, who received a higher education or had the opportunity to study abroad, the majority of Japanese were taught that Japan was indeed the country of the gods, ruled directly by a direct descendent of the sun goddess (Kuno and Tsurumi 2015: 132).

The late nineteenth century had seen the introduction of modern scientific disciplines to Japan, including folklore studies, archaeology, and physical anthropology/scientific racism. The ethnic nation of the Japanese, whose origin was now explored with the new techniques and concepts introduced, was named the Yamato people (*yamato minzoku*), after the country's archaic name in the *Nihon Shoki*. This differentiation between "true" Japanese and other imperial subjects such as Chinese, Koreans, or the Indigenous Ainu of Hokkaidō, but not the people of the Ryūkyū Islands, was made explicit in the textbooks employed in the empire's schools (e.g., Monbushō 1935: 5–6, 143–44).

A Really Existing Country of the Gods

By the early twentieth century, the political, economic, and social modernization through the selective adoption of Western institutions and practices had turned Japan into an industrial power at the center of a colonial empire. Yet the archipelago remained a sentient landscape shaped by gods, ranging from imperial ancestors to one's own as well as to local tutelary deities. In this regard, the myths of state ideology, official national history, and anthropological research into the "racial" origins of the Japanese mutually confirmed each other.

But while Japan had become the only non-Western country recognized as an equal by the European and North American colonial empires at the end of the nineteenth century, it became increasingly isolated after World War I. In East Asia, the empire became the main competitor to the British, resulting in 1923 in the end of the Anglo-Japanese alliance agreed upon in 1902.

Anglo-Saxon countries banned immigration of Japanese with legislation based on racist arguments, while domestically, Japan suffered from Great Depression. In the countryside, villages depended on additional income derived from raising silkworms, the silk of which would be exported. Radical nationalism gained ground at this time, especially among young officers who had experienced poverty in the countryside and had been indoctrinated at preparatory schools and military academies. Conspiracies were formed to overthrow the government and usher in direct imperial rule by Emperor Hirohito (1901–1989). Significantly, the members of a clandestine group behind a failed coup in 1933 called themselves the *shinpeitai*, or "band of divine soldiers," explicitly using the term from the *Nihon Shoki* that also appears in Aizawa's *New Theses*. Attempted coups and the assassination of civilian politicians and industrialists failed to open the doors to utopia. Rather, the killing of a Chinese warlord in Manchuria and the subsequent invasion thereof led to the Japanese exit from the League of Nations, increased international isolation, and finally to full-blown war in China and Japan's entry into World War II. At the same time, the murder of politicians allowed militarists in the armed forces and the bureaucracy to take the helm and steer the country toward war with the willing support of the industrial conglomerates.

Against this backdrop, what political scientist Maruyama Masao has called ultranationalism and what Walter Skya referred to as Shinto fundamentalism not only took firm hold in Japanese society but was actively propagated by the state (Skya 2009: 354). As an official summary of the state ideology, the ministry of education published in 1937 a booklet titled *Kokutai no hongi* (国体の本義), translated after the war as the *Cardinal Principles of the National Entity* (Gauntlett and Hall 1949). One of its authors was the scholar Yamada Yoshio 山田孝雄 (1873–1958), a self-taught man who had ascended through the ranks of the education system to become the president of the Kogakkan University, an institute for the education of Shinto Priests, in 1940. Skya refers to a magazine essay published by

Yamada in 1943 as exemplary of the author's political ideas and of wartime ideology in general. Yamada understood the Japanese creation myth literally. Japan was the country of the gods because the Japanese emperors and the Japanese people had indeed descended from the gods, who had created the world. "Being a divine country," he wrote, "is not just a metaphor, or a figure of speech, but a fact and a reality in our country." On this fundamental belief, then, rested the conviction that Japan was destined to unite the "eight corners of the word," as a wartime slogan derived from the *Nihon Shoki* went, under benevolent imperial rule (Skya 2009: 301–10).

Under the benevolent emperor, the various ethnicities of the empire were hierarchally ordered, with the Yamato people, the true people of the country of the gods, on top and other ethnicities and minorities subject to different degrees of discrimination and exploitation. For them, only in death was equality and full acceptance into the sentient landscape of the gods achievable. From 1869 onward, fallen soldiers were enshrined in the newly founded Yasukuni Shrine in Tokyo to be worshiped as tutelary deities of the nation and therefore to became part of its sentient landscape (Harootunian 1999: 145, 150–53).

Nihonjinron: The Sentient Landscape of the Gods as a Cultural Heritage

The policies of the American occupation of Japan after the empire's surrender in August 1945 were outlined in the *United States Initial Post-Surrender Policy* for Japan, issued on 6 September 1945 (State-War-Navy Coordinating Committee 1945). To democratize the country, the document made clear that religion was not to be used for nationalist and militarist purposes. Accordingly, the so-called *Shinto Directive*, issued by the Supreme Command of the Allied Powers in Japan on 15 December 1945, separated Shinto from the government, abolished institutions that had supported the imperial cult, and banned religious instruction in state schools. Private institutions remained free to teach, however, as long as their doctrines were not considered "militaristic or ultranationalistic." The *Kokutai no hongi* was officially outlawed as was "the doctrine that the islands of Japan are superior to other lands because of divine or special origin" (GHQ of the Allied Powers 1960). The American written constitution then enshrined a strict separation of state and religion in Article 20. While rewriting the constitution has been a declared goal of Japanese conservatives ever since, they so far have not been able to mobilize a large enough share of the electorate to amend it, proving popular support for the document.

Defeat in World War II and outlawing of the wartime ideology made a reconceptualization of Japanese national identity necessary. This led to the emergence of *nihonjinron*, a literary genre exploring the uniqueness of the Japanese, but now understood culturally rather than religiously or racially (Morris-Suzuki 1998: 204). Ironically, the war-time study of Japanese culture by Ruth Benedict, *The Chrysanthemum and the Sword* made available to the public in 1946, is widely understood today as having been the "ur-text" of the nihonjinron literature (Lie 2001: 249).

Shinto is here understood as the authentic and original religion of Japan, an essential element of Japanese culture that distinguishes the country from other countries in Asia. This religious tradition links the nation or people of Japan through the mediation of the emperor to the state and its institutions. Nihonjinron does not consider the Japanese as superior per se, nor does the literature assume a really existing sentient landscape of the country of the gods. Rather, the practices and beliefs related to the shinkoku concept are thought to make Japan culturally unique. This is linked to the belief in an essential cultural homogeneity of the Japanese, which remains widespread. The exclusionary nature of this conception of the Japanese nation is evident from the results of the 2019 World Values Survey. Only 0.2 percent of Japanese participants answered that they would trust individuals of another nationality completely, and 29.1 percent did not want to have foreign workers as their neighbors (World Values Survey 2019: Q21, 63).

Present in the Sentient Landscape of the Gods, Yet Excluded from the National Community: Discrimination against Minorities Based on Shinkoku Thought

Every construction of a nation as culturally and ethnically homogenous rests on the identification of a boundary marking outsiders to the national community. As mentioned in the introduction, in post-World War II Japan there are four main groups of outsiders within the nation's borders: the Ainu, the Burakumin, the Ryūkyū Islanders, and immigrants from Okinawa or Korea as well as their descendants. (CERD 2018; Lie 2004: 3; Ohnuki-Tierney 1998: 31–32). What these diverse groups have in common is that they were originally not considered to be people of the country of the gods and thus were not considered to belong in its sentient landscape. The nature and degree of their discrimination has changed, of course, from imperial Japan to the postwar period to the present. Their common exclusion from the national community was—and partly remains—spatially visible through their concentration in segregated neighborhoods and their occupying the lowest tier in the urban labor market. It must be stressed, however, that much has been achieved in the last three decades to overcome these discriminations and their economic consequences for the minorities.

Burakumin 部落民, *the Outcast "Hamlet People"*

After the resignation over a fundraising scandal of Prime Minister Mori Yoshirō (b. 1937), who as mentioned above had made international headlines with his description of Japan as the "country of the gods," a leadership contest among high-ranking members of the Liberal Democratic Party of Japan took shape. Chief Cabinet Secretary Nonaka Hiromu 野中廣務 (1925–2018) was a top contender until, according to credible rumors, Minister of Economic and Fiscal Policy Asō Tarō 麻生太郎 (b. 1940) remarked, "We are not going to let someone from the *buraku* become the prime minister of Japan, are we?" It took no more than this reference to Nonaka's membership in the minority group of the Burakumin to reduce his chances of being elected enough for him to drop out (Yamaguchi 2009).

The Burakumin, or "hamlet people," are a disadvantaged minority of about 1.2 million people living in approximately 4,600 communities or *buraku* 部落 (hamlets) throughout Japan. This group arose in imperial Japan through the merging of former members of outcast groups in the feudal order with a newly emerging lumpenproletariat, and through the appearance of segregated settlements for them. The former outcasts were a heterogenous group, but they shared two characteristics. First, they engaged in nonagricultural work. Second, the nature of their occupations made them impure or defiled based on pre-Buddhist as well as Buddhist ideas, as they were engaged with the killing and disposal of animals and humans. The words used to name the two best known groups, commonly referred to when discussing the Burakumin, make this clear. These are *eta* 穢多 (abundant filth/pollution) and *hinin* 非人 (nonhumans). Members of these groups were, for example, leatherworkers, butchers, or executioners (Kobayakawa 2021: 112–14; Ohnuki-Tierney 1998: 34–43). But Eiko Ikegami has also related the emergence of the outcast groups to the rise of the samurai to power. Previously, the court nobility had considered the warriors to be similar to these outcast groups due to their violent occupation and hunting culture. The rise of the former to the apex of power necessitated a more rigid segregation of the latter (Bialock 2007: 54; Ikegami 1995: 57 – 60, 113 – 116). Their segregation become most rigid in the Tokugawa period, when social mobility in general was considered a danger to the feudal order.

Their existence in Japan was a conceptual problem for Japanese scholars in the Tokugawa period, who were convinced of a pure Japanese identity linked to their divine homeland. They therefore came to the conclusion that the Burakumin were not just "lowly people" but not even people of the country of the gods. They were from a "different stock," possibly descending from the "barbarous" Ezo (Ooms 1996: 300–5). This discursive exclusion from the sentient landscape of Japan was made visible in the practice of omitting their villages in maps and leaving out the sections of a road passing through their settlements when calculating the distance between places (Ooms 1996: 287).

Following the Meiji Restoration and the introduction of a new system of family registration, the feudal status system was abolished in 1871. Outcast groups became commoners but were administratively kept separate as "new commoners" (*shin heimin*). This and their living in separate settlements opened a door for continued discrimination that lasted throughout the postwar period. As the Burakumin lost their monopolies on their traditional occupations, most of them remained impoverished (Kobayakawa 2021: 113–14). Embracing scientific racism, Japanese anthropologists also translated *kokugaku* beliefs about the origins of the former outcasts into the new era by advancing that they were "racially" different from—and morally inferior to—the Yamato people (Taïeb 2019).

In 1922 the Levelers Association of Japan (*Suiheisha* 水平社) was founded as a self-emancipatory movement to fight discrimination against the Burakumin. It remained unsuccessful until its dissolution during World War II. After the war, the "new commoner" designation was dropped for Burakumin, but their discrimination based on family records and neighborhoods continued. Against the backdrop of the Cold War, however, the Buraku Liberation League (*Buraku Kaihō Dōmei* 部落解放同盟), with the support of left-wing parties, was able to pressure the government to decide more comprehensive measures. Fearing a radicalization, the government enacted the Special Measures Law for Assimilation Projects in 1969 (Law No. 60 of 10 July 1969). It provided the legal basis for large-scale investments into buraku districts to lift standards of living and increase educational achievements, thereby assimilating them into mainstream society. In the same year, family registration records were made inaccessible to outsiders, making the background checks allowing for discrimination illegal (Neary 2003: 270–71; Hah and Lapp 1978: 494–99). The Assimilation Projects were discontinued in 2002 after USD 136 billion had been spent and economic and educational gaps significantly narrowed. Yet Burakumin still show lower educational achievements and economic disadvantages in the present (Tsumaki 2012; Uchida 2008; Alabaster 2009; Lie 2001: 85–89).

Additionally, the twenty-first century saw the rise of hate speech, especially online, targeting Burakumin as well as other communities. Recorded instances of such dehumanizing hate speech have explicitly used the term *eta* and referenced the animals commonly considered dirty, showing a continuity with the prejudices of the feudal past (Yamamoto 2021: 107–9). In 2016 the government acknowledged this ongoing discrimination and discursive exclusion by enacting the Law on the Promotion of the Elimination of Discrimination against Buraku (Law No. 199 of 16 December 2016). A recent survey by the Ministry of Justice shows that while discrimination and hate speech are still not uncommon, identifiable perpetrators are now nearly exclusively over fifty years of age (Hōmushō jinken yōgo-kyoku 2020: 9, 10–11, 13, 14, 16, 19, 21).

Japan's Indigenous People, the Ainu

On 13 January 2020, Deputy Prime Minister of Japan and Minister of Finance Asō Tarō remarked in Fukuoka that there was no other country which, over a two-thousand-year history, had had only one ethnicity and one dynasty. Japan was therefore a splendid country (Kakihana and Tōyama 2020; Kakihana 2020). Commentators were quick to point out that this statement contradicted the official policy of his own government. Only in April 2019, it had enacted the Law on the Implementation of the Policies to Realize a Society Where the Pride of Ainu People are Respected (Law No. 16 of 19 April 2019), which for the first time recognized the approximately two hundred thousand Ainu, mainly living on the northern island of Hokkaidō, as an Indigenous people with their own distinct culture (Tsutsui 2017: 1061).

In premodern Japan, the Ainu were referred to as Emishi or Ezo and Hokkaidō as the land of the Ezo *(Ezo-chi* 蝦夷地*)*. The Ainu were thus linked to the "barbarians" in eastern or northern Japan mentioned in the historical chronicles, whose lands were conquered by the imperial court. With shinkoku in the medieval period not being a clearly bounded geobody but the realm of the emperor, the expansion of the country of the gods was only possible through conquest and the subsequent exclusion of these people and the simultaneous integration of the tutelary deities into the sentient landscape of the realm. This point was made implicitly in Aizawa's *New Theses* (Wakabayashi 1999: 173–74). Until the early seventeenth century, still little was known about the geography of Hokkaidō and a connection to the Eurasian continent was considered possible (Walker 2001: 31–33). Here, it is noteworthy that in the medieval period the use of the term Ezo overlapped with a word used for a type of outcast group. Cultural practices provided the linkage as the Ezo were known first of all as hunters (Bialock 2007: 53). Some scholars imagined an Ezo genealogy for the Burakumin as mentioned above (Ooms 1996: 305).

In the Tokugawa period, the feudal lords of Matsumae residing in Southern Hokkaidō were given a trading monopoly used to economically exploit the Ainu. This necessitated making it possible to differentiate between Japanese and these "barbarians." The Ainu were therefore explicitly banned from adopting Japanese customs such as speaking Japanese or dressing like Japanese. This policy was reversed in the early nineteenth century, when Russian ships began exploring Hokkaidō. This assimilation policy failed, however, due to a lack of funds (Howell 2004: 327, 330).

In 1869, the year after the Meiji Restoration, *Ezo-chi* was annexed as Hokkaidō. The island was to be actively developed through the Hokkaidō Development Commission, a government agency, to prevent a Russian intrusion on Japan's northern frontier. The new territory was merged ritually into the sentient landscape of imperial Japan through the construction of new shrines, including ones for pioneers, who became tutelary deities for the region (Hardacre 2017: 392–95). In 1899, the Imperial Diet in Tokyo enacted the Former Natives Protection Act, which provided the Ainu with Japanese citizenship and aimed to assimilate the Ainu to majority Japanese culture, turning them into farmers. They were, however, not considered to be members of the Yamato people but of their own inferior "race." As land was handed out to immigrants from the other islands, and Hokkaidō's natural resources were exploited by companies from these islands, the Ainu became impoverished and were reduced legally to being wards of the state (Siddle 2005: 70–75).

Only after World War II, in 1946, was the Hokkaidō Ainu Association, a mutual assistance group, founded by members of the Indigenous minority. Significantly, in 1961, the group dropped their people's name due to its derogatory associations in Japanese society (Tsutsui 2017: 1060–61). In postwar Japan, the Ainu found themselves in a paradoxical situation. They were at the same time discriminated against for having no (or only part) Japanese "blood," and they were officially considered nonexistent as the Japanese nation was said to be ethnically homogenous after the loss of the colonial empire (Siddle 2005: 156–57). A sense of Indigenous pride emerged only in the 1970s following collaborations with Indigenous people in other parts of the world leading to a campaign against the negative portrayal of Ainu in official textbooks and for a new Ainu law (Tsutsui 2017: 1063–67). In 1997, the government responded with the Act on the Promotion of Ainu Culture and Dissemination and Enlightenment of Knowledge about Ainu Tradition (Law No. 52 of 14 May 1997), which nevertheless failed to recognize the Ainu as an Indigenous people. Following the adoption of the UN Declaration on the Rights of Indigenous Peoples in 2007 and questions regarding the status of the Ainu in Japan's Universal Periodic Review at the UN Human Rights Council the following year, pressure was finally successful. In June 2008, the Japanese Diet recognized the Ainu as an Indigenous people of Japan, leading to the law of 2019 referred to above (Tsutsui 2017: 1068–69; Lewallen 2016: 27).

The Ainu's embrace of an identity distinct from mainstream Japanese society and its recognition by the Japanese state is mirrored in the closing of the economic gap between the two demographics, which nonetheless remains significant. While at the turn of the millennium Ainu in Hokkaidō were twice as likely to receive social welfare, in 2017 this was down to a mere 10 percent difference. During the same time period, the percentage of Ainu entering senior high school approximately doubled from 16.1 percent to 33.3 percent. This remains, however, significantly lower than the average percentage for their communities which is 45.8 percent (Hokkaidō Kankyō Seikatsubu 2017: 5, 7).

From Foreigners to True Japanese: The Ryūkyū Islanders

The Ryūkyū Islands are an island chain stretching roughly from the south of Kyūshū to the north of Taiwan. Okinawa is the largest of these islands. In the early fifteenth century, the islands were united as the Ryūkyū Kingdom, a tributary to Ming China. In 1609, Okinawa was invaded by the feudal domain of Satsuma in Southern Kyūshū, who forced its king to be a vasal to both the lord of Satsuma and the shogun in Edo. Throughout the Tokugawa period, the Ryūkyū Islands continued to be regarded as a foreign country and therefore not as a part of Japan conceived of as the country of the gods (Toby 1984: 45–52).

After the Meiji Restoration of 1868, the future status of the islands within the Japanese Empire was unsettled, with leading members of the political oligarchy considering their inhabitants to be not Japanese. Due to the island chain's strategic location, however, a policy of political integration was adopted. And so, political leaders, anthropologists, and historians alike discovered the Ryūkyū Islanders to be "racially" Japanese (Oguma 2014: 19–35). Nevertheless, the people of the islands were not considered to be equals of the inhabitants of Japan's main islands after the integration of the kingdom as a prefecture in 1879. They were considered backward relative to the Japanese of the main islands, and an assimilation policy was enforced that was aimed at eradicating the island's distinct culture. Due to this backwardness, conscription was introduced only in 1898 and the limited suffrage was extended to the prefecture of Okinawa only in 1912. A colonial plantation economy was introduced that extracted wealth from the Ryūkyū Islands, while those migrating to the main islands, to Japanese colonies, or even to foreign lands suffered from discrimination (Matsuda 2018: 32–39; Oguma 2014: 47, 58; Lie 2004: 98–99).

This marginalized position of the islands and of their population was made most evident in the closing days of World War II, when the military chose Okinawa as the main battle site to resist the American advance. The 150,000 civilians who were killed in the fighting, committed suicide, or were massacred by both militaries amounted to a third of Okinawa's population. The islands were sacrificed once again in 1947, when Emperor Hirohito, for the sake of peace in the Far East, advised the US government to continue its occupation after the return of sovereignty to Japan in 1952. The Ryūkyū Islands would remain a quasi colony of the United States until 1972. During this period, most US military bases were shifted from the Japanese main islands to Okinawa, where they remain today (Oguma 2014: 137, 157, 313).

At the same time, Ryūkyū Islanders continued to be considered ethnically Japanese. The two hundred thousand who had settled on the main islands where thus legally treated just as other Japanese citizens, who nonetheless pejoratively considered them to be "third country people" (Oguma 2014: 171, 178; Kalicki, Murakami, and Fraser 2013: 217, 222–23).

While at present the vast majority of the islands' people are in favor of at least a drastic reduction of the American presence, the future of the military bases in the prefecture is determined by the national government in Tokyo (Kōno 2017: 20). It is therefore not surprising that there is an active protest movement against the bases, against violent crimes committed by soldiers against women, and against the risks that accidents of military airplanes pose, a burden on the community that has been recognized by the UN Committee on the Elimination of Racial Discrimination (CERD 2018). Ironically, members of the far right have come to consider such activities, which essentially aim to achieve a return of the islands to complete Japanese sovereignty, as "anti-Japanese" (Ealey and Norimatsu 2018). This is an interpretation that arguably once again points to Ryūkyū Islanders not being fully considered part of the Japanese people.

Today, the prefecture of Okinawa remains one of the least developed prefectures in Japan, with the second-highest unemployment rate and the lowest gross prefectural product per capita (Sōmushō Tōkeikyoku 2021; Keizai Shakai Sōgō Kenkyūjo 2017).

Conclusion

The sentient landscapes of Indigenous communities are usually considered to be distinct from the ethnoscapes of modern nation-states. Most importantly, sacred national homelands are mostly not imagined to be sentient. But both sentient Indigenous landscapes and modern nation-state ethnoscapes have in common that they shape the collective identities of communities—Indigenous ones in the former, national in the latter case—and that these collective identities are dependent on these lands for their reproduction. This chapter has argued that Japan may offer a unique vantage point to interrogate the supposed conceptual differences between Indigenous sentient landscapes and modern national ethnoscapes, as well as their necessary exclusionary nature that both share.

At least since the early eighth century, Japan has been referred to as *shinkoku*, "the country of the gods." This was not simply because Japan was created by the Japanese gods but because the gods and their descendants and especially the imperial house have shaped the history of the archipelago and remain present in the myriad shrines throughout the country. This idea of the country of the gods was always a political one. It was first employed to carve out a distinct identity for a court that only recently had created a kingdom in central Japan and appears to have had territorial ambitions on the continent, while establishing the legitimacy of the dynasty. The eastward and northward expansion increased the size of the country of the gods but only by excluding—through the conquest of their lands—the *Ezo*, and by pacifying and including tutelary deities into the sentient landscape.

These people were later interpreted as having been the ancestors of the Ainu, the Indigenous people of Hokkaidō, and they were speculated to have been the forefathers of the outcast Burakumin. When Hokkaidō was incorporated into the newly founded Japanese nation-state and empire in the late nineteenth century, the Ainu were integrated as a separate and less developed race and their land was annexed into the sentient country of the gods through the building of new shrines. In the postwar period the Ainu found themselves at once excluded through discriminatory practices in labor and marriage markets as well as officially cast out from the ethnoscape through an official discourse that denied their very existence. Only in 2019 did the Japanese state officially recognize them as an Indigenous people within its boundaries.

The Burakumin mostly likely emerged as a group in modern Japan. But they inherited and became defined through the prejudices against occupational groups that were considered impure in medieval Japan at a time when shinkoku implied Japanese inferiority vis-à-vis the continent. Their existence in the country of the gods became problematic once shinkoku was interpreted as signifying a superior status. Interestingly, even before the introduction of scientific racism from Europe, Japanese scholars hypothesized that the Burakumin must have come from somewhere else, that they were of a different "stock," to explain their existence in the sentient landscape of the Japanese islands. These prejudices lasted long into the postwar period, as is evident from the issuance of a law in 2016 to combat hate speech and discrimination against this minority.

The outsider status of Ryūkyū Islanders is more straightforward. The Ryūkyū Islands had not been considered part of the country of the gods in premodern times. For the Japanese of the main islands, they would remain foreigners. Suffrage was granted to the islanders only in 1912. After World War II, Ryūkyū Islanders residing on the Japanese main islands were not deprived of their rights. But the Ryūkyū Islands as a whole were sacrificed, first to achieve Japanese sovereignty after the US occupation and then to have US troops largely redeployed from the land of the gods to military bases in places like Okinawa, where they remain today.

The society of imperial Japan was recognized as a multiethnic one, in which various people could live together harmoniously in a hierarchical order—with the Yamato people of the Japanese main islands at the top—under the benevolent rule of the emperor. There were of course important differences in how these groups were integrated into the unequal social structure. Yet there was also the commonality that there was only one way for Burakumin, Ainu, Ryūkyū Islanders, and Korean or Taiwanese colonial subjects to be recognized as true equals to their Yamato peers, and thus to be fully integrated into the sentient landscape of the gods. This path was dying as soldiers for the emperor and becoming enshrined in Yasukuni Shrine as deities protecting the sentient landscape by becoming part of it. In an eerie echo of the days of World War II, present-day right-wing commentators imply that for the people of the prefecture of Okinawa to be recognized as true Japanese, they cannot argue for a reduction or dissolution of the American military bases.

David M. Malitz joined the German Institute for Japanese Studies (DIJ) in Tokyo as Senior Research Fellow in September 2021. Previously, he taught at Chulalongkorn University in Bangkok. David obtained a dual master's degree in business administration and Japanese studies from the Universities of Mannheim and Heidelberg and a doctoral degree in Japanese studies from Munich's Ludwig Maximilian University. He conducted his doctoral research on the history of Japanese-Thai relations at Kyoto University's Center for Southeast Asian Studies with a JSPS fellowship and at Thammasat and Chulalongkorn Universities in Bangkok. At the DIJ, David is working on the past, present, and future of Japan's relations with Southeast Asia.

References

Alabaster, Jay. 2009. "Google Crosses Line with Controversial Old Tokyo Maps." *Japan Times*, 5 May.
Antoni, Klaus. 1998. *Shintô und die Konzeption des japanischen Nationalwesens kokutai: Der religiöse Traditionalismus in Neuzeit und Moderne Japans*. Leiden: Brill.
Aston, William George. 1896a. *Nihongi: Chronicles of Japan from the Earliest Times to A.D. 697*, vol. 1. London: Kegan Paul, Trench, Trübner & Co.
———. 1896b. *Nihongi: Chronicles of Japan from the Earliest Times to A.D. 697*, vol. 2. London: Kegan Paul, Trench, Trübner & Co.
Bialock, David T. 2007. *Eccentric Spaces, Hidden Histories: Narrative, Ritual, and Royal Authority from the Chronicles of Japan to the Tale of the Heike*. Stanford: Stanford University Press.
Breen, John, and Mark Teeuwen. 2010. *A New History of Shinto*. Malden: Wiley-Blackwell.
Committee on the Elimination of Racial Discrimination (CERD). 2018. Concluding observations on the combined tenth and eleventh periodic reports of Japan. 26 September.
Como, Michael. 2008. *Shotoku: Ethnicity, Ritual, and Violence in the Japanese Buddhist Tradition*. New York: Oxford University Press.
Cruikshank, Julie. 2005. *Do Glaciers Listen? Local Knowledge, Colonial Encounters, and Social Imagination*. Vancouver: University of British Columbia Press.
Ealey, Mark, and Satoko Oka Norimatsu. 2018. "Japan's Far-right Politicians, Hate Speech and Historical Denial—Branding Okinawa as 'Anti-Japan.'" *The Asia-Pacific Journal: Japan Focus* 16 (3), No. 2, Article ID 5111, February 1, 2018. Available at https://apjjf.org/2018/03/Ealey-Norimatsu.html.
Earhart, H. Bayron. 2011. *Mount Fuji: Icon of Japan*. Columbia, SC: University of South Carolina Press.
Ethington, Philip J., and Nobuko Toyosawa. 2015. "Inscribing the Past: Depth as Narrative in Historical Spacetime." In *Deep Maps and Spatial Narratives*, ed. D. J. Bodenhamer, J. Corrigan, and T. M. Harris, 72–101. Bloomington: Indiana University Press.
Gauntlett, J. Owen, and Hall, Robert King. 1949. *Kokutai no Hongi: Cardinal Principles of the National Entity of Japan*. Cambridge: Harvard University Press.
GHQ of the Allied Powers. 1960. The Shinto Directive. *Contemporary Religions in Japan* 2(3) (15 December 1945), 85–89.
Gordon, Andrew. 2009. *A Modern History of Japan: From Tokugawa Times to the Present*. 2nd edn. New York: Oxford University Press.
Hah, Chong-do, and Christopher C. Lapp. 1978. "Japanese Politics of Equality in Transition: The Case of the Burakumin." *Far Eastern Survey* 18(5): 487–504.
Hardacre, Helen. 2017. *Shinto: A History*. New York: Oxford University Press.
Harootunian, Harry. 1999. "Memory, Mourning, and National Morality: Yasukuni Shrine and the Reunion of State and Religion." In *Nation and Religion: Perspectives on Europe and Asia*, ed. P. v. d. Veer and H. Lehmann, 144–60. Princeton: Princeton University Press.

Hokkaidō Kankyō Seikatsubu [Department of Environment and Social Development, Government of Hokkaidō]. 2017. *Hokkaidō Ainu seikatsu jittai chōsahō: Hōkokusho* [Report of the Fact-finding investigation about the livelihood of the Ainu in Hokkaidō]. Sapporo: Hokkaidō Kankyō Seikatsubu.

Hōmushō jinken yōgo-kyoku [Human Rights Bureau, Ministry of Justice]. 2020. *Buraku sabetsu no jittai ni kakaru chōsa* [Investigation of the actual situation of Burakumin discrimination]. Tokyo: Hōmushō jinken yōgo-kyoku.

Howell, David L. 2004. "Ainu Ethnicity and the Boundaries of the Early Modern Japanese State." In *Race, Ethnicity and Culture in Modern Japan*, ed. M. Weiner, 316–36. London: Routledge Curzon

Ichijō Kaneyoshi. 1480. *Shōdanchiyō* [Principles of ruling the realm according to a humble woodcutter]. Available at: https://colbase.nich.go.jp/collection_items/kyohaku/B percentE7 percent94 percentB2689?locale=ja#&gid=null&pid=1.

Ikegami, Eiko. 1995. *The Taming of the Samurai: Honorific Individualism and the Making of Modern Japan*. Cambridge: Harvard University Press.

Itō, Satoshi. 2003. "The Medieval Period: The Kami Merge with Buddhism." In *Shinto, A Short History*, ed. M. Teeuwen and J. Breen, 63–107. London: Routledge Curzon.

Josephson, Jason Ānanda. 2012. *The Invention of Religion in Japan*. Chicago: University of Chicago Press.

Kakihana, Masahiro. 2020. "Aso Apologizes if 'Single-race Nation' Remark Misunderstood." *The Asahi Shinbun*, 14 January.

Kakihana Masahiro and Tōyama Takeshi. 2020. "Asō Tarō -shi: 'Nihon ha nisen nen, hitotsu no minzoku' seifu hōshin to mujun" [Asō Tarō: "Japan has been a homogenous ethnic nation for two thousand years". A contradiction with the government's stance]. *Asahi Shinbun*, 13 January.

Kalicki, Konrad, Go Murakami, and Nicholas A. R. Fraser. 2013. "The Difference that Security Makes: The Politics of Citizenship in Postwar Japan in a Comparative Perspective." *Social Science Japan Journal* 16(2): 211–34.

Kang, Etsuko Hae-Jin. 1997. *Diplomacy and Ideology in Japanese-Korean Relations: From the Fifteenth to the Eighteenth Century*. Basingstoke: Macmillan.

Keizai Shakai Sōgō Kenkyūjo [Economic and Social Research Institute]. 2017. *Kenmin keizai keisan* [Prefectural economic accounts]. Available at: https://www.esri.cao.go.jp/jp/sna/data/data_list/kenmin/files/contents/main_h15.html.

Kitabatake Chikafusa. 1914. *Jinnō Shōtōki* [Chronicles of the Authentic Lineages of the Divine Emperors]. Tokyo: Yūhōdō Bunko.

Kobayakawa, Akira. 2021. "Japan's Modernization and Discrimination: What are Buraku and Burakumin?" *Critical Sociology* 47(1): 111–32.

Kōno Kei. 2017. "Okinawa beigun kichi wo meguru ishiki: Okinawa to zenkoku" [Attitudes toward the US military bases in Okinawa: Okinawa and nationwide]. *Hōsō kenkyū to chōsa* [The NHK Monthly Report on Broadcast Research] 67(8) (1 August): 18–31.

Kōtoku Shūsui. 1901. *Teikokushugi: Nijū seiki no kaibutsu* [Imperialism, the monster of the 20th century]. Tokyo: Keiseisha.

Kuno Osamu and Tsurumi Shunsuke. 2015. *Gendai Nihon no shisō: Sono itsutsu no uzu* [Modern Japanese thought: it's fivefold maelstorm]. Tokyo: Iwanami Shinsho.
Kuroita Katsumi. 1962a. *Kunyomi Nihon Shoki, Chūkan* [Kunyomi-version of the Nihongi, vol. 2]. Tokyo: Iwanami Shoten.
———. 1962b. *Kunyomi Nihon Shoki, Gekan* [Kunyomi-version of the Nihongi, vol. 3]. Tokyo: Iwanami Shoten.
Lefebvre, Henri. 1991. *The Production of Space*. Trans. D. Nicholson-Smith. Malden: Blackwell.
Lewallen, Ann-Elise. 2016. *The Fabric of Indigeneity: Ainu Identity, Gender, and Settler Colonialism in Japan*. Santa Fe: School for Advanced Research Press, University of New Mexico Press.
Lie, John. 2001. "Ruth Benedict's Legacy of Shame: Orientalism and Occidentalism in the Study of Japan." *Asian Journal of Social Science* 29(2): 249–61.
———. 2004. *Multiethnic Japan*. Cambridge: Harvard University Press.
Maeda Tsutomu. 2014. "Hirata Atsutane no kōsetsu: 'Ibuki Oroshi' wo chūshin ni" [Lecture on Hirata Atsutane: with a focus on the 'Ibuki Oroshi']. *Nihon Bunka Ronsō [Essays on Japanese culture]* 22: 37–55.
Matsuda, Hiroko. 2018. *Liminality of the Japanese Empire: Border Crossings from Okinawa to Colonial Taiwan*. Honolulu: University of Hawaii Press.
McNally, Mark. 2005. *Proving the Way: Conflict and Practice in the History of Japanese Nativism*. Cambridge: Harvard University Press.
Monbushō [Ministry of Education]. 1935. *Jinjō shōgaku chirisho, Maki ichi* [Geography textbook for primary schools, vol. 1]. Tokyo: Ministry of Education.
———. 1937. *Kokutai no hongi* [Cardinal principles of the national entity of Japan]. Tokyo: Monbushō.
Mori, Mizue. 2003. "Ancient and Classical Japan: The Dawn of Shinto." In *Shinto, a Short History*, ed. N. Inoue, 12–62. London: Routledge Curzon.
Morris-Suzuki, Tessa. 1998. *Re-Inventing Japan: Time, Space, Nation*. Armonk: M. E. Sharpe.
Neary, Ian. 2003. "Burakumin at the End of History." *Social Research* 70(1): 269–94.
Nora, Pierre. 1989. "Between Memory and History: Les Lieux de Mémoire." *Representations* 26 (Special Issue: Memory and Counter-Memory): 7–24.
Oguma, Eiji. 2002. *A Genealogy of "Japanese" Self-images*. Melbourne: Transpacific Press.
———. 2014. *The Boundaries of the Japanese, vol. 1: Okinawa 1868–1972—Inclusion and Exclusion*. Melbourne: Transpacific Press.
Ohnuki-Tierney, Emiko. 1998. "A Conceptual Model for the Historical Relationship Between the Self and the Internal and External Others: The Agrarian Japanese, the Ainu, and the Special-Status People." In: *Making Majorities: Constituting the Nation in Japan, Korea, China, Malaysia, Fiji, Turkey, and the United States*, ed. D. C. Gladney, 31–51. Stanford: Stanford University Press.
Oka Norimatsu, Satoko. 2013. "The Emperor's Army and Japan's Discrimination against Okinawa." *The Asia-Pacific Forum—Japan Focus* 15 (11), No. 2, Article ID 5044, June 1 2017. Available at https://apjjf.org/2017/11/Norimatsu.html.

Ooms, Herman. 1996. *Tokugawa Village Practice: Class, Status, Power, Law*. Berkeley: University of California Press.
Peterson, Nicolas. 2011. "Is the Aboriginal Landscape Sentient? Animism, the New Animism and the Warlpiri." *Oceania* 81(2): 167–79.
Povinelli, Elizabeth A. 1993. *Labor's Lot: The Power, History, and Culture of Aboriginal Action*. Chicago: University of Chicago Press.
Saitō Hirō. 2006. *Shinkoku Nihon* [Japan, the land of the gods]. Tokyo: Chikuma Shinsho.
Sharp, Nonie. 2002. *Saltwater People: The Waves of Memory*. Crow's Nest: Allen & Unwin.
Shimazono Susumu. 2010. *Kokka shintō to nihonjin* [State-Shintō and the Japanese]. Tōkyō: Iwanami Shoten.
Siddle, Richard. 2005. *Race, Resistance, and the Ainu of Japan*. Abingdon: Routledge.
Skya, Walter A. 2009. *Japan's Holy War: The Ideology of Radical Shintō Ultranationalism*. Durham: Duke University Press.
Smith, Anthony D. 2009. *Ethno-symbolism and Nationalism: A Cultural Approach*. Abingdon: Routledge.
Sōmushō Tōkeikyoku [Statistics Bureau of the Ministry of Internal Affairs and Communications]. 2021. *Rōdōryoku chōsa (kihon shūkei) todōfuken-betsu kekka* [Results of the prefectural labor force survey (basic tabulation)]. Available at: https://www.stat.go.jp/data/roudou/pref/index.html.
State-War-Navy Coordinating Committee. 1945. *United States Initial Post-Surrender Policy for Japan* (SWNCC150/4). Available at: https://www.ndl.go.jp/constitution/shiryo/01/022/022tx.html.
Taïeb, Caroline. 2019. "La discrimination des burakumin au Japon." *La Vie des Idées*, 6 September.
Teeuwen, Mark and Fabio Rambelli. 2003. "Introduction: Combinatory religion and the honji suijaku paradigm in pre-modern Japan." In: *Buddhas and Kami in Japan: Honji Suijaku as a Combinatory Paradigm*, ed. M. Teeuwen and F. Rambelli, 1–53. London: Routledge Curzon.
Tierney, Robert Thomas. 2015. *Monster of the Twentieth Century: Kōtoku Shūsui and Japan's First Anti-Imperialist Movement*. Oakland: University of California Press.
Toby, Ronald P. 1984. *State and Diplomacy in Early Modern Japan: Asia in the Development of the Tokugawa Bakufu*. Princeton: Princeton University Press.
Tsumaki Shingo. 2012. "Hinkon-shakaiteki haijo no chiikiteki kengen: Sai-fuanteika suru toshibu buraku" [Local manifestation of poverty and social exclusion: unstable life of urban Burakumin]. *Shakaigaku Hyoron* [Japanese Sociological Review] 62(4): 489–503.
Tsutsui, Kiyoteru. 2017. "Human Rights and Minority Activism in Japan: Transformation of Movement Actorhood and Local-Global Feedback Loop." *American Journal of Sociology* 122(4): 1050–103.
Uchida Ryūshi. 2008. "Shakaiteki haijo-hōsetsu to shakaiteki nettowāku: Dōwa taisaku jigyō to hisabetsu buraku no wakamono no shūrō wo megutte" [Social exclusion/inclusion and social networks: Dōwa-policies and the employment of disadvantaged young Burakumin]. *Riron to dōtai* [Social theory and dynamics] 1: 55–71.

United Nations. 2007. *United Nations Declaration on the Rights of Indigenous Peoples*. Available at: https://www.un.org/development/desa/indigenouspeoples/declaration-on-the-rights-of-indigenous-peoples.html.

Varley, H. Paul. 1980. *A Chronicle of Gods and Sovereigns: Jinnō Shōtōki of Kitabatake Chikafusa / translated by H. Paul Varley*. New York: Columbia University Press.

Vlastos, Stephen. 1998. "Tradition: Past/Present Culture and Modern Japanese History." In *Mirror of Modernity: Invented Traditions of Modern Japan*, ed. S. Vlastos, 1–16. Berkeley: University of California Press.

Wakabayashi, Bob Tadashi. 1999. *Anti-Foreignism and Western Learning in Early-Modern Japan: The New Theses of 1825*. Council of East Asian Studies. Cambridge: Harvard University Press.

Walker, Brett L. 2001. *The Conquest of Ainu Lands: Ecology and Culture in Japanese Expansion, 1590–1800*. Berkeley: University of California Press.

Watts, Jonathan. 2000. "Japan divine, claims PM." *Guardian*, 17 May.

Wehler, Hans-Ulrich. 2007. *Nationalismus: Geschichte, Formen, Folgen*. Munich: C. H. Beck.

World Values Survey Wave 7: 2017–2020. Data for Japan from 2019. Available at: https://www.worldvaluessurvey.org/WVSOnline.jsp.

Yamaguchi, Mari. 2009. "Discrimination claims die hard in Japan: Despite official claims, prejudice against former 'buraku' outcasts said active from bottom to top." *Japan Times*, 25 January.

Yamamoto, Takanori. 2021. "Buraku Discrimination and Hate Speech: Complex Situations of Classical and Contemporary Discrimination in Japan." In *Hate Speech in Japan: The Possibility of a Non-Regulatory Approach*, ed. S. Higaki and Y. Nasu, 107–24. Cambridge: Cambridge University Press.

CHAPTER 8

Imagining Chile's South
The Making of a Phobic Landscape of Prestige in the Forests

Georg T. A. Krizmanics

This chapter is about the relation between nature and culture (Descola 2013a, 2013b) and its role for imagining Chile's south during colonial times and the first decades after independence (1818). Until the mid-nineteenth century the south, the region that stretches from Chillán southwards, was largely independent and controlled by Mapuche peoples, with two exceptions: the enclaves of Valdivia and Chiloé.[1]

For central Chileans this made the south a landscape of resistance that was not broken until the 1880s by military defeat (Crow 2013: 19–50). Landscapes emerge out of the tensions that bind nature and culture inseparably together (Schama 1996: 3–19), and thus they are "cultural image[s], a pictorial way of representing, structuring or symbolizing surroundings" (Daniels and Cosgrove 1988: 1). Landscapes are an essential part of a nation's imaginary and are core to local, regional, and national identification(s) (Smith 1988: 183–90).[2]

In the following, I am interested in examining, through an analysis of key documents, how conquistadores, missionaries, and Creoles have related to sentient landscapes in the context of their efforts to "civilize" Mapuches.[3] It will become evident that the narratives of the colonial period present the strength of Indigenous resistance as a result of a privileged relationship between humans (Mapuche) and nonhumans (nature, especially forests). From a "modern" point of view it was a savage relationship unsuitable for the so-called civilized part of the world. This contrast provides evidence for the end of an age and the rise of a new Western cosmology, where nature ceased to be understood as being one and reigning everywhere, "distributing equally among humans and nonhumans a multitude of technical skills, ways of life, and modes of reasoning." By introducing the difference between human and nonhuman, "[m]oderns were discovering the lazy propensity of barbaric and savage peoples to judge everything according to their own particular norms." At the same time, with this very same difference "they were masking their own ethnocentricity behind a rational approach to knowledge, the errors of which at that time escaped notice" (Descola 2013b: xv).

Second, I argue that the Creole elites that carried out Chile's independence were eager to resignify the special relationship between Mapuches and nature in order to break indigenous resistance and obtain access to Mapuche land. Creoles desired Mapuches to become like Germans, as both were deemed to have a similarly privileged relationship with nature and especially with forests. From the outside this special relationship meant that it was believed Germans felt and understood the sentient character of nature in a way that was inconceivable for a civilized person. It was due to this ancient relationship, which dated from Roman times and was followed by an impressive civilizing record, that Chilean elites deemed German settlers to be extraordinarily suited to civilize nature and transform the southern landscape of resistance into a landscape of progress,[4] just as they had done in central Europe. In other words, Germans were admired for conserving their special relationship with nature and at the same time for using their wisdom against nature, thus overcoming the condition of savagery. At the same time this constitutes the making of a phobic landscape that excludes Mapuches and their way of relating to nature. My analysis aims at fostering the understanding of mechanisms of inclusion and exclusion that operate through landscapes and nourish and feed back into the ongoing social, political, and economic conflict in Chile's south (Miller Klubock 2014).

The Eye of the Observer Makes the Landscape

A narrative regarding a determined territory is never fixed, instead it steadily evolves and (re)signifies the associated landscape. Even a hegemonic narrative about a territory still signifies just one of many possible landscapes—something nationalists deny. For them there is just one unique landscape that truly represents the nation's essence and identity. This exclusiveness, the focus on identity and not identification, is what makes a landscape's phobic character. Nationalists are keen to present this phobic heritage as "an acquisition, a possession that grows and solidifies" (Foucault 1977: 146), with little interest in highlighting the ambiguity and contingence inherent even in hegemonic narratives. Analyzing the genealogy of narratives is not the search for "a timeless and essential secret" but is instead the effort to show that narratives "have no essence or that their essence was fabricated. . . . What is found at the historical beginning of things is not the inviolable identity of their origin; it is the dissension of other things. It is disparity" (ibid.: 142).

Uncovering this disparity "disturbs what was previously considered immobile; it fragments what was thought unified; it shows the heterogeneity of what was imagined consistent with itself" (ibid.: 147). Thus, the emergence of landscapes is not the result of an innocent process; rather, it is dependent on power relations and the outcome of ideological disputes over how to envision the world. This explains why, by analyzing landscape, "we discover its links to broader historical structures and processes and are able to locate landscape study within a progressive debate about society and culture." Furthermore, research on the social construction of landscapes helps us to better understand how "people have signified themselves and their world through their imagined relationship with nature, . . . through which they have underlined and communicated their own social role and that of others with respect to external nature." In this relationship the "terrestrial space [is] both subject and object of human agency" (Cosgrove 1998: 15).

Communities are also imagined through landscapes (Anderson 2006), and the narrative that structures a determined landscape at a certain moment combines what is perceived as real and what is understood as imagined. Consider, for example, the experience of the Polish scholar Ignacio Domeyko,[5] whose detailed descriptions of the virgin forests south of the Biobío River awakened the interest of central Chileans in a territory they were previously little aware of. Domeyko prepared for the trip in 1845 by reading *La Araucana*, an epic poem written by the Spanish nobleman and soldier Alonso de Ercilla y Zúñiga. He had participated during 1557 and 1559 in the military campaigns led by the Captaincy General of Chile to subdue the Mapuche, or Araucanians, as Spaniards then referred to them.[6]

Before the arrival of Spanish conquistadors to Chile in 1536, Mapuches had already resisted Incan attempts to conquer them. Due to their spirit of resistance, the Inca called them in Quechua *purumaucas*, which means wild and indomitable enemies. Most likely the Spaniards derived Araucanian from the abbreviation *aucas* (Rinke 2007: 14), as they too experienced the spirit of resistance that resulted in roughly a century of intense warfare. The impossibility of defeating Mapuches militarily made the Crown's representatives in the captaincy change their approach and pursue a different strategy. In the symbolically important Quilín peace agreement from 1641, Spaniards acknowledged Mapuches' independence, and it was agreed to establish the Biobío River as the frontier. In return, the natives accepted the activities of Christian missionaries on their territory. Although afterward there were still skirmishes between both parties, the intensity of the conflict diminished considerably, especially after the abolition of "Indian" slavery in 1674. This opened up the space for peaceful coexistence, with mutual benefits and transculturation.[7] This exchange gave Mapuches an advantage over neighboring tribes on the other side of the Andes, and while Mapuches extended their influence over their neighbors, Spaniards established an economy based on agriculture and trade (ibid.: 17ff.).

Despite this lasting and largely peaceful coexistance that culminated in Mapuches' backing of the royalist cause during the wars of independence at the beginning of the nineteenth century (Pinto Rodríguez 2003: 67), Domeyko was expecting to encounter a landscape of resistance, as described by Ercilla almost three hundred years earlier. He was hoping to meet the invincible, indomitable warriors (ibid.: 55) and (re)discover a "territory that has never surrendered to the yoke of a central government" (Domeyko 1846: 16).[8] Instead, he found a people "in its *normal* state, that is, in time of peace, because man was created for peace and not for war." Domeyko describes a Mapuche in this normal state as being "affable, honest, susceptible of the noblest virtues, hospitable, a friend of quiet and order, a lover of his country and therefore of the independence of his homes, circumspect, serious, energetic: he seems born to be a good citizen" (ibid.: 75).[9] His scholarly view of this landscape is dominated by Ercilla's account, and Domeyko constantly compares the landscape he travels through with the imagined landscape that became real to his mind's eye while reading *La Araucana*. "Passing now further of the aforementioned plains, mountains and ridges," he writes, "we find ourselves in the classic land of Arauco, at every step stumbling upon the memories of times gone by and with the riversides sung by the zealous Ercilla" (ibid.: 15).[10]

Domeyko (ibid.: 31) experienced his insertion into "a rain forest so dense and difficult to walk through" that it were as if he had traveled through time. It felt "as if no one had passed through it since the time when the first conquistadors set foot on Araucanian soil."[11] For Domeyko the words that still most accurately described the territory he traversed were Ercilla's, as the landscape "involuntarily reminds us of what [he] said when passing through [it]." So much so, that he could not resist quoting a verse from the third part of *La Araucana*:

Ne'er did Nature block man's footsteps / Nunca con tanto estorbo a los humanos
With a barrier so obstructive; / Quiso impedir el paso la natura,
Ne'er did trees and creepers measure / I que así de los cielos soberanos
So the height of sovereign heavens; / Los árboles midiesen la altura:
Nor amidst such cliffs and gullies / Ni entre tantos peñascos i pantanos
Were such scrub and lichens mingled / Mezcló tanta maleza i espesura,

As on this trail-path forbidden, / Como en este camino defendido
Woven close with trees and bracken. / De zarzas, breñas i arboles tejido.
(Ercilla quoted in Domeyko 1846: 31)[12]

Finally, Domeyko (ibid.: 98) also had another landscape constantly on his mind: the European one that he had left behind. For him, the climate in the south "is the one of all provinces in Chile that most resembles the temperament of northern Europe." This led Domeyko to consider that one of the most convenient means for civilizing the territory and its people was European immigration. He claimed that ancient Gauls and Teutons had a proven civilizing record in Roman times and under much worse climatic conditions than those of Valdivia, "when immense forests and swamps covered a large part of central Europe" (ibid.: 99).[13] Therefore, European settlers in Chile's south should do the same as their ancestors in ancient Europe, with the most beneficial effects for the local climate. The settlement of those forests and mountains would improve the climate "due to the cutting of the trees and the cultivation of the land that until now just attracts and conserves humidity and exhales evil miasmas" (ibid.: 98–99).[14]

The idea of landscape is of European origin (Schama 1996: 10), and Spanish conquistadors and missionaries as well as Creoles and European immigrants were keen to impose this European idea in Chile. The dispute was and is not about the form of landscape but the underlying European idea that humans and (nonhuman) nature are separate spheres, with the former dominant and understood to be superior to the latter. For Mapuches—at around a million people one of the most populous Indigenous populations on the American continent (Museo Chileno de Arte Precolombino 2002: vi)—"the dividing line between human, animal, tree and mountain is not clear-cut. They do not distinguish 'at a glance' between 'animate' and 'inanimate,' 'sentient' and 'non-sentient,' 'thinking' and 'non-thinking'" (Böning quoted in Le Bonniec 2013). For them, natural elements are not just matter but have a social existence; they are imagined as forceful tutelary spirits that are the forest, the volcano, the river, and so forth. Ewald Böning, a missionary of the Society of the Divine Word, noted in the early 1970s that when his informant from Pucura in Southern Chile saluted fauna and flora, like a bird, a tree, or a stone, he did not give thought to whether it possessed an intellect or not. For him, "a European, who does not know this Mapuche thinking, or rather this feeling, would relate these greetings and prayers to spirits and belief in gods; but that would be a misinterpretation" (Le Bonniec 2013).

The Mapuche poet Leonel Lienlaf explains that this way of understanding stems from envisioning the world with *az mogen*. This Mapuche way of seeing life is about "how you 'live with' the territory.... The land does not belong to us, but we belong to the land" (Le Bonniec 2013). The *lonko* (Mapuche chief) and academic José Quidel Lincoleo (2016: 716–18) describes how the relationship between human and nonhuman life in a place is established. He refers among other works to an account by Jimena Pichinao, who illustrates the relationship by alluding to the *anülmapun* ceremony. The term means to put down roots or to settle in a place, and from the Mapuche point of view, to inhabit a space implies knowing everything that is alive in it, be it human or not. Formerly, when a family settled on a land, they performed this ceremony, which consisted of a formal greeting to the nonhuman entities living there. This was considered to be the first necessary protocol in order to gain a balanced coexistence between humans and the places' other beings. Thus introduced, the beings would let them live, accompanying them without negatively interfering in the family's daily life (Pinchinao cited in Quidel Lincoleo 2016: 718). Therefore, land is not conceived of as a dead object to be owned but is full of (immaterial) life that mutually defines people and landscapes (di Giminiani 2018). McFall (2002: 306) describes this relationship with the analogy of a spider web that has to be maintained in order for Mapuche communities to prosper.[15] They depended on vast lands and these lands had their purpose, function, and cultural, sociopolitical, and economical meaning, as the Mapuche art historian José Ancán argues. "Those lands always were an indispensable part of the collective imaginary" (Ancán cited in Le Bonniec 2013).

Although this way of life "does not follow the canons relating to landscapes," it does include an "aesthetic concept of the idea of inhabiting a territory," as Leonel Lienlaf states (Le Bonniec 2013). However, Europeans and their descendants did not recognize these spaces as landscapes but as wilderness and unoccupied land, or as territory with a culturally inferior human imprint that was the result of an inefficient and unprofitable way of doing agriculture (McFall 2002: 308–14; Miller Klubock 2014: 31).[16] This argument that "the land belongs to those who make it productive and not exclusively to those who occupy it" (Marimán et al. 2006: 12) is still made today. At the beginning of the twentieth century the supposedly unproductive ways Mapuche related to their land were linked to "natural laziness," but now the formerly "weak and drunk" Mapuche are discredited as terrorists by Chilean elites (Quidel Lincoleo 2016: 714) in order to undermine their land claims (di Giminiani 2018: 50). The magnitude of this ideological dispute and its impacts become evident when looking for an adequate translation for landscape into Mapudungun (the Mapuche language). As Le Bonniec (2008: 58–59) shows, there are two expressions used for landscape in Mapudungun that are constructed around the core notion of *az mapu*, which describes the shape of the land. On the one hand, landscape is referred to as *azy chi mapu*, which means "the earth is beautiful." This expression describes the land as it should be, in a state of harmony bounded by "the law of nature," *ad-mapu*. The other term that is used for landscape, *azwentulay mapu fantepu*, expresses the transformation of the earth's shape. It means that "at this point the earth is out of shape," or "in these days, the earth is no longer beautiful."

Germans, Araucanians, and the Forest: A Special Relationship

From the time of independence onward Creole ideologues intimately linked the destiny of Chile to a national project based on the idea of progress—a project for which European immigration was considered necessary in order to complete the state's de facto takeover of a large part of the southern territory, then mostly still controlled by Mapuche peoples. Although in the long term "education and enlightenment" were to ensure the country's civilizing progress (O'Higgins 1822: x),[17] Chilean elites were convinced that in the short term this progress could only be achieved through European immigration. "Attracting foreign farmers, industrialists, and capitalists is not possible," Chile's founding father Bernardo O'Higgins claimed in a speech during a constitutional assembly, "without offering them a great guarantee, and all the freedom they enjoy in other regions: this is the most important acquisition, the fertile surface of our soil is still virgin, and intact its entrails, they alone will soon provide us with new fruits and treasures" (ibid.: xi).[18]

In other words, since the elites' expectations were that Indigenous people would not become civilized as quickly as required, importing already educated and enlightened people was seen as the short-term remedy. In the eyes of the Chilean authorities and based on the *Report on Foreign Immigration*, presented to the Chilean government in 1865, Germans were the kind of civilized people deemed most suitable for the colonization of the country's southern territories.

> The German, because of the nature and climate of the country he inhabits, is more suitable for the hard work that our agriculture and mining requires. He also possesses with greater perfection than our farmers the methods of cultivation and is more experienced in the exploitation of mines than our workers. These advantages are of great value in Chile's present condition, since the country is not so much in need of arms to increase its productive force but rather intelligence that takes advantage of the robust ones that it possesses by itself and that it now wastes by ignorance or by our insurmountable attachment to routine. (Vicuña Mackenna 1865: 27)[19]

Additionally, one of the concerns Chilean governments had regarding the influx of immigrants was the threat they could pose to the territorial unity of the state. It was feared that concentrated immigration from a single nation-state could provoke a future annexation of settlements by the nation of their origin. As there was no German nation-state until the proclamation of the German Empire in 1871, *The Report on Immigration* from 1865 considered that German immigration would reduce this risk of colonial intervention:

> [T]he German—unlike the Englishman whose first pride is the homeland, the Frenchman who loves it out of vanity and enthusiasm, the Spaniard who binds all his concerns and all his virtues to it—dispenses more easily with these attractions, and forms his homeland in the forest where he builds his home and in which he sees his children grow up freely and happily. (Vicuña Mackenna 1865: 26)[20]

The belief among Chilean decision makers that Germans had a special innate relationship with nature seems to stem also from a deeper cultural history. There are indeed striking similarities between the descriptions of "Indians" by Spanish conquistadors and the representations of German tribes by Romans. An important document in this respect is the Roman historian Cornelius Tacitus's *Germania, or, On the Origin and Situation of the Germans*. He wrote it around the year AD 98 when the empire's troops were undertaking a series of military campaigns to "pacify" the Teutons. Tacitus created an account of civilization versus barbarism, in which Germanic tribes had managed to remain innocent children of nature, "clad in the skins of wild beasts or, according to the first-century geographer Pomponius Mela, in a garment made from tree bark" (Schama 1996: 76–77). Garments made of tree bark, albeit among the Chilean "Indians," would also be noticed by Spanish chroniclers some fifteen hundred years later. There, Mapuches used the Maque tree,[21] as its "bark is thin and long and consistent strands come out of it. . . . [T]he Indians used to make garments out of [its] threads before they had sheep's wool" (Rosales 1877: 224).[22] Tacitus's descriptions represented Germans as ferocious but noble primitives, due to their essentially natural purity, which made them instinctively indifferent and immune "to the vices that had corrupted Rome: luxury, secrecy, property, sensuality, slavery" (Tacitus cited in Schama 1996: 77).

Tacitus's criticism—as Schama (1996: 76–77) shows—aimed at explaining the Roman Empire's failure to subdue the Germans, an effort that had already been underway for two hundred and ten years. If it had not been for the empire's decadent aberrations, the argument goes, Germans would not have been in a position to teach Romans lessons time and again.

Tacitus's interest in the Germans was motivated by his desire to criticize the Roman Empire and thus bring about the necessary change in order to make civilization prevail over barbarism. In his descriptions of German tribes, he was clear that what they represented, after all, was the opposite of Rome. As Schama (1996: 81) argues, Tacitus's aims are especially clear when he writes about German topographies by describing them as shapeless and dismal: "For a Roman, the sign of a pleasing landscape was necessarily that which had been formed, upon which man had left his civilizing and fructifying mark."

Fast forward some fifteen hundred years to the Captaincy General of Chile, where Alonso de Ercilla participated in the Spanish Crown's military campaigns to subdue the Mapuche. This experience inspired his epic poem *La Araucana*, the foundational work of Chile's national literary imaginary (Oyarzún Peña 1967: 12). In this context it is interesting to note with Goic (1992: 342) that Ercilla most probably had also been inspired in his writing by Tacitus's *Germania*. In a way similar to Tacitus, Ercilla idealizes Araucanians. There is no better example of Ercilla's instrumentalization of the Mapuches than his invention of the term Araucanian to refer to the Indigenous peoples of Arauco. The term's power becomes evident through the words of the ethnologist Ricardo E. Latcham, whose works were published in the first third of the twentieth century. Latcham admitted that his objects of study are known "by the name Araucanian" not because it did them justice but because it was "invented by Ercilla to refer to the Indians of Arauco." Its use then had been "extended to cover all the Indians of war, becoming generic for all the Indians of the area" (Latcham quoted in Parentini Gayani 1996: 28).[23]

Monsalve (2015: 127, 130) explains that Ercilla exploits the figure of the violent and diabolical Araucanian to make it appear as if the defeats the Spaniards suffered were nothing more than a divine punishment for the dangerous moral decadence that had spread among the conquistadors. When Ercilla criticizes greed and laments the excesses of war, he does not do so due to concerns regarding the fate of Araucanians and their "admirable" warriors. Rather, he does so because he believes that moral corruption threatens the stability of the state by interfering with the proper functioning of colonial governance (ibid.: 129). Thus, Ercilla's objective is arguably to rescue the colonial enterprise and ensure the longevity of an ever-stronger Spanish Empire (ibid.: 130).

Mapuche resistance lasted until the 1880s, when "pacification" attempts succeeded and Creole elites extended the state's control over Mapuche territories. At the moment of defeat, Mapuches had been struggling to maintain autonomy for approximately four hundred years. At the time the conquistadors arrived, they had already been put under pressure by the Incan Empire. In both Tacitus's and Ercilla's stories of civilization versus barbarism, an element that reinforced this difference was the privileged proximity the noble primitives had to nature. As savages they were represented "as the social equivalent of a force of nature" (Schama 1996: 89). Both Germans and Araucanians appeared to belong to and somehow be an extension of the woods by "suddenly . . . rushing from the forest" (ibid.: 89) and by "retreating into the woods" during the engagement in "hit-and-run attacks" (ibid.: 90). Indeed Ercilla presents the forest as one with the "savages," as becomes evident in the context of a Mapuche ambush, where the natives "were buried in the brushwood" for "concealment" and a "safe covert":

> Here the Indians lurked in ambush / Aquí estaban los indios emboscados
> Waiting for our band's arrival / Esperando a los nuestros si viniesen
> Whom they thought to catch, disordered, / Por cogerlos sin orden descuidados
> Ere they grew aware of danger. / Antes que del peligro se advirtiesen:
> They were buried in the brushwood / De un bosque a mano hecho rodeados,
> So that they might have concealment, / Para que más cubiertos estuviesen,
> And by ruse that none suspected / Hasta que, inadvertidos del engaño,
> From safe coverts work their mischief. / Pudiesen a su salvo hacer el daño.
>
> Down the fourteen Spaniards hastened, / Los catorce españoles abajaban
> Down the slope and toward the valley / Por un repecho, al valle enderezando,
> Where the savages lay hidden, / Donde ocultos los bárbaros estaban
> Waiting, covered o'er with leafage. / Cubiertos de los ramos aguardando:
> Ours had not yet reached the thicket / Los nuestros con el bosque aún no igualaban
> When the Indians, beating, blowing / Cuando los indios, súbito sonando
> Tabor drums and hoarse-lunged trumpets / Bárbaras trompas, roncos tamborinos.
> Occupied the roads and passes. (Ercilla 1945: 40) / Los pasos ocuparon y caminos. (Ercilla 1910: 61–62)

Finally, there existed also the belief among Creole elites and scholars that the first people to settle in Chile belonged to the German tribe of the Frisians. This was put forward, for example, by José Toribio Medina (1852–1930), one of the most renowned Chilean intellectuals at the turn of the twentieth century.[24] In *The Aborigines of Chile,* he refers to sources that show the origins and extension of this belief dating back to the early days of the conquistadors' arrival, as a reference to *La Araucana* shows. Medina (1882: 15) mentions an author of the seventeenth century who explained that Glaura, an Araucanian native noble, would have confessed to Ercilla her Frisian descent, and he quotes the following verse for evidence:

Glaura am I named, engendered / Mi nombre es Glaura,
In a fatal hour, and daughter / en fuerte hora nacida,
Of good chieftain Quilacura, / Hija del buen cacique Quilacura
Of the noble blood of Friso (Ercilla 1945: 230) / De la sangre de Frisio
esclarecida. (Ercilla cited in Medina (1882: 16).

The Prodigious Tree That Grew in the Shape of a Crucifix

Apart from *La Araucana* there exist additional accounts that build on the same equation between the forest and Araucanians, corroborating the use of this trope outside the lyric and epic traditions. The Jesuit chronicler Diego de Rosales (1877: 221) wrote in his 1674 book *General History of the Kingdom of Chile. Indian Flanders* the most complete work on his time.[25] He introduces the chapter titled "Different species of trees, their utilities and medicinal virtues" by noticing that "the trees and thick forests that the mountains and valleys of this kingdom produce are everywhere extremely dense and grow more and multiply with greater vigor" the closer they are to the Antarctic (ibid.).[26] These "forests have been the most impregnable fortresses where the Indians have defended themselves, because they go into them when the Spaniards come to look for them, without wanting to fight hand to hand, unless some forced occasion demands it." These fortresses were their refuge, whence "they go out to make raids to our lands" (ibid.).[27]

This idea of savages being an organic part of nature, in this case part of the woods, was also exploited by Jesuits for Catholic proselytizing among Mapuches in rural areas. "It is about the prodigious tree that grew in the shape of a crucifix in one of the mountains of Chile,"[28] as the title of one of Alonso de Ovalle's (1646: 58) chapters announces. According to this chronicler's written testimony (ibid.: 59), it all began in 1636, when an "Indian" went into the woods of the central Chilean Limache Valley near Valparaiso to fell trees for construction purposes. Completely immersed in his work, he first cut down various trees and then diligently set about wielding the axe in order to obtain the beams he needed. Without noticing, he started to work the miraculous tree first on one side and then on the other until he suddenly realized the perfect shape of the cross the tree hand grown in and stopped. Ovalle (ibid.: 59) states that the perfection of the cross alone would have sufficed to cause admiration in everyone lucky enough to see it, but the miracle was even more astounding: "On top of this thusly formed cross the very same tree had formed a crucifix of the thickness and size of a perfect man." Everything, every single part of the body with all its details, seemed "as if a sculptor had formed them."[29]

Figure 8.1. Limache Cross. Source: Alonso de Ovalle's 1646 *Histórica Relación del Reyno de Chile* (Historical account of the kingdom of Chile) (between pp. 58 and 59). © memoriachilena.

For Ovalle (ibid.: 59) and his contemporaries this prodigious tree represented "such a great and new argument for [their] faith" that it reassured them in their missionary efforts. It symbolized in a meaningful and moving way "how faith begins to take root in that new world and that the author of nature wants the roots of the trees themselves to sprout and bear witness to faith no longer in hieroglyphs, but in the true representation of the death and passion of our Redeemer, as he was the only and effective means by which faith was planted" (ibid.: 59).[30]

The big unsolved mystery of Ovalle's account is the reaction of the native woodcutter when he discovered the prodigious tree. A description thereof is completely absent, as if his response did not matter. For Ovalle, the most important part for the "Indian" in this story seems to be his discovering the tree, and thereby his faith. At the same time Ovalle makes the reader understand that the "Indian" by himself was not able to keep, watch over, and strengthen his faith. The need for spiritual tutelage is reinforced by Ovalle's behavioral description of the native woodcutter's rashness and inattentiveness. He somehow reproaches him for not having noticed the divine providence immediately, which led him to damage the crucifix, as "the part that belonged to the head and face was taken away with an axe blow" (ibid.: 59).[31]

The Jesuit Ovalle tells that after the unearthing of the venerable tree the "word of such a great prodigy spread and a very noble lady, who was very devoted to the Holy Cross and had her haciendas in the very same valley of Limache, did great diligences to have this treasure" (ibid.: 59). When everything was prepared "she took it to her ranch where she built a church and placed it on the altar" (ibid.: 59).[32] Thus, the forest was the appropriate place for the divine to become manifest and the tree to be discovered, but not a suitable site for it to be venerated. Veneration had to be done in the institutional framework of the church, which made the difference between barbaric paganism and civilized faith. Ovalle (ibid.: 59) made this clear by stating that among all those who went to visit the cross was also "the bishop of Santiago, [who] granted the indulgences he could for those who visited the sanctuary."[33]

This was the way Ovalle (ibid.: 59) himself approached the crucifix: "From the doorstep of the church I saw this prodigious tree and at the first sight that celestial figure was represented to me in a mystified whole." He goes on by describing how impressed he was by this spiritual experience and how he "felt moved on the inside and [at the same time] as if outside myself, recognizing with the naked eye what can hardly be believed if it is not seen. I myself had not expected it to be that much."[34] Seemingly, what baffled Ovalle (ibid.: 59) the most was that divine providence could become manifest in nature and in insensible things, as those are the thoughts he expresses in the closing part of the chapter. In order to assist the "devout reader" in retracing this extraordinary experience, he enclosed a picture card that was as authentic as possible (figure 8.1). This should bring the reader to "admire the divine wisdom of our God and his most high providence in the means and motives that he has given us even in natural and insensible things for the confirmation of our faith and the increase of the piety and devotion of his faithful" (ibid.: 59).[35]

"The" Araucanian invented by Ercilla had a threatening resemblance to "the" native that was reborn as Araucanian by graceful divine providence, as described by Ovalle: both were imagined as a people that were naturally deprived of speaking for themselves. Of course, "Araucanians" appear in *La Araucana*, but it is Ercilla who imagines their words and idealizes them. And with these words, speaking through them, he "not only distances himself from the Indian's cause, but also rebukes the Araucanian rebellion, which he deems illegitimate" (Monsalve 2015: 125). The crucifix did not stay in the Limache Valley; it was brought to Renca, San Luis, in Argentina, and although it did not remain preserved as Ovalle had seen it, veneration never stopped. The Lord of Renca, as the crucifix is now known, is a firm part of the regional religious folklore, and in a song called "Zamba del Señor de Renca," devoted parishioners and pilgrims cheerfully haunt the Mapuche soul by chanting "Christ you were born Araucanian."[36]

The Triumph of Civilized Nature

The resurrection of imaginaries was easier than the establishment of a dialogue eye to eye between Creole and Mapuche elites during the struggle for independence from Spain. Creole elites became interested in the glorious past of Mapuche resistance because they identified similarities between the Indigenous struggles against Spaniards in the sixteenth century and their own (Collier 1967: 212). This interest was strongly guided by Ercilla's *La Araucana*, which after a hundred years without any reprinting had been republished in Europe four times between 1733 and 1804 (ibid.: 28). Heroic Mapuche military leaders, such as Michimalonko, Lincoyán, Colo Colo, Caupolicán, and Lautaro, were idealized in an artificial way as role models for Creole elites' own military endeavors without feeling the need to harmonize the past and present realities of Mapuche lives (ibid.: 213). A representative example is provided by the priest, journalist and revolutionary Camilo Henríquez, who founded the country's first newspaper *Aurora de Chile*, in 1812:[37]

> Oh, patriots . . . recover your rights, imitating in unity and constancy your Araucanian ancestors, whose ashes repose in the urn of the sacred cause of liberty. . . . May Colo Colo, Caupolicán, and the immortal Lautaro (the American Scipio) be reborn amongst us, so that their patriotism and valor can serve . . . to frighten the tyrants. (Camilo Henríquez quoted in Collier 1967: 212)

This time the native reborn as Araucanian (as described above) became the Araucanian reborn as Chilean. And once again the rebirth was imagined as an event that had to take place in the forest with all its consequences for nature and natives. This is exemplified by the introductory part of the tragedy *The Triumph of Nature*, written by the author of the lyrics to Chile's first national anthem, Bernando de Vera y Pintado.[38] It was performed on 20 August 1819, O'Higgins's birthday (Collier 1967: 215). The scene is set at the mouth of the Biobío River, where the last descendent of the Araucanian lineage of heroes watches the sun set over the sea. Behind him dominates the "thick forest" (Anrique 1899: 113).[39] While he speaks to the sun, he sees a Chilean frigate approaching: "O universal life, O soul of the world, O heart of nature, O progenitor sun of our fathers, at whose sight there is no new species!" (ibid.: 114). The closer the frigate comes the better he hears the crew's shouting of patriotic slogans, and when they go ashore, he decides to hide behind the willows (ibid.: 116). Then the captain continues to ignite his crew with an emotive speech invoking the *maitén* trees in front of them:

> Oh, sturdy *maitenes*, whose trunks were once watered by unmixed blood—the indomitable Araucanian's blood with which he sealed his eternal independence. Today behold beneath thy shade the patriots who are renewing liberty in all the land. A day will come when, associated with the natives of this beautiful forest, we shall form a single family together. Her brilliant ferocity softened, Araucania will then taste the fruits of trade, the arts and the sciences. Agrarian laws will regulate her fields. Industry, and those connections which bring pleasure and wealth, will replace rusticity and indigence. (Vera y Pintado quoted in Collier 1967: 215)

The idealized Mapuche leader of course agrees to be reborn into civilization and takes the irresistible fruits—apples?—of trade, the arts, and the sciences, as it will be Eden on earth. The "natives of this beautiful forest" will swallow the tempting apple that will change savage life in the forest to civilized eternity in Eden. No more resistance.

Conclusion

Although the abovementioned scene is fiction, it does anticipate and further develop a dominant narrative present during the conquest of Araucanía in the second half of the nineteenth century by the Chilean state. As Crow (2013: 19–50) has shown, there are multiple and contested histories of this occupation, and she identifies two as the most dominant for the time of the military campaigns: on the one hand, stories of peace and friendship between Chileans and Mapuches, and on the other hand, shocking accounts of violent conflict (ibid.: 22). The former were state sponsored, leading to the dominant view that prevailed until the end of the twentieth century and presented the occupation of Araucanía as a peaceful process. The latter version began to prevail at the beginning of the twenty-first century, when the Commission for Historical Truth and New Treatment of Indigenous Peoples determined that Santiago's society at the time had become "convinced that it was [only going to be possible] to occupy Araucanía through violent means" (quoted in ibid.: 34).

In the tragic play *The Triumph of Nature*, the idea expressed by the captain aims at making the land productive by means of trade, arts, and sciences. Mapuches that approve the idea seem to have to trade in their own laws for new agrarian laws that do not take into consideration landscape's sentience, which makes the play really an absolute triumph of so-called civilization over the Mapuche. In the play there is no space for manifold indigene agency that would allow for adoption and cultural survival, as described by Crow (2013). There seems just one inevitable proceeding, the violently friendly absorption of the Mapuche by "civilization" that grew to the magnitude of a ruthless war of extermination (Bengoa 1996: 205–248)). Is this how "the fortunate copy of Eden" was thought to be made? That copy of Eden praised in the fifth verse of the second Chilean national anthem from 1847 is still sung during official ceremonies today:

> Pure, Chile, is your azure sky, / Puro, Chile, es tu cielo azulado,
> Pure breezes also blow across you, / Puras brisas te cruzan también,
> And your field, embroidered with flowers, / Y tu campo de flores bordados
> It is the fortunate copy of Eden: / Es la copia feliz del Edén:
> Majestic is the snow-white mountain, / Majestuosa es la blanca montaña
> That was given to you by the Lord as a bastion, / Que te dio por baluarte el Señor,
> And this sea that tranquilly washes your shore, / Y ese mar que tranquilo te baña
> Promises you future splendor. / Te promete futuro esplendor. (Lillo quoted in Pedemonte 2008: 156)

Georg T. A. Krizmanics is a political scientist and historian. As adjunct professor at IE Law School he teaches contemporary political and economic history. Dr. Krizmanics holds a PhD in social sciences from the Complutense University in Madrid, an MA in Latin American studies from the University Institute Ortega y Gasset in Madrid, and an MA in political sciences from the University of Vienna. He is a member of the Research Group on Global and Transnational History (Complutense University), and of the Research Group on Memory and History in the Contemporary World (National University of Distance Education, Madrid).

Dr. Krizmanics would like to thank Prof. José Antonio Sánchez Román for his thoughtful comments on an early version of this chapter; and the editors, Dr. Alexandra Coțofană and Dr. Hikmet Kuran, for their trust in his initial proposal, and their tireless efforts in bringing this volume together.

Notes

1. It was not until the second half of the nineteenth century that the several Indigenous peoples that had Mapudungun as a common language decided to use Mapuche (people of the earth) as their common and unifying denomination. Mapuches were organized in a decentralized way, unlike the Inca and Spaniards (Rinke 2007: 19).
2. For example, coats of arms often include scenic details and they are frequently referred to in official anthems.
3. For a conquistador's account, I use Alonso de Ercilla y Zúñiga's *La Araucana*, the foundational work of Chile's national literary imaginary. It was translated into English by Charles Maxwell Lancaster and Paul Thomas Manchester (Ercilla y Zúñiga 1945). Two Jesuit chroniclers account for missionary views. On the one hand, there is Ovalle's *Histórica Relación del Reyno de Chile*, the first chronicle dedicated exclusively to the country, printed in 1646. This work established a long tradition of Jesuit historians, which would be continued by Diego de Rosales and others. On the other hand, Rosales wrote in 1674 the *General History of the Kingdom of Chile. Indian Flanders*, the most complete chronicle on his time. Finally, *The Triumph of Nature* (Anrique 1899), written by the author of the lyrics to Chile's first national anthem, Bernardo de Vera y Pintado, makes for the Creole account.
4. I understand this landscape of resistance without clear distinction between nature and culture. The landscape was perceived as hostile by creoles, mainly because of the imagined alliance between nature and Mapuche peoples.
5. Ignacio Domeyko (1802–1889) was hired by the Chilean government in 1838 as a secondary school teacher for chemistry and mineralogy. He became a renown scholar and dean of the Universidad de Chile. Due to his merits he was granted Chilean nationality. See "Ignacio Domeyko," Biblioteca Nacional de Chile, http://www.memoriachilena.gob.cl/602/w3-article-646.html#presentacion, 18.06.2022.
6. Alonso de Ercilla y Zúñiga (1533–1594) was educated at Emperor Charles V's court. After the publication of the first of three parts of *La Araucana* in 1574, he was ordained knight of the Order of Santiago. See "Alonso de Ercilla y Zúñiga," and "La Araucana," Bilbioteca Nacional de Chile, http://www.memoriachilena.gob.cl/602/w3-article-3285.html; http://www.memoriachilena.gob.cl/602/w3-article-3286.html, 18.06.2022.
7. On the beneficial economic transformations for Indigenous and colonial communities after the peace agreement, see Pinto Rodríguez 2003: 34–53.
8. The original reads: "un territorio que nunca se ha rendido al yugo de un gobierno fijo."
9. The original reads: "Este carácter, si se le examina en su estado *normal*, es decir, en tiempo de paz, porque el hombre ha sido creado para la paz i no para la guerra, este carácter es afable, honrado, susceptible de las más nobles virtudes, hospitalario, amigo de la quietud i del órden, amante de su patria i por consiguiente de la independencia de sus hogares, circunspecto, serio, enérjico: parece nacido para ser buen ciudadano."

10. The original reads: "Pasando ahora más al sur de las citadas llanuras, montañas y cordilleras, nos hallamos en la tierra clásica de Arauco, dando a cada paso con los recuerdos de tiempos que fueron y con las riberas cantadas por el esforzado Ercilla."
11. The original reads: "entramos en una selva tan tupida i difícil de transitar, como si por ella nadie hubiese pasado desde los tiempos en que los primeros conquistadores pisaron el suelo Araucano."
12. The English translation is from Charles Maxwell Lancaster and Paul Thomas Manchester (Ercilla y Zúñiga 1945: 292).
13. The original reads: "Mucho mas ingratos que el temperamento de Valdivia habian sido los de la antigua Galia i Jermania en tiempo de los Romanos, cuando inmensos bosques i pantanos cubrian una gran parte del centro de Europa."
14. The original reads: "Uno de los efectos mas benéficos que pudieran resultar de la colonizacion de aquellas selvas i montañas, consistiría en la mejora del temperamento de toda la provincia de Valdivia, mejora que se debería al corte de los árboles i al cultivo de los terrenos que hasta ahora no hacen otra cosa mas que atraer i conservar la humedad i exhalar miasmas maléficos."
15. Descola (2013b: 5) explains this relationship in a similar way for the Achuar living on both sides of the frontier between Ecuador and Peru. "Conjugal harmony depend[s] on the relationship that the Achuar have managed to establish with many different interlocutors, both human and nonhuman—relations that ensure that these others are well disposed to them."
16. This relates also to experiences elsewhere, as the testimony of a leader of the Jawoyn of the Australian Northern Territory expressed after part of their land was converted into a natural reserve. "Nitmiluk national park is not a wilderness, . . . it is a human artefact. It is a land constructed by us over tens of thousands of years through our ceremonies and ties of kinship, through fire and through hunting" (Descola 2013b: 35 f.).
17. Bernardo O'Higgins Riquelme (1778–1842) carried out Chile's independence in 1818 and consolidated the nation in its early years. See "Bernardo O'Higgins Riquelme," Bilbioteca Nacional de Chile, http://www.memoriachilena.gob.cl/602/w3-article-562.html, 18.06.2022.
18. The original reads: "Atraher extrangeros agricultores, industriosos y capitalistas, no es posible sin ofrecerles una gran garantía, y toda la libertad de que gozan en otras regiones: esta es la adquisición más importante, virgen todavía la feraz superficie de nuestro suelo, é intactas sus entrañas, solo ellos nos procurarán en breve nuevos frutos y tesoros."
19. The original reads: "[E]l aleman por la naturaleza i el clima del país que habita, es mas idóneo para las fuertes labores que nuestra labranza i nuestra minería requiere, posee ademas con mayor perfeccion que nuestros labriegos los métodos de cultivo i es mas espertos en la esplotacion de las minas que nuestros operarios, ventajas de gran valía en la actual condicion de Chile, pues el país no tanto requiere brazos para aumentar su fuerza productora, sino inteligencias para aprovechar las robustas que posee por sí mismo i que ahora malgasta por ignorancia o por nuestro invencible apego a la rutina."

20. The original reads: "[E]l aleman, a diferencia del ingles cuyo primer orgullo es la patria, del frances que la ama por vanidad i por entusiasmo, del español que vincula en ella todas sus preocupaciones i todas sus virtudes, prescinde con mas facilidad de estos atractivos, i forma su patria en el bosque donde levanta su hogar i en el que vé crecer sus hijos libres i felices." (Vicuña Mackenna 1865: 26).
21. The scientific name for the Maque (also Maqui or Clon) is *Aristotelia chilensis*, and it is known as Chilean wineberry (Cordero, Abello, and Galvez 2017: 36–37).
22. The original reads: "La corteza es delgada y salen de ella ebras largas y de consistencia, tal que antiguamente hazian los indios vestidos de sus ilos antes que tubiessen lana de ovejas" (Rosales 1877: 224).
23. It is important to state, as the Chilean Government–employed German linguist Rodolfo Lenz (1895–1897: xxi, footnote p. 2) did, that Mapuche "is the only term the Indians themselves use."
24. See "José Toribio Medina," Biblioteca Nacional de Chile, http://www.memoriachilena.gob.cl/602/w3-article-663.html, 18.06.2022.
25. The *Historia general del reino de Chile. Flandes Indiano* was first published by Benjamín Vicuña Mackenna in three volumes between 1877 and 1878. Although it does not go beyond the first 117 years after the conquistadors arrived, it does range far beyond the purely military chroniclers who have dealt with this period, such as Alonso de Góngora Marmolejo, who finishes his account in 1575, or Pedro Mariño de Lobera, who goes only slightly further. See, "Historia general del reino de Chile. Flandes Indiano," Biblioteca Nacional de Chile, http://www.memoriachilena.gob.cl/602/w3-article-3356.html, 18.06.2022.
26. The original reads: "Los arboles y espesos bosques que producen las cerranias y valles deste Reyno, son en todas partes espesissimos y crecen mas y se multiplican con mayor lozania en las tierras de mayor altura polar."
27. The original reads: "Y estos bosques an sido las mas inexpugnables fortalezas donde los indios se han defendido, porque en ellas se meten quando los van a buscar los españoles, sin que alguna ocasión forzosa lo pida, y della salen a hazer correrías y malocas a nuestras tierras, volviéndose luego a su guardia de la montaña, donde tienen sus casas."
28. The original reads: "se trata del prodigioso arbol que en forma de Crucifixo nacio en una delas Montañas de Chile."
29. The original reads : "sobre esta cruz assi formada, se ve un bulto de un Crucifixo del mesmo arbol, del greusso, y tamaño de un hombre perfecto . . . como si un escultor [lo] hubiera formado" (Ovalle 1646: 59).
30. The original reads: "aquel santuario [left the admirer] consolado de ver un tan grande, y nuevo argumento de nuestra fee, que como comiença en aquel nuevo mundo a hechar sus raizes quiere el autor dela naturaleza, que las delos mesmos arboles broten y den testimonio de ella, no ya en jeroglificos, sino en la verdadera representacion dela muerte, y passion de nuestro Redentor, que fue el unico, y efficaz medio con que ella se planto."

31. The original reads: "y assi se llevo de un hachazo a quella parte, que correspondía ala cabeza, y rostro."
32. The original reads: "Corrio luego la voz de tan grade prodigio, y una señora muy noble, y muy devota dela Santa Cruz, que tiene sus haziendas en el mesmo valle de Limache hizo grandes diligencias por haver este thesoro, y haviendole alcançado, lo llevo a su estancia, y alli la edifico una Yglesia, y la coloco en un altar."
33. The original reads: "de todos los que van a visitarla fue entre otros el señor obispo de Santiago y la concedió las indulgencias que pudo para quien visite aquel santuario."
34. The original reads: "luego, que delos Umbrales de la Yglesia vi este prodigioso arbol, y a la primera vista seme representò en un todo confuso aquella celestial figura del Crucifixo, me sentí movido interiormente, y como fuera de mi, reconociendo a vista de ojo lo que a penas se puede creer sino se ve, ni yo havia pensado que era tanto."
35. The original reads: "he querido juntamente añadir una estampa [...] y esta ajustada con su original todo lo possible, para que el piadoso lector tenga en que admirar la divina sabiduria de nuestro Dios, y su altissima providencia en los medios, y motivos, que nos dado, aun en las cosas naturales, y insensibles confirmacion de nuestra fee, y aumento dela piedad, y devocion de sus fieles."
36. For the lyrics of the song and current veneration accounts about the Lord of Renca, see http://elcristoderenca.blogspot.com/2007, 18.06.2022. Mulhall (2003, 133) states that the song was ordered to be composed by the priest Miguel Rocha in 1963.
37. See "Camilo Henríquez," Biblioteca Nacional de Chile, http://www.memoriachilena.gob.cl/602/w3-article-564.html, 18.06.2022.
38. The anthem was sung from 1820 until 1828. See "Primer Himno Nacional," Biblioteca Nacional de Chile, http://www.memoriachilena.gob.cl/602/w3-article-94806.html, 18.06.2022.
39. I became aware of the existence of *The Triumph of Nature* through Collier (1967) and use his translations. Mine are indicated by referring to the original source in Anrique (1899).

References

Anderson, Benedict. 2006. *Imagined Communities*. London: Verso.

Anrique, Nicolás. 1899. *Ensayo de una Bibliografía Dramática Chilena* [Essay of a Chilean dramatic bibliography]. Santiago de Chile: Imprenta Cervantes.

Bengoa, José. 1996. *Historia del Pueblo Mapuche (Siglo XIX y XX)* [History of the Mapuche people (nineteenth and twentieth century). Santiago de Chile: Ediciones Sur.

Collier, Simon. 1967. *Ideas and Politics of Chilean Independence, 1808–1833*. Cambridge: Cambridge University Press.

Comisionado Presidencial para Asuntos Indígenas, ed. 2008. *Informe de la Comisión Verdad Histórica y Nuevo Trato con los Pueblos Indígenas* [Report on historical truth and new treatment of Indigenous peoples]. Santiago de Chile: Comisionado Presidencial para Asuntos Indígenas. Available at: http://www.corteidh.or.cr/tablas/27374.pdf.

Cordero, Sebastián, Lucía Abello, and Francisca Galvez. 2017. *Plantas Silvestres Comestibles y Medicinales de Chile y Otras Partes del Mundo* [Edible and medicinal wild plants of Chile and other parts of the world]. Guía de Campo. Concepción: CORMA.

Cosgrove, Denis E. 1998. *Social Formation and Symbolic Landscape*. Madison: University of Wisconsin Press.

Crow, Joanna. 2013. *The Mapuche in Modern Chile. A Cultural History*. Gainesville, FL: University Press of Florida.

Daniels, Stephen, and Denis Cosgrove. 1988. "Introduction: Iconography and Landscape." In *The Iconography of Landscape,* ed. Denis Cosgrove and Stephen Daniels, 1–10. Cambridge: Cambridge University Press.

Descola, Philippe. 2013a. *The Ecology of Others*. Translated by Geneviève Godbout and Benjamin P. Luley. Chicago: Prickly Paradigm.

———. 2013b. *Beyond Nature and Culture*. Translated by Jante Lloyd. Chicago: University of Chicago Press.

di Giminiani, Piergiorgio. 2018. *Sentient Lands: Indigeneity, Property, and Political Imagination in Neoliberal Chile*. Tucson: The University of Arizona Press.

Domeyko, Ignacio. 1846. *Araucania y sus Habitantes* [Araucania and its population]. Santiago de Chile: Imprenta Chilena.

Ercilla y Zúñiga, Alonso de. 1945. *The Araucaniad*. Translated by Charles Maxwell Lancaster and Paul Thomas Manchester. Nashville, TN: Vanderbilt University Press.

———. 1910. *La Araucana* [The Araucaniad]. Santiago de Chile: Imprenta Elzeviriana.

Foucault, Michel. 1977. "Nietzsche, Genealogy, History." In: *Language, Counter-Memory, Practice: Selected Essays and Interviews*, ed. D. F. Bouchard, 139–64. Ithaca: Cornell University Press.

Goic, Cedomil. 1992. *Los Mitos Degradados. Ensayos de Comprensión de la Literatura Hispanoamericana* [Degraded myths: essays on the understanding of Spanish-American literature]. Amsterdam and Atlanta, GA: Rodopi.

Le Bonniec, Fabien. 2008. "Del 'Territorio Independiente Araucano' al Wallmapu." In *Paisaje, espacio y territorio,* ed. Nicolas Ellison and Mònica Martínez Mauri, 47–67. Quito: Abya-Yala.

———. 2013. "What is a Landscape for the Mapuche?" *VideoArtResearch*. Retrieved from https://videoartresearch.org/what-is-a-landscape-for-the-mapuche.

Lenz, Rodolfo. 1895–1897. "De la Lengua Araucana [On the Araucanian language]. In *Estudios Araucanos. Materiales para el Estudio de la Lengua, la Literatura i las Costumbres de los Indios Mapuche o Araucanos*, ed. Rodolfo Lenz, xiii–xxxi. Santiago de Chile: Imprenta Cervantes.

Marimán, Pablo, Sergio Caniuqueo, José Millalén, and Rodrigo Levil. 2006. "Introducción" [Introduction]. In: *¡ . . . Escucha, Winka . . . ! Cuatro Ensayos de*

Historia National Mapuche y un Epílogo sobre el Futuro, ed. Pablo Marimán, Sergio Caniuqueo, José Millalén, and Rodrigo Levil, 11–16. Santiago: LOM Ediciones.
McFall, Sara. 2002. "Paisajes Visuales, Ópticas Distintas: Cambios en el Medio Ambiente y la Territorialidad Mapuche" [Visual landscapes, different views: changes in Mapuche environment and territoriality]. In *Territorialidad Mapuche en el Siglo XX* [Mapuche territoriality in the twentieth century], ed. Roberto Morales Urra, 301–23. Concepción: Escaparate Ediciones.
Medina, José Toribio. 1882. *Los Aboríjenes de Chile* [The aborigenes of Chile]. Santiago de Chile: Imprenta Gutenberg.
Miller Klubock, Thomas. 2014. *La Frontera. Forests and Ecological Conflict in Chile's Frontier Territory*. Durham: Duke University Press.
Monsalve, Ricardo. 2015. "The Scourge of God in the New World: Alonso de Ercilla's Araucanians." *Romance Notes* 55: 199–232.
Mulhall, María Graciela. 2003. *San Luís, Hombres y Mujeres Constructores de su Historia* [San Luís, men and women builders of their own history]. Digital Public Library San Luis website. Retrieved from http://bpd.sanluis.gov.ar:8383/greenstone3/sites/localsite/collect/literatu/index/assoc/HASH0159.dir/doc.pdf.
Museo Chileno de Arte Precolombino. 2002. "Introducción" [Introduction]. In *Voces Mapuches. Mapuche Dungu*, ed. Carlos Aldunate and Leonel Lienlaf, vi–vii. Santiago de Chile: Trineo.
O'Higgins, Bernardo. 1822. "Mensaje del Poder Ejecutivo. Honorable Convencion, del 23 de Julio [Message from the executive power, honorable convention of July 23rd]." In *Constitución Política del Estado de Chile. Promulgada el 23 de octubre*, Bernardo O'Higgins, vii–xii. Santiago de Chile: Imprenta del Estado.
Ovalle, Alonso de. 1646. *Histórica Relación del Reyno de Chile* [Historical account of the kingdom of Chile]. Rome: Francisco Cavallo.
Oyarzún Peña, Luis. 1967. *Temas de la Cultura Chilena* [Themes of Chilean culture]. Santiago de Chile: Editorial Universitaria.
Parentini Gayani, Luis Carlos. 1996. *Introducción a la Etnohistoria Mapuche* [Introduction to Mapuche ethnohistory]. Santiago de Chile: Ediciones de la Dirección de Bibliotecas, Archivos y Museos.
Pedemonte, Rafael. 2008. *Los Acordes de la Patria. Música y Nación en el Siglo XIX Chileno* [The chords of the homeland: music and nation in the Chilean nineteenth century]. Santiago de Chile: Globo.
Pinto Rodríguez, Jorge. 2003. *La Formación del Estado y el Pueblo Mapuche. De la Inclusión a la Exclusión* [State formation and the Mapuche people: from inclusion to exclusion]. Santiago de Chile: Dirección de Bibliotecas, Archivos y Museos.
Quidel Lincoleo, José. 2016. "El Quiebre Ontológico a Partir del Contacto Mapuche Hispano" [The ontological break since Mapuche-Hispano contact]. *Chungara: Revista de Antropología Chilena* 48(4): 713–19.
Rinke, Stefan. 2007. *Kleine Geschichte Chiles* [A Short History of Chile]. Munich: C. H. Beck.
Rosales, Diego de. (1674) 1877. *Historia General de el Reyno de Chile. Flandes Indiano* [General history of the kingdom of Chile. Indian Flanders]. Valparaíso: Imprenta del Mercurio.

Schama, Simon. 1996. *Landscape and Memory*. London: HarperCollins.
Smith, Anthony D. 1988. *The Ethnic Origin of Nations*. Oxford: Blackwell.
Vicuña Mackenna, Benjamín. 1865. *Bases del Informe Presentado al Supremo Gobierno Sobre la Inmigración Estranjera por la Comisión Especial Nombrada con este Objeto i Redactada por el Secretario de Ella Don Benjamín Vicuña Mackenna* [Bases of the report presented to the supreme government on foreign immigration by the special commission appointed for this purpose and drafted by its secretary, Mr. Benjamín Vicuña Mackenna]. Santiago de Chile: Imprenta Nacional.

Part III.
The Skeptics

CHAPTER 9

Can the Forests be Xenophobic?
Migrant Pathways through Croatia and the Forest as Cover

Sarah Czerny, Marijana Hameršak,
Iva Pleše, and Sanja Bojanić

According to research by forestry scientists, the forests in the most forested region in Croatia, Gorski Kotar, are a mixture of fir and beech trees, where the coniferous trees slightly outnumber the deciduous ones.[1] One important feature of these so-called natural forests" is their dense network of forest roads, which are very often used by people working in the forestry industry (Klepac 1997) as well as by walkers, hikers, and mushroom and fruit pickers—both from the local areas and beyond. In the last few years these forests have also become a part of the landscape for migrants, mostly from the Global South, who pass through them on their journey to Western Europe. They move along the so called "Balkan route." Since 2018 one of the most used northern parts of the Balkan route traverses northwest Bosnia and Herzegovina (Beznec and Kurnik 2020; Hameršak et al. 2020; Stojić Mitrović et al. 2020), and then clandestinely proceeds into the EU via the Republic of Croatia.

Croatia, while a member of the EU, is not yet a Schengen state and sits at the EUs external border. The migrants' journey then continues into Slovenia, which is also an EU member state but, unlike Croatia, a part of the Schengen area. It is here that the migrants' transit from Croatia to Slovenia frequently passes through the Gorski Kotar region, since it is located in northern Croatia and sits on the border with Slovenia. Thus, as a result of its specific geopolitical position, the Gorski Kotar region and its forests are a locus of intense migratory movement. Attempts by migrants to cross the borders are systematically prevented by the European Union acting through local state authorities, and differing border strategies and tactics are employed. These include mass pushbacks or fast-track deportations back to Bosnia and Herzegovina or to Serbia. These deportations are extensively documented in different forms (by journalists, NGOs and activists' reports, individual testimonies of different actors, and indirectly by gaps in official statistics), but they are also systematically covered up and denied by Croatian authorities.

The aim of this chapter is to explore how recent migratory movement through the forest landscape has shaped social relations in the forests, where we want to consider *how* the forests are responding to the migrants as they pass through them. The reason we take this approach is because in the Croatian social context the loudest narratives about the effect that migrants have on the forests are ones that are offered by far-right groups. In their accounts, they offer examples of how they think the migrants are disrupting both human and animal social life in the forests. But we argue for caution when considering the alleged disruptiveness of the migrants to "forest life," especially when bearing in mind accounts from other social contexts. As we explain in the first part of the chapter, in other social contexts where scholars have analyzed the relation between "nature" and right-wing and far-right narratives, and also in writing by some biologists about invasive species, it is clear that these are all *human* representations of how nonhuman life responds. Furthermore, they are selective, in that these representations are based on specific human interests. Due to this, in this chapter we consider alternative narratives about human-forest relations, based on published reports about pushbacks and borrowing Kohn's (2013) suggestion to read the forests in a semiotic way. In our analysis of these narratives we analytically approach the forests as agents, asking whether there is evidence that the forests themselves are making a distinction between the migrants, residents, or police who pass through them. Based on this analysis, we offer the conclusion that what is shared is that the forests are providing to all the human figures who pass through them a form of cover that conceals their activities when they are in the forests. Notably, when offering this cover, the forests do not discriminate between these human figures based on human concerns, such as their origin or residency. Consequently, we argue that the forests cannot be determined to be intrinsically xenophobic. However, the way that the forests are represented by humans *can* be xenophobic, and they are represented in a multiplicity of different ways that are often conflicting.

Forest Entanglements

When one considers the narratives circulating in the Croatian media about the relation between migrants and the forests, one sees that migrants are often depicted as being a problem for the forests. As a result of this relatively recent change in terms of "who" is walking in the forests, there is an apparent tension between local inhabitants and those passing through them. Members of local far-right groups inform the public via social media about the activities of migrants passing through the region (c.f. Goreta 2020). They criticize the Croatian government for not actively engaging the armed forces to defend Croatian national borders or the property of Croatian citizens, claiming that migrants are devastating the property of people in the local area on a large scale. In a newspaper report at the end of 2020, images were published that had been taken by a surveillance camera on a forest path, which showed many people walking through the forest in the dark. In the text that accompanied these images, a member of a far-right group spokespersons described his own experience of walking in the forest when migrants were present, claiming that they are armed and that they attack and rob other people who are in the forests. In his account, he explained that the way he and other locals act in the forests has changed because of the migrants' presence, saying, "While we walk through the woods, if there are not many of us, we do this in silence. But this is not good at all because of the wild animals. For example, if a wolf or bear hears us then it will take cover. [Making noise] is how you should walk through the forest. But now we are quiet because the migrants move in large groups, from twenty, thirty, to fifty people." Referring to the migrants, he continued: "I have met animals in the forest a million times, and never had any problems, but it is better to not have anything to do with these ones." "I would rather meet a bear in the forest," he concluded, "than a group of migrants." Similar narratives are voiced not just by actors from far-right groups, who are actively agitating for a "solution" to the "migrant problem." On social media, such as Facebook, it is also possible to find many photographs of food wrappers, containers, and clothing that are presented as having been left by the migrants. If such photographs are shared digitally where it is possible for readers to leave comments, often the comments are derogatory concerning the plight of migrants.

Nevertheless, such narratives are not unique to Gorski Kotar. The role that far-right groups in Gorski Kotar have given themselves—propagating narratives that suggest people walking through the forests are harmful to the local environment—is one that groups in other locations have also given themselves. As Biehl and Staudenmaier (2011) have argued, there is a long history of entanglements between ecological movements and right-wing exclusionary ideologies. In their account, Biehl and Staudenmaier discuss the important role that "nature" had in nineteenth-century ideologies developed by figures such as Ernst Moritz Arndt, who wrote *On the Care and Conservation of Forests* in 1815. They also draw out how such lines of thinking developed into National Socialist ideology, where "ecological themes played a vital role in German fascism" (ibid.: 30). Biehl and Staudenmaier make it very clear that the relation between nature and far-right ideologies is not a new one. As they explain, these far-right ideologies are supported by an underlying conceptual framework that proposes the presence of a natural order of things that subsumes all other interests, including human ones. These ideologies propose that it is this natural order of things that humans should respect and protect, and that society should be organized around nature's processes in order to preserve "social-ecological harmony" (ibid.: 27). From this emerges the key idea of needing to *defend* this natural balance.

Furthermore, there is not only a historical interest in "defending nature." Recent research (Darwish 2018; Hage 2017) on far-right ideologies and their relation to nature has identified the presence of a similar trope. Present-day ideologies seek to defend nature's balance and to represent nature, with far-right ideologues as not only self-appointed defenders of nature but also its self-appointed spokespersons. For instance, Darwish (2018) has written about the neo-Nazi Nordic Resistance Movement, exploring the relation between far-right subcultures, masculinity, and environmentalism in a narrative analysis of the podcast *Nordic Frontier*. In her account, she has described how members of the Nordic Resistance Movement offer themselves as self-appointed protectors of the Nordic forests (50) and set themselves up against a series of "significant others." One of the groups that she suggests is treated by the Nordic Resistance Movement as a significant other is the group she terms "Racial Strangers," which includes immigrants, Jews, and all non-Aryan people (72). In Darwish's analysis of the podcast, she describes how the hosts portray the Racial Strangers as having "little or no respect for Nordic nature" (73) and present them "as a foreign species outside its 'habitat' that lacks the necessary means to understand the Nordic flora and fauna" (73). Thus, like the nineteenth century ideologies that Biehl and Staudenmaier (2011) have described, these narratives also promote the idea that Racial Strangers in the Nordic natural habitat disrupt the balance of the "natural world," which in turn should be protected.

Bearing all this in mind and returning to consider those narratives about migrants in the forests of Gorski Kotar, we suggest that a similar structure is visible. Like Darwish's (2018) discussion of how the Nordic Resistance Movement describes Racial Strangers as a "mass," far-right activists in Croatia talk about the masses passing through the forest and about migrants in terms of their disruptiveness to the local social context of Gorski Kotar. In these accounts, they are not only considered to be disruptive to the property and activities of the local people, which includes their interest in developing the region as a tourist area, but they also disrupt the relation between the local people and the forests. As we have just mentioned, some claim that the way local inhabitants walk through the forests has changed since migrants have started walking in them. Yet perhaps the most important and notable similarity is how far-right activists present themselves as defenders of the forests, as well as defenders of the people who live in and near them. They declare they are defending the forests and local areas because no one else will, a point they constantly refer to in their calls for the Croatian government to "wake up to the migrant problem." Thus, there are notable parallels between these historical accounts, figures in the Nordic Resistance Movement, and those who want to "defend" Gorski Kotar.

It is important to also point out here that this interest in defending or protecting the forests, or even the "natural world" in its entirety, from incoming non-native species, is not exclusive to right-wing discourse. There are accounts within biological literature about how non-native or invasive species have not adapted to the "natural habitat" in the same way as native species have. For instance, Hettinger (2012: 7) describes non-native species as those species that are "foreign to an ecological assemblage in the sense that they have not significantly adapted with the biota constituting that assemblage, or to the local abiotic conditions, and the local biota have not significantly adapted to them." The question of how troublesome these non-native species are to the local environment remains unresolved and open for debate. Brown and Sax (2004: 530) maintain that in environmental and scientific communities, invasive species tend to elicit a "visceral emotional response," which they suggest is because there appears to be "something deep in our biological nature, related to xenophobia toward other humans, that colours our view of alien plants and animals."

Brown and Sax claim that this shares many parallels with those ideologies and discourses that determine "nature" to be something untouched, and that harbor "a tendency to view some prior condition as 'pristine' or most natural, and therefore the state that should be preserved" (530). From this they go on to say that while they do not want to claim that invasive species are "good," they do "plead for more scientific objectivity and less emotional xenophobia" (531). They conclude that it is the analytical work of scientists that creates this xenophobic response to invasive species, rather than invasive species being a problem per se.[2] They propose that not all native species should be treated in a uniform way, whereby they are all treated as "good," and in turn all non-native species are treated as "bad." They offer examples of native species, such as malaria-carrying mosquitoes, that cause enormous damage to local habitats, and of invasive species that have purposefully been introduced to benefit humans, such as crop plants that bring great benefits (483). While these scholars discuss the role of invasive species for quite different reasons from those of far-right activists or agitators, one aspect that is shared is how these self-appointed spokespersons' construction of the relation between incomers and local habitats has a fundamental influence on the way both are perceived. Irrespective of their positions, they are all speaking *for* nature. As Comaroff has concluded in a discussion about invasive species in South Africa:

> The fetishism of alien species and the dangerous politics of enmity it begets should alert us to the consequences, in these times, of the all-too-human effort to enrol nature as alibi in the effort to address vexed questions of sovereignty, belonging, entitlement, and distribution—to draw lines, sometimes necropolitical lines—in what is an increasingly border-less, yet unequal, world. (Comaroff 2017: 46)

Thus, as he describes, the concept of "nature" is appropriated for discussions of "sovereignty, belonging, entitlement, and distribution." In sum what becomes visible from these accounts is that it is human interpretations, as well as human re-presentations of "natural" landscapes, that determine who is welcome and who is unwelcome in them. Furthermore, it is clearly a human interest to label certain actors, be they human, plant, or animal, as "invasive" or as "unwanted" in a particular landscape.

"Reading the Forests"

It is because of this point that we now turn to consider how the forests themselves are responding to the human actors who are inhabiting them, either permanently or temporarily. Here we ask how the forests are responding to those figures who have joined this "multispecies muddle" (Haraway 2016).[3] This requires taking an analytical perspective that treats the forests as agents, rather than as objects to which humans are doing things. To our minds, Eduardo Kohn's (2013) work on how forests think offers a way to read the forest's response. Using the example of anteaters' snouts, he suggests that over time anteaters have adapted to the need to have longer noses to be able to access ant tunnels. In doing so, in an evolutionary sense, they have adapted to the environment. It is through the "logic of evolutionary adaptation," which Kohn argues takes a semiotic form, that it becomes possible to read meaning into these adaptations. In this sense, it is possible to consider "nonhuman organisms as selves and biotic life as a sign process, albeit one that is often highly embodied and nonsymbolic" (Kohn 2013: 75). As a result, if one accepts Kohn's ideas about reading forest life in this semiotic way, an observational window is opened through which we can explore how forest life might be responding to human activity.

Just to give an example from the social context of Gorski Kotar to further illustrate this approach, in 2014 the forests of Gorski Kotar were victim to an ice storm, when due to a set of specific weather conditions ice glazed the branches of the trees of the forest causing them to snap because of the weight. The damage caused to the trees by the storm was so extensive that it was declared a natural disaster and the forests are still recovering. Scholars who have studied this event (Teslak et al. 2020) argue that one of the main causes of this storm is climate change since the warmer air temperatures are creating the conditions for these meteorological events. Thinking about this in terms of Kohn's (2013) suggestion that we can read the signs of the forests to see what they are "thinking" through the way they adapt or respond, we can conclude that in this case the trees in the forests are suffering in these human-forest relations. It is also not just the trees, since other forms of life in the forests are also suffering due to not having the benefit of the cover that the trees once offered them. Therefore, in terms of how the forests in Gorski Kotar respond to the migrants passing through them, we argue that it is possible to see their responses in the migrants' accounts of their experiences in the forests and their interactions with the forests.

To do this, we explore representations of the forests in published pushback reports since, while they are scarce, they are also the most diverse accessible sources about migrants' movements taking place in these forests. More precisely, we will refer to reports gathered in the Border Violence Monitoring Testimony Database, the most comprehensive and still active collection of reports for the so-called Balkan route and Croatia. Before we discuss this further, it is important to point out two specificities of the pushback reports that we are going to analyze in detail.[4] First, these reports only outline the spatial configuration. When they try to label and geographically situate the space, it is done in a rudimentary way, for example: *the first motorway* (14 August 2018, No Name Kitchen), *the road no. 1* (13 August 2018, No Name Kitchen), *E65 motorway* (11 October 2018, Balkan Info Van), *B road* (6 September 2018, Balkan Info Van), and so forth. The reports also represent the forests in general terms such as *forest, river, wooded hills,* and *mountains,* or *small path in a forested area* (24 July 2019, No Name Kitchen), *some open woodland* (1 September 2018, Balkan Info Van), *nearby woodland* (25 August 2018, Balkan Info Van), *forests of Croatia* (27 July 2019, Border Violence Monitoring), as well as *wooded hills of the Croatian forest* (6 September 2018, Balkan Info Van), *woods in the mountains of Croatia* (1 September 2018, Balkan Info Van), *forest in Croatia* (26 July 2019, Border Violence Monitoring), or as formulated in a pushback report from 27 February 2019: "We walked a lot in forests, sometimes through small villages, sometimes we even crossed high mountains" (No Name

Kitchen). This kind of representation of space leads us to the second specificity of the pushback reports in terms of offering material for analysis. The abstract and rudimentary representation of space in these reports is because the reports tend to be in an administrative style and have specific goals (ones that do not focus on the description of landscape if it does not have "forensic" value). Moreover, both the people on the move as well as the activists who are documenting their experiences, who are also very often foreigners, are not familiar with the spaces they are discussing, such as the toponyms and the configurations of the terrain. This is evident in mistakes in naming places that reflect the position of people on the move but also the position of activists as foreigners, outsiders, and intruders.[5]

Despite such representations of space in these reports, it is possible to discern ones related to the Gorski Kotar area. Some reports refer to toponyms in Gorski Kotar, some of them to toponyms in Slovenia or in other regions in Croatia that indicate that the route probably went through Gorski Kotar, and some of them include toponyms or refer to walking distances, which makes it possible (although in some cases less probable) that the route went through Gorski Kotar. For some reports one can be sure, and for others one can only suppose with more or less certainty, that they refer to Gorski Kotar.

The Forest as Cover

From our readings of these reports what becomes visible is that although the forests necessarily represent an obstacle for people on the move, since they are something else that migrants must overcome on their way to their final destination, they are also an environment that enables people to move unnoticed by authorities or residents of the area, which has become the heavily guarded EU external border. This means that in the forests people can hide from unwelcome encounters, and (almost) every encounter is unwelcome and has the potential to result in a pushback. In fact, such encounters with others are one of the few mandatory elements of every pushback report since a pushback is the result of an encounter with authorities. The use of forests as a cover is implicitly presented in all the reports dealing with the movement through forests. Some reports explicitly name the forest as such: "The group of eleven males left Velika Kladuša on foot and crossed the Croatian border through the forest. They walked during the day using the cover of the forest and waited for the night to cross exposed areas" (7 August 2018, Balkan Info Van, emphasized by authors). Here they explicitly equate the cover of the forest with the cover of night or darkness. Where there is no forest, people must wait until night fall to offer them cover in order to be able to cross "exposed areas" and, vice versa, during the daylight they use the forest as the cover for their movement.

It is important to note that forests do not provide consistent cover but are interrupted by *open woodland* (1 September 2018, Balkan Info Van), *rivers* (8 July 2018, No Name Kitchen), *roads* (23 November 2018, No Name Kitchen), *houses* (30 November 2018, No Name Kitchen), and other objects constructed by humans. The diversity of this environment can also offer additional cover as in the case of houses. People sometimes, for instance because of the cold, leave the forest environment, in the strictest sense of the term, and hide in empty houses and shelters dispersed within the forest (1 December 2018, No Name Kitchen). More often leaving the forest and the cover of the trees increases the danger by making people on the move literally more visible, uncovered (25 August 2018, Balkan Info Van; 23 November 2018, No Name Kitchen). The covering function of the forest is even more evident in those descriptions of situations in which people are spotted by the police (or locals) near to but outside of the forest. It is in these descriptions that the forest becomes a place where people hide from immediate danger: "The larger group was spotted attempting to cross the stretch of river, protected by a border fence. The police spotted the interviewee and his companions by the river and began to shout at them. The group was scared and fled into the nearby woodland (back into the Croatian interior)" (25 August 2018, Balkan Info Van).

We will later consider the forest as a place of trailing and capturing people, but what is important to note here is that the forest offers such conditions for people on the move today. Such descriptions of the forest as a place of escape from danger are visible not only in reports that refer to traveling on foot (predominantly through the forest) but also in those that refer to traveling by vehicle in the region, which is greatly forested and where roads mostly go near or through the woods:

> After three days of walking, they reached a forest in Croatia where they were picked up by two vans that were supposed to take them further north. At this point they separated into two groups, with fifteen people in each van. During their ride to Slovenia, a police car tried to stop them. One of the van's drivers jumped out of the moving vehicle and accordingly one of the individuals pulled the hand brake to stop the vehicle. All the individuals exited the van and ran into a forest. (2 November 2018, No Name Kitchen)

Here, the forest terrain offers cover in the sense that it cannot be easily accessed by those forms of transportation that are usually used for following and capturing people on the roads.

The two fragments cited above about escaping from the police to the forest continue with sentences that reveal an ambiguity in the forest's role in migrants' clandestine movements through this region. We have already referred to this ambiguity by using the terms "cover" on the one hand and "obstacle" on the other when describing the forest. While the already quoted parts of two passages speak about forests offering cover and a place to escape from danger, the rest of these sections speak about forests as a dangerous place—"It was dark and hard to see anything in the forest" (25 August 2018, Balkan Info Van)—and a place that is limited in resources required for survival. "Thirteen of them reached the forest and hid there for two days, during which time they ran out of food. *'We were starving, and we were so thirsty'*" (2 November 2018, No Name Kitchen). Because of these difficult conditions in the forests, in both cases people were stopped from moving onward. In the first case "the group became dispersed and consequently the interviewee and two other young males were caught" (25 August 2018, Balkan Info Van), and in the second "they [the migrants] decided [....] to search for the authorities" (2 November 2018, No Name Kitchen). How demanding forests are for people who are forced to cross them clandestinely can be seen in these reports when they explicitly appear as a place of struggle: "They struggled in the forests because they ran out of food after four days. For five days they walked without eating and [for] three days without water" (7 June 2019, Border Violence Monitoring). Although a lack of food and water does not necessarily lead to people surrendering themselves, which did not happen in the abovementioned case, it can be a reason for this (28 November 2019, Border Violence Monitoring, No Name Kitchen; 14 September 2020, No Name Kitchen). In addition to a lack of food and water, another reason for people giving up is bad weather in the forests:

> After they entered Croatia, they walked through the deeply snow-covered forests, which hindered their progress significantly. Although they had enough food with them, the snow remained a persistent problem for them, and they considering giving up. On the fifth day of walking, in the afternoon of 18 January, they decided to walk into a nearby town, hoping to find some authorities who might take them back to Bosnia. They all felt very cold and their clothes and sleeping bags were wet. (18 January 2019, No Name Kitchen)

Referring to this and similar situations, the No Name Kitchen's monthly report of January 2019 employs the term self-deportation for such practice: "The hard conditions of the walking 'game' prove challenging enough that groups sometimes purposefully alert authorities to their location in the hopes of being 'rescued'" (No Name Kitchen and Balkan Info Van 2019: 7). Due to the hard conditions in the forests during the winter period and bearing in mind the regularity of pushbacks, alerting the authorities and "surrendering" can be understood not only as an essential way to save life but also as a "reliable, albeit dangerous, means of transport and return to BiH [Bosnia and Herzegovina]" (ibid.).

Thus, one of the dangers of the forests for migrants lies, paradoxically, in their covering possibilities. In addition to the forests offering cover for people on the move, they also offer a cover for police just before making arrests. According to the reports, in order to hide their presence in the forest the police dress themselves in casual clothes as a form of camouflage or cover. Dressed as civilians, wearing the same clothes as local residents or hikers, they can be conceived as being, if not "natural," then at least, in contrast to police officers, a regular element of the forest. Aside from dressing as local residents, police can take on the guise of smugglers, who for migrants are also not a "foreign element" of the forests but, on the contrary, at least in some cases, are expected and waited for.

> The group spent one night in the forest. The following day around 3 PM, a man appeared close to them, wearing casual clothes, and signaling them to come out of the forest to enter a van that would transport them to Italy. *"This man said to us: 'Come, come, come. We are not police and no police is coming. We will take you to Italia.' Okay, so we went into the car. When we were inside of it, the man said to us: 'Wait until the next car is coming.' Okay, [we] were waiting. But two or three minutes later we could hear some voices and see some men who had guns. And one of them said: 'Sit down here, we are police,' but they did not have police ID cards. We sat for one hour on a road, it was raining heavily, while he called to the police station."* (31 August 2018, No Name Kitchen)

Encounters with the authorities are, of course, not the only encounters that take place in this precarious context of escape. The reports highlight encounters with officials, but they also refer to encounters with locals, smugglers, and hunters, among others. For example, one group in the forest encountered "a number of hunters, whom they begged not to inform the authorities" (11 November 2018, No Name Kitchen). It is not known in this case whether the hunters reported their encounter with migrants to the police, but other reports suggest that encounters with locals or other civilians in the forest can be a prelude to pushback, since they alert the police. The implicit cooperation of local people is an important element of the multilevel European border apparatus.

In addition to encounters with others in the forests, the detection of migrants or discovery of their presence by others who remained unnoticed can, according to the reports, also lead to pushbacks. As one of the reports says:

> After about one week of walking, they approached the Kolpa river bordering Slovenia in the early morning hours. When they arrived, they found the river to be flowing much stronger than they had anticipated. . . . As the rest of the nine were already tired, they decided to light a fire to make tea. . . . They

saw flashlights coming down from the mountain and inferred that someone had seen their fire and informed the authorities about their presence. They immediately put out the fire. While several officers passed close to their campsite, they remained undetected and the officers proceeded past them unaware of their presence. . . . As several individuals were preparing to inflate plastic bags to use as flotation devices on the river, they turned their heads and saw again several officers coming down from the mountain with their pistols drawn. They ordered the group of eight to stop, which they did. (11 November 2018, No Name Kitchen)

The police apprehension of migrants, described in the report we cite below, has the same structure of the police failing and then succeeding in discovering people. It began as a siege of an otherwise empty "building in a forest next to a road," which migrants used that night "to shelter from the cold."

> Several officers approached the building and shot three times into the air. The seven of them remained silent. *"We are silent when police are coming, when they were shooting. They say 'Go! Go! Go!'* [but] *we didn't do anything."* The officers didn't enter the building and eventually ended up leaving. Still, it seemed that they were aware, or suspicious, of the presence of people in the house. Despite the respondent's insistence on leaving, the group decided to stay for the night. *"We must change this place; the police know where we are."* Ultimately, however, the group stayed in the house because they were so cold and so wet that they saw no other option. (1 December 2018, No Name Kitchen)

The next morning, the police returned, and the group was apprehended. (1 December 2018, No Name Kitchen). These descriptions in the reports and in other accounts show that the forests are not only presented as the place of cover for migrants moving forward but also as the place of their interception and arrest. According to the reports, people can be intercepted and arrested by the police at a *river side* (11 November 2018, No Name Kitchen) or *in a forest close to the Slovenian border* (23 September 2018, No Name Kitchen). In this context, the forests are depicted as a "crime scene," with a focus on the authorities and on police misconduct. In line with this, the reports offer detailed descriptions of police (mis)conduct, while the forest as a distinctive setting completely disappears and it is usually not even mentioned after the interception. At such crime scenes, according to the reports, the police order people to sit down on the ground; interrogate, frisk, and strip them; take or destroy their documents, mobile phones, and power sources; confiscate their money; ignore their requests; refuse to let them speak; use electric shocks (stun gun), guns, and pepper spray; burn their clothes; set dogs on them; and physically attack and beat them. Nevertheless, if forests disappear, they reappear again in these reports on pushbacks. When these reports start with an account about an arrest they start with the forests and end with expulsions in another forest. These forests are never a forest in the region of Gorski Kotar but forests on the eastern borders of Croatia and external borders of the European Union. Bearing in mind that most of the expulsions that take place in Croatia are not done by standard readmission procedures but clandestinely and often violently, the forest functions as a cover for these practices. Furthermore, the reports note that the "pushback points are most often close to streams or downward sloping hills, which serve as natural tools of assistance for the police officers carrying out these actions. People are pushed into the streams or down the hills" (No Name Kitchen 2018: 9).

Thus, when one responds to the question of what the forests offer to those passing through, our analysis of pushback reports suggests that the forests offer a form of cover to different actors on the migrant route that runs through Gorski Kotar. In this sense, the forests appear to take a neutral stance in terms of how they relate to those who are in their midst. In the first instance, they provide a way for people to move without being noticed, where the cover they offer helps people to continue their journeys without being seen. Secondly, and it is here that the neutral stance of forests becomes most visible, forests do not discriminate among those to *whom* they offer this cover. Just as they offer cover to migrants passing through, they also offer cover to other human figures, such as the police, local populations, and smugglers. What is notable here is that their activities also occur under the cover of the forests, and in this sense they are camouflaged. Thirdly, the cover offered by forests presents a challenge for all human figures passing through, irrespective of whether they are migrants or police or local people.

The dense foliage and difficult terrain slow down migrants' journeys and also make the forests a difficult place to navigate. Their terrain is sometimes difficult to identify and a challenge for humans to orient themselves in, which as we have shown is visible in the way that people describe them. It is here that local human knowledge takes a privileged form in the sense that people who are familiar with the terrain are more easily able to navigate through it. For this reason, we argue that from this perspective it appears that the forests are neither unwelcoming to visitors and xenophobic by "nature," nor are they welcoming. Instead, they do not discriminate in terms of those to whom they offer cover, whether they are figures who are frequently in the forests or just people passing through. Indeed, the point that we want to end on is that when one considers forests in this way, the issue of whether they are xenophobic or unwelcoming to visitors from the standpoint of cover becomes very clearly a human interest. When one tries to read the forests in the way that Kohn (2013) has suggested, rejecting or welcoming outsiders does not seem to be an interest of the forests at all. Rather, the question of whether landscapes are xenophobic is one that belongs firmly in the human realm and is clearly a focus of human interest and discussion.

Conclusion

In this chapter we have set out to consider whether we could describe the forests of Gorski Kotar as xenophobic toward outsiders, such as the migrants who pass through them on their escape to Western Europe. Our point has been that it is very important to not unwittingly get caught up in xenophobic debates about who, or what, is welcome in a specific landscape. As we have discussed there is a long history of the far right appropriating "nature" to shore up their racist narratives. Clearly, therefore, the role that scholars have is an essential one in determining whether landscapes, or in our case forests, can be deemed xenophobic or not. As we have discussed in this chapter, the forests of Gorski Kotar appear to be neutral regarding those to whom they offer cover. But it can also be argued that the cover they offer is actually revealing in that it discloses the status and perception of migrants and current migration practices in local societies, at both the official and unofficial levels.

Sarah Czerny holds a doctorate in anthropology from the University of Edinburgh, where her doctoral work was funded by a scholarship from the Economic and Social Research Council, UK. She is assistant professor in social anthropology at the Department of Cultural Studies, Faculty of Humanities and Social Sciences, University of Rijeka, where she also serves as head of department. Sarah is a member of the Expert Council for the Disability Office, University of Rijeka, and a member of the European Association of Social Anthropologists and of the International Union of Anthropological and Ethnographic Sciences.

Marijana Hameršak is a senior research associate at the Institute of Ethnology and Folklore Research in Zagreb and a titular assistant professor of the University of Zagreb. She graduated in comparative literature and general linguistics from the Faculty of Humanities and Social Sciences, University of Zagreb, in 2000, and earned her PhD from the same faculty in 2008 with the thesis "Formations of Childhood and Transformations of Fairy Tales in Croatian Children's Literature."

Iva Pleše graduated with a degree in comparative literature and ethnology from the Faculty of Humanities and Social Sciences, University of

Zagreb, in 1997. She gained her MA (2005) and PhD (2010) from the Department of Ethnology and Cultural Anthropology at the Faculty of Humanities and Social Sciences, University of Zagreb. Since 2001, she has worked at the Institute of Ethnology and Folklore Research, currently as a research associate.

Sanja Bojanić is a researcher who studied philosophy at the University of Belgrade and expanded and tailored her interests as a graduate student at the University of Paris 8, where she obtained an MA in hypermedia studies in the Department of Science and Technology of Information, and an MA and PhD at the Centre d'etudes féminines et d'etude de genre. Her studies ultimately led to interdisciplinary research based on experimental artistic practices, queer studies, and particularities of Affect Theory.

Notes

This work has been supported in part by Croatian Science Foundation under the project *The European Irregularized Migration Regime at the Periphery of the EU: From Ethnography to Keywords* (IP-2019-04-6642).

1. As well as beech and fir trees, the forests also consist of mountain beech trees, mountain spruce trees, and premountain spruce trees, among others.
2. When considering the issue of whether it is the analytical work of scholars that elicits this xenophobic response to the invasive species, it might be initially tempting to want to take a deconstructive approach. But Jean-Klein's (2001) writing on a closely related field, nationalism studies, offers a cautionary tale about taking this path. She has argued that in the field of nationalism studies there is a split posture on the part of scholars. On the one hand, when considering Western nationalist projects, scholars have taken "a determined, condemnational, and 'deconstructive' ethnographic stance," engaging in a "quasi redemptive exercise" (85). On the other hand, scholars have taken quite a different approach to "other" nationalisms that unfold in non-Western settings, and in post-colonial settings, where they are considered to be "subaltern, self-liberational, and virtuous," and scholarship appears to be "going out of its way" to assist these kinds of nationalist efforts (85). Furthemore, Hage (2017) has written about something similar in his account of whether racism is an environmental threat, where he has considered the relation between racism and speciesism, and the way that humans are represented as animals in racist narratives. Something that Hage points out is that our deconstructivist interests might be of no interest whatsoever to those persons whose narratives we seek to challenge. Hage argues that antiracist academics try to judge racists on the "logical contradictions, inconsistencies, and discrepancies in their arguments" as if they "are students or fellow academics with whom they are having

disagreements in a tutorial room about how to interpret reality" (2017: 5). As he writes, "it is as if the racists' greatest sin is that they are bad thinkers: they are 'essentialists,' they deviate from 'classical biological racism,' or they make false empirical statements about reality that the antiracist academics work for long hours to correct by highlighting a lot of statistical data that proves them correct" (ibid.). It is for this reason that we argue there is much to think about when considering *how* we might analytically approach such narratives.

3. Rather than considering forests as a unified singular form we propose they should be considered along the lines of what Haraway (2016) has termed a "multispecies muddle." Even though forests are often thought of as a singular living being, they are actually a habitat that hosts a wide range of different species. One of the many definitions that can be found in the *Šumarski list*, a Croatian journal dedicated to forestry, states: "A forest is characterized by harmony and mutual relationships between the living community or biocenosis (plants, animals, microorganisms) and site (soil, climate, relief)." Therefore, when we talk about forests, we talk about "air, water, climate, soil, landscape and the plant and animal world." [Editorial board, "Croatian Forestry at the Crossroads." 2012. *Šumarski list* (3, 4): 119.]. To this list we also add the human world.

4. The Border Violence Monitoring Testimony Database is available at https://www.borderviolence.eu/violence-reports/. Specific reports published in this database are quoted or referred to here in parentheses by date and name of the organization that recorded the report. For example: (7 November 2018, No Name Kitchen).

5. Furthermore, the term forest in the reports does not necessarily correspond to the dictionary sense of "a dense growth of trees and underbrush covering a large tract." (See "Forest." *Merriam-Webster.com Dictionary*, Merriam-Webster, https://www.merriam-webster.com/dictionary/forest.) "Forest" and similar terms can also denote nature in general or unpopulated or sparsely populated green areas. For example: "*I asked him, why did they act like that to me? I am not dangerous; I am not a thief. I don't want to stay in Croatia, only* [to pass through the] *jungle*" (7 November 2018, No Name Kitchen). The term *jungle*, used in this and other pushback reports, supposedly comes from the Pashto *dzjangal*, and it was also used for the name of the makeshift migrant camp in Calais, France (Hicks and Mallet 2019: 2). In pushback reports it can be used with or without translation, mostly in parentheses, to mean *forest* or, more broadly, *wooded terrain* (26 July 2019, Border Violence Monitoring) or *woodland* (5 December 2019, No Name Kitchen). Furthermore, boundaries between the forest (understood as an unpopulated area) and an urban area can blur in reports. It is not unusual that reports name as forest even those places that are close to highly urbanized or at least populated areas, such as in the following example: "The family was walking in a forest close to the town called Črnomelj, where they were seen by a man on a motorbike, who called the police. The family noticed the man calling the police and wanted to escape but the local people surrounded them and did not let them leave until the police arrived" (21 August 2018, No Name Kitchen; cf. 2 September 2020, No Name Kitchen).

References

Biehl, Janet, and Peter Staudenmaier. 2011. *Ecofascism Revisited: Lessons from the German Experience*. Porsgrunn, Norway: New Compass Press.

Beznec, Barbara, and Andrej Kurnik. 2020. "Old Routes, New Perspectives. A Postcolonial Reading of the Balkan Route." *movements: Journal for Critical Migration and Border Regime Studies* 5(1): 33–54.

Border Violence Monitoring. n.d. Testimony Database. Retrieved from *https://www.borderviolence.eu/violence-reports/*.

Brown, James H., and Dov F. Sax. 2004. "An Essay on Some Topics Concerning Invasive Species." *Austral Ecology* 29: 530–36.

Brown, James H., and Dov F. Sax. 2005. "Biological invasions and scientific objectivity: Reply to Cassey et al." *Austral Ecology* 30: 481–83.

Comaroff, John. 2017. "Invasive Aliens: The Late-Modern Politics of Species Being." *Social Research: An International Quarterly* 84(1): 29–52.

"Croatian Forestry at the Crossroads." 2012. *Šumarski list* (3, 4): 119.

Darwish, Maria. 2018. *Green Neo-Nazism: Examining the Intersection of Masculinity, Far-right Extremism and Environmentalism in the Nordic Resistance Movement*. Trykk: Reprosentralen, Universitetet i Oslo.

Editorial board, "Croatian Forestry at the Crossroads." 2012. *Šumarski list* (3, 4): 119.

Goreta, Mirela. 2020. "Nož pod vrat: kolone izbjeglica prestravile Gorski kotar: grupe naoružanih ljudi pljačkaju planinare, slučajne prolaznike, provaljuju u vikendice." ["A knife on the throat: Columns of refugees terrify Gorski kotar: Groups of armed people rob mountaineers, and passers-by, and break into holiday homes"] *Slobodna Dalmacija*, Accessed on 16. November, 2021.

Hage, Ghassan. 2017. *Is Racism an Environmental Threat?* Cambridge: Polity.

Hameršak, Marijana, Sabine Hess, Marc Speer, and Marta Stojić Mitrović. 2020. "The Forging of the Balkan Route: Contextualizing the Border Regime in the EU Periphery." *movements: Journal for Critical Migration and Border Regime Studies* 5(1): 9–29.

Haraway, Donna. 2016. "Staying with the Trouble. Anthropocene, Capitalocene, Chthulucene." In *Anthropocene or Capitalocene? Nature, History, and the Crisis of Capitalism*, ed. Jason W. Moore, 34–77. Oakland, CA: PM Press/Kairos.

Hettinger, Ned. 2012. "Conceptualizing and Evaluating Non-Native Species." *Nature Education Knowledge* 3(10): 7.

Hicks, Dan, and Sarah Mallet. 2019. *Lande. The Calais "Jungle" and Beyond*. Bristol: Bristol Univesity Press

Jean-Klein, Iris. 2001. "Nationalism and Resistance: The Two Faces of Everyday Activism in Palestine during the Intifada." *Cultural Anthropology* 16: 83–126.

Klepac, Dušan. 1997. *Iz šumarske povijesti Gorskoga kotara u sadašnjost* [From the forestry history of the Gorski Kotar into the present]. Zagreb: Hrvatske šume.

Kohn, Eduardo. 2013. *How Forests Think: Toward an Anthropology Beyond the Human*. Berkeley: University of California Press.

No Name Kitchen, etc. 2018. *Border Violence on The Balkan Route. May 2017–December 2018*. Not available online anymore. Private archive.

No Name Kitchen Velika Kladuša and Balkan Info Van. 2019. *Illegal Pushbacks and Border Violence Reports. Bosnia-Herzegovina, January 2019*. Not available online anymore. Private archive.

Stojić Mitrović, Marta, Nidžara Ahmetašević, Barbara Beznec, and Andrej Kurnik. 2020. *Dark Side of Europeanization. Serbia, Bosnia and Herzegovina and The European Border Regime*. Belgrade and Ljubljana: Rosa Luxemburg Stiftung and Inštitut Časopis za kritiko znanosti.

Teslak, Krunoslav, Karlo Beljan, Mislav Vedriš, Marijana Žunić, Mario Komarčević, and Jura Čavlović. 2020. "Štetni utjecaj ledoloma na stanje i strukturu šuma Gorskog kotare" [Harmful impact of icebreaks on the condition and structure of forests in Gorski Kotar]. In *ssa*, [*A collection of works from the scientific conference of Forest Management during climate change and natural disasters*]. ed. Igor Anić, 77–101. Zagreb: Hrvatska akademija znanosti i umjetnosti.

CHAPTER 10

Footsteps through the City
Encounters with Social Justice in Czech Urban Landscapes

Susanna Trnka

This chapter follows the footsteps of residents of three Czech cities, examining how history and social justice come to be experienced as embedded in urban landscapes.[1] It develops a phenomenological examination of perspectives and sensibilities of time, national identity, and state politics, examining how Czechs both create a sense of collective belonging and exercise powers of exclusion in order to enact their visions of a "just society." We start by walking through the streets of Prague, following along with pilgrims and city dwellers alike as they celebrate the religious holiday of Saint Václav, with a view to understanding how the Czech Republic, the country known for having the largest number of atheists and agonistics in the world, is revitalizing its "Christian heritage." We then consider the legacies of visions of social justice that emerged during World War II and in the Communist period through the lens of both the industrial landscape of Ostrava and the UNESCO heritage site of Český Krumlov.

In all three cases, my analysis focuses on how urban landscapes are experienced as imbued with a deeply historicized national identity that is increasingly being employed by the contemporary state to energize dividing lines between "Czechs" and "others." Utilizing Heideigger's conceptualization of "thrownness" alongside Czech phenomenologist Jan Patočka's work on perception and movement, I explore how Czechs actively create and deconstruct history, contemporary notions of how social justice might be achieved, and how these dynamics come to underpin the positioning of Muslim refugees and other "outsiders," including the Roma, as "alien" or undesirable by both nation and state.

The 28th of September is a public holiday in the Czech Republic, honoring the life and death of the tenth-century political and religious leader,

Saint Václav. Public processions, Christian masses, and historical reenactments of the saint's life are held in cities and towns across the nation. Pilgrims from around the country congregate in Prague before embarking on a thirty-kilometer procession to attend mass in the town of Stará Boleslav, where Saint Václav died. Simultaneously, the nation celebrates "Czech Statehood Day" as, since 2000, 28 September doubles as the commemoration of the founding of the Czech state.

In 2016, the Czech president, Miloš Zeman, originally an outspoken critic of moves to couple Czech Statehood Day with a major religious holiday, made his first-ever appearance at Stará Boleslav's mass. In his speech, he cited the Biblical verses "God is love" and "[if I do not have] love, I am nothing," before declaring: "Remember these words in a time when all of Europe is looking again for its cultural roots in the fight against Islamic fundamentalism. We must do all we can to make sure we truly return to these roots" ("Den" 2016).

What was the president suggesting? Was he advocating for greater tolerance and love towards others, or for closing the doors to those deemed as threatening Europe's "cultural roots"? Given Zeman's well-known antipathy toward refugees, summoning the nation's Christian roots was part of an ongoing effort to bolster antipathy toward Muslims. But as the possible double meaning of Zeman's use of Biblical verses demonstrates, his invocation of the nation's history could lend itself to various moral framings. As I suggest in this chapter, walking through towns and cities, be it as part of a pilgrimage or simply traversing from one place to another, highlights the multiplicity of ways that morality and social justice can be constituted with respect to historical events and the contemporary. What *we must do*, to echo Zeman, and how we must do it are radically contested issues that draw upon a range of historical narratives that we meet up with as we move through urban spaces.

As Barbara Bender asserts, landscapes—including urban ones—are always inherently subjective, "historically particular, imbricated in social relations and deeply political" (2002: S104). Tim Ingold adds to this the understanding that landscapes not only become a part of us, but we become a part of them as "each component enfolds within its essence the totality of its relations with each and every other" (2000: 191).

One way of examining how we politicize and historicize landscapes—and ourselves—is to walk our way through them. While much has been said of how narrative imbues landscapes with significance (Cruikshank 2001), so too do movement and sensory engagement (Anzoise 2017; Di Giminiani 2018; Ingold 2000). Landscapes are not only interpreted or "read" as cultural texts but evoke and provide different ways of being in the world (Brown 2019; Descola 2013). Many Czech urban spaces were intentionally constructed to convey nationalist visions (Bažant 2017), but to be effective, they must be experienced in particular ways. Contemporary activation and resignification of nationalist imaginaries of urban spaces is, as I examine here, accomplished via both discourse and movement, from pilgrimages to shopping expeditions. As Julie Cruikshank notes, sentient landscapes do not stand alone, ready to be discovered, but are created via interrelations with people; our engagements with landscapes are both referential and constitutive, with "the power to create or to establish what they signify" (2001: 391).

In the Czech case, urban landscapes were, at times, consciously constructed to "speak" very particular nationalist narratives. Today these messages often come to be embodied in ways that tend to reinforce exclusionist and racist ideologies of white, "traditionally" Christian, Slavic identity as ostensibly inherently in opposition to other national, ethnic, or "racial" and religious categories. In this chapter I draw together phenomenological theory and walking ethnographies of three cities to probe how this has come to be so, how and why such narratives are naturalized, and what means there may be to overturn or at least disrupt such claims.

Walking through Prague, Walking through Time

At the top of Prague's Wenceslaus Square stands a massive statue of Saint Václav on horseback. Legend has it that should the Czech lands be under threat, the statue of the Good King and his steed will spring to life, hurtling down the boulevard and assembling his many hidden knights, before leading Czechs to victory.

Consciously invoking such legends is one way of explicitly conjuring up historical narratives and placing oneself among them. Such gestures to the past can be fleeting, as when walking up Prague's Petřín Hill my friends wave toward the Hunger Wall, reminding everyone assembled that during the fourteenth century famine King Charles IV ordered the wall's construction to provide employment for the poor and relieve their hunger.

Others are self-consciously elaborate, as when my friends Jarda and Veronika, both in their early sixties, took me on a five-hour historical walking tour of Prague. Each step was punctuated with multiple, crisscrossing historical legends. At Vyšehrad we stood on the fortress ramparts overlooking the river as they narrated the story of Libuše, the prophet and female founder of the ruling Přemyslid dynasty, who in the eighth century had a vision of where to build the city of Prague. "Look at the curve of the river and how the landscape opens up before you," Jarda prompted, "you can see why this particular spot would be most advantageous for building a fortification." Crossing Charles Bridge provoked accounts of the exploits of King Charles IV, who initiated its construction, just as Prague Castle's Saint Vitus Cathedral spurred stories about how Saint Václav oversaw the building of the first church there. So it went, the account of one legendary leader following another. Each of these leaders not only helped make the city into what it is today, but, as their stories attest, were thought to be endowed with extraordinary physical, mystical, or intellectual abilities and with a deep sense of justice and a willingness to work for the collective good.

While I was fascinated by how our journey made the historical landscape come alive, this feeling was not new to them. Our footsteps retraced a walk that Jarda and Veronika used to do annually with their children. Each child was tasked with learning a new story or legend to share when they reached a particular spot, be it at one of the thirty-one statues of saints and historical personages who line Charles Bridge (or, in the case of Prince Bruncvík's statue, stand on the bridge's pier) or at the cannonball embedded in Vyšehrad's eleventh-century rotunda. The walk became not just a history lesson but a process of linking stories and legends to the material realities in their midst, enabling an old building, statue, or monument to rise to new significance while remaining part of the contemporary landscape.

How we come to commemorate events and connect them to a specific place is as much about the present as it is about any given place's actual past. Places are always imbued with history, whether we recognize it or not. History resides in the buildings, the turns of the street, the cobblestones we slip on in the rain. Prague's Old Town, inhabited since the nineth century, reflects more than a millennium of urban development. Malá Strana (the Lesser Town) is the setting for movies needing an eighteenth-century backdrop while also the space of buses, commuters, playgrounds, bars, and ice cream shops. How then do these streets and buildings convey history? In addition to commemorative rituals, how do we actively encounter history in specific places, coming to embody historical narratives through more mundane movements such as our daily traversing through time and space? Here the work of Martin Heidegger and Czech philosopher Jan Patočka on thrownness, movement, and perception is helpful.

One way Heidegger described the work of history was through the concept of thrownness, or how as human beings we are thrown into a particular time and place and that is where we must enact our lives. Thrownness, according to Heidegger, is at the heart of the human struggle as it results in inevitable feelings of guilt. We are never at the beginning of an event but are instead thrust into a time and place already constituted.

As such, we enter a situation ripe with choices, paths, options—not only those we opt to embrace, but also those we cannot take. We make choices, we feel guilt. The truly knowledgeable self is the one who can reconcile this tension, accepting their place in history while shaping their destiny. Heidegger thus viewed our existence as historically and spatially prescribed, but he also emphasized how grasping our sense of place in history vests us with the ability to choose our responses to the exigencies of space and time.

One of Heidegger's key points is that the spaces in which we dwell are always marked by time. Technology—buildings, bridges, agricultural divisions of land—is a part of these histories, reconfiguring the landscape, the world in which we live, and thus reconfiguring who we are and can be. Heidegger's image of the bridge that actively gathers both sides of the river to create a meaningful space is a good example:

> The bridge swings over the stream "with ease and power." It does not just connect banks that are already there. The banks emerge as banks only as the bridge crosses the stream. The bridge designedly causes them to lie across from each other. . . . It brings stream and bank and land into each other's neighborhood. ([1971] 2001a: 150)

Part of dwelling in the spaces created by buildings or bridges is moving through them. As Patočka (1998) (and Husserl before him) emphasized, our perception of the world and thus ultimately our understanding of it, is dependent on acts of movement. Walking can be a central facet of this. Whether a formal procession or a pragmatic means of getting from one place to another, walking is a way of dwelling and finding one's footing in the world. In the cities we live in or in foreign locales, walking is a means of dynamically creating a sense of place (de Certeau 1984), while also opening up to the possibilities of incorporating it within us. Like other forms of movement, walking enacts and throws into relief our passage through space and time, simultaneously constituting our presence and absence through a series of spaces (Lepecki 2004).

Walking is interrelational, a means of bringing us into, or out of, pace with others. As Tim Ingold and Jo Lee Vergunst suggest:

> That walking is social may seem obvious. . . . However to hold . . . that social life is walked is to make a far stronger claim, namely for the rooting of the social in the actual ground of lived experience, where the earth we tread interfaces with the air we breathe. It is along this ground, and not in some ethereal realm of discursively constructed significance, over and above the material world, that lives are paced on in their mutual relations. (2008: 2)

Walking is also a means of embodying culture. Marcel Mauss noted how English soldiers had a different gait from French ones, remarking,

"You all know that the British infantry marches with a different step from our own: with a different frequency and a different stride" ([1935] 2007: 52). Through an examination of what he called our "techniques du corps," Mauss highlighted how our bodily enactments are marked by our social and cultural milieu, so that any movement, be it dancing, skipping, walking, or digging a ditch, not only carries cultural meaning but is culturally mediated.

In the city, walking has its own rhythms, movements, and possibilities for engagement. Walking in the footsteps of those who came before us, traversing along their pathways, moving between the buildings they erected, our bodies respond. We may no longer need to leap out of the way of horse-drawn carriages but instead move aside for Segways and motor scooters. As we move through life, what the city requires from us changes. Cobblestones and high heels have their own ways of accommodating one another, requiring a new sense of balance. Pushing a baby pram along city streets requires yet another kind of attentiveness to the existence (or not) of sidewalks and curbs. For some of the elderly, spaces seem to shift, making new demands on old bodies. My friend Anežka, who is eighty and walks at a brisk pace, jokingly complained, "I go to the graveyard every year, and it seems to me the path and the steps are changing—every year they get steeper and wider!" The city lives through our bodies and we are continually relearning how to accommodate it.

Nor are we alone on these streets. Buildings have plaques reminding us of the lives of noteworthy occupants—"in this house lived, and on December 31, 1958, died, opera singer in the National Theatre of Prague, Milada Ševcovicová." Even more imposingly, statues that are life-size (or larger) seemingly prop up architectural facades—strong men with barrel chests, semiclad women, or fat, bucolic infants—staring down at us as we walk along. One feels their presence, as our feet find themselves tracing down paths well worn by those who came before us, seeing some similar vistas, feeling a similar sense of cold or warmth, a simulacrum of the past, necessarily incomplete, conjured up by the sedimentation of time under our feet. This kind of walking is an act of tethering, of getting to know the ground beneath our feet and, in doing so, recognizing how it anchors us to a particular space and time, interlinking a moment in the life of a city with a moment in our lifespan, interconnecting a progression of lives and generations that are always flux but never interchangeable.

For Heidegger ([1959] 1966), such reflective activity necessarily leads to embracing a particular kind of belonging, known as autochthony. The logical slippage between feeling anchored in a specific time and place and the privileging of autochthony is, however, not self-evident and is worth considering in detail.

Heidegger opened his *Discourse on Thinking* by suggesting that we need to make a distinction between calculative thinking—the thinking of planning or organizing for future profit—and meditative thinking or reflecting on "the meaning which reigns in everything that is" ([1959] 1966: 46). He then recounted that anyone can follow the path of meditative thinking in his own manner and within his own limits: "It is enough if we dwell on what lies close and meditate on what is closest; upon that which concerns us, each one of us, here and now; here, on this patch of home ground; now, in the present hour of history. . . . We grow thoughtful and ask: does not the flourishing of any genuine work depend upon its roots in a native soil?" ([1959] 1966: 47).

Heidegger's next step was to suggest that "the rootedness, the autochthony, of man is threatened today at its core!" ([1959] 1966: 48–49). Invoking his interpretation of the work of the poet Johann Peter Hebel, Heidegger asserted we should heed Hebel's message that "[f]or a truly joyous and salutary human work to flourish, man must be able to mount from the depth of his home ground up into the ether" ([1959] 1966: 47). As is well known, for Heidegger the search for and valorization of soil, ground, and rootedness led to his embrace of the Nazi Party, deploring those whom he, and the Nazis, viewed as "rootless," namely Jews (Lapidot and Brumlik 2017). While there is much controversy over just how involved Heidegger was in Nazi politics, many have convincingly argued that his philosophical writing promotes views of German nationalism that align with Nazi Party rhetoric (e.g., Smith 1995).

Contra Heidegger, as anthropologists have long demonstrated, autochthony or being the "first people" of the land (sometimes conceptualized as being born out of the earth) is, however, never just about finding the soil under one's feet. Autochthony is actively constructed, and as Zeman's invocation of belonging in the Czech Republic and, more broadly, in Europe as a decidedly Christian endeavor demonstrates, it is a selective enterprise that includes inclusion of those who see and feel the soil between their feet but also exclusion of those who do not. Autochtony reflects, only for some, the feeling that "here, on this patch of home ground; now, in the present hour of history." There are other ways to cut these histories, and, as Heidegger himself elsewhere highlighted, the end point to which any given path may lead is never guaranteed ([1971] 2001b: 181–84).

The historical accounts that are articulated by pointing out architectural features or undertaking pilgrimages, reenactments, or historical walking tours offer a select slice of the past, asserting very specific linkages between time, space, ethnicity, and national identity (cf. Alonso 1994). Such selectiveness can be quite obvious: despite professing to have "no religion" like the majority of Czechs, Jarda and Veronika's tour of the city reflects a distinctively Christian perspective. Notably, their passion for history did not extend to Josefov, the city's large, renowned Jewish Quarter, about which they said they know little.

Instead, "history," as they describe it and which we came to embody during our five-hour journey, focuses closely on the activities of legendary leaders, patrons, and saints recognized for bringing Christianity to Eastern and Central Europe, but even more so for their contributions to developing the Czech state, in terms of its political power and its cultural and educational foundations. Saint Václav united Christians and overturned the rule of his (baptized, but at heart still pagan) mother; he is most highly regarded, however, for his generous and just treatment of the poor. King Charles IV is similarly noted for being the Holy Roman Emperor, but more importantly for expanding Prague, making Bohemia a center of European political power, founding Charles University, and taking care of his starving people by building the Hunger Wall. Both rulers are most valued for their development of a just, generous, and inclusive monarchist politics, propelling the development of a nation whose inhabitants prospered and stayed on par with, or led, the rest of Europe.

In popular discourse, the development of such a just society is often depicted as a teleological progression: the city founded by the prophet Libuše became the capital of the state developed by Saint Václav, which was further refined by King Charles IV. Each step in this process is portrayed as part of a natural evolution of society toward being more just and fair. As sites of commerce, politics, higher education, and cosmopolitan exchange, cities are often viewed as embodying the ongoing refinement of knowledge and, therefore, moral development. They are thus linked with a vision of social justice as it will one day be achieved if only history keeps unfolding.

At the same time, many narratives include historical interruptions that derailed the momentum toward ever-increasing progress and social justice. These include such moments as the imposition of Austro-Hungarian rule, placing Czechs under foreign domination, the Nazi occupation during World War II when social justice morphed into dogged survival, and the period of state socialism, when moral progress was stalled by silence, fear, and collaboration with Communist authorities. As my sixty-year-old friend Kryštof once explained, "The country's morality was left undeveloped because we were stifled by forty years of Communism. So, while the West was moving forward [morally], we were stagnant and that is why there is all this corruption here now."

Jarda and Veronika are undoubtedly aware of such counterpoints to the narrative arc of national development and social justice they espouse. But neither alternative perspectives nor major moments of breakage dominate how they experience and narrate (their place in) their city's history. They may have trouble recounting Jewish histories of Prague, though I suspect they know more than they think they do, but they could have capably traced Communist or Nazi pasts in the landscapes before us. Instead, they offer a particular framing—of kings and saints and (a certain kind of) social justice—that feels to them as indisputable as the cobblestones under our feet. Indeed, it is this intertwining of history and the sensory, embodied realities of moving through the place where specific events once happened that makes other possibilities challenging to recognize. Nonetheless, other narrators and other cities foreground different kinds of historical consciousness.

Walking through Dust, Christianity, and Totalitarianism in Ostrava

Ostrava, in the eastern part of Moravia, represents a different kind of urbanity. Home to approximately 294,000 inhabitants, Ostrava was founded in the mid-thirteenth century and rose to prominence with the development of mining and steelworks in the early 1800s. Under state socialism, these industries rapidly expanded. Post-1989, however, the mines and many of the steelworks began to close and jobs became increasingly insecure.

Everywhere one goes, the city is marked by its industrial past and present. The Czech Republic's largest steelworks, Liberty Ostrava—previously ArcelorMittal Ostrava—dominates local employment and the city's skyline. As part of an official tour of what was then ArcelorMittal Ostrava, I was led around the steelworks' premises by Viktor, a retired foreman, rehired as a company tour guide. I was the only visitor that day and Viktor was delighted to give the tour in Czech. About an hour into it, he began to deviate from the company-approved script. Standing outside the main production buildings, he drew attention to the haze in the air, explaining it was composed of dust that hadn't been caught by the plant's de-dusters. He had already informed me about the company's ecological awareness and the plant's advanced de-dusting procedures, following which he noted that the Human Resources department always checked afterward to make sure that he did not forget to include that part. "The part they don't tell me to show you is the black stuff coating the ground," he now murmured. We both stared at the thick layer of dust. "The company cleans it up all the time," he stated, "otherwise it would be worse." "But without dust," he added wryly, "it wouldn't be Ostrava."

We continued walking until we came to a large, empty warehouse. Viktor took a quick look inside and then pulled me in, shutting the door behind us. "I looked you up on the Internet," he asserted. "You wrote about Christianity in Fiji?" I nodded, feeling confused. It took me a while to realize he wanted to know my stance on "believers" before recounting to me his life story.

Hidden away in the warehouse together, Viktor told me he was born in 1946 so had effectively spent half his life under Communism (that is, after 1948) and the other half (after 1989) living under democracy, and so he could attest that both have their good and bad aspects. Under Communism the state took care of the people, he said. The steelworks' premises once included a bank, a health center, a post office, and a dormitory. The company even organized holidays for its employees.

But under Communism, life was difficult for Catholics, and as a believer, Viktor ran into trouble when he wanted to go to university, being instead forced to work as a laborer. He asked if I had read George Orwell's novels, explaining his fascination with how Orwell captured the Communist mindset so well. "That is because totalitarianism is the same wherever it is," he asserted, "[whether] it is in the police force that Orwell worked for, in the Communist state, or under Nazism." He added:

> Communism could happen again. The Bible tells us where all these things come from. It tells us it's human nature and human nature hasn't changed over time. . . . People don't remember how bad it was and it is possible it will come again. Look, even Auschwitz is not so far from here—only eighty kilometers or so from Ostrava. Who is to say that won't happen again?

We were heading back to the company headquarters when Viktor grabbed me by the shoulders, declaring:

> Stand here and look at the building just next to the headquarters, the scientific research building. Look at the top floor and you'll see another floor, set back under the roof, almost hidden. Can you see the two small windows, just at the end, facing the main road and the entryway? And on the other side, there are another two, just in the same place but facing the other direction. Do you know what they are?

They looked like gun slots to me, but I let him answer.

> They are for shooting. This building was built in the 1960s, fifteen years after the end of the war. Yet they still built gun holes so that if an enemy came down the street and tried to enter the premises, they could gun them down. . . . I don't show that to everyone.

It was supposed to be a company tour highlighting ArcelorMittal's productivity and environmental sensitivity. But Viktor read the landscape differently. His was a conflicted story of the steelworks for which he'd worked for decades, which he held complicit in the violence of socialism, still visible through the research building's gun slots, and in the environmental destruction of capitalism, evident in the layers of dust. Rather than a teleological movement towards social justice (from Libuše to Saint Václav to King Charles IV), his account focused on coming to terms with the Communist and Nazi pasts—and perhaps even their potential futures—through an understanding of the Bible's reflections on the immutable nature of good and evil.

Viktor was one of many persecuted by the socialist regime due to their religion. While not illegal, Christianity was frowned upon and strictly regulated by state socialist authorities, with numerous crackdowns on priests and other religious authorities for their purported anti-Communist sentiments. Most believers hid their religious affiliation as much as possible to protect their education and employment opportunities.

Christianity is no longer targeted. The Czech Republic has, however, never been a particularly religious nation—according to a Pew Research Center (2017) poll, 72 percent of the population describe themselves as atheist, agnostic, or believing in "nothing in particular." Another 26 percent describes themselves as "Christians," mostly Catholics. Some parts of the country, including Moravia where Ostrava is located, are considered more religious than others (Willoughby 2003). That said, religious rites once conducted in hushed tones now openly take place throughout the country, and plenty of those who believe "nothing in particular" ally with Christianity as part of their national tradition.

But when it comes to debating political morality, apart from the very faithful such as Viktor, people generally do not invoke the Bible to determine what is or is not socially just. Rather, ideas about what makes a fair society tend to draw on a multiplicity of framings, among which (teleological) narratives of national development, socialist ideals, and free-market rhetoric figure prominently. Implicit throughout these is a more diffuse sense that it is the role of society to promote the greater good and enable, or at least not hinder, individuals' opportunities to live a good life, while requiring of citizens some level of responsibility either directly for one another or back towards the state (Trnka 2017a, 2017b). Such views on social justice may be crystallized in the platforms of political parties, but they also emerge in public discourse as loosely framed historical reminiscences about the "good leaders" of the past or in shared notions of how reciprocal relations between citizens and states should (but may not) operate.

Today, public discourse has largely been overtaken by a singular vision of the state socialist past as politically, economically, and morally damaging. The socialist regime is often referred to by the same term—*totalita*, or totalitarianism—used to describe the Nazi protectorate. But not everyone shares this predominantly negative view.

Like Viktor, many Czechs recount positive aspects of the previous regime, including free healthcare, subsidized housing, and secure employment. This is not to dilute the impact of the 1989 revolution, which is widely viewed as indeed a revolutionary step forward in granting citizens' increased freedom and the potential to have a real role in governance and civil society. But while state socialism as a mode of governance is widely, but not entirely, rejected, the economic ideals of state socialism reverberate through social discourse. As one working-class man in Prague stated to me, "the country is full of corruption as 30 percent of the people own all the wealth." He stated this disparity as if it is an obvious, fundamental injustice. For him, and many others on the left end of the political spectrum, the socialist promise of equal distribution of resources holds strong.

For others on the right, injustice isn't manifest through the existence of class difference per se but rather through the unequal opportunities that are thought to enable some to rise to the top while others flounder in the new economy. Their disquiet is often voiced through complaints about corruption, an idiom used to suggest a broader lack of equal opportunities.

In either iteration, left or right, efforts to create a just society are depicted as thwarted by the government's lack of interest in fostering society's evolution toward an increasingly moral and just community. Unlike the rulers of the past—Libuše, Saint Václav, and King Charles IV—who focused on building a great and just society, the leaders in this political system, many contend, are out to line their pockets.

If, however, social justice is widely viewed as promoting equality, either in terms of resources or opportunity, and having one's wellbeing protected by the state, there are those, such as Muslim migrants and the Roma (otherwise known as "Gypsies")—both depicted as decidedly "Other" in public discourse—for whom the possibility of social justice seems far off.

Building Boundaries in Český Krumlov

Just as my Prague friends enjoy historical walking tours, so do many of the people I know in the historic southern city of Český Krumlov. A small city of about thirteen thousand people, Český Krumlov is famous for its historic thirteenth-century castle. On one of my visits there, I arrived just as a newly restored part of the castle garden was opened to the public. My friends, sixty-year-old Martina and her husband, seventy-year-old Ladislav, were eager to tour the garden, as were many locals. As we walked, we met a small crowd of people engaged in lively discussion about the course of the path that ran through the newly reconstructed area. "How much of this path is merely restored and how much is brand new?"

"Wasn't there once a gate at that end of the garden, where there is now a cement wall, which the path used to pass through?" Ladislav eagerly joined in, all the while carefully calculating the distance from his house of the various features under discussion, murmuring that the missing gate was so many kilometers from his house, the original start of the path was so far off from his front door.

The group, which we had now joined, kept walking. At an overlook that afforded excellent views of the city, the loose collection of people began to recount how the landscape had changed over the years. The most vocal, perhaps because of his seniority, was a man who had settled in Český Krumlov during the 1950s. "This street used to have houses that stood facing that direction, not like the way they are now. And that building that is now a gallery used to be the old brewery," he proclaimed. Ladislav and Martina drew my attention to other landmarks, pointing out a synagogue visible in the distance. People in the crowd who overhead them joined in, speaking sympathetically about the fate of the Jews who had been sent to concentration camps during the war.

The conversation turned to a collective lamentation over the "destruction of the city." To my surprise, it was neither Germans nor Communists but the Roma who were singled out for blame. In the 1950s, said the stranger who had moved to Český Krumlov at that time, "there were so many Gypsies living in the center of town, they took over the buildings." Martina interjected, explaining to me that, predominantly inhabited by Germans before the war, the city had been a Nazi stronghold. When the Nazis left, Roma from other cities who had survived the Nazis' anti-Roma purges moved in.

The man then related how, in the 1950s, if you walked into the city at night, "You could see Gypsies who weren't wearing any pants, just shirts, so when they ran around their naked buttocks were visible." He recounted seeing an Austrian visitor "reach into his pocket, pull out a handful of chocolate candies, and throw them into the center of a group of Gypsies, and the Gypsies ran around like chickens, picking them all up." He laughed and I was struck by the animosity of portraying the Roma as akin to animals, in contrast to the civilized Czech, Jew, or German.

Nothing more was said of "Gypsies" until the next day when we were walking to Ladislav and Martina's church for Sunday services. Ladislav told me,

> The Gypsies got used to not working during Communism. They were given money by the state and got used to that. At the same time, the Communists put up the Iron Curtain so the Gypsies could not go anywhere. They were used to traveling in their caravans, but the Communists forced them to live in *paneláky* (state-run, prefabricated apartments). So they broke down the

walls and threw everything out and generally made a mess. Nobody else in the panelák could sleep when the Gypsies were up all night singing! It's fine for the Gypsies to sleep all day because they don't work, but they keep everyone else up too! . . . The Gypsies should be removed from the cities. They destroy everything and should be gotten rid of.

Later that evening Ladislav, Martina, and I took another walk through the city, on our way to a documentary film premiere. We arrived early so they pointed out more of the city's sights, including the castle library where Martina's grandfather had worked and a nearby Communist memorial to the proletariat where Martina used to dance at May Day. But in the midst of all the remembrances, there were also histories to be forgotten.

The film we saw that evening was the biography of a local photographer, Josef Seidel. It briefly mentioned how his son, František, who took numerous photos around the Šumava Mountains during World War II, had about five thousand of his negatives seized by the Communists after the war.

It was a minor moment in the film but it dominated the Q&A session that followed, as a young man in the audience wanted to know why the photographs had been seized. Our host, the museum curator, suggested there might be two possible reasons, the first being that new censorship laws that had just been passed meant that all publications needed to be cleared by the government authorities—thus the seizure. He briefly paused and the young man hurried to supply the second reason: "The other possibility was that there were photos of people who had collaborated with the Germans on the negatives." Not exactly, the curator shrugged, it was more likely the photos contained information about various settlements in the district and could have been used as a record of where the Germans had lived before their villages were wiped out. (The Sudetenland expulsions following World War II led to the removal of approximately three million Germans. The death toll is widely disputed, with estimates ranging from 30,000 to 250,000) (Cordell and Wolff 2005).

The film focused on Josef and František Seidel's photography, but in doing so, it had referred to the often uncomfortable and elided history of the Germans expelled from this territory. But most of the audience was not interested in this narrative thread. At the end of the Q&A, they wandered around the gallery, gazing at the accompanying exhibition of Seidel's photos and drawing the images of the past captured by the photographs into their own knowledge of Český Krumlov. Around the room, I could hear exclamations of "Look, that picture was taken from just over there!" and "That used to be such-and-such place, but it isn't there anymore." Ladislav had another history in mind and rushed up to the curator, declaring, "Seidel photographed our wedding!" He thus inserted himself and Martina into the Seidels' story, much the same way as he had calculated the distance from his house to each of the castle garden's features.

Ladislav had, however, yet another connection with the film, which remained private until the next morning when I found him pouring over an old map. I asked him what he was looking at and he pointed to the Sudetenland, tracing his finger over the sites of the nearly invisible, not-to-be-remembered, predominantly German villages. "Have you ever been there?" I asked. "Sure, I grew up in a house there, taken from the Germans," he laughed. "It was really big."

He refused, however, to say more on this subject, despite my encouragement. It was a momentary breakthrough of a history not often openly articulated. In fact, when Václav Havel in December 1989, just before taking up the post of president, suggested that Czechs apologize for the Sudetenland expulsions, the idea was met with hostility and derision.

Exclusion

Ladislav and Martina's awareness of geography and its historical linkages is almost overwhelming. "Look, our house is over here in relation to the castle garden over there." "Look, there used to be a gate here; it isn't here anymore but you can just see its outline." It is as if they are constantly trying to locate themselves in relation to places and times in history. It is as if they are saying "Look, we are here, and this is where this here is in relation to everything else that has happened in this space." It is as if their lives are preoccupied with the fact of thrownness and the need to determine exactly where and when they are living.

Ladislav, Martina, and many others derive a sense of solidarity through remembered and forgotten aspects of the Christian, nationalist, state socialist and World War II pasts as manifest in local, historical connections— one's precise geographic, temporal, and kinship relation to the castle in Český Krumlov, for example. But this solidarity is also created out of exclusions (as Heidegger's own politics so clearly attests). Some exclusions are represented with sadness, such as remembrances of the destruction of Český Krumlov's Jewish community. Others are hidden, such as the ejection of Sudetenland Germans, relegated to the quiet edges of family histories. Yet others are pointed critiques directed at those viewed as not participating fairly in social and economic life.

Martina and Ladislav's rejection of the Roma as just and equitable partners in the Czech nation echo a much broader discourse. Repeatedly,

Czechs tell me "the problem with Gypsies" is that "they don't know how to work." Or: "They want all the rights, but no responsibilities. They have twelve children so that they can take social welfare all their lives." Or: "They are prone to violence—they beat up people and steal. The good ones are the exceptions." When a friend of mine laments that her seven-year-old son forgot his lunch box at school that day and it might get stolen overnight, her son attempts to console her by stating that "it won't get stolen as there aren't any Gypsies at my school."

Elsewhere, I have described how Czech racism toward the Roma tends to focus on issues of labor (Trnka 2017b). Following classic models of state-citizen social contracts, many Czechs envision themselves as taking part in a reciprocal relationship with the state, whereby their labor contributes to the economic vitality of the nation, and in return, they are guaranteed rights to healthcare, housing, and education. In contrast, they view the Roma as largely taking from the state while being not only unproductive but disruptive of others' abilities to work. The social contract is, however, seen as encompassing only those who have appropriate relations with the state—who give enough and do not take too much—thus casting the Roma as necessarily outside of the nation. The public voicing of such sentiments, as well as their explicit invocation in right-wing politics, erupted after the 1989 revolution (Hockenos 1993).

While the Roma have been an ongoing focus of racial animosity, in recent years Muslim refugees are increasingly sharing this role. The reasoning behind their exclusion is different but garners a similar level of intense racial prejudice. This need not surprise us. As Fredrik Barth ([1969] 1998) argued long ago, ethnic and racial prejudice does not stem from one's response to a particular objective characteristic of the Other (such as skin color, diet, or language) but from the desire to draw firm boundaries between who is "us" and who is not. The point of focusing on differences in skin color or food practices is to use these facets to construct a racial or ethnic boundary rather than any intrinsic meaningfulness these characteristics may contain. Arguments about place-based attachments—"belonging" to a certain piece of land or soil, for example—are, however, particularly difficult to dislodge as landscapes that come to be invested with nationalist characteristics are not only thought of as historically having been built by a particular group or groups of people but are experientially seen and felt as linking some people into a historical, present, and future collectivity of resemblance, i.e., "a people," whilst necessarily excluding those deemed different (Herzfeld 2005, ch. 4). The embodied sensoriality of such experiences of inclusion/exclusion makes them much harder to argue against (Trnka, Dureau, and Park 2013).

"We Will Make Them Sick"

Public sentiments against Muslims were galvanized in September 2015 when thousands of Syrian refugees began walking across Europe and Czechs braced themselves against an imagined onslaught. Since then, the othering of Muslims has become ubiquitous in public and private discourse. One Czech after another told me that they do not like the idea of refugees from the Middle East. Unlike refugees from Slavic countries, "who are fine because we can talk with them," Syrian refugees would never be understood. "Who of us can learn Arabic?"

Fears are expressed in classic clichés: "They are another civilization." "They will never fit in." "They are dirty and will make us sick." Occasionally, a new concern is raised: "We will make them sick." In discussing the refugee crisis with friends over dinner, my fifty-five-year-old friend Matěj revealed that he supports the Czech government's refusal to accept European refugee quotas because "these people don't want to be here. They want to go to Germany." "It seems very organized," his twenty-four-year-old son Alexandr added. "They don't seem like war-torn people."

"The main reason these people don't want to stay here is because they don't like our food," Běta, Matěj's wife, explained. "We put špek [a Czech version of prosciutto] in everything, and even if they don't know it, they end up eating it! They stay away from [consuming] pork but inadvertently eat something with špek, and suddenly it makes them feel sick."

Alexandr joked, "So we should have a quota and just give them 'enzyme therapy' so they can eat our food!"

Such assertions of corporeal difference inevitably lead to paranoia over possible embodied breakdowns between self and other. In 2015, Zeman went on record telling academics who criticized his antirefugee rhetoric that if they wanted to welcome refugees into the country, they should open the doors of their own homes to them (Tománek 2015). Some Czechs responded willingly. For others, it was an invitation to scaremonger.

When the European Union refugee quota system was introduced in 2015, the Czech Republic stood apart with Hungary, Poland, and Slovakia (the Vysegrád Four) for refusing to accept their allotted number of Syrian asylum seekers. It became a fraught political issue as the former socialist states opposed the demands of their EU counterparts, who responded with allegations of racism and xenophobia. Neither wanting to relent nor wanting to be seen as kowtowing to Europe, especially to Germany, the Czechs turned the humanitarian crisis into a political assertion of national self-determination. At the time, a ministry of foreign trade official explained to me that, "like everyone else," she thought the refugee crisis was terrible, but surely Czechs have the right to protect their borders "and the way the Vysegrád Four are being represented in the foreign press is appalling." Referring back to Soviet rule, she added, "Having a foreign power telling you what to do—it's like state socialism all over again." Two years on, as the quota system was due to expire, even left-leaning newspapers lauded how, in 2015, the "rebels" from Central and Eastern Europe stood up against a system that "today no-one [in Europe] wants to see continued" (Hruška 2017: 1).

We now have a clearer sense of the significance of Zeman's 2016 involvement in Saint Václav's pilgrimage as well as his invocations that "God is love." Zeman's participation was intended to shore up the image of the Czech nation as united against infidels; new boundary lines between the Czech state and the EU were being drawn through the employment of old religious divisions. The pilgrimage became not just an invocation of Christian tradition but an attempt to, however briefly, Christianize contemporary politics, employing the vision of the Czech Republic as a Christian nation to stand strong against asylum seekers and thus, it was presumed, to keep the Czech economy buoyant. Having previously fought against the Christianization of "Czech Statehood Day," Zeman made a U-turn, promoting the image of a Christian heritage uniting Europe against the tide of Islam as a politically expedient way of bolstering state autonomy. Moreover, while representing himself primarily as a leader striving for the greater good of the Czech people, he also tried to take on the mantle of speaking on behalf of "Europe," suggesting his position was backed by European-wide, Christian tradition.

But despite its Christian heritage, the Czech Republic is not a Christian state. Notwithstanding the Catholic Church's willingness to get involved in state politics, the country is unlikely to head in this direction, though ultimately it is up to its citizens to decide. It is also up to them to determine how they envision social justice, as there are multiple, competing, and complementary histories of this concept that can be invoked, be they of legendary leaders, the economic and social equalities promised by state socialism, companies as providers, or biblical depictions of good and evil. It is, moreover, largely up to the nation how porous and malleable it wants the boundary lines to be between those who "belong" and those who do not, or if such boundary lines are even salient.

In turning to Christianity to shut the door on asylum seekers, Zeman courted and received support from sympathetic members of the church. Indeed, the state and church appeared firmly on the same page, with Czech Cardinal Dominik Duka proclaiming in February 2017, "The current situation in the countries of Western Europe is a warning to us. . . . The whole history of humanity shows how uncontrolled migration causes violence and conflict, as well as economic and cultural collapse" (Luxmore 2017). Nonetheless, even before the first refugees crossed into the Czech Republic, there were those in the church, such as priest and theologian Tomáš Halík, who decried the rise of Islamophobia and called on Czech Christians to consider their "moral obligation" to offer refugees sanctuary ("Přijímat" 2014). One could, moreover, easily reinterpret Zeman's invocations of God's love in the spirit of welcoming refugees rather than rejecting them, suggesting two competing responses—both drawing on Christianity for their historical underpinnings. As Heidegger reminds us, we must necessarily make choices as to how to respond to our historical conditions.

Autochthony is an active endeavor. Heidegger recognized this when he suggested we look at the soil under our feet and meditate upon its meaning. However, Heidegger's invitation in *Discourse on Thinking* is precisely to think. And as thinking can never be predetermined, it opens up multiple directions where it might lead. Heidegger's mistake lay in the steps he took in pondering the meaning of the soil of his homeland, as well as in his attempt to lead his readers along the path of his own thinking about autochthony in relation to German nationalism. But the choice of whether or not to follow in his, or in Zeman's, footsteps is implicitly ours to take.

As anthropologists and geographers have long pointed out, our relation with (sentient or nonsentient) landscapes is not some atemporal, unchanging bedrock (Li 2013; Howitt 2001); rather, there is a multiplicity of ways of doing and being in history within a single place (Bacigalupo 2018). Electing whether to accept the dominant modes in which "belonging" is constituted in our societies, or to listen to the more minor chords that are being played in the background, is our moment of taking charge of thrownness and determining which direction we walk in.

Susanna Trnka is Professor of Social Anthropology and director of the Health and Society major at the University of Auckland, New Zealand. Her primary research areas are the body, state-citizen relations, and subjectivity. She has conducted research in the Czech Republic and New Zealand, and she has in the past worked in Fiji. She is currently the Editor-in-Chief of *American Ethnologist*.

Note

1. This chapter is a revised version of chapter 1 of *Traversing: Embodied Lifeworlds in the Czech Republic* (Cornell University Press, 2020). Reprinted with permission of Cornell University Press.

References

Alonso, Ana María. 1994. "The Politics of Space, Time and Substance: State Formation, Nationalism and Ethnicity." *Annual Review of Anthropology* 23: 379–405.

Anzoise, Valentina. 2017. "Perception and (Re)framing of Urban Environments: A Methodological Reflection toward Sentient Research." *Visual Anthropology* 30(3): 191–205.

Bacigalupo, Ana Mariella. 2018. "The Mapuche Undead Never Forget: Traumatic Memory and Cosmopolitics in Post-Pinochet Chile." *Anthropology and Humanism* 43(2): 228–48.

Barth, Fredrik. (1969) 1998. "Introduction." In *Ethnic Groups and Boundaries: The Social Organization of Cultural Difference*, ed. Fredrik Barth, 9–38. Long Grove, Illinois: Waveland Press.

Bažant, Jan. 2017. "The Classical Tradition and Nationalism: The Art and Architecture of Prague, 1860–1900." In *A Handbook to Classical Reception in Eastern and Central Europe*, ed. Zara Martirosova Torlone, Dana LaCourse Munteanu, and Dorota Dutsch, 133–45. Chichester, West Sussex: John Wiley & Sons.

Bender, Barbara. 2002. "Time and Landscape." *Current Anthropology*. 43(S4): S103–S112.

Brown, Jason M. 2019. "Worlds and Worldviews: Resource Management, Re-enchantment and Landscape." Dwelling in *Political Landscapes*, ed. A. Lounela, E. K. Berglundand, and T. P. Kallinen, 264–83. Helsinki: Suomalaisen Kirjallisuuden Seura.

Cordell, Karl, and Stefan Wolff. 2005. "Ethnic Germans in Poland and the Czech Republic: A Comparative Evaluation." *Nationalities Papers* 33(2): 255–76.

Cruikshank, Julie. 2001. "Glaciers and Climate Change: Perspectives from Oral Tradition." *Arctic* 54(4): 377–93.

de Certeau, Michel. 1984. *The Practice of Everyday Life*. Berkeley: University of California Press.

"Den české státnosti oslavily ve Staré Boleslavi tisíce lidí, mezi nimi i Zeman a Klaus" [Thousands of People Celebrated the Day of Czech Statehood in Stará Boleslav, among Them Zeman and Klaus.]. 2016. *iRozhlas*, 28 September. Retrieved from https://www.irozhlas.cz/zpravy-domov/obrazem-den-ceske-statnosti-oslavily-ve-stare-boleslavi-tisice-lidi-mezi-nimi-i-zeman-a-klaus_201609281923_dpihova.

Descola, Phillipe. 2013. *Beyond Culture and Nature*. Chicago: University of Chicago Press.Di Giminiani, Piergiorgio. 2018. *Sentient Lands: Indigeneity, Property, and Political Imagination in Neoliberal Chile*. Tucson: University of Arizona Press.

Heidegger, Martin. (1959) 1966. *Discourse on Thinking*. Translated by John M. Anderson and E. Hans Freund. New York: Harper & Row.

———. (1971) 2001a. "Building Dwelling Thinking" In *Poetry, Language, Thought*. Translated by Albert Hofstadter, 143–59. New York: Harper & Row.

———. (1971) 2001b. "Epilogue: Letter for a Young Student." In *Poetry, Language, Thought*. Translated by Albert Hofstadter, 181–84. New York: Harper & Row.

Herzfeld, Michael. 2005. *Cultural Intimacy: Poetics in the Nation-State*. New York: Routledge.

Hockenos, Paul. 1993. *Free to Hate: The Rise of the Right in Post-communist Eastern Europe*. New York: Routledge.
Howitt, Richie. 2001. "Frontiers, Border, Edges: Liminal Challenges to the Hegemony of Exclusion." *Australian Geographical Studies* 39(2): 233–45.
Hruška, Blahoslav. 2017. "Kvóty končí. Nahradí je africká centra? [Quotas Are Ending. Will African Centers Replace Them?]" *Lidové Noviny* [*The People's Newspaper*], 5 September, pp. 1, 3.
Ingold, Tim. 2000. *The Perception of the Environment: Essays on Dwelling, Livelihood and Skill*. London: Routledge.
Ingold, Tim, and Jo Lee Vergunst. 2008. "Introduction." In *Ways of Walking Ethnography and Practice on Foot*, ed. Tim Ingold and Jo Lee Vergunst, 1–20. Hampshire and Burlington, UK: Ashgate.
Lapidot, Elad, and Micha Brumlik, eds. 2017. *Heidegger and Jewish Thought: Difficult Others*. London: Rowan and Littlefield.
Lepecki, André. 2004. "Introduction: Presence and Body in Dance and Performance Theory." In *Of the Presence of the Body: Essays on Dance and Performance Theory*, ed. André Lepecki, 1–13. Middletown, CT: Wesleyan University Press.
Li, Fabiana. 2013. "Relating Divergent Worlds: Mines, Aquifers and Sacred Mountains in Peru." *Anthropologica* 55: 399–411.
Luxmore, Johnathan. 2017. "Eastern Europe's church leaders face growing criticism over refugees." *National Catholic Reporter*, 9 March. Retrieved from https://www.ncronline.org/news/world/eastern-europes-church-leaders-face-growing-criticism-over-refugees.
Mauss, Marcel. (1935) 2007. "Techniques of the Body." In *Beyond the Body Proper*, ed. Margaret M. Locke and Judith Farquhar, 50–68. Durham, NC: Duke University Press.
Patočka, Jan. 1998. *Body, Community, Language, World*. Translated by Erazim Kohák. Chicago: Open Court.
Pew Research Center. 2017. "Religious Belief and National Belonging in Central and Eastern Europe." *Assets*. Retrieved from http://assets.pewresearch.org/wp-content/uploads/sites/11/2017/05/15120244/CEUP-FULL-REPORT.pdf.
"Přijímat uprchlíky je morální povinnost, míní teolog Tomáš Halík" [Accepting Refugees is a Moral Obligation, Says Theologist Tomáš Halík.]. 2014. *iDNES. cz*, 14 December. Retrieved from http://zpravy.idnes.cz/tomas-halik-o-prijimani-uprchliku-drf-/domaci.aspx?c=A141214_144827_domaci_cen.
Smith, Steven B. 1995. "Heidegger and Political Philosophy." *Nomos* 27: 440–63.
Tománek, Tomáš. 2015. "Zeman: Vědci by si měli vzít běženci domů. [Zeman: Academics Should Take Refugees into Their Homes]." *Lidové Noviny* [*The People's Newspaper*], 1 September.
Trnka, Susanna. 2017a. *One Blue Child: Asthma, Responsibility and the Politics of Global Health*. Palo Alto, CA: Stanford University Press.
———. 2017b. "Reciprocal Responsibilities: Struggles over (New and Old) Social Contracts, Environmental Pollution, and Childhood Asthma in the Czech Republic." In *Competing Responsibilities: The Ethics and Politics of Contemporary Life*, ed. Susanna Trnka and Catherine Trundle, 71–95. Durham, NC: Duke University Press.

Trnka, Susanna, Christine Dureau, and Julie Park, eds. 2013. *Senses and Citizenships: Embodying Political Life*. New York: Routledge.

Willoughby, Ian. 2003. "Czechs May Go to Mass on Christmas Eve, but Are They Really Religious?" *Czech Radio*, 16 December. Retrieved from http://www.radio.cz/en/section/curraffrs/czechs-may-go-to-mass-on-christmas-eve-but-are-they-really-religious.

Epilogue

Why Is It Vital to Scrutinize the Connection between Landscape, Sentience, and Xenophobia in the Age of Deepening Crises of Democracy and Ecology?

Hikmet Kuran

There is a rich and growing literature about the perception, conceptualization, and imaginaries of organic entities (flora, fauna) and inorganic entities (rivers, mountains, glaciers, rocks, landscapes, etc.)—a literature which indicates quite disruptive approaches elaborating those entities' roles, values, importance, or "sentience" (e.g., Povinelli 1995; Cruikshank 2006; Janowski and Ingold 2012; Rogaski 2018; Peterson 2011; Kohn 2013; Mathieu 2006; Backhaus, Reichler, and Stremlow 2008; Gordillo 2018). Methodological perspectives from the fields of political geography, environmental studies, anthropology, and their cognate disciplines are employed to explore alternative logics of sentient landscapes. These perspectives deal with human-nature interaction through political, ecological, and cultural dimensions, with specific interrogations or analysis focusing on concepts such as subjectivity, intentionality, indigeneity, and colonialism. Moreover, the scope can range from anthropological engagements to political considerations in spatiotemporal context.

Often romanticized as pure, good, and just, sentient landscapes are mainly imagined and analyzed as protectors of those who are powerless, Indigenous, and colonized. Yet indigeneity is a social construct that has traditionally been claimed by political factions with wildly different agendas. Arguments against romanticizing others and their political agendas have long been made in gender theory (Ortner 1995; Mohanty 2003; Mahmood 2005; Abu-Lughod 2013) yet are still in need of development where human/nonhuman binaries are concerned. However, despite the field of sentient landscapes gaining attention in academia, the literature rarely seems to question their intentionality. Questioning the mainstream understanding and perception of nature and its entities as passive objects, many studies have criticized and countered the dualist essence of that perception by blaming the controversies and issues it involves. They have not only elicited a new way of thinking about nature but also created a new platform to discuss human-nature interaction through political and social imaginaries.

However, it can be stated that in a great majority of those studies nature's constructive, protective, peaceful, and friendly interaction with humans is taken for granted by sentient-based conceptualizations. Thinking forests, talking rivers or mountains, and helping deserts reverberate in the literature organized around this perspective, displaying a self-affirmative approach associated with natural entities. This volume, though, asks provocatively, What if they talk, think, help, or communicate in a way that asserts a content not at all positive or friendly? To answer this question to the full, the concept of "sentience" needs to be explained by tackling both theoretical and practical dimensions.

Reconsidering Sentience through Landscape

Coming from the Latin word *sentire*, sentience means "the ability to feel" and is employed "to characterize certain cosmologies, as in animism, where the status of personhood is extended to different categories of nonhuman beings" (Di Giminiani 2018: 11). While speaking about a sacred mountain called Paektu/Changbai, Rogaski (2018: 747, 749) defines a sentient being as "a thinking, emoting subject capable of benevolence and malice" and as "a sensing, thinking, powerful entity that command[s] awe, fear, and worship." By extension, the concept of sentient landscape refers to the natural entities bearing sentient characteristics. Sentient landscape is "sensuous to those who can recognize it and know it" (Biddle 2007: 12–13), "always potentially liable to act for its own reasons" (Povinelli 1995: 133), extending "the ability for intentional and affective action to topographic elements" (Di Giminiani 2018: 11). As such, sentient landscape is critical for rethinking the object-subject divide and human-nature dualism.

Going through another phase, new animism creates a distinctive perspective regarding human and nonhuman entities. It offers a recognition that avers that "the world is full of persons, only some of whom are human" (Harvey 2005: xi). From this point onward, new animism proposes an alternative discourse on the object-subject divide. This is the point where discussions about intentionality—a concept that is related to the ethnic, Indigenous, colonial, and sentient issues—get on the stage. Contrary to Western modernity and the mechanistic worldview, new animism point to a broader perspective to rethink the anthropological, political, cultural, and ecological engagements regarding human-nature interaction by ascribing intentionality and agency, defining nonhuman entities as persons and "subjects."

According to Harvey, "discussion of these discourses, points of view, practices and possibilities aids attempts to understand worldviews and lifeways that are different in various ways from those typically inculcated and more or less taken for granted in Western modernity." Such discussions put in question false claims about the facts or assumptions that preserve colonialist and dualist worldviews (Harvey 2005: xi–xii; Peterson 2011: 169), and which are also undeniably linked with the dominant economical paradigm; capitalism. Speaking about a land commissioner from Australia who "thinks" through this mainstream paradigm, Povinelli (1995: 505) states that:

> The culture of progress, productivity, and political economy that subtends his evaluations remains, in the policy world, an unassailable totem.... [T]he cultural frameworks subtending political economy (not the disputable ways of assessing political-economic systems) were long ago transmuted into neutral, natural, and objective fact.

The social sciences and humanities still partly inhabit a tradition that imagines a dialectical relationship between an Indigenous culture, on one hand, and that of moderns/Westerners, on the other, where the latter is obstructing the natural development of the former. We treat this logic as universal, without analyzing what Western means. In the case of a political age like the one we are currently in, the death or corruption of Indigenous knowledge might look different. When we speak of Western values meddling in Indigenous affairs, we imagine a secularized or Christian West that aims to annihilate local beliefs, often deemed superstitious. But what happens when we turn the lens on landscapes where human political and military power has often found a home?

Therefore, this volume intends to reconsider the human-nature interaction from the standpoint of a sentient-based perspective that can be constructive in going beyond mainstream, deterministic, or reductionist discourse and overcoming the restricting dualisms.

However, it should be noted that the other side of the story might turn out to be problematic as well and create contestations especially in more popular political trends and discourses. With the dominance of a mechanistic worldview, the modern epistemological perspective began to be shaped by pure "reason," through deactivating "sentience." Romanticism, an antithesis of the scientific perspective, claims that reason cannot explain every phenomenon by itself and glorifies sentience and intuition by asserting that those are the only way to reach the truth (Pepper 2001). As Zimmer (2010) and Fischer (2019: 134) point out, believing a "statement to feel true, even it is not supported by factual evidence," is one of the very basic elements of the post-truth era. Keeping the post-truth conceptualization in mind, we can see that the rise of a political and cultural ambience that prefers emotions over reason and scientific evidence (Groves 2019) can be traced back to the romanticized and racialized claims concerning nature. In this regard, it is reasonable to define another ontological bridge between fascist/ecofascist and far-right values, which are dominantly based on racial claims and the trivialization of "reason."

This connection might also be observed in climate change denials and their influence on far-right political discourse about environmental protection (Boussalis and Coan 2016; Jacques, Dunlap, and Freeman 2008; Fischer 2019; Cook 2019). For this reason, the threat of creating another dualism while trying to overcome one is a crucial and challenging issue, to which this volume also pays attention. In order to avoid that danger, the very "boundary" and "substance" of the sentience of natural entities should be clarified in both its theoretical and practical senses.

Suggesting the "mutual constitution of people and land as political subjects" (2018: 6) in a discussion of Mapuche land claims in Chile, Di Giminiani discusses the landscape's subjectivity by criticizing essentialist and constructivist approaches and by defining an alternative conceptualization. He offers the intersubjective relation as the pivotal understanding in analyzing land ontologies. Defining this intersubjectivity as "a relation between two subjects, land and people, both endowed with sentient abilities" (ibid.: 7), he emphasizes that it is critical "to grasp that territories are neither pre-political (that is, spaces where attachment is unaffected by the dynamic formation of new subjectivities and relations through politics) nor post-political (in other words, spaces signified exclusively through collective action)" (ibid.: 10).

Reconsidering Landscape Through Xenophobia

With regard to sentient landscapes, this approach can be fruitful to apprehend a way of thinking and understanding that avoids the limits or inefficacies of ascribing intentionality only to human beings. With this step, we can expect to create a more comprehensive perspective that deals not only with political economy issues, such as land claims or Indigenous property rights, but also with nationalistic, far-right arguments and policies that might also include ecological issues.

While scholars have explored the field of sentient landscapes and political geographies (e.g., Povinelli 1995; Peterson 2011; Kohn 2013; Gordillo 2018), little has been said about sentient landscapes embodying right-wing values. What can we gain from analyzing the subversive politics of sentient landscape as siding with those who have historically used their power to abuse? Could we imagine cosmopolitics where the moral agent is a far-right, xenophobic, racist landscape?

In most ethnographic situations where landscape is understood as sentient, we see, on the one hand, moral panics surrounding the use and abuse of land by foreigners and corrupt local politicians (e.g., Cruikshank 2006; Bacigalupo 2018), and on the other hand, the affective geographies that terrain can create to express the tensions of this reality (e.g., Di Giminiani 2018; Gordillo 2018). This present volume aims to also explore the troubles with the way that concepts of "indigeneity" and feeling "colonized" are being used, particularly when they are claimed by the privileged population of a certain national space, or in the national discourse of countries that have traditionally been on the giving end of racial, colonial, and gender violence. In such cases, the classical terminology used in social sciences and the humanities does not fully cover all realities of the current world.

In the national spaces examined in this volume, the reigning histories and their relationship with the governing of others do not neatly fit the colonial model that scholarship has learned to think with, in terms of who abuses and who is being abused. Europe, for example, has a never-ending practice of creating hierarchies and shades of whiteness within its own geography (Bartlett 1993). While non-Christians have historically suffered the most from this racial othering, the recent Brexit referendum showed that those who find themselves at the physical margins of Europe are also perceived as being on the darker end of the racial spectrum—and with this, of course, comes a plethora of Orientalizations, stereotypes, and conspiracies. This further highlights the failure of the core/periphery model from the 1960s. Countries outside of the imagined West were to copy the model of the prosperous, industrialized countries, thinking this would advance the economies of all the nations. In this process, specific expectations and models were created for newly imagined regions such as Eastern Europe, the Balkans, and the Baltics. We see similar political chronologies taking place in former colonies of European empires, where entire racial imaginaries are being restructured and remodeled to mirror, or at least translate, European models.

The not-elsewhereness-and-not-insideness of many of the national identities in this volume makes classical models of postcolonial theory hard to apply. The logics of indigeneity from interwar Germany call on very different political values than the logics of indigeneity of the Mapuche. The social categories that academics created by building their disciplines in colonized spaces have not been updated to help scholars speak about the realities of the land in nation-states where categories like "indigeneity" could be employed by social groups to further their xenophobia. Furthermore, these social groups are not historically subjected to the sorts of victimhood that anthropological research commonly sees associated with most understandings of the concept of indigeneity.

What counts as foreign for the national imaginaries examined here? What are the histories, the myths, the redrawn borders that inform who counts as a dangerous other? In the absence of traditional colonialism—where the people drawing up the institutional framework are from elsewhere and are occupying the land of an Indigenous, collective self—the conceptual grounds of the self/other binary and its hegemonic practices must be rethought. Bearing these points in mind, and with a close look at recent political events, it can be easily noticed that far-right parties and so-called populist promises are growing globally. Therefore, examining the theoretical premises of xenophobic natural entities is a sine qua non for analyzing existing—and growing—political discourse as well.

As Forchtner (2019) points out, in an age of two intersecting crises unfolding globally—the crisis of liberal democracy and the environmental crisis—the correlation and interaction between them are both critical and understudied. Considering the growth of far-right imaginaries and the rise of a particular brand of populism (see Bergmann 2020; Thorleifsson 2019; Pasieka 2017; Gingrich and Banks 2006; Hage 2000, 2017; Kalb 2009; Shoshan 2016), their association with the catastrophic ecological breakdown and destruction found in climate change, biodiversity loss, air pollution, and food security make the interaction between political actors and the environment a matter of importance, worthy of attention. Nature-based constructions of national identity and political knowledge, and their implementation in the far-right spectrum, are tied not only to historical conceptualizations but also to present ecofascist revulsions about ecological problems. As the far-right ruling parties employ and reimagine concepts of "historical heritage," they combine xenophobic claims with a racist perception of nature. Therefore, unraveling the "national" imaginaries of natural entities seems vital as well to comprehend such far-right political agendas.

Another essential objective of analyzing sentience is to reveal existing and shifting relationships between racism and xenophobic perceptions of nature. In other words, the examination of historic roots might lead the way to understand the role of environmental entities in far-right policies.

As can be seen in various chapters of this volume, the sentient bridge between nature and nation is constructed as racial othering, which is mainly the result of a mentality centering and at the same time romanticizing Indigenous identity, creating the very ground of racial superiority and hierarchy claims. Understanding this construction process is vital to illuminating the theoretical correlation between nature and nation.

As one of the very prominent examples of this construction process, the National Socialist reign in Germany (1933–1945) offers a substantial "data set," both theoretically and practically, to decode the connection points of otherness, racial hierarchy, national identity, and natural entities. The Blood and Soil approach, for example, exemplifies the historical construction of a correlation between natural and national identity in a quite clear ethnographic understanding that would later create substantial ground for Nazi ideology to build a fascist doctrine (Dominick 1992). The role of sentience is important in revealing social imaginaries employed by historical and political discourses, allowing us to rethink the self/other binary, ethnopolitics, and ongoing political discourse. To do that, not only the imaginaries but also the politics of nature must be taken into account since the "politics of nature is at the same time a politics of identity" (Olsen 1999: 29). As Di Giminiani (2018) reveals, in order to fully recognize and perceive the elements that affect landscape imaginaries, essentialist or constructivist approaches come short, especially in colonial agendas.

The process of self-making and relatedly "nation building" should be analyzed through a more comprehensive understanding than ones that produce or reproduce the self/other binary or are based on deterministic approaches to human-nature interaction, as briefly discussed above with reference to intentionality. Furthermore, we can observe via several case studies that it is not only the case for Nazi, colonial, or Indigenous imaginaries but also for European modernity. Jon Mathieu's (2006) study for instance, reveals the nexus between sacralization, nation building, industrialization, and landscape by focusing on the Alpine landscape. Therefore, reading human-nature interaction oriented around sentience and through situating intersubjectivity and reciprocity will serve as a critical step to reconsider the political context.

As Rogaski (2018) elaborated in her detailed study, the role of knowledge about sentient entities—in her case, Mount Paektu/Changbai—is historically conditioned by the political context. She explicitly investigates the role of imaginaries and knowledge about the mountain for national independence and resistance. Turning back to Di Giminiani (2018), the case of the Mapuche also points out the quite similar implication that "land and its dwellers have bodies that are continuously constituted" (84) and that "involvement of land in the process of self-making both preexists and is produced with the very act of navigating the environment" (58). This perspective thus plays a vital role in overcoming the subject/object division and the deterministic perception of human-nature relations by emphasizing "the mutual affect between these two entities" (74), which indisputably puts forward the vitality of sentience.

This book takes a new stance on sentient landscapes with the intention of dispelling the denial of coevalness represented by their scholarly romanticization. At the end of the day, the big takeaway of the volume is this: if we truly engage with the idea that landscape is sentient (thus human-like), then we must also allow ourselves, as scholars, to imagine sentient landscapes as covering the entire spectrum when it comes to intentionality and political values. We argue that the denial of coevalness, a term famously coined by Johannes Fabian, works in this case as a social imaginary where sentient landscapes maintain a purely good, premodern logic, similar to how non-European societies were traditionally seen by European colonizers. This volume includes chapters from scholars in all fields engaging with sentient landscapes (anthropology, history, political ecology, environmental studies, etc.) to helps us deeply reconsider the theoretical basis with which we operate.

With its overarching multidisciplinary scope, this volume intends to touch on a wide range of conceptual, practical, historical, and contemporary considerations from colonial, Indigenous issues to environmental, fascist, far-right, and migration studies. Moreover, this volume takes a step further to better evaluate and analyze the aforementioned conceptualizations by also expanding the theoretical ground, defining and implementing a new perspective on human-nature interaction based on sentience and natural entities, namely landscapes. With these rewarding contributions, I believe several disciplines, such as anthropology, ecology, environmental studies, history, politics, and cultural studies, can benefit from this book, and it can also serve as a fruitful ground to further research and analysis discussing contemporary issues, especially ones in the nexus of environmental catastrophe and rise of the far right.

Unveiling the tangled relationship between sentient landscapes and xenophobia points out a crucial task in a world that is facing both an ecological crisis and an unsettling rise of far-right values and racist discourses. Taking the ecofascist assumptions claiming affinities between ecology and fascism into consideration, the task of unveiling and disclosure becomes more vital for two reasons. First, because those assumptions have been increasingly spoken out loud by several far-right organizations and entities.[1] And second, because of the increasing post-truth way of thinking that directly interacts not only with the liberal democratic establishment and its concepts but also with ecological crisis, which can be observed through environmental skepticism, anti-vaccination, and climate denial. Given the urgency of tackling climate change and autocratic regimes, two of the most powerful threats humanity faces today, it is clear how relevant and vital it is to decipher the connection between xenophobia and sentient landscapes in our political and ecological affairs.

Hikmet Kuran is assistant professor at Cappadocia University in the Department of Urban, Environmental, and Local Government Policies. He has research and teaching interests in environmental ethics, environmental politics, and Nazi ecology. Hikmet received his PhD in political science from Ankara University, and his most recent monograph, *Sehir Hakki; Neoliberal Kentlesme Ve Sinif Mücadelesi* (Right to the city: neoliberal urbanization and class struggle), came out in 2021 with the Turkish publishing house Nika Yayinevi.

Note

1. Please see an example in https://www.vice.com/en/article/wxqmey/neo-nazis-eco-fascism-climate-change-recruit-young-people.

References

Abu-Lughod, Lila. 2013. *Do Muslim Women Need Saving?*. Cambridge MA: Harvard University Press.
Bacigalupo, Ana Mariella. 2018. "The Mapuche Undead Never Forget: Traumatic Memory and Cosmopolitics in Post-Pinochet Chile. *Anthropology&Humanism* 43(2): 228-248.
Backhaus, Norman, Claude Reichler, and Matthias Stremlow. 2008. "Conceptualizing Landscape: An Evidence-based Model with Political Implications." *Mountain Research and Development* 28(2): 132–39.
Bergmann, Eirikur. 2020. *Neo-Nationalism: The Rise of Nativist Populism*. London: Palgrave Macmillan.
Biddle, Jennifer. 2007. *Breasts, Bodies, Canvas: Central Desert Art as Experience*. Sydney: UNSW Press.
Boussalis, Constantine, and Travis G. Coan. 2016. "Text-mining the Signals of Climate Change Doubt." *Global Environmental Change* 36: 89–100.
Cook, John. 2019. "Understanding and Countering Misinformation About Climate Change." In *Handbook of Research on Deception, Fake News and Misinformation Online*, ed. I. Chiluwa and S. Samoilenko, 281–306. Hershey, PA: IGI-Global.
Cruikshank, Julie. 2006. *Do Glaciers Listen? Local Knowledge, Colonial Encounters, and Social Imagination*. Vancouver: UBC Press.
Di Giminiani, Piergiorgio. 2018. *Sentient Lands: Indigeneity, Property, and Political Imagination in Neoliberal Chile*. Tucson: University of Arizona Press.

Dominick III, Raymond. 1992. *The Environmental Movement in Germany: Prophets and Pioneers, 1871–1971*. Bloomington: Indiana University Press.

Fischer, Frank. 2019. "Knowledge Politics and Post-Truth in Climate Denial: On the Social Construction of Alternative Facts." *Critical Policy Studies* 13(2): 133–52.

Forchtner, Bernard. 2019. *The Far Right and the Environment: Politics, Discourse and Communication*. London: Routledge.

Gingrich, Andre, and Marcus Banks. 2006. *Neo-Nationalism in Europe and Beyond: Perspectives from Social Anthropology*. New York: Berghahn.

Gordillo, Gaston. 2018. "Terrain as Insurgent Weapon: An Effective Geometry of Warfare in the Mountains of Afghanistan." *Political Geography* 64: 53–62.

Groves, Christopher. 2019. "Post-Truth and Anthropogenic Climate Change: Asking the Right Questions." *WIREs Climate Change* 10(6): 1–12.

Hage, Ghassan. 2000. *White Nation: Fantasies of White Supremacy in a Multicultural Society*. London: Routledge.

———. 2017. *Is Racism an Environmental Threat?* Cambridge: Polity Press.

Harvey, Graham. 2005. *Animism: Respecting the Living World*. London: Hurst.

Jacques, Peter J., Riley E. Dunlap and Mark Freeman. 2008. "The Organization of Denial: Conservative Think Tanks and Environmental Scepticism." *Environmental Politics* 17(3): 349–385.

Janowski, Monica, and Tim Ingold. 2012. *Imagining Landscapes: Past, Present and Future*. London: Ashgate Publishing.

Kalb, Don. 2009. "Conversations with a Polish Populist: Tracing Hidden Histories of Globalization, Class and Dispossession in Postsocialism." *American Ethnologist* 36(2): 207–23.

Kaufmann, Eric. 1998. "Naturalizing the Nation: The Rise of Naturalistic Nationalism in the United States and Canada." *Comparative Studies in Society and History* 40(4): 666–95.

Kohn, Eduardo. 2013. *How Forests Think? Toward an Anthropology Beyond the Human*. Berkeley: University of California Press.

Mathieu, Jon. 2006. "The Sacralization of Mountains in Europe during the Modern Age." *Mountain Research and Development* 26(4): 343–49.

Mohanty, Chandra Talpade. 2003. *Feminism without Borders: Decolonizing Theory, Practicing Solidarity*. North Carolina: Duke University Press.

Olsen, Jonathan. 1999. *Nature and Nationalism: Right-Wing Ecology and the Politics of Identity in Contemporary Germany*. Basingstoke, UK: Palgrave.

Ortner, Sherry B. 1995. "Resistance and the Problem of Ethnographic Refusal." *Comparative Studies in Society and History* 37(1): 173-193.

Pasieka, Agnieszka. 2017. "Taking Far-Right Claims Seriously and Literally: Anthropology and the Study of Right-Wing Radicalism." *Slavic Review* 76(1): 19–29.

Pepper, David. 2001. *Roots of Modern Environmentalism*. London: Croom Helm.

Peterson, Nicolas. 2011. "Is the Aboriginal Landscape Sentient? Animism, the New Animism and the Warlpiri." *Oceania* 81: 167–79.

Povinelli, Elizabeth A. 1995. "Do Rocks Listen? Cultural Politics of Apprehending Australian Aboriginal Labor." *American Anthropologist* 97(3): 505–18.

Rogaski, Ruth. 2018. "Knowing a Sentient Mountain: Space, science and the sacred in ascents of Mount Paektu/Changbai." *Modern Asian Studies* 52(2): 716–52.

Shoshan, Nitzan. 2016. *The Management of Hate: Nation, Affect, and the Governance of Right-Wing Extremism in Germany.* Princeton, NJ: Princeton University Press.
Thorleifsson, Cathrine. 2019. "In Pursuit of Purity: Populist Nationalism and the Racialization of Difference." *Global Studies in Culture and Power* 28(2): 186-202.
Zimmer, Ben. 2010. "Truthiness." *The New York Time Magazine* 13 October.

Index

Adamastor, 23, 25–31, 34, 38
Ainu, 160, 162, 169, 172, 175–77, 179–80
agency, 8, 24, 27, 31, 38, 122, 167, 176, 188, 201, 253
Almería, 142, 145, 147–56
Alonso de Ercilla y Zúñiga, 188
Anthropocene, 6, 7,
Anthropology, 3, 45, 57, 143, 169, 251, 258
anti-colonialism, 79
anti-immigration, 16, 43–44
anti-imperialism, 53
anti-Muslim/islamophobia, 100, 105–6, 111, 247
anti-Semitism, 70–73, 79–80, 121, 123, 131
apartheid, 3, 16, 23, 25–26, 28, 30–34
Arauco, 189, 192, 194–96, 198–201
Arnt, Ernst Moritz, 127–30, 132
Austro-Hungarian Empire, 16, 78, 90
autarky, 138

Bacigalupo, Ana Mariella, 247, 255
Bhāratīya Janatā Party (BJP), 102–4
Blood and Soil, 131, 133–35, 138, 257
Bramwell, Anna, 133–34
Buddhism, 16, 98–110, 112–14, 173
Burakumin, 160, 162, 172–75, 179–80

Canada, 16, 43–53, 59–60
capitalism, 5, 7, 8, 121–22, 124, 131, 142–43, 157, 161, 166, 192, 239, 253
Chile, 16–17, 186–97, 199–201

Christianity, 3, 4, 8, 13, 27, 70–74, 76–77, 79, 81, 114, 122, 128, 166, 188, 199, 229–31, 235–39, 243, 246–47, 253, 255
city/urban, 25–26, 35, 40, 44, 46, 49, 70, 130–31, 133–34, 148–49, 173, 226, 229, 223–32, 234–237, 240–42
climate, 6, 51, 99, 121, 144, 190, 192, 217, 226, 254, 256, 259
colonialism, 2–3, 6–8, 12, 15–16, 23–25, 27–31, 34–38, 44–47, 49, 50, 52–54, 56, 58, 60–61, 68, 76, 78, 87–90, 100, 102, 104, 112, 148–49, 168, 170, 176–78, 180, 186, 192–94, 251, 253, 255–58
conspiracy theories, 69, 170, 255
Cree, 45–46, 54–55, 59
Croatia, 17. 211–15, 217–20, 223
Cruikshank, Julie, 11, 230–31, 255
Cyril Coetzee, 25, 28–31
The Czech Republic, 17, 229–32, 235–37, 239–41, 243–47

Dalai Lama, 106, 110
Dauerwald, 14, 133, 135–38
Darre, R. Walter, 133–35
decolonialism, 12, 36, 38, 52, 148
deforestation, 5, 164
desert, 16, 34, 125, 142, 144–48, 150–52, 155–58, 252
Descola, Phillipe, 3, 11–12, 58, 111, 186–87, 230
Di Giminiani, Piergiorgio, 10, 24, 191, 252, 254–55, 257

Düesberg, Rudolf, 121–22, 132
Ecology(-ies), 5, 6, 24, 44–45, 51, 55, 59, 61, 83, 138–39, 153–54, 213–15, 237, 251, 253, 255–56, 258–59
empire(s), 3, 16, 27, 69, 124, 169–71, 177, 179, 193–95, 255
environment, 7, 14, 16, 35–36, 39, 44, 58, 123, 128–29, 131–32, 134–35, 138–39, 143–46, 149, 153, 155–57, 213, 215–16, 218–19, 238, 251, 254, 256, 258–59
ethnicity, 23, 39, 60, 69–70, 72, 79, 86, 102, 130, 132, 139, 169, 171–72, 175–76, 178, 180, 231, 235, 244, 253
Europe/European, 4–5, 23–24, 26–28, 30–31, 36, 38, 46, 60, 70, 73, 125–26, 142, 144–45, 147, 150, 154, 156–58, 166, 169–70, 179, 190–92, 199, 211, 221, 223–25, 230, 235–36, 245–46, 255, 257–58
extractivism, 5, 12, 53, 56–57, 142, 149, 177

fascism, 4, 13–16, 31, 52, 89, 135, 138, 143, 156, 213, 254, 256–58
far-right, 13,44, 68–70, 91, 94, 122, 178, 212–16, 224, 254–56, 258
Fichte, Johann Gottlieb, 125–36, 130
Forchtner, Bernhard, 13, 256
forest, 6, 13–15, 17, 25, 86, 46, 48–49, 51–54, 81, 86, 89, 121–125, 127–33, 135–39, 142, 144, 186–93, 195–96, 198–200, 211–24, 252
Francisco Franco, 142, 148, 150, 153

Germania, 123, 129, 193, 194
Germany, 13–17, 122, 127–30, 132, 136, 187, 192–95, 213, 235, 241–43, 245, 247, 256–57
Gordillo, Gaston, 10, 57, 251, 255
Gorski Kotar, 211, 213–215, 217–18, 223–24
Gottlieb Fichte, 125–26, 130
Göring, Hermann, 136–37
Himalayas, 16, 98
Hinduism, 102–4, 112–13

Hokkaidō, 160, 162, 169, 175–177, 179
hostility, 15, 16, 34, 98, 100–1, 106, 109–10, 112–13, 126, 145, 150–51, 156, 167, 243
Hage, Ghassan, 46, 100, 214, 225, 256

Ignacio Domeyko, 188–190
imperialism, 7, 17, 23–24, 27, 53, 56, 58, 90, 160–61, 164–65, 167, 175–76, 179–80
indigeneity, 2–3, 11, 15–17, 24, 26, 28, 30, 56–57, 60–61, 70, 73, 101, 112–13, 160–61, 164, 169, 175–77, 179–80, 187, 192, 194, 199, 201, 251, 253–58
Ingold, Tim, 4, 7, 100, 143–44, 157, 230, 233, 251
Islam, 16, 69–70, 76, 98–100, 102–6, 108–13, 230, 246

Japan, 15–17, 160–80
Japanese Empire, 169–71, 176–77, 179
Judaism, 15–16, 52, 70–73, 80–81, 92, 122, 125, 130, 214, 235–37, 241, 243

Kanien'kehá:ka, 43, 46, 48, 60
Karoo, 25, 34–37
Kashmir, 98, 102, 103, 108, 112–13
Kohn, Eduardo, 58, 212, 216–17, 223, 251, 255
Korean residents, 160, 162, 169

Ladakh, 16, 98–114
Latour, Bruno, 2, 101, 111

Mapuche, 186–, 199, 200–1
modern(ity), 2, 8, 24, 30, 37–38, 52, 54, 56, 58, 60, 81, 92, 100–1, 104–6, 108, 108–13, 122, 129–31, 133, 135, 144, 148–52, 156–57, 178–80, 186, 253, 257–58
migrant(s), 16, 43, 45, 49, 59–61, 99, 150–155, 157, 162–63, 165, 170, 172, 176–77, 190, 192–93, 211–215, 217–18, 220–25, 240, 246, 258
Mihai Eminescu, 69–71, 73, 79–83, 91–92

military, 10, 15, 44, 69–70, 86, 90, 164, 170–71, 178, 180, 186, 188, 193–94, 199–200, 253
Miloš Zeman, 230, 235, 245–47
Mircea Eliade, 71, 92, 93
Modersohn, A.W., 137–38
Mohawk(s), 43–44, 48, 60–61
Montreal, 43, 50, 57
mountain, 6, 8–13, 23, 27, 48, 50–51, 75, 77–78, 84–85, 88–89, 92, 98–99, 101, 107, 126, 128, 142, 146, 167, 189–90, 192, 196, 201, 217, 222, 225, 242, 257

National Socialist, 123, 125, 133, 136–138, 213, 257
nature, 3, 8, 14, 27, 46, 49–552, 54, 58, 68–69, 73–74, 79–81, 83, 121–28, 130–36, 156, 161–62, 165, 167, 172–73, 179, 186–90, 192–93, 195–201, 212–16, 223–24, 226, 238–39, 251–54, 256–59
Nazi, 13, 16, 121, 124, 128, 130–31, 133–138, 214, 235–239, 241, 257
Nicolae Ceaușescu, 81
nomadic, 45–46, 48–49, 53, 55, 61, 122
nonhuman, 3, 44, 55–56, 58, 100, 108, 111, 156, 173, 187, 190–91, 203, 212, 216, 252–53
Nordic Resistance Movement, 214–15

occupation, 37, 45, 67, 86, 124–30, 166, 169, 171, 173–74, 178, 180, 191, 195, 200–1, 236, 256
Ottoman Empire, 16, 67–69, 75–76, 79, 82, 86

Peterson, Nicolas, 11, 161, 251, 253, 255
Plastic Sea, 147–52, 154–55
populism, 17, 130, 256
post-colonialism, 37, 38, 225, 255
post-socialism/post-communism/ post-1989, 81, 91, 237
post-war, 162, 171–72, 174, 176, 179–80
Povinelli, Elizabeth A, 9, 11, 24, 161, 251–53, 255

Prague, 229–32, 234, 236–37, 240
Pretoria, 31–34

Quebec, 43–46, 48, 50–56, 59–60

race, 7, 14, 23, 25, 27, 32, 51, 122–24, 130, 132–33, 137–38, 176–77, 179, 214
racial purity, 13–14, 25, 28, 34, 49, 51, 122, 123, 127, 129–30, 134, 174
racism, 6, 14, 17, 25, 27, 32, 39, 51, 81, 121–22, 128, 131, 135–36, 151–53, 162, 170, 172, 224, 231, 244–45, 254–258
Riehl, Wilhelm Heinrich, 128–130, 132
refugee(s), 16, 108, 229–30, 244–45, 247
Rogaski, Ruth, 8, 12, 251–52
Romania, 16, 67–92
Romanticism, 2–4, 13, 45, 50–51, 104, 124–25, 129–31, 146, 148–49, 251, 254, 257–58
Rroma, 70, 229, 240–244
Rudolf Düesberg, 121–22, 132

Saint Václav, 229–32, 236, 239–40, 246
Schama, Simon, 11, 122, 186, 190, 193–95,
segregation, 25, 26, 172–73
sentient landscape(s), 1–8, 10–17, 24, 37, 56, 67–71, 74, 79, 82–84, 86, 90–91, 98, 100–1, 106, 108–10, 112–13, 122, 132, 160–64, 166–72, 174–76, 179–180, 186, 231, 247, 252, 255, 258–59
sentient river, 74, 76, 79
settler/settler-colonialism, 11, 16–17, 23–24, 27–28, 37–38, 43–47, 49–51, 59, 61, 112, 161, 173, 178, 187, 190–91, 193, 195
Shinkoku, 160, 162, 164, 172, 179
Shintoism, 170–72
silviculture, 12–13, 133, 136, 138
socialism/communism, 12–14, 52, 68–69, 71, 73, 79, 81, 83–84, 91, 161, 229, 236–41, 243, 245–46
South Africa, 16, 23–35, 37–38
Spain, 142–43, 147–51, 154–56, 199

urban, 25–26, 49, 70, 125, 130–31, 133–35, 148–49, 173, 226, 229–32, 237

Viveiros de Castro, Eduardo, 6, 12, 60
Völkisch, 121, 124, 130–31, 136–38
wilderness, 13, 46, 50–52, 74, 124, 129, 144,–45, 156, 188, 213

Wilson, Jeffrey K., 15, 121–22, 124–25, 132–33
Wilhelm Heinrich Riehl, 128–30, 132

xenophobic forest, 14, 212
xenophobic landscape(s), 6–7, 15–16, 24, 36, 50, 61, 67–71, 78–79, 83, 86, 91, 123, 133, 135–36, 139, 224, 255

www.ingramcontent.com/pod-product-compliance
Lightning Source LLC
Chambersburg PA
CBHW051532020426
42333CB00016B/1892